KU-568-127

Beginning Programming with Python®

FOR

DUMMIES®

A Wiley Brand

3 0116 01971915 0

Beginning Programming with Python® FOR DUMMIES®

A Wiley Brand

by John Paul Mueller

Beginning Programming with Python® For Dummies®

Published by: **John Wiley & Sons, Inc.,** 111 River Street, Hoboken, NJ 07030-5774, www.wiley.com

Copyright © 2014 by John Wiley & Sons, Inc., Hoboken, New Jersey

Media and software compilation copyright © 2014 by John Wiley & Sons, Inc. All rights reserved.

Published simultaneously in Canada

No part of this publication may be reproduced, stored in a retrieval system or transmitted in any form or by any means, electronic, mechanical, photocopying, recording, scanning or otherwise, except as permitted under Sections 107 or 108 of the 1976 United States Copyright Act, without the prior written permission of the Publisher. Requests to the Publisher for permission should be addressed to the Permissions Department, John Wiley & Sons, Inc., 111 River Street, Hoboken, NJ 07030, (201) 748-6011, fax (201) 748-6008, or online at http://www.wiley.com/go/permissions.

Trademarks: Wiley, For Dummies, the Dummies Man logo, Dummies.com, Making Everything Easier, and related trade dress are trademarks or registered trademarks of John Wiley & Sons, Inc. and may not be used without written permission. Python is a registered trademark of Python Software Foundation Corporation. All other trademarks are the property of their respective owners. John Wiley & Sons, Inc. is not associated with any product or vendor mentioned in this book.

LIMIT OF LIABILITY/DISCLAIMER OF WARRANTY: THE PUBLISHER AND THE AUTHOR MAKE NO REPRESENTATIONS OR WARRANTIES WITH RESPECT TO THE ACCURACY OR COMPLETENESS OF THE CONTENTS OF THIS WORK AND SPECIFICALLY DISCLAIM ALL WARRANTIES, INCLUDING WITHOUT LIMITATION WARRANTIES OF FITNESS FOR A PARTICULAR PURPOSE. NO WARRANTY MAY BE CREATED OR EXTENDED BY SALES OR PROMOTIONAL MATERIALS. THE ADVICE AND STRATEGIES CONTAINED HEREIN MAY NOT BE SUITABLE FOR EVERY SITUATION. THIS WORK IS SOLD WITH THE UNDERSTANDING THAT THE PUBLISHER IS NOT ENGAGED IN RENDERING LEGAL, ACCOUNTING, OR OTHER PROFESSIONAL SERVICES. IF PROFESSIONAL ASSISTANCE IS REQUIRED, THE SERVICES OF A COMPETENT PROFESSIONAL PERSON SHOULD BE SOUGHT. NEITHER THE PUBLISHER NOR THE AUTHOR SHALL BE LIABLE FOR DAMAGES ARISING HEREFROM. THE FACT THAT AN ORGANIZATION OR WEBSITE IS REFERRED TO IN THIS WORK AS A CITATION AND/OR A POTENTIAL SOURCE OF FURTHER INFORMATION DOES NOT MEAN THAT THE AUTHOR OR THE PUBLISHER ENDORSES THE INFORMATION THE ORGANIZATION OR WEBSITE MAY PROVIDE OR RECOMMENDATIONS IT MAY MAKE. FURTHER, READERS SHOULD BE AWARE THAT INTERNET WEBSITES LISTED IN THIS WORK MAY HAVE CHANGED OR DISAPPEARED BETWEEN WHEN THIS WORK WAS WRITTEN AND WHEN IT IS READ.

For general information on our other products and services, please contact our Customer Care Department within the U.S. at 877-762-2974, outside the U.S. at 317-572-3993, or fax 317-572-4002. For technical support, please visit www.wiley.com/techsupport.

Wiley publishes in a variety of print and electronic formats and by print-on-demand. Some material included with standard print versions of this book may not be included in e-books or in print-on-demand. If this book refers to media such as a CD or DVD that is not included in the version you purchased, you may download this material at http://booksupport.wiley.com. For more information about Wiley products, visit www.wiley.com.

Library of Congress Control Number: 2014935516

ISBN 978-1-118-89145-2 (pbk); ISBN 978-1-118-89147-6 (ebk); ISBN ePDF 978-1-118-89149-0 (ebk)

Manufactured in the United States of America

10 9 8 7 6 5 4 3 2 1

Contents at a Glance

Introduction 1

Part I: Getting Started with Python 5

Chapter 1: Talking to Your Computer 7
Chapter 2: Getting Your Own Copy of Python 21
Chapter 3: Interacting with Python 39
Chapter 4: Writing Your First Application 57

Part II: Talking the Talk 81

Chapter 5: Storing and Modifying Information 83
Chapter 6: Managing Information 93
Chapter 7: Making Decisions 117
Chapter 8: Performing Repetitive Tasks 133
Chapter 9: Dealing with Errors 149

Part III: Performing Common Tasks 181

Chapter 10: Interacting with Modules 183
Chapter 11: Working with Strings 205
Chapter 12: Managing Lists 223
Chapter 13: Collecting All Sorts of Data 243
Chapter 14: Creating and Using Classes 267

Part IV: Performing Advanced Tasks 291

Chapter 15: Storing Data in Files 293
Chapter 16: Sending an E-Mail 309

Part V: The Part of Tens 327

Chapter 17: Ten Amazing Programming Resources 329
Chapter 18: Ten Ways to Make a Living with Python 339
Chapter 19: Ten Interesting Tools 347
Chapter 20: Ten Libraries You Need to Know About 357

Index 365

Table of Contents

Introduction **1**

About This Book 1
Foolish Assumptions 2
Icons Used in This Book 3
Beyond the Book 3
Where to Go from Here 4

Part I: Getting Started with Python **5**

Chapter 1: Talking to Your Computer **7**

Understanding Why You Want to Talk to Your Computer 7
Knowing that an Application is a Form of Communication 9
    Thinking about procedures you use daily 9
    Writing procedures down 10
    Seeing applications as being like any other procedure 11
    Understanding that computers take things literally 11
Defining What an Application Is 12
    Understanding that computers use a special language 12
    Helping humans speak to the computer 13
Understanding Why Python is So Cool 14
    Unearthing the reasons for using Python 15
    Deciding how you can personally benefit from Python 16
    Discovering which organizations use Python 17
    Finding useful Python applications 18
    Comparing Python to other languages 18

Chapter 2: Getting Your Own Copy of Python **21**

Downloading the Version You Need 21
Installing Python 24
    Working with Windows 25
    Working with the Mac 27
    Working with Linux 29
Accessing Python on Your Machine 32
    Using Windows 32
    Using the Mac 35
    Using Linux 36
Testing Your Installation 36

Chapter 3: Interacting with Python **39**

Opening the Command Line..40

    Starting Python 41

    Using the command line to your advantage....................................42

    Using Python environment variables to your advantage 44

Typing a Command 45

    Telling the computer what to do 46

    Telling the computer you're done 46

    Seeing the result..46

Using Help...48

    Getting into help mode..48

    Asking for help 49

    Leaving help mode...52

    Obtaining help directly 52

Closing the Command Line 54

Chapter 4: Writing Your First Application. **57**

Understanding the Integrated DeveLopment Environment (IDLE).........58

Starting IDLE...59

    Using standard commands 60

    Understanding color coding..61

    Getting GUI help 62

    Configuring IDLE 63

Creating the Application..67

    Opening a new window 67

    Typing the command 68

    Saving the file 69

Running the Application 71

Understanding the Use of Indentation...72

Adding Comments 74

    Understanding comments...74

    Using comments to leave yourself reminders.................................75

    Using comments to keep code from executing................................75

Loading and Running Existing Applications 78

    Using the command line or terminal window 78

    Using the Edit window...79

    Using the Python Shell window or Python command line 79

Closing IDLE 80

Part II: Talking the Talk.. **81**

Chapter 5: Storing and Modifying Information. **83**

Storing Information 83

    Seeing variables as storage boxes 84

    Using the right box to store the data 84

Defining the Essential Python Data Types 85
   Putting information into variables.................................. 85
   Understanding the numeric types 85
   Understanding Boolean values 89
   Understanding strings... 90
Working with Dates and Times 91

Chapter 6: Managing Information. 93

Controlling How Python Views Data...................................... 94
   Making comparisons 94
   Understanding how computers make comparisons 95
Working with Operators 95
   Defining the operators 96
   Understanding operator precedence 103
Creating and Using Functions 104
   Viewing functions as code packages 104
   Understanding code reusability................................... 104
   Defining a function.. 105
   Accessing functions.. 107
   Sending information to functions 108
   Returning information from functions 112
   Comparing function output 114
Getting User Input 114

Chapter 7: Making Decisions 117

Making Simple Decisions Using the if Statement.......................... 118
   Understanding the if statement 118
   Using the if statement in an application 119
Choosing Alternatives Using the if...else Statement 124
   Understanding the if...else statement 124
   Using the if...else statement in an application 124
   Using the if...elif statement in an application 125
Using Nested Decision Statements....................................... 129
   Using multiple if or if...else statements......................... 129
   Combining other types of decisions.............................. 130

Chapter 8: Performing Repetitive Tasks 133

Processing Data Using the for Statement................................. 134
   Understanding the for statement................................. 134
   Creating a basic for loop... 135
   Controlling execution with the break statement 136
   Controlling execution with the continue statement............... 138
   Controlling execution with the pass clause 140
   Controlling execution with the else statement 141

Processing Data Using the while Statement 143
Understanding the while statement 143
Using the while statement in an application 144
Nesting Loop Statements 145

Chapter 9: Dealing with Errors 149

Knowing Why Python Doesn't Understand You 150
Considering the Sources of Errors 151
Classifying when errors occur 152
Distinguishing error types 153
Catching Exceptions 155
Basic exception handling 156
Handling more specific to less specific exceptions 167
Nested exception handling 170
Raising Exceptions 174
Raising exceptions during exceptional conditions 174
Passing error information to the caller 175
Creating and Using Custom Exceptions 176
Using the finally Clause 178

Part III: Performing Common Tasks 181

Chapter 10: Interacting with Modules 183

Creating Code Groupings 184
Importing Modules 185
Using the import statement 187
Using the from...import statement 188
Finding Modules on Disk 191
Viewing the Module Content 193
Using the Python Module Documentation 198
Opening the pydoc application 198
Using the quick-access links 200
Typing a search term 202
Viewing the results 203

Chapter 11: Working with Strings 205

Understanding That Strings Are Different 206
Defining a character using numbers 206
Using characters to create strings 207
Creating Stings with Special Characters 208
Selecting Individual Characters 211
Slicing and Dicing Strings 213
Locating a Value in a String 217
Formatting Strings 219

Chapter 12: Managing Lists **223**

Organizing Information in an Application 224
  Defining organization using lists 224
  Understanding how computers view lists 225
Creating Lists 226
Accessing Lists 228
Looping Through Lists 231
Modifying Lists 232
Searching Lists 236
Sorting Lists 238
Working with the Counter Object 240

Chapter 13: Collecting All Sorts of Data **243**

Understanding Collections 243
Working with Tuples 245
Working with Dictionaries 248
  Creating and using a dictionary 249
  Replacing the switch statement with a dictionary 253
Creating Stacks Using Lists 256
Working with queues 260
Working with deques 263

Chapter 14: Creating and Using Classes **267**

Understanding the Class as a Packaging Method 268
Considering the Parts of a Class 269
  Creating the class definition 269
  Considering the built-in class attributes 271
  Working with methods 273
  Working with constructors 275
  Working with variables 277
  Using methods with variable argument lists 281
  Overloading operators 282
Creating a Class 284
Using the Class in an Application 285
Extending Classes to Make New Classes 287
  Building the child class 287
  Testing the class in an application 289

Part IV: Performing Advanced Tasks *291*

Chapter 15: Storing Data in Files **293**

Understanding How Permanent Storage Works 294
Creating Content for Permanent Storage 295
Creating a File 298

Reading File Content 301
Updating File Content 303
Deleting a File..308

Chapter 16: Sending an E-Mail **309**

Understanding What Happens When You Send E-Mail.........................310
Viewing e-mail as you do a letter 311
Defining the parts of the envelope 312
Defining the parts of the letter...318
Creating the E-mail Message 322
Working with a text message...323
Working with an HTML message 324
Seeing the E-mail Output 325

Part V: The Part of Tens **327**

Chapter 17: Ten Amazing Programming Resources **329**

Working with the Python Documentation Online 330
Using the LearnPython.org Tutorial 331
Performing Web Programming Using Python 332
Getting Additional Libraries...332
Creating Applications Faster Using an IDE...................................334
Checking Your Syntax with Greater Ease 334
Using XML to Your Advantage..335
Getting Past the Common Python Newbie Errors 336
Understanding Unicode 337
Making Your Python Application Fast 338

Chapter 18: Ten Ways to Make a Living with Python **339**

Working in QA...340
Becoming the IT Staff for a Smaller Organization.......................341
Performing Specialty Scripting for Applications 342
Administering a Network...343
Teaching Programming Skills..343
Helping People Decide on Location 344
Performing Data Mining..344
Interacting with Embedded Systems 345
Carrying Out Scientific Tasks...345
Performing Real-Time Analysis of Data 346

Chapter 19: Ten Interesting Tools. 347

Tracking Bugs with Roundup Issue Tracker 348
Creating a Virtual Environment Using VirtualEnv 349
Installing Your Application Using PyInstaller 350
Building Developer Documentation Using pdoc 351
Developing Application Code Using Komodo Edit 352
Debugging Your Application Using pydbgr 353
Entering an Interactive Environment using IPython 354
Testing Python Applications using PyUnit 354
Tidying Your Code Using Isort 355
Providing Version Control Using Mercurial 355

Chapter 20: Ten Libraries You Need to Know About. 357

Developing a Secure Environment Using PyCrypto 358
Interacting with Databases Using SQLAlchemy 358
Seeing the World Using Google Maps 359
Adding a Graphical User Interface Using TkInter 359
Providing a Nice Tabular Data Presentation Using PrettyTable 360
Enhancing Your Application with Sound Using PyAudio 360
Manipulating Images using PyQtGraph 361
Locating Your Information Using IRLib 362
Creating an Interoperable Java Environment Using JPype 363
Accessing Local Network Resources Using Twisted Matrix 364
Accessing Internet Resources Using Libraries 364

Index 365

Introduction

. . . .

*Q*uick! Which programming language will get you up and running writ-ing applications on every popular platform around? Give up? Yes, it's Python. The amazing thing about Python is that you really can write an appli-cation on one platform and use it on every other platform that you need to support. Unlike the other programming languages that promised to provide platform independence, Python really does make that independence pos-sible. In this case, the promise is as good as the result you get.

Python emphasizes code readability and a concise syntax that lets you write applications using fewer lines of code than other programming languages require. In addition, because of the way Python works, you find it used in all sorts of fields that are filled with nonprogrammers. Some people view Python as a scripted language, but it really is so much more. (Chapter 18 provides you with just an inkling of the occupations that rely on Python to make things work.)

About This Book

Beginning Programming with Python For Dummies is all about getting up and running with Python quickly. You want to learn the language fast so that you can become productive in using it to perform your real job, which could be anything. Unlike most books on the topic, this one starts you right at the beginning by showing you what makes Python different from other languages and how it can help you perform useful work in a job other than program-ming. As a result, you gain an understanding of what you need to do from the start, using hands-on examples and spending a good deal of time performing actually useful tasks. You even get help with installing Python on your par-ticular system.

When you have a good installation on whatever platform you're using, you start with the basics and work your way up. By the time you finish working through the examples in this book, you'll be writing simple programs and performing tasks such as sending an e-mail using Python. No, you won't be an expert, but you will be able to use Python to meet specific needs in the job environment. To make absorbing the concepts even easier, this book uses the following conventions:

- ✔ Text that you're meant to type just as it appears in the book is **bold**. The exception is when you're working through a step list: Because each step is bold, the text to type is not bold.

- ✔ When you see words in *italics* as part of a typing sequence, you need to replace that value with something that works for you. For example, if you see "Type ***Your Name*** and press Enter," you need to replace *Your Name* with your actual name.

- ✔ Web addresses and programming code appear in monofont. If you're reading a digital version of this book on a device connected to the Internet, note that you can click the web address to visit that website, like this: www.dummies.com.

- ✔ When you need to type command sequences, you see them separated by a special arrow, like this: File⇨New File. In this case, you go to the File menu first and then select the New File entry on that menu. The result is that you see a new file created.

Foolish Assumptions

You might find it difficult to believe that I've assumed anything about you — after all, I haven't even met you yet! Although most assumptions are indeed foolish, I made these assumptions to provide a starting point for the book.

It's important that you're familiar with the platform you want to use because the book doesn't provide any guidance in this regard. (Chapter 2 does provide Python installation instructions for various platforms.) In order to provide you with maximum information about Python, this book doesn't discuss any platform-specific issues. You really do need to know how to install applications, use applications, and generally work with your chosen platform before you begin working with this book.

This book also assumes that you can find things on the Internet. Sprinkled throughout are numerous references to online material that will enhance your learning experience. However, these added sources are useful only if you actually find and use them.

Icons Used in This Book

As you read this book, you see icons in the margins that indicate material of interest (or not, as the case may be). This section briefly describes each icon in this book.

Tips are nice because they help you save time or perform some task without a lot of extra work. The tips in this book are time-saving techniques or pointers to resources that you should try in order to get the maximum benefit from Python.

I don't want to sound like an angry parent or some kind of maniac, but you should avoid doing anything marked with a Warning icon. Otherwise, you could find that your program only serves to confuse users, who will then refuse to work with it.

Whenever you see this icon, think advanced tip or technique. You might find these tidbits of useful information just too boring for words, or they could contain the solution you need to get a program running. Skip these bits of information whenever you like.

If you don't get anything else out of a particular chapter or section, remember the material marked by this icon. This text usually contains an essential process or a bit of information that you must know to write Python programs successfully.

Beyond the Book

This book isn't the end of your Python programming experience — it's really just the beginning. I provide online content to make this book more flexible and better able to meet your needs. That way, as I receive e-mail from you, I can do things like address questions and tell you how updates to either Python or its associated libraries affect book content. In fact, you gain access to all these cool additions:

- ✔ **Cheat sheet:** You remember using crib notes in school to make a better mark on a test, don't you? You do? Well, a cheat sheet is sort of like that. It provides you with some special notes about tasks that you can do with Python that not every other developer knows. You can find the cheat sheet for this book at `http://www.dummies.com/cheatsheet/beg inningprogrammingwithpython`. It contains really neat information like the top ten mistakes developers make when working with Python and some of the Python syntax that gives most developers problems.

✔ **Dummies.com online articles:** A lot of readers were skipping past the parts pages in the book, so I decided to remedy that. You now have a really good reason to read the parts pages, and that's online content. Every parts page has an article associated with it that provides additional interesting information that wouldn't fit in the book. You can find the articles for this book at `http://www.dummies.com/extras/begi nningprogrammingwithpython`.

✔ **Updates:** Sometimes changes happen. For example, I might not have seen an upcoming change when I looked into my crystal ball during the writing of this book. In the past, that simply meant the book would become outdated and less useful, but you can now find updates to the book at `http://www.dummies.com/extras/beginningprogrammin gwithpython`.

In addition to these updates, check out the blog posts with answers to reader questions and demonstrations of useful book-related techniques at `http://blog.johnmuellerbooks.com/`.

✔ **Companion files:** Hey! Who really wants to type all the code in the book? Most readers would prefer to spend their time actually working through coding examples, rather than typing. Fortunately for you, the source code is available for download, so all you need to do is read the book to learn Python coding techniques. Each of the book examples even tells you precisely which example project to use. You can find these files at `http:// www.dummies.com/extras/beginningprogrammingwithpython`.

Where to Go from Here

It's time to start your Programming with Python adventure! If you're a complete programming novice, you should start with Chapter 1 and progress through the book at a pace that allows you to absorb as much of the material as possible.

If you're a novice who's in an absolute rush to get going with Python as quickly as possible, you could skip to Chapter 2 with the understanding that you may find some topics a bit confusing later. Skipping to Chapter 3 is possible if you already have Python installed, but be sure to at least skim Chapter 2 so that you know what assumptions were made when writing this book.

Readers who have some exposure to Python can save time by moving directly to Chapter 5. You can always go back to earlier chapters as necessary when you have questions. However, it's important that you understand how each example works before moving to the next one. Every example has important lessons for you, and you could miss vital content if you start skipping too much information.

Part I
Getting Started with Python

Visit www.dummies.com for great Dummies content online.

In this part . . .

- ✔ Discover what programming is all about and why you need Python to do it.

- ✔ Get your own copy of Python and install it on your system.

- ✔ Work with the interactive environment that Python provides.

- ✔ Create your first application using Python.

- ✔ Understand the benefits of adding comments to your application.

Chapter 1

Talking to Your Computer

· ·

In This Chapter

▶ Talking to your computer

▶ Creating programs to talk to your computer

▶ Understanding what a program does and why you want to create it

▶ Considering why you want to use Python as your programming language

· ·

*H*aving a conversation with your computer might sound like the script of a science fiction movie. After all, the members of the *Enterprise* on *Star Trek* regularly talked with their computer. In fact, the computer often talked back. However, with the rise of Apple's Siri (http://www.apple.com/ios/siri/) and other interactive software, perhaps you really don't find a conversation so unbelievable.

Asking the computer for information is one thing, but providing it with instructions is quite another. This chapter considers why you want to instruct your computer about anything and what benefit you gain from it. You also discover the need for a special language when performing this kind of communication and why you want to use Python to accomplish it. However, the main thing to get out of this chapter is that programming is simply a kind of communication that is akin to other forms of communication you already have with your computer.

Understanding Why You Want to Talk to Your Computer

Talking to a machine may seem quite odd at first, but it's necessary because a computer can't read your mind — yet. Even if the computer did read your mind, it would still be communicating with you. Nothing can occur without an exchange of information between the machine and you. Activities such as

✔ Reading your e-mail

✔ Writing about your vacation

✔ Finding the greatest gift in the world

are all examples of communication that occurs between a computer and you. That the computer further communicates with other machines or people to address requests that you make simply extends the basic idea that communication is necessary to produce any result.

In most cases, the communication takes place in a manner that is nearly invisible to you unless you really think about it. For example, when you visit a chat room online, you might think that you're communicating with another person. However, you're communicating with your computer, your computer is communicating with the other person's computer through the chat room (whatever it consists of), and the other person's computer is communicating with that person. Figure 1-1 gives you an idea of what is actually taking place.

Figure 1-1:
Commu-
nication
with your
computer
may be
invisible
unless you
really think
about it.

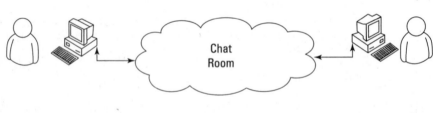

Notice the cloud in the center of Figure 1-1. The cloud could contain anything, but you know that it at least contains other computers running other applications. These computers make it possible for your friend and you to chat. Now, think about how easy the whole process seems when you're using the chat application. Even though all these things are going on in the background, it seems as if you're simply chatting with your friend and the process itself is invisible.

Knowing that an Application is a Form of Communication

Computer communication occurs through the use of applications. You use one application to answer your e-mail, another to purchase goods, and still another to create a presentation. An *application* (sometimes called an *app*) provides the means to express human ideas to the computer in a manner the computer can understand and defines the tools needed to shape the data used for the communication in specific ways. Data used to express the content of a presentation is different from data used to purchase a present for your mother. The way you view, use, and understand the data is different for each task, so you must use different applications to interact with the data in a manner that both the computer and you can understand.

It's possible to obtain applications to meet just about any general need you can conceive of today. In fact, you probably have access to applications for which you haven't even thought about a purpose yet. Programmers have been busy creating millions of applications of all types for many years now, so it may be hard to understand what you can accomplish by creating some new method for talking with your computer through an application. The answer comes down to thinking about the data and how you want to interact with it. Some data simply isn't common enough to have attracted the attention of a programmer, or you may need the data in a format that no application currently supports, so you don't have any way to tell the computer about it unless you create a custom application to do it.

The following sections describe applications from the perspective of working with unique data in a manner that is special in some way. For example, you might have access to a video library database but no method to access it in a way that makes sense to you. The data is unique and your access needs are special, so you may want to create an application that addresses both the data and your needs.

Thinking about procedures you use daily

A *procedure* is simply a set of steps you follow to perform a task. For example, when making toast, you might use a procedure like this:

1. Get the bread and butter from the refrigerator.

2. Open the bread bag and take out two pieces of toast.

3. Remove the cover from the toaster.

4. Place each piece of bread in its own slot.

5. Push the toaster lever down to start toasting the bread.

6. Wait for the toasting process to complete.

7. Remove toast from the toaster.

8. Place toast on a plate.

9. Butter the toast.

Your procedure might vary from the one presented here, but it's unlikely that you'd butter the toast before placing it in the toaster. Of course, you do actually have to remove the bread from the wrapper before you toast it (placing the bread, wrapper and all, into the toaster would likely produce undesirable results). Most people never actually think about the procedure for making toast. However, you use a procedure like this one even though you don't think about it.

Computers can't perform tasks without a procedure. You must tell the computer which steps to perform, the order in which to perform them, and any exceptions to the rule that could cause failure. All this information (and more) appears within an application. In short, an application is simply a written procedure that you use to tell the computer what to do, when to do it, and how to do it. Because you've been using procedures all your life, all you really need to do is apply the knowledge you already possess to what a computer needs to know about specific tasks.

Writing procedures down

When I was in grade school, our teacher asked us to write a paper about making toast. After we turned in our papers, she brought in a toaster and some loaves of bread. Each paper was read and demonstrated. None of our procedures worked as expected, but they all produced humorous results. In my case, I forgot to tell the teacher to remove the bread from the wrapper, so she dutifully tried to stuff the piece of bread, wrapper and all, into the toaster. The lesson stuck with me. Writing about procedures can be quite hard because we know precisely want we want to do, but often we leave steps out — we assume that the other person also knows precisely what we want to do.

Many experiences in life revolve around procedures. Think about the checklist used by pilots before a plane takes off. Without a good procedure, the plane could crash. Learning to write a great procedure takes time, but it's doable. You may have to try several times before you get a procedure that works completely, but eventually you can create one. Writing procedures down isn't really sufficient, though — you also need to test the procedure by using someone who isn't familiar with the task involved. When working with computers, the computer is your perfect test subject.

Seeing applications as being like any other procedure

A computer acts like the grade school teacher in my example in the previous section. When you write an application, you're writing a procedure that defines a series of steps that the computer should perform to accomplish whatever task you have in mind. If you leave out a step, the results won't be what you expected. The computer won't know what you mean or that you intended for it to perform certain tasks automatically. The only thing the computer knows is that you have provided it with a specific procedure and it needs to perform that procedure.

Understanding that computers take things literally

People eventually get used to the procedures you create. They automatically compensate for deficiencies in your procedure or make notes about things that you left out. In other words, people compensate for problems with the procedures that you write.

When you begin writing computer programs, you'll get frustrated because computers perform tasks precisely and read your instructions literally. For example, if you tell the computer that a certain value should equal 5, the computer will look for a value of exactly 5. A human might see 4.9 and know that the value is good enough, but a computer doesn't see things that way. It sees a value of 4.9 and decides that it doesn't equal 5 exactly. In short, computers are inflexible, unintuitive, and unimaginative. When you write a procedure for a computer, the computer will do precisely as you ask absolutely every time and never modify your procedure or decide that you really meant for it to do something else.

Defining What an Application Is

As previously mentioned, applications provide the means to define express human ideas in a manner that a computer can understand. To accomplish this goal, the application relies on one or more procedures that tell the computer how to perform the tasks related to the manipulation of data and its presentation. What you see onscreen is the text from your word processor, but to see that information, the computer requires procedures for retrieving the data from disk, putting it into a form you can understand, and then presenting it to you. The following sections define the specifics of an application in more detail.

Understanding that computers use a special language

Human language is complex and difficult to understand. Even applications such as Siri have serious limits in understanding what you're saying. Over the years, computers have gained the capability to input human speech as data and to understand certain spoken words as commands, but computers still don't quite understand human speech to any significant degree. The difficulty of human speech is exemplified in the way lawyers work. When you read legalese, it appears as a gibberish of sorts. However, the goal is to state ideas and concepts in a way that isn't open to interpretation. Lawyers seldom succeed in meeting their objective precisely because human speech is imprecise.

Given what you know from previous sections of this chapter, computers could never rely on human speech to understand the procedures you write. Computers always take things literally, so you'd end up with completely unpredictable results if you were to use human language to write applications. That's why humans use special languages, called *programming languages,* to communicate with computers. These special languages make it possible to write procedures that are both specific and completely understandable by both humans and computers.

Computers don't actually speak any language. They use binary codes to flip switches internally and to perform math calculations. Computers don't even understand letters — they understand only numbers. A special application turns the computer-specific language you use to write a procedure into binary codes. For the purposes of this book, you really don't need to worry too much about the low-level specifics of how computers work at the binary level. However, it's interesting to know that computers speak math and numbers, not really a language at all.

Helping humans speak to the computer

It's important to keep the purpose of an application in mind as you write it. An application is there to help humans speak to the computer in a certain way. Every application works with some type of data that is input, stored, manipulated, and output so that the humans using the application obtain a desired result. Whether the application is a game or a spreadsheet, the basic idea is the same. Computers work with data provided by humans to obtain a desired result.

When you create an application, you're providing a new method for humans to speak to the computer. The new approach you create will make it possible for other humans to view data in new ways. The communication between human and computer should be easy enough that the application actually disappears from view. Think about the kinds of applications you've used in the past. The best applications are the ones that let you focus on whatever data you're interacting with. For example, a game application is considered immersive only if you can focus on the planet you're trying to save or the ship you're trying to fly, rather than the application that lets you do these things.

 One of the best ways to start thinking about how you want to create an application is to look at the way other people create applications. Writing down what you like and dislike about other applications is a useful way to start discovering how you want your applications to look and work. Here are some questions you can ask yourself as you work with the applications:

✔ What do I find distracting about the application?

✔ Which features were easy to use?

✔ Which features were hard to use?

✔ How did the application make it easy to interact with my data?

✔ How would I make the data easier to work with?

✔ What do I hope to achieve with my application that this application doesn't provide?

Professional developers ask many other questions as part of creating an application, but these are good starter questions because they begin to help you think about applications as a means to help humans speak with computers. If you've ever found yourself frustrated by an application you used, you already know how other people will feel if you don't ask the appropriate questions when you create your application. Communication is the most important element of any application you create.

You can also start to think about the ways in which you work. Start writing procedures for the things you do. It's a good idea to take the process one step at a time and write everything you can think of about that step. When you get finished, ask someone else to try your procedure to see how it actually works. You might be surprised to learn that even with a lot of effort, you can easily forget to include steps.

The world's worst application usually begins with a programmer who doesn't know what the application is supposed to do, why it's special, what need it addresses, or whom it is for. When you decide to create an application, make sure that you know why you're creating it and what you hope to achieve. Just having a plan in place really helps make programming fun. You can work on your new application and see your goals accomplished one at a time until you have a completed application to use and show off to your friends (all of whom will think you're really cool for creating it).

Understanding Why Python is So Cool

Many programming languages are available today. In fact, a student can spend an entire semester in college studying computer languages and still not hear about them all. (I did just that during my college days.) You'd think that programmers would be happy with all these programming languages and just choose one to talk to the computer, but they keep inventing more.

Programmers keep creating new languages for good reason. Each language has something special to offer — something it does exceptionally well. In addition, as computer technology evolves, so do the programming languages in order to keep up. Because creating an application is all about efficient communication, many programmers know multiple programming languages so that they can choose just the right language for a particular task. One language might work better to obtain data from a database, and another might create user interface elements especially well.

As with every other programming language, Python does some things exceptionally well, and you need to know what they are before you begin using it. You might be amazed by the really cool things you can do with Python. Knowing a programming language's strengths and weaknesses helps you use it better as well as avoid frustration by not using the language for things it doesn't do well. The following sections help you make these sorts of decisions about Python.

Unearthing the reasons for using Python

Most programming languages are created with specific goals in mind. These goals help define the language characteristics and determine what you can do with the language. There really isn't any way to create a programming language that does everything because people have competing goals and needs when creating applications. When it comes to Python, the main objective was to create a programming language that would make programmers efficient and productive. With that in mind, here are the reasons that you want to use Python when creating an application:

- ✔ **Less application development time:** Python code is usually 2–10 times shorter than comparable code written in languages like C/C++ and Java, which means that you spend less time writing your application and more time using it.

- ✔ **Ease of reading:** A programming language is like any other language — you need to be able to read it to understand what it does. Python code tends to be easier to read than the code written in other languages, which means you spend less time interpreting it and more time making essential changes.

- ✔ **Reduced learning time:** The creators of Python wanted to make a programming language with fewer odd rules that make the language hard to learn. After all, programmers want to create applications, not learn obscure and difficult languages.

It's important to realize that, although Python is a popular language, it's not the most popular language out there. In fact, it currently ranks eighth on sites such as TIOBE (http://www.tiobe.com/index.php/content/paperinfo/tpci/index.html), an organization that tracks usage statistics (among other things). If you're looking for a language solely for the purpose of obtaining a job, Python is a good choice, but C/C++, Java, C#, or Visual Basic would be better choices. Make sure you choose a language you like and one that will address your application development needs, but also choose on the basis of what you intend to accomplish. Python was the language of the year in both 2007 and 2010 and has ranked as high as the fourth most popular language in February 2011. So, really, it's a good choice if you're looking for a job, but not necessarily the best choice. However, it may surprise you to know that many colleges now use Python to teach coding, and it has become the most popular language in that venue. Check out my blog post at http://blog.johnmuellerbooks.com/2014/07/14/python-as-a-learning-tool for details.

Deciding how you can personally benefit from Python

Ultimately, you can use any programming language to write any sort of application you want. If you use the wrong programming language for the job, the process will be slow, error prone, bug ridden, and you'll absolutely hate it — but you can get the job done. Of course, most of us would rather avoid horribly painful experiences, so it's important to know what sorts of applications people typically use Python to create. Here's a list of the most common uses for Python (although people do use it for other purposes):

✔ **Creating rough application examples:** Developers often need to create a *prototype,* a rough example of an application, before getting the resources to create the actual application. Python emphasizes productivity, so you can use it to create prototypes of an application quickly.

✔ **Scripting browser-based applications:** Even though JavaScript is probably the most popular language used for browser-based application scripting, Python is a close second. Python offers functionality that JavaScript doesn't provide (see the comparison at `https://blog.glyphobet.net/essay/2557` for details) and its high efficiency makes it possible to create browser-based applications faster (a real plus in today's fast-paced world).

✔ **Designing mathematic, scientific, and engineering applications:** Interestingly enough, Python provides access to some really cool libraries that make it easier to create math, scientific, and engineering applications. The two most popular libraries are NumPy (`http://www.numpy.org/`) and SciPy (`http://www.scipy.org/`). These libraries greatly reduce the time you spend writing specialized code to perform common math, scientific, and engineering tasks.

✔ **Working with XML:** The eXtensible Markup Language (XML) is the basis of most data storage needs on the Internet and many desktop applications today. Unlike most languages, where XML is just sort of bolted on, Python makes it a first-class citizen. If you need to work with a Web service, the main method for exchanging information on the Internet (or any other XML-intensive application), Python is a great choice.

✔ **Interacting with databases:** Business relies heavily on databases. Python isn't quite a query language, like the Structure Query Language (SQL) or Language INtegrated Query (LINQ), but it does do a great job of interacting with databases. It makes creating connections and manipulating data relatively painless.

✔ **Developing user interfaces:** Python isn't like some languages like C# where you have a built-in designer and can drag and drop items from a toolbox onto the user interface. However, it does have an extensive array of graphical user interface (GUI) frameworks — extensions that make graphics a lot easier to create (see `https://wiki.python.org/moin/GuiProgramming` for details). Some of these frameworks do come with designers that make the user interface creation process easier. The point is that Python isn't devoted to just one method of creating a user interface — you can use the method that best suits your needs.

Discovering which organizations use Python

Python really is quite good at the tasks that it was designed to perform. In fact, that's why a lot of large organizations use Python to perform at least some application-creation (development) tasks. You want a programming language that has good support from these large organizations because these organizations tend to spend money to make the language better. Here's a list of the large organizations that use Python the most:

✔ Alice Educational Software – Carnegie Mellon University (`http://www.cmu.edu/corporate/news/2007/features/alice.shtml`): Educational applications

✔ Fermilab (`https://www.fnal.gov/`): Scientific applications

✔ Go.com (`http://go.com/`): Browser-based applications

✔ Google (`https://www.google.com/`): Search engine

✔ Industrial Light & Magic (`http://www.ilm.com/`): Just about every programming need

✔ Lawrence Livermore National Library (`https://www.llnl.gov/`): Scientific applications

✔ National Space and Aeronautics Administration (NASA) (`http://www.nasa.gov/`): Scientific applications

✔ New York Stock Exchange (`https://nyse.nyx.com/`): Browser-based applications

✔ ObjectDomain (`http://case-tools.org/tools/objectdomain.html`): Computer Aided Software Engineering (CASE) tools

✔ Redhat (`http://www.redhat.com/`): Linux installation tools

- ✔ Yahoo! (`https://www.yahoo.com/`): Parts of Yahoo! mail
- ✔ YouTube (`http://www.youtube.com/`): Graphics engine
- ✔ Zope – Digital Creations (`http://www.zope.com/`): Publishing application

These are just a few of the many organizations that use Python extensively. You can find a more complete list of organizations at `http://www.python.org/about/success/`. The number of success stories has become so large that even this list probably isn't complete and the people supporting it have had to create categories to better organize it.

Finding useful Python applications

You might have an application written in Python sitting on your machine right now and not even know it. Python is used in a vast array of applications on the market today. The applications range from utilities that run at the console to full-fledged CAD/CAM suites. Some applications run on mobile devices, while others run on the large services employed by enterprises. In short, there is no limit to what you can do with Python, but it really does help to see what others have done. You can find a number of places online that list applications written in Python, but the best place to look is `https://wiki.python.org/moin/Applications`.

As a Python programmer, you'll also want to know that Python development tools are available to make your life easier. A *development tool* provides some level of automation in writing the procedures needed to tell the computer what to do. Having more development tools means that you have to perform less work in order to obtain a working application. Developers love to share their lists of favorite tools, but you can find a great list of tools broken into categories at `http://www.python.org/about/apps/`.

Of course, this chapter describes a number of tools as well, such as NumPy and SciPy (two scientific libraries). The remainder of the book lists a few other tools; make sure that you copy down your favorite tools for later.

Comparing Python to other languages

Comparing one language to another is somewhat dangerous because the selection of a language is just as much a matter of taste and personal preference as it is any sort of quantifiable scientific fact. So before I'm attacked by the rabid protectors of the languages that follow, it's important to realize that I also use a number of languages and find at least some level of overlap among them all. There is no best language in the world, simply the language that works best for a particular application. With this idea in mind, the following sections provide an overview comparison of Python to other languages. (You can find comparisons to other languages at `https://wiki.python.org/moin/LanguageComparisons`.)

C#

A lot of people claim that Microsoft simply copied Java to create C#. That said, C# does have some advantages (and disadvantages) when compared to Java. The main (undisputed) intent behind C# is to create a better kind of C/C++ language — one that is easier to learn and use. However, we're here to talk about C# and Python. When compared to C#, Python has these advantages:

- ✔ Significantly easier to learn
- ✔ Smaller (more concise) code
- ✔ Supported fully as open source
- ✔ Better multiplatform support
- ✔ Easily allows use of multiple development environments
- ✔ Easier to extend using Java and C/C++
- ✔ Enhanced scientific and engineering support

Java

For years, programmers looked for a language that they could use to write an application just once and have it run anywhere. Java is designed to work well on any platform. It relies on some tricks that you'll discover later in the book to accomplish this magic. For now, all you really need to know is that Java was so successful at running well everywhere that other languages have sought to emulate it (with varying levels of success). Even so, Python has some important advantages over Java, as shown in the following list:

- ✔ Significantly easier to learn
- ✔ Smaller (more concise) code
- ✔ Enhanced variables (storage boxes in computer memory) that can hold different kinds of data based on the application's needs while running (dynamic typing)
- ✔ Faster development times

Perl

PERL was originally an acronym for Practical Extraction and Report Language. Today, people simply call it Perl and let it go at that. However, Perl still shows its roots in that it excels at obtaining data from a database and presenting it in report format. Of course, Perl has been extended to do a lot more than that — you can use it to write all sorts of applications. (I've even used it for a Web service application.) In a comparison with Python, you'll find that Python has these advantages over Perl:

- ✔ Simpler to learn
- ✔ Easier to read
- ✔ Enhanced protection for data
- ✔ Better Java integration
- ✔ Fewer platform-specific biases

Chapter 2

Getting Your Own Copy of Python

* *

In This Chapter

▶ Obtaining a copy of Python for your system

▶ Performing the Python installation

▶ Finding and using Python on your system

▶ Ensuring your installation works as planned

* *

*C*reating applications requires that you have another application, unless you really want to get low level and write applications in machine code — a decidedly difficult experience that even true programmers avoid if at all possible. If you want to write an application using the Python programming language, you need the applications required to do so. These applications help you work with Python by creating Python code, providing help information as you need it, and letting you run the code you write. This chapter helps you obtain a copy of the Python application, install it on your hard drive, locate the installed applications so that you can use them, and test your installation so that you can see how it works.

Downloading the Version You Need

Every *platform* (combination of computer hardware and operating system software) has special rules that it follows when running applications. The Python application hides these details from you. You type code that runs on any platform that Python supports, and the Python applications translate that code into something the platform can understand. However, in order for the translation to take place, you must have a version of Python that works on your particular platform. Python supports these platforms:

✔ Advanced IBM Unix (AIX)

✔ Amiga Research OS (AROS)

- ✔ Application System 400 (AS/400)
- ✔ BeOS
- ✔ Hewlett-Packard Unix (HP-UX)
- ✔ Linux
- ✔ Mac OS X (comes pre-installed with the OS)
- ✔ Microsoft Disk Operating System (MS-DOS)
- ✔ MorphOS
- ✔ Operating System 2 (OS/2)
- ✔ Operating System 390 (OS/390) and z/OS
- ✔ PalmOS
- ✔ Playstation
- ✔ Psion
- ✔ QNX
- ✔ RISC OS (originally Acorn)
- ✔ Series 60
- ✔ Solaris
- ✔ Virtual Memory System (VMS)
- ✔ Windows 32-bit (XP and later)
- ✔ Windows 64-bit
- ✔ Windows CE/Pocket PC

Wow, that's a lot of different platforms! This book is tested with the Windows, Mac OS X, and Linux platforms. However, the examples could very well work with these other platforms, too, because the examples don't rely on any platform-specific code. Let me know if it works on your non-Windows, Mac, or Linux platform at John@JohnMuellerBooks.com. The current version of Python at the time of this writing is 3.3.4. I'll talk about any Python updates on my blog at http://blog.johnmuellerbooks.com. You can find the answers to your Python book-specific questions there, too.

To get the right version for your platform, you need to go to http://www.python.org/download/releases/3.3.4/. The download section is initially hidden from view, so you need to scroll halfway down the page. You see a page similar to the one shown in Figure 2-1. The main part of the page contains links for Windows, Mac OS X, and Linux downloads. These links provide you with the default setup that is used in this book. The platform-specific links on the left side of the page show you alternative Python configurations that you can use when the need arises. For example, you may want to use a more advanced editor than the one provided with the default Python package, and these alternative configurations can provide one for you.

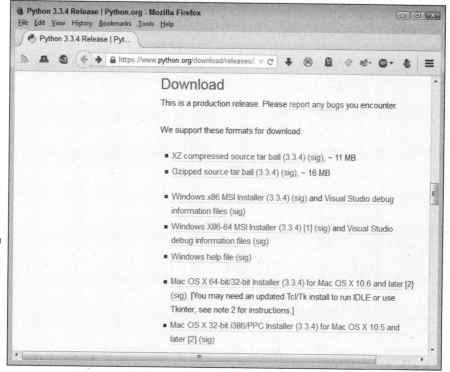

Figure 2-1:
The Python download page contains links for all sorts of versions.

If you want to work with another platform, click the Other link on the left side of the page. You see a list of Python installations for other platforms, as shown in Figure 2-2. Many of these installations are maintained by volunteers rather than by the people who create the versions of Python for Windows, Mac OS X, and Linux. Make sure you contact these individuals when you have installation questions because they know how best to help you get a good installation on your platform.

Figure 2-2:
Volunteers
have made
Python
available on
all sorts of
platforms.

Installing Python

After you download your copy of Python, it's time to install it on your system. The downloaded file contains everything needed to get you started:

- Python interpreter
- Help files (documentation)
- Command-line access
- Integrated DeveLopment Environment (IDLE) application
- Uninstaller (only on platforms that require it)

This book assumes that you're using one of the default Python setups found at `http://www.python.org/download/releases/3.3.4/`. The following sections describe how to install Python on the three platforms directly supported by this book: Windows, Mac OS X, and Linux.

Working with Windows

The installation process on a Windows system follows the same procedure that you use for other application types. The main difference is in finding the file you downloaded so that you can begin the installation process. The following procedure should work fine on any Windows system, whether you use the 32-bit or the 64-bit version of Python.

1. **Locate the downloaded copy of Python on your system.**

   The name of this file varies, but normally it appears as `python-3.3.4.msi` for 32-bit systems and `python-3.3.4.amd64.msi` for 64-bit systems. The version number is embedded as part of the filename. In this case, the filename refers to version 3.3.4, which is the version used for this book.

2. **Double-click the installation file.**

   (You may see an Open File – Security Warning dialog box that asks whether you want to run this file. Click Run if you see this dialog box pop up.) You see a Python Setup dialog box similar to the one shown in Figure 2-3. The exact dialog box you see depends on which version of the Python installation program you download.

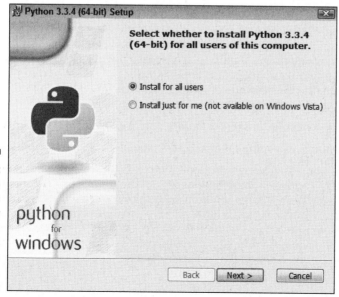

Figure 2-3:
The setup process begins by asking you who should have access to Python.

3. **Choose a user installation option (the book uses the default setting of Install for All Users) and click Next.**

   Install asks you to provide the name of an installation directory for Python, as shown in Figure 2-4. Using the default destination will save you time and effort later. However, you can install Python anywhere you desire.

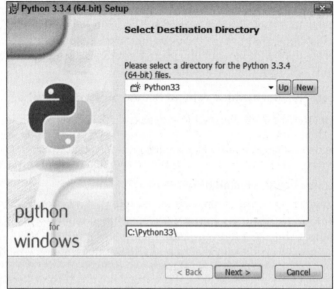

Figure 2-4: Decide on an installation location for your copy of Python.

Using the Windows \Program Files or \Program Files (x86) folder is problematic for two reasons. First, the folder name has a space in it, which makes it hard to access from within the application. Second, the folder usually requires administrator access, so you'll constantly battle the User Account Control (UAC) feature of Windows if you install Python in either folder.

4. **Type a destination folder name, if necessary, and click Next.**

   Python asks you to customize its installation, as shown in Figure 2-5.

Enabling the Add python.exe to Path option will save you time later. This feature makes it possible to access Python from the Command Prompt window. Don't worry too much about how you use this feature just yet, but it really is a good feature to have installed. The book assumes that you've enabled this feature. Don't worry about the other features you see in Figure 2-5. They're all enabled by default, which provides you with maximum access to Python functionality.

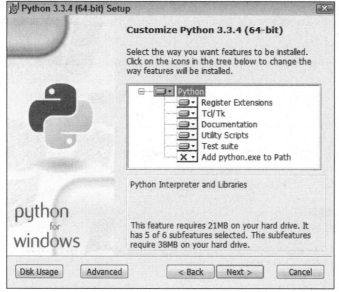

Figure 2-5:
Customize
your instal-
lation to
meet your
needs.

5. **(Optional) Click the down arrow next to the Add python.exe to Path option and choose the Will Be Installed On Local Drive option.**

6. **Click Next.**

   You see the installation process start. At some point, you might see a User Account Control dialog box asking whether you want to perform the install. If you see this dialog box, click Yes. The installation continues and you see an Installation Complete dialog box.

7. **Click Finish.**

   Python is ready for use.

Working with the Mac

Your Mac system likely already has Python installed on it. However, this installation is normally a few years old — or whatever the age of your system happens to be. For the purposes of this book, the installation will likely work fine. You won't be testing the limits of Python programming technology — just getting a great start using Python.

The Leopard version of OS X (10.5) uses a really old version of Python 2.5.1. This particular version lacks direct access to the IDLE application. As a result, you may find that some book exercises won't work properly. The article at https://wiki.python.org/moin/MacPython/Leopard tells you more about how to overcome this particular issue. The newest version of OS X at the time of this writing (Mavericks, or 10.9) comes with Python 2.7, which is just fine for working through the examples in the book.

Depending on how you use Python, you might want to update your installation at some point. Part of this process involves installing the GNU Compiler Collection (GCC) tools so that Python has access to the low-level resources it needs. The following steps get you started with installing a new version of Python on your Mac OS X system.

1. **Navigate to** http://www.python.org/download/releases/3.3.4/ **with your browser.**

   You see information regarding the latest version of Python, as shown in Figure 2-1.

2. **Click the appropriate link for your version of OS X:**

   a. Python 3.3.4 Mac OS X 64-bit/32-bit x86-64/i386 Installer for 32-bit or 64-bit versions on the Intel processor

   b. Python 3.3.4 Mac OS X 32-bit i386/PPC Installer for 32-bit versions on the Power PC processor

   The Python disk image begins downloading. Be patient: The disk image requires several minutes to download. Most browsers provide a method for monitoring the download process so that you can easily see how long the download will take. When the download is complete, your Mac automatically opens the disk image for you.

   The disk image actually looks like a folder. Inside this folder, you see a number of files, including python.mpkg. The python.mpkg file is the one that contains the Python application. The text files contain information about the build, licensing, and any late-breaking notes.

3. **Double-click** python.mpkg.

   You see a Welcome dialog box that tells you about this particular Python build.

4. **Click Continue three times.**

   The installation program displays late-breaking notes about Python, licensing information (click Agree when asked about the licensing information), and, finally, a destination dialog box.

5. **Select the Volume (hard drive or other media) that you want to use for installing Python and click Continue.**

   The Installation Type dialog box appears. This dialog box performs two tasks:

   - Click Customize to change the feature set that is installed on your system.
   - Click Change Install Location to modify the place where the installer places Python.

   The book assumes that you're performing a standard installation and that you haven't changed the installation location. However, these options are available in case you want to use them.

6. **Click Install.**

   The installer may request your administrator password. Type the administrator name and password, if required, into the dialog box and click OK. You see an Installing Python dialog box. The contents of this dialog box will change as the installation process proceeds so that you know what part of Python the installer is working with.

   After the installation is completed, you see an Install Succeeded dialog box.

7. **Click Close.**

   Python is ready to use. (You can close the disk image at this point and remove it from your system.)

Working with Linux

Some versions of Linux come with Python installed. For example, if you have a Red Hat Package Manager (RPM)-based distribution (such as SUSE, Red Hat, Yellow Dog, Fedora Core, and CentOS), you likely already have Python on your system and don't need to do anything else.

Depending on which version of Linux you use, the version of Python varies and some systems don't include the Interactive DeveLopment Environment (IDLE) application. If you have an older version of Python (2.5.1 or earlier), you might want to install a newer version so that you have access to IDLE. Many of the book exercises require use of IDLE.

You actually have two techniques to use to install Python on Linux. The following sections discuss both techniques. The first technique works on any Linux distribution; the second technique has special criteria that you must meet.

Using the standard Linux installation

The standard Linux installation works on any system. However, it requires you to work at the Terminal and type commands to complete it. Some of the actual commands may vary by version of Linux. The information at `http://docs.python.org/3/install/` provides some helpful tips that you can use in addition to the procedure that follows.

1. **Navigate to** `http://www.python.org/download/releases/3.3.4/` **with your browser.**

   You see information regarding the latest version of Python, as shown in Figure 2-1.

2. **Click the appropriate link for your version of Linux:**

   a. Python 3.3.4 compressed source tarball (any version of Linux)

   b. Python 3.3.4 xzipped source tarball (better compression and faster download)

3. **When asked whether you want to open or save the file, choose Save.**

   The Python source files begin downloading. Be patient: The source files require a minute or two to download.

4. **Double-click the downloaded file.**

   The Archive Manager window opens. After the files are extracted, you see the `Python 3.3.4` folder in the Archive Manager window.

5. **Double-click the** `Python 3.3.4` **folder.**

   The Archive Manager extracts the files to the `Python 3.3.4` subfolder of your home folder.

6. **Open a copy of Terminal.**

   The Terminal window appears. If you have never built any software on your system before, you must install the build essentials, SQLite, and bzip2 or the Python installation will fail. Otherwise, you can skip to Step 10 to begin working with Python immediately.

7. **Type** sudo apt-get install build-essential **and press Enter.**

   Linux installs the Build Essential support required to build packages (see `https://packages.debian.org/squeeze/build-essential` for details).

8. **Type** sudo apt-get install libsqlite3-dev **and press Enter.**

   Linux installs the SQLite support required by Python for database manipulation (see `https://packages.debian.org/squeeze/libsqlite3-dev` for details).

9. **Type** sudo apt-get install libbz2-dev **and press Enter.**

   Linux installs the bzip2 support required by Python for archive manipulation (see `https://packages.debian.org/sid/libbz2-dev` for details).

10. **Type** CD Python 3.3.4 **in the Terminal window and press Enter.**

    Terminal changes directories to the `Python 3.3.4` folder on your system.

11. **Type** ./configure **and press Enter.**

    The script begins by checking the system build type and then performs a series of tasks based on the system you're using. This process can require a minute or two because there is a large list of items to check.

12. **Type** make **and press Enter.**

    Linux executes the make script to create the Python application software. The make process can require up to a minute — it depends on the processing speed of your system.

13. **Type** sudo make altinstall **and press Enter.**

    The system may ask you for your administrator password. Type your password and press Enter. At this point, a number of tasks take place as the system installs Python on your system.

Using the graphical Linux installation

All versions of Linux support the standard installation discussed in the "Using the standard Linux installation" section of this chapter. However, a few versions of Debian-based Linux distributions, such as Ubuntu 12.*x* and later, provide a graphical installation technique as well. You need the administrator group (sudo) password to use this procedure, so having it handy will save you time. The following steps outline the graphical installation technique for Ubuntu, but the technique is similar for other Linux installations:

1. **Open the** Ubuntu Software Center **folder. (The folder may be named** Synaptics **on other platforms.)**

   You see a listing of the most popular software available for download and installation.

2. **Select Developer Tools (or Development) from the All Software drop-down list box.**

   You see a listing of developer tools, including Python.

3. **Double-click the Python 3.3.4 entry.**

   The Ubuntu Software Center provides details about the Python 3.3.4 entry and offers to install it for you.

4. **Click Install.**

   Ubuntu begins the process of installing Python. A progress bar shows the download and installation status. When the installation is complete, the Install button changes to a Remove button.

5. **Close the** `Ubuntu Software Center` **folder.**

   You see a Python icon added to the desktop. Python is ready for use.

Accessing Python on Your Machine

After you have Python installed on your system, you need to know where to find it. In some respects, Python does everything it can to make this process easy by performing certain tasks, such as adding the Python path to the machine's path information during installation. Even so, you need to know how to access the installation, which the following sections describe.

Using Windows

A Windows installation creates a new folder in the Start menu that contains your Python installation. You can access it by choosing Start⇨All Programs⇨ Python 3.3. The two items of interest in the folder when creating new applications are IDLE (Python GUI) and Python (command line).

A word about the screenshots

As you work your way through the book, you'll use either IDLE or the Python command-line shell to work with Python. The name of the graphical (GUI) environment, IDLE, is precisely the same across all three platforms, and you won't even see any significant difference in the presentation. The differences you do see are minor, and you should ignore them as you work through the book. With this in mind, the book does rely heavily on Windows screenshots — all the screenshots you see were obtained from a Windows system for the sake of consistency.

The command-line shell also works precisely the same across all three platforms. The presentation may vary a little more than IDLE does simply because the shell used for each platform varies slightly. However, the commands you type for one platform are precisely the same on another platform. The output is the same as well. When viewing the screenshot, look at the content rather than for specific differences in the presentation of the shell.

Clicking IDLE (Python GUI) produces a graphical interactive environment like the one shown in Figure 2-6. When you open this environment, IDLE automatically displays some information so that you know you have the right application open. For example, you see the Python version number (which is 3.3.4 in this case). It also tells you what sort of system you're using to run Python.

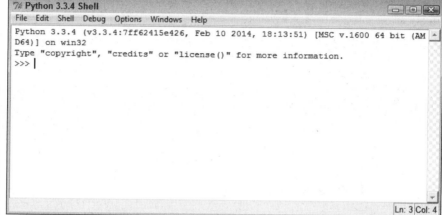

Figure 2-6:
Use IDLE when you want the comforts of a graphical environment.

The Python (command line) option opens a command prompt and executes the Python command, as shown in Figure 2-7. Again, the environment automatically displays information such as the Python version and the host platform.

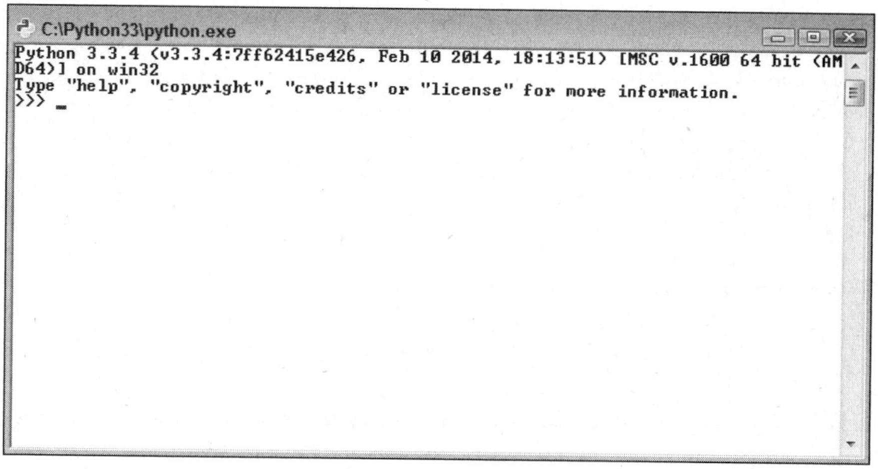

Figure 2-7:
Use the command prompt when you want the speed and flexibility of a command-line interface.

A third method to access Python is to open a command prompt, type **Python**, and press Enter. You can use this approach when you want to gain additional flexibility over the Python environment, automatically load items, or execute Python in a higher-privilege environment (in which you gain additional security rights). Python provides a significant array of command-line options that you can see by typing **Python /?** at the command prompt and pressing Enter. Figure 2-8 shows what you typically see. Don't worry too much about these command-line options — you won't need them for this book, but it's helpful to know they exist.

```
Administrator: Command Prompt

Microsoft Windows [Version 6.1.7601]
Copyright (c) 2009 Microsoft Corporation.  All rights reserved.

C:\Windows\system32>Python /?
usage: Python [option] ... [-c cmd | -m mod | file | -] [arg] ...
Options and arguments (and corresponding environment variables):
-b     : issue warnings about str(bytes_instance), str(bytearray_instance)
         and comparing bytes/bytearray with str. (-bb: issue errors)
-B     : don't write .py[co] files on import; also PYTHONDONTWRITEBYTECODE=x
-c cmd : program passed in as string (terminates option list)
-d     : debug output from parser; also PYTHONDEBUG=x
-E     : ignore PYTHON* environment variables (such as PYTHONPATH)
-h     : print this help message and exit (also --help)
-i     : inspect interactively after running script; forces a prompt even
         if stdin does not appear to be a terminal; also PYTHONINSPECT=x
-m mod : run library module as a script (terminates option list)
-O     : optimize generated bytecode slightly; also PYTHONOPTIMIZE=x
-OO    : remove doc-strings in addition to the -O optimizations
-q     : don't print version and copyright messages on interactive startup
-s     : don't add user site directory to sys.path; also PYTHONNOUSERSITE
-S     : don't imply 'import site' on initialization
-u     : unbuffered binary stdout and stderr, stdin always buffered;
         also PYTHONUNBUFFERED=x
         see man page for details on internal buffering relating to '-u'
-v     : verbose (trace import statements); also PYTHONVERBOSE=x
         can be supplied multiple times to increase verbosity
-V     : print the Python version number and exit (also --version)
-W arg : warning control; arg is action:message:category:module:lineno
         also PYTHONWARNINGS=arg
-x     : skip first line of source, allowing use of non-Unix forms of #!cmd
-X opt : set implementation-specific option
file   : program read from script file
-      : program read from stdin (default; interactive mode if a tty)
arg ...: arguments passed to program in sys.argv[1:]

Other environment variables:
PYTHONSTARTUP: file executed on interactive startup (no default)
PYTHONPATH   : ';'-separated list of directories prefixed to the
               default module search path.  The result is sys.path.
PYTHONHOME   : alternate <prefix> directory (or <prefix>;<exec_prefix>).
               The default module search path uses <prefix>\lib.
PYTHONCASEOK : ignore case in 'import' statements (Windows).
PYTHONIOENCODING: Encoding[:errors] used for stdin/stdout/stderr.
PYTHONFAULTHANDLER: dump the Python traceback on fatal errors.
PYTHONHASHSEED: if this variable is set to 'random', a random value is used
   to seed the hashes of str, bytes and datetime objects.  It can also be
   set to an integer in the range [0,4294967295] to get hash values with a
   predictable seed.

C:\Windows\system32>_
```

Figure 2-8:
Using a standard command line offers the flexibility of using switches to change the way Python works.

To use this third method of executing Python, you must include Python in the Windows path. This is why you want to choose the Add python.exe to Path option when installing Python on Windows. If you didn't add the path during installation, you can add it afterward using the instructions found in the Adding a Location to the Windows Path article on my blog at `http://blog.johnmuellerbooks.com/2014/02/17/adding-a-location-to-the-windows-path/`. This same technique works for adding Python-specific environment variables such as

✔ PYTHONSTARTUP

✔ PYTHONPATH

✔ PYTHONHOME

✔ PYTHONCASEOK

✔ PYTHONIOENCODING

✔ PYTHONFAULTHANDLER

✔ PYTHONHASHSEED

None of these environment variables is used in the book. However, you can find out more about them at `http://docs.python.org/3.3/using/cmdline.html#environment-variables`.

Using the Mac

When working with a Mac, you probably have Python already installed and don't need to install it for this book. However, you still need to know where to find Python. The following sections tell you how to access Python depending on the kind of installation you performed.

Locating the default installation

The default OS X installation doesn't include a Python-specific folder in most cases. Instead, you must open Terminal by choosing Applications⇨Utilities⇨Terminal. After Terminal is open, you can type **Python** and press Enter to access the command-line version of Python. The display you see is similar to the one shown in Figure 2-7. As with Windows (see the "Using Windows" section of the chapter), using Terminal to open Python offers the advantage of using command-line switches to modify the manner in which Python works.

Locating the updated version of Python you installed

After you perform the installation on your Mac system, open the `Applications` folder. Within this folder, you find a `Python 3.3` folder that contains the following:

✔ `Extras` folder

✔ IDLE application (GUI development)

✔ Python Launcher (interactive command development)

✔ Update Sh... command

Double-clicking IDLE application opens a graphical interactive environment that looks similar to the environment shown in Figure 2-6. There are some small cosmetic differences, but the content of the window is the same. Double-clicking Python Launcher opens a command-line environment similar to the one shown in Figure 2-7. This environment uses all the Python defaults to provide a standard execution environment.

Even if you install a new version of Python on your Mac, you don't have to settle for using the default environment. It's still possible to open Terminal to gain access to the Python command-line switches. However, when you access Python from the Mac Terminal application, you need to ensure that you're not accessing the default installation. Make sure to add `/usr/local/bin/ Python3.3` to your shell search path.

Using Linux

After the installation process is complete, you can find a `Python 3.3` sub-folder in your home folder. The physical location of Python 3.3 on your Linux system is normally the `/usr/local/bin/Python3.3` folder. This is important information because you may need to modify the path for your system manually. Linux developers need to type **Python3.3**, rather than just **Python**, when working at the Terminal window to obtain access to the Python 3.3.4 installation.

Testing Your Installation

To ensure that you have a usable installation, you need to test it. It's important to know that your installation will work as expected when you need it. Of course, this means writing your first Python application. To get started, open a copy of IDLE. As previously mentioned, IDLE automatically displays the Python version and host information when you open it (refer to Figure 2-6).

To see Python work, type **print("This is my first Python program.")** and press Enter. Python displays the message you just typed, as shown in Figure 2-9. The `print()` command displays onscreen whatever you tell it to display. You see the `print()` command used quite often in this book to display the results of tasks you ask Python to perform, so this is one of the commands you work with frequently.

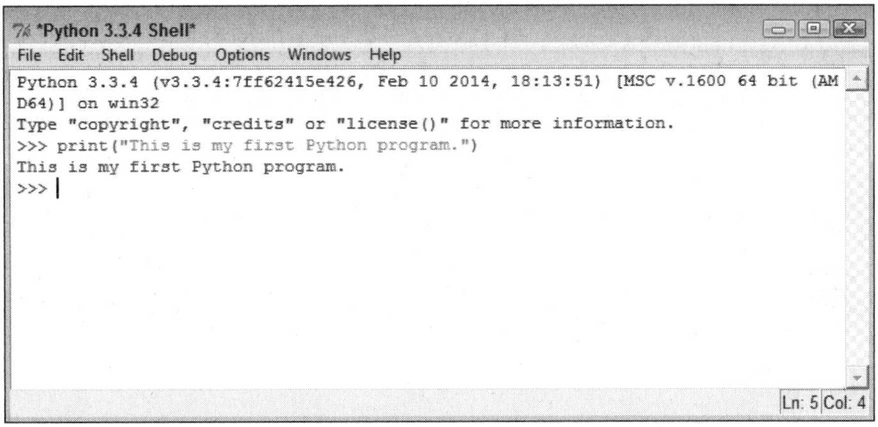

Figure 2-9:
The
`print()`
command
displays
whatever
information
you tell it
to print.

Notice that IDLE color codes the various entries for you so that they're easier to see and understand. The colors codes are your indicator that you've done something right. Four color codes are shown in Figure 2-9 (although they're not visible in the print edition of the book):

- **Purple:** Indicates that you have typed a command
- **Green:** Specifies the content sent to a command
- **Blue:** Shows the output from a command
- **Black:** Defines non-command entries

You know that Python works now because you were able to issue a command to it, and it responded by reacting to that command. It might be interesting to see one more command. Type **3 + 4** and press Enter. Python responds by outputting 7, as shown in Figure 2-10. Notice that 3 + 4 appears in black type because it isn't a command. However, the 7 is still in blue type because it's output.

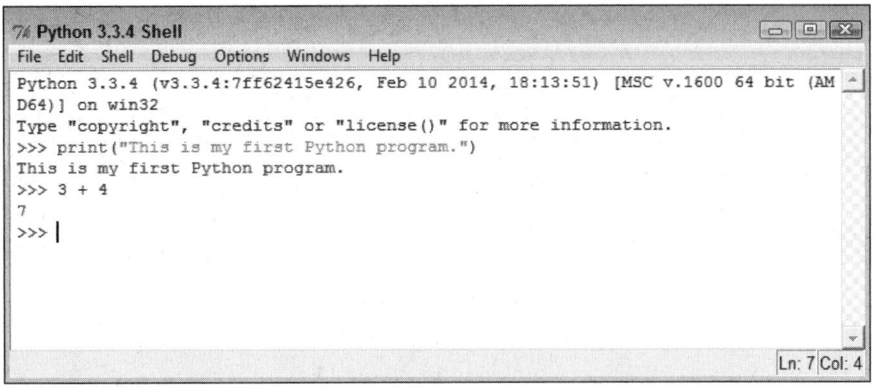

Figure 2-10:
Python sup-
ports math
directly as
part of the
interactive
environment.

It's time to end your IDLE session. Type **quit()** and press Enter. IDLE may display a message such as the one shown in Figure 2-11. Well, you never intended to kill anything, but you will now. Click OK, and the session dies.

Figure 2-11:
IDLE seems
to get a little
dramatic
about
ending a
session!

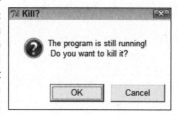

Notice that the quit() command has parentheses after it, just as the print() command does. All commands have parentheses like these two. That's how you know they're commands. However, you don't need to tell the quit() command anything, so you simply leave the area between the parentheses blank.

Chapter 3

Interacting with Python

- -

In This Chapter

▶ Accessing the command line

▶ Using commands to perform tasks

▶ Obtaining help about Python

▶ Ending a command-line session

- -

*U*ltimately, any application you create interacts with the computer and the data it contains. The focus is on data because without data, there isn't a good reason to have an application. Any application you use (even one as simple as Solitaire) manipulates data in some way. In fact, the acronym CRUD sums up what most applications do:

- ✔ Create
- ✔ Read
- ✔ Update
- ✔ Delete

If you remember CRUD, you'll be able to summarize what most applications do with the data your computer contains (and some applications really are quite cruddy). However, before your application accesses the computer, you have to interact with a programming language that creates a list of tasks to perform in a language the computer understands. That's the purpose of this chapter. You begin interacting with Python. Python takes the list of steps you want to perform on the computer's data and changes those steps into bits the computer understands.

Understanding the importance of the README file

Many applications include a README file. The README file usually provides updated information that didn't make it into the documentation before the application was put into a production status. Unfortunately, most people ignore the README file and some don't even know it exists. As a result, people who should know something interesting about their shiny new product never find out. Python has a README.txt file in the \Python33 directory. When you open this file, you find all sorts of really interesting information:

✔ How to build a copy of Python for Linux systems

✔ Where to find out about new features in this version of Python

✔ Where to find the latest version of the Python documentation

✔ How to convert your older Python applications to work with Python 3.3.x

✔ What you need to do to test custom Python modifications

✔ How to install multiple versions of Python on the same system

✔ How to access bug and issue tracking for Python

✔ How to request updates to Python

✔ How to find out when the next version of Python will come out

Opening and reading the README file will help you become a Python genius. People will be amazed that you really do know something interesting about Python and will ask you all sorts of questions (deferring to your wisdom). Of course, you could always just sit there, thinking that the README is just too much effort to read.

Opening the Command Line

Python offers a number of ways to interact with the underlying language. For example, you worked a bit with the Integrated DeveLopment Environment (IDLE) in Chapter 2. IDLE makes it easy to develop full-fledged applications. However, sometimes you simply want to experiment or to run an existing application. Often, using the command-line version of Python works better in these cases because it offers better control over the Python environment through command-line switches, uses fewer resources, and relies on a minimalistic interface so that you can focus on trying out code rather than playing with a GUI.

Starting Python

Depending on your platform, you might have multiple ways to start the command line. Here are the methods that are commonly available:

- ✔ Select the Python (command-line) option found in the `Python 3.3` folder. This option starts a command-line session that uses the default settings.

- ✔ Open a command prompt or terminal, type **Python**, and press Enter. Use this option when you want greater flexibility in configuring the Python environment using command-line switches.

- ✔ Locate the Python folder, such as `C:\Python33` in Windows, and open the `Python.exe` file directly. This option also opens a command-line session that uses the default settings, but you can do things like open it with increased privileges (for applications that require access to secured resources) or modify the executable file properties (to add command-line switches).

No matter how you start Python at the command line, you eventually end up with a prompt similar to the one shown in Figure 3-1. (Your screen may look slightly different from the one shown in Figure 3-1 if you rely on a platform other than Windows, you're using IDLE instead of the command-line version of Python, your system is configured differently from mine, or you have a different version of Python.) This prompt tells you the Python version, the host operating system, and how to obtain additional information.

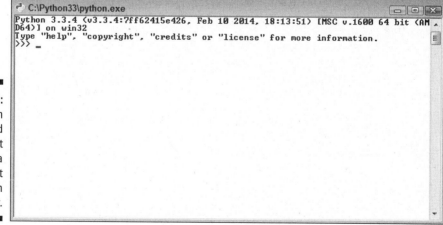

Figure 3-1:
The Python command prompt tells you a bit about the Python environment.

Using the command line to your advantage

This section will seem a little complicated at first, and you won't normally need this information when using the book. However, it's still good information, and you'll eventually need it. For now, you can browse the information so that you know what's available and then come back to it later when you really do need the information.

To start Python at a command prompt, type **Python** and press Enter. However, that's not all you can do. You can also provide some additional information to change how Python works:

✔ **Options:** An option, or command-line switch, begins with a minus sign followed by one or more letters. For example, if you want to obtain help about Python, you type **Python –h** and press Enter. You see additional information about how to work with Python at the command line. The options are described later in this section.

✔ **Filename:** Providing a filename as input tells Python to load that file and run it. You can run any of the example applications from the downloadable code by providing the name of the file containing the example as input. For example, say that you have an example named `SayHello.py`. To run this example, you type **Python SayHello.py** and press Enter.

✔ **Arguments:** An application can accept additional information as input to control how it runs. This additional information is called an argument. Don't worry too much about arguments right now — they appear later in the book.

Most of the options won't make sense right now. They're here so that you can find them later when you need them (this is the most logical place to include them in the book). Reading through them will help you gain an understanding of what's available, but you can also skip this material until you need it later.

Python uses case-sensitive options. For example, `-s` is a completely different option from `-S`. The Python options are

✔ `-b`: Add warnings to the output when your application uses certain Python features that include: `str(bytes_instance)`, `str(bytearray_instance)`, and comparing `bytes` or `bytearray` with `str()`.

✔ `-bb`: Add errors to the output when your application uses certain Python features that include: `str(bytes_instance)`, `str(bytearray_instance)`, and comparing `bytes` or `bytearray` with `str()`.

✔ `-B`: Don't write `.py` or `.pyco` files when performing a module import.

✔ -c *cmd*: Use the information provided by *cmd* to start a program. This option also tells Python to stop processing the rest of the information as options (it's treated as part of the command).

✔ -d: Start the debugger (used to locate errors in your application).

✔ -E: Ignore all the Python environment variables, such as PYTHONPATH, that are used to configure Python for use.

✔ -h: Display help about the options and basic environment variables onscreen. Python always exits after it performs this task without doing anything else so that you can see the help information.

✔ -i: Force Python to let you inspect the code interactively after running a script. It forces a prompt even if stdin (the standard input device) doesn't appear to be a terminal.

✔ -m *mod*: Run the library module specified by *mod* as a script. This option also tells Python to stop processing the rest of the information as options (the rest of the information is treated as part of the command).

✔ -O: Optimize the generated bytecode slightly (makes it run faster).

✔ -OO: Perform additional optimization by removing doc-strings.

✔ -q: Tell Python not to print the version and copyright messages on interactive startup.

✔ -s: Force Python not to add the user site directory to sys.path (a variable that tells Python where to find modules).

✔ -S: Don't run 'import site' on initialization. Using this option means that Python won't look for paths that may contain modules it needs.

✔ -u: Allow unbuffered binary input for the stdout (standard output) and stderr (standard error) devices. The stdin device is always buffered.

✔ -v: Place Python in verbose mode so that you can see all the import statements. Using this option multiple times increases the level of verbosity.

✔ -V: Display the Python version number and exit.

✔ --version: Display the Python version number and exit.

✔ -W *arg*: Modify the warning level so that Python displays more or fewer warnings. The valid *arg* values are

- action
- message
- category
- module
- lineno

✔ -x: Skip the first line of a source code file, which allows the use of non-Unix forms of #!cmd.

✔ -X opt: Set an implementation-specific option. (The documentation for your version of Python discusses these options, if there are any.)

Using Python environment variables to your advantage

Environment variables are special settings that are part of the command line or terminal environment for your operating system. They serve to configure Python in a consistent manner. Environment variables perform many of the same tasks as do the options that you supply when you start Python, but you can make environment variables permanent so that you can configure Python the same way every time you start it without having to manually supply the option.

As with options, most of these environment variables won't make any sense right now. You can read through them to see what is available. You find some of the environment variables used later in the book. Feel free to skip the rest of this section and come back to it later when you need it.

Most operating systems provide the means to set environment variables temporarily, by configuring them during a particular session, or permanently, by configuring them as part of the operating system setup. Precisely how you perform this task depends on the operating system. For example, when working with Windows, you can use the Set command (see my blog post at http://blog. johnmuellerbooks.com/2014/02/24/using-the-set-command-to-your-advantage/ for details) or rely on a special Windows configuration feature (see my post at http://blog.johnmuellerbooks.com/2014/02/17/adding-a-location-to-the-windows-path/ for setting the Path environment variable as an example).

Using environment variables makes sense when you need to configure Python the same way on a regular basis. The following list describes the Python environment variables:

✔ PYTHONCASEOK=x: Forces Python to ignore case when parsing import statements. This is a Windows-only environment variable.

✔ PYTHONDEBUG=x: Performs the same task as the -d option.

✔ PYTHONDONTWRITEBYTECODE=x: Performs the same task as the -B option.

✔ PYTHONFAULTHANDLER=*x*: Forces Python to dump the Python traceback (list of calls that led to an error) on fatal errors.

✔ PYTHONHASHSEED=*arg*: Determines the seed value used to generate hash values from various kinds of data. When this variable is set to random, Python uses a random value to seed the hashes of str, bytes, and datetime objects. The valid integer range is 0 to 4294967295. Use a specific seed value to obtain predictable hash values for testing purposes.

✔ PYTHONHOME=*arg*: Defines the default search path that Python uses to look for modules.

✔ PYTHONINSPECT=*x*: Performs the same task as the -i option.

✔ PYTHONIOENCODING=*arg*: Specifies the encoding[:errors] (such as utf-8) used for the stdin, stdout, and stderr devices.

✔ PYTHONNOUSERSITE: Performs the same task as the -s option.

✔ PYTHONOPTIMIZE=*x*: Performs the same task as the -O option.

✔ PYTHONPATH=*arg*: Provides a semicolon (;) separated list of directories to search for modules. This value is stored in the sys.path variable in Python.

✔ PYTHONSTARTUP=*arg*: Defines the name of a file to execute when Python starts. There is no default value for this environment variable.

✔ PYTHONUNBUFFERED=*x*: Performs the same task as the -u option.

✔ PYTHONVERBOSE=*x*: Performs the same task as the -v option.

✔ PYTHONWARNINGS=*arg*: Performs the same task as the -W option.

Typing a Command

After you start the command-line version of Python, you can begin typing commands. Using commands makes it possible to perform tasks, test ideas that you have for writing your application, and discover more about Python. Using the command line lets you gain hands-on experience with how Python actually works — details that could be hidden by an Interactive Development Environment (IDE) such as IDLE. The following sections get you started using the command line.

Telling the computer what to do

Python, like every other programming language in existence, relies on commands. A *command* is simply a step in a procedure. In Chapter 1, you saw how "Get the bread and butter from the refrigerator" is a step in a procedure for making toast. When working with Python, a command, such as print(), is simply the same thing: a step in a procedure.

To tell the computer what to do, you issue one or more commands that Python understands. Python translates these commands into instructions that the computer understands, and then you see the result. A command such as print() can display the results onscreen so that you get an instant result. However, Python supports all sorts of commands, many of which don't display any results onscreen but still do something important.

As the book progresses, you use commands to perform all sorts of tasks. Each of these tasks will help you accomplish a goal, just as the steps in a procedure do. When it seems as if all the Python commands become far too complex, simply remember to look at them as steps in a procedure. Even human procedures become complex at times, but if you take them one step at a time, you begin to see how they work. Python commands are the same way. Don't get overwhelmed by them; instead, look at them one at a time and focus on just that step in your procedure.

Telling the computer you're done

At some point, the procedure you create ends. When you make toast, the procedure ends when you finish buttering the toast. Computer procedures work precisely the same way. They have a starting and an ending point. When typing commands, the ending point for a particular step is the Enter key. You press Enter to tell the computer that you're done typing the command. As the book progresses, you find that Python provides a number of ways to signify that a step, group of steps, or even an entire application is complete. No matter how the task is accomplished, computer programs always have a distinct starting and stopping point.

Seeing the result

You now know that a command is a step in a procedure and that each command has a distinct starting and ending point. In addition, groups of commands and entire applications also have a distinct starting and ending point. So, take a look at how this works. The following procedure helps you see the result of using a command:

1. **Start a copy of the Python command-line version.**

   You see a command prompt where you can type commands, as shown in Figure 3-1.

2. **Type** print("This is a line of text.") **at the command line.**

   Notice that nothing happens. Yes, you typed a command, but you haven't signified that the command is complete.

3. **Press Enter.**

   The command is complete, so you see a result like the one shown in Figure 3-2.

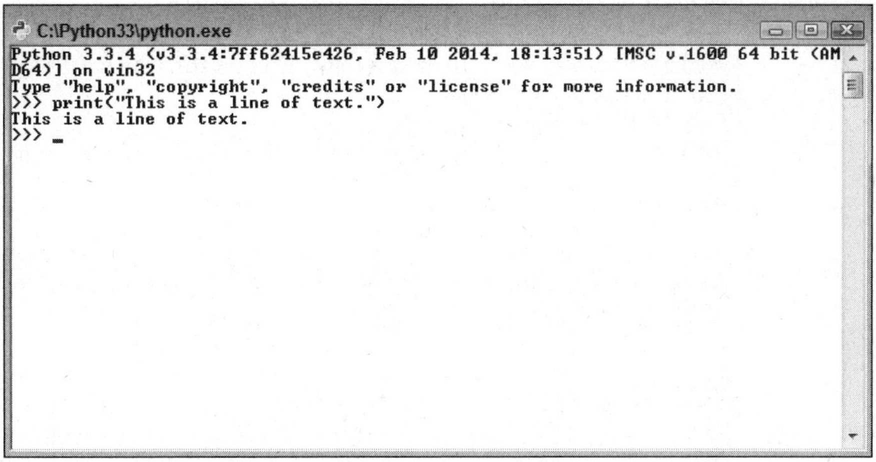

```
C:\Python33\python.exe
Python 3.3.4 (v3.3.4:7ff62415e426, Feb 10 2014, 18:13:51) [MSC v.1600 64 bit (AM
D64)] on win32
Type "help", "copyright", "credits" or "license" for more information.
>>> print("This is a line of text.")
This is a line of text.
>>>
```

Figure 3-2: Issuing commands tells Python what to tell the computer to do.

This exercise shows you how things work within Python. Each command that you type performs some task, but only after you tell Python that the command is complete in some way. The print() command displays data onscreen. In this case, you supplied text to display. Notice that the output shown in Figure 3-2 comes immediately after the command because this is an interactive environment — one in which you see the result of any given command immediately after Python performs it. Later, as you start creating applications, you notice that sometimes a result doesn't appear immediately because the application environment delays it. Even so, the command is executed by Python immediately after the application tells Python that the command is complete.

Using Help

Python is a computer language, not a human language. As a result, you won't speak it fluently at first. If you think about it for a moment, it makes sense that you won't speak Python fluently (and as with most human languages, you won't know every command even after you do become fluent). Having to discover Python commands a little at a time is the same thing that happens when you learn to speak another human language. If you normally speak English and try to say something in German, you find that you must have some sort of guide to help you along. Otherwise, anything you say is gibberish and people will look at you quite oddly. Even if you manage to say something that makes sense, it may not be what you want. You might go to a restaurant and order hot hubcaps for dinner when what you really wanted was a steak.

Likewise, when you try to speak Python, you need a guide to help you. Fortunately, Python is quite accommodating and provides immediate help to keep you from ordering something you really don't want. The help provided inside Python works at two levels:

- ✓ **Help mode,** in which you can browse the available commands
- ✓ **Direct help,** in which you ask about a specific command

There isn't a correct way to use help — just the method that works best for you at a particular time. The following sections describe how to obtain help.

Getting into help mode

When you first start Python, you see a display similar to the one shown in Figure 3-1. Notice that Python provides you with four commands at the outset (which is actually your first piece of help information):

- ✓ help
- ✓ copyright
- ✓ credits
- ✓ license

All four commands provide you with help, of a sort, about Python. For example, the copyright() command tells you about who holds the right to copy, license, or otherwise distribute Python. The credits() command tells you who put Python together. The license() command describes the usage agreement between you and the copyright holder. However, the command you most want to know about is simply help().

To enter help mode, type **help()** and press Enter. Notice that you must include the parentheses after the command even though they don't appear in the help text. Every Python command has parentheses associated with it. After you enter this command, Python goes into help mode and you see a display similar to the one shown in Figure 3-3.

Figure 3-3:
You ask
Python
about other
commands
in help
mode.

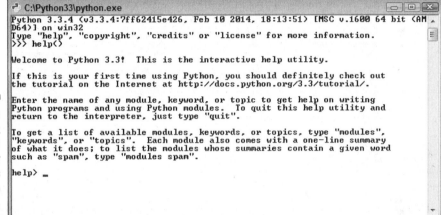

```
C:\Python33\python.exe
Python 3.3.4 (v3.3.4:7ff62415e426, Feb 10 2014, 18:13:51) [MSC v.1600 64 bit (AM
D64)] on win32
Type "help", "copyright", "credits" or "license" for more information.
>>> help()

Welcome to Python 3.3! This is the interactive help utility.

If this is your first time using Python, you should definitely check out
the tutorial on the Internet at http://docs.python.org/3.3/tutorial/.

Enter the name of any module, keyword, or topic to get help on writing
Python programs and using Python modules. To quit this help utility and
return to the interpreter, just type "quit".

To get a list of available modules, keywords, or topics, type "modules",
"keywords", or "topics". Each module also comes with a one-line summary
of what it does; to list the modules whose summaries contain a given word
such as "spam", type "modules spam".

help> _
```

You can always tell that you're in help mode by the help> prompt that you see in the Python window. As long as you see the help> prompt, you know that you're in help mode.

Asking for help

To obtain help, you need to know what question to ask. The initial help message that you see when you go into help mode (refer to Figure 3-3) provides some helpful tips about the kinds of questions you can ask. If you want to explore Python, the three basic topics are

✔ modules
✔ keywords
✔ topics

The first two topics won't tell you much for now. You won't need the `modules` topic until Chapter 10. The `keywords` topic will begin proving useful in Chapter 4. However, the `topics` keyword is already useful because it helps you understand where to begin your Python adventure. To see what topics are available, type **topics** and press Enter. You see a list of topics similar to those shown in Figure 3-4.

Figure 3-4: The `topics` help topic provides you with a starting point for your Python adventure.

```
C:\Python33\python.exe
help> topics

Here is a list of available topics.  Enter any topic name to get more help.

ASSERTION          DELETION            LITERALS           SEQUENCES
ASSIGNMENT         DICTIONARIES        LOOPING            SHIFTING
ATTRIBUTEMETHODS   DICTIONARYLITERALS  MAPPINGMETHODS     SLICINGS
ATTRIBUTES         DYNAMICFEATURES     MAPPINGS           SPECIALATTRIBUTES
AUGMENTEDASSIGNMENT ELLIPSIS           METHODS            SPECIALIDENTIFIERS
BASICMETHODS       EXCEPTIONS          MODULES            SPECIALMETHODS
BINARY             EXECUTION           NAMESPACES         STRINGMETHODS
BITWISE            EXPRESSIONS         NONE               STRINGS
BOOLEAN            FILES               NUMBERMETHODS      SUBSCRIPTS
CALLABLEMETHODS    FLOAT               NUMBERS            TRACEBACKS
CALLS              FORMATTING          OBJECTS            TRUTHVALUE
CLASSES            FRAMEOBJECTS        OPERATORS          TUPLELITERALS
CODEOBJECTS        FRAMES              PACKAGES           TUPLES
COMPARISON         FUNCTIONS           POWER              TYPEOBJECTS
COMPLEX            IDENTIFIERS         PRECEDENCE         TYPES
CONDITIONAL        IMPORTING           PRIVATENAMES       UNARY
CONTEXTMANAGERS    INTEGER             RETURNING          UNICODE
CONVERSIONS        LISTLITERALS        SCOPING
DEBUGGING          LISTS               SEQUENCEMETHODS

help>
```

When you see a topic that you like, such as FUNCTIONS, simply type that topic and press Enter. To see how this works, type **FUNCTIONS** and press Enter (you must type the word in uppercase — don't worry, Python won't think you're shouting). You see help information similar to that shown in Figure 3-5.

Figure 3-5: You must use uppercase when requesting topic information.

```
C:\Python33\python.exe
CODEOBJECTS        FRAMES              PACKAGES           TUPLES
COMPARISON         FUNCTIONS           POWER              TYPEOBJECTS
COMPLEX            IDENTIFIERS         PRECEDENCE         TYPES
CONDITIONAL        IMPORTING           PRIVATENAMES       UNARY
CONTEXTMANAGERS    INTEGER             RETURNING          UNICODE
CONVERSIONS        LISTLITERALS        SCOPING
DEBUGGING          LISTS               SEQUENCEMETHODS

help> FUNCTIONS
Functions
*********

Function objects are created by function definitions.  The only
operation on a function object is to call it: "func(argument-list)".

There are really two flavors of function objects: built-in functions
and user-defined functions.  Both support the same operation (to call
the function), but the implementation is different, hence the
different object types.

See *Function definitions* for more information.

Related help topics: def, TYPES

help>
```

As you work through examples in the book, you use commands that look interesting, and you might want more information about them. For example, in the "Seeing the result" section of this chapter, you use the print() command. To see more information about the print() command, type **print** and press Enter (notice that you don't include the parentheses this time because you're requesting help about print(), not actually using the command). Figure 3-6 shows typical help information for the print() command.

Figure 3-6: Request command help information by typing the command using whatever case it actually uses.

```
C:\Python33\python.exe
operation on a function object is to call it: "func(argument-list)".

There are really two flavors of function objects: built-in functions
and user-defined functions.  Both support the same operation (to call
the function), but the implementation is different, hence the
different object types.

See *Function definitions* for more information.

Related help topics: def, TYPES

help> print
Help on built-in function print in module builtins:

print(...)
    print(value, ..., sep=' ', end='\n', file=sys.stdout, flush=False)

    Prints the values to a stream, or to sys.stdout by default.
    Optional keyword arguments:
    file:  a file-like object (stream); defaults to the current sys.stdout.
    sep:   string inserted between values, default a space.
    end:   string appended after the last value, default a newline.
    flush: whether to forcibly flush the stream.

help>
```

Unfortunately, reading the help information probably doesn't help much yet because you need to know more about Python. However, you can ask for more information. For example, you might wonder what sys.stdout means — and the help topic certainly doesn't tell you anything about it. Type **sys.stdout** and press Enter. You see the help information shown in Figure 3-7.

Figure 3-7: You can ask for help on the help you receive.

```
C:\Python33\python.exe
Help on TextIOWrapper in sys object:

sys.stdout = class TextIOWrapper(_TextIOBase)
 |  Character and line based layer over a BufferedIOBase object, buffer.
 |
 |  encoding gives the name of the encoding that the stream will be
 |  decoded or encoded with. It defaults to locale.getpreferredencoding(False).
 |
 |  errors determines the strictness of encoding and decoding (see
 |  help(codecs.Codec) or the documentation for codecs.register) and
 |  defaults to "strict".
 |
 |  newline controls how line endings are handled. It can be None, '',
 |  '\n', '\r', and '\r\n'.  It works as follows:
 |
 |  * On input, if newline is None, universal newlines mode is
 |    enabled. Lines in the input can end in '\n', '\r', or '\r\n', and
 |    these are translated into '\n' before being returned to the
 |    caller. If it is '', universal newline mode is enabled, but line
 |    endings are returned to the caller untranslated. If it has any of
 |    the other legal values, input lines are only terminated by the given
 |    string, and the line ending is returned to the caller untranslated.
 |
 |  * On output, if newline is None, any '\n' characters written are
-- More  --
```

You may still not find the information as helpful as you need, but at least you know a little more. In this case, help has a lot to say and it can't all fit on one screen. Notice the following entry at the bottom of the screen:

```
-- More  --
```

To see the additional information, press the spacebar. The next page of help appears. As you read to the bottom of each page of help, you can press the spacebar to see the next page. The pages don't go away — you can scroll up to see previous material.

Leaving help mode

At some point, you need to leave help mode to perform useful work. All you have to do is press Enter without typing anything. When you press Enter, you see a message about leaving help, and then the prompt changes to the standard Python prompt, as shown in Figure 3-8.

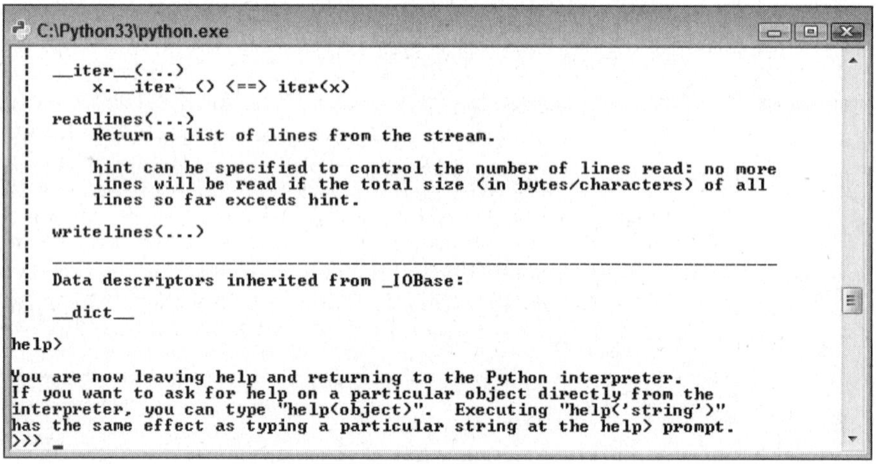

Figure 3-8: Exit help mode by pressing Enter without typing anything.

```
C:\Python33\python.exe

    __iter__(...)
        x.__iter__() <==> iter(x)

    readlines(...)
        Return a list of lines from the stream.

        hint can be specified to control the number of lines read: no more
        lines will be read if the total size (in bytes/characters) of all
        lines so far exceeds hint.

    writelines(...)

    ----------------------------------------------------------------------
    Data descriptors inherited from _IOBase:

    __dict__

help>
You are now leaving help and returning to the Python interpreter.
If you want to ask for help on a particular object directly from the
interpreter, you can type "help(object)".  Executing "help('string')"
has the same effect as typing a particular string at the help> prompt.
>>>
```

Obtaining help directly

Entering help mode isn't necessary unless you want to browse, which is always a good idea, or unless you don't actually know what you need to find. If you have a good idea of what you need, all you need to do is ask for help directly (a really nice thing for Python to do). So, instead of fiddling with help mode, you simply type the word *help*, followed by a left parenthesis and single quote, whatever you want to find, another single quote, and the right parenthesis. For example, if you want to know more about the `print()` command, you type **help('print')** and press Enter. Figure 3-9 shows typical output when you access help this way.

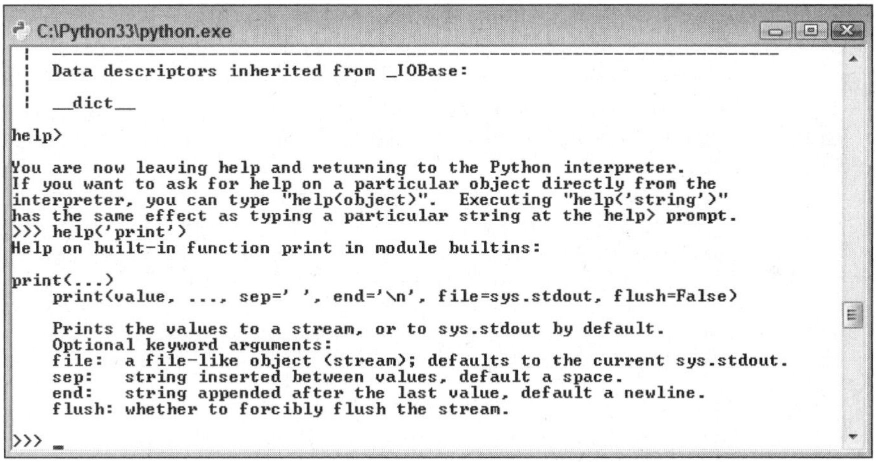

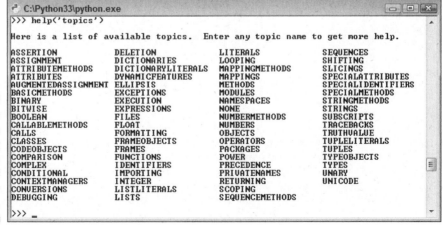

Figure 3-9:
Python makes it possible to obtain help whenever you need it without leaving the Python prompt.

You can browse at the Python prompt, too. For example, when you type **help('topics')** and press Enter, you see a list of topics like the one that appears in Figure 3-10. You can compare this list with the one shown in Figure 3-4. The two lists are identical, even though you typed one while in help mode and the other while at the Python prompt.

Figure 3-10:
It's possible to browse at the Python prompt if you really want to.

You might wonder why Python has a help mode at all if you can get the same results at the Python prompt. The answer is convenience. It's easier to browse in the help mode. In addition, even though you don't do a lot of extra typing at the prompt, you do perform less typing while in help mode. Help mode also provides additional helps, such as by listing commands that you can type, as shown in Figure 3-3. So you have all kinds of good reasons to enter help mode when you plan to ask Python a lot of help questions.

No matter where you ask for help, you need to observe the correct capitalization of help topics. For example, if you want general information about functions, you must type **help('FUNCTIONS')** and not `help('Functions')` or `help('functions')`. When you use the wrong capitalization, Python will tell you that it doesn't know what you mean or that it couldn't find the help topic. It won't know to tell you that you used the wrong capitalization. Someday computers will know what you meant to type, rather than what you did type, but that hasn't happened yet.

Closing the Command Line

Eventually, you want to leave Python. Yes, it's hard to believe, but people have other things to do besides playing with Python all day long. You have two standard methods for leaving Python and a whole bunch of nonstandard methods. Generally, you want to use one of the standard methods to ensure that Python behaves as you expect it to, but the nonstandard methods work just fine when you simply want to play around with Python and not perform any productive work. The two standard methods are

✔ `quit()`

✔ `exit()`

Either of these methods will close the interactive version of Python. The *shell* (the Python program) is designed to allow either command.

Both of these commands can accept an optional argument. For example, you can type **quit(5)** or **exit(5)** and press Enter to exit the shell. The numeric argument sets the command prompt's ERRORLEVEL environment variable, which you can then intercept at the command line or as part of a batch file. Standard practice is to simply use `quit()` or `exit()` when nothing has gone wrong with the application. To see this way of exiting at work, you must

1. **Open a command prompt or terminal.**

   You see a prompt.

2. **Type** Python **and press Enter to start Python.**

   You see the Python prompt.

3. Type quit(5) **and press Enter.**

You see the prompt again.

4. Type echo %ERRORLEVEL% **and press Enter.**

You see the error code, as shown in Figure 3-11. When working with plat-forms other than Windows, you may need to type something other than echo %ERRORLEVEL%. For example, when working with a bash script, you type **echo $** instead.

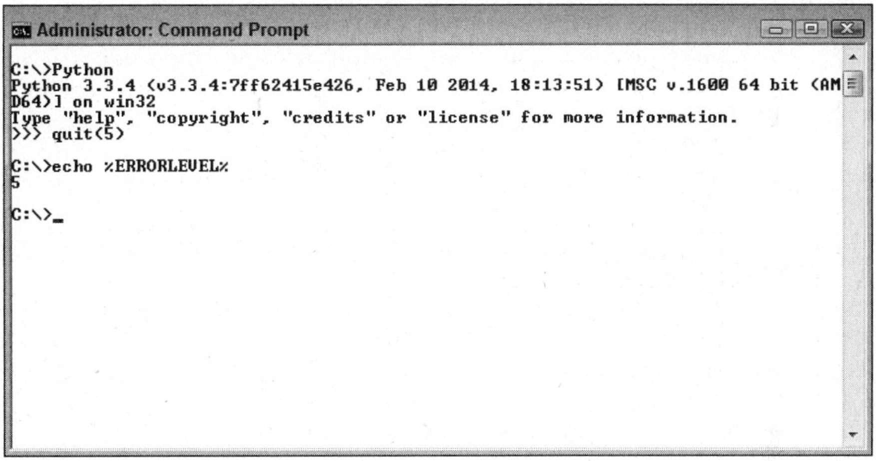

```
Administrator: Command Prompt

C:\>Python
Python 3.3.4 (v3.3.4:7ff62415e426, Feb 10 2014, 18:13:51) [MSC v.1600 64 bit (AM
D64)] on win32
Type "help", "copyright", "credits" or "license" for more information.
>>> quit(5)

C:\>echo %ERRORLEVEL%
5

C:\>_
```

Figure 3-11:
Add an error code when needed to tell others the Python exit status.

One of the most common nonstandard exit methods is to simply click the command prompt's or terminal's Close button. Using this approach means that your application may not have time to perform any required cleanup, which can result in odd behaviors. It's always better to close Python using an expected approach if you've been doing anything more than simply browsing.

You also have access to a number of other commands for closing the command prompt when needed. In most cases, you won't need these special commands, so you can skip the rest of this section if desired.

When you use quit() or exit(), Python performs a number of tasks to ensure that everything is neat and tidy before the session ends. If you sus-pect that a session might not end properly anyway, you can always rely on one of these two commands to close the command prompt:

✔ sys.exit()

✔ os._exit()

Both of these commands are used in emergency situations only. The first, `sys.exit()`, provides special error-handling features that you discover in Chapter 9. The second, `os._exit()`, exits Python without performing any of the usual cleanup tasks. In both cases, you must import the required module, either `sys` or `os`, before you can use the associated command. Consequently, to use the `sys.exit()` command, you actually use this code:

```
import sys
sys.exit()
```

You must provide an error code when using `os._exit()` because this command is used only when an extreme error has occurred. The call to this command will fail if you don't provide an error code. To use the `os._exit()` command, you actually use this code (where the error code is 5):

```
import os
os._exit(5)
```

Chapter 10 discusses importing modules in detail. For now, just know that these two commands are for special uses only and you won't normally use them in an application.

Chapter 4

Writing Your First Application

· ·

In This Chapter

▶ Working with the Integrated DeveLopment Environment (IDLE)

▶ Getting started with IDLE

▶ Writing the first application

▶ Seeing how the first application works

▶ Formatting your application code

▶ Using comments effectively

▶ Working with existing applications

▶ Ending your IDLE session

· ·

*M*any people view application development as some sort of magic practiced by wizards called geeks who wave their keyboard to produce software both great and small. However, the truth is a lot more mundane.

Application development follows a number of processes. It's more than a strict procedure, but is most definitely not magic of any sort. As Arthur C. Clark once noted, "Any sufficiently advanced technology is indistinguishable from magic." This chapter is all about removing the magic from the picture and introducing you to the technology. By the time you're finished with this chapter, you too will be able to develop a simple application (and you won't use magic to do it).

As with any other task, people use tools to write applications. In the case of Python, you don't have to use a tool, but using a tool makes the task so much easier that you really will want to use one. In this chapter, you use a tool that comes with Python, the Integrated DeveLopment Environment (IDLE). In the previous chapter, you use the command-line tool to play around with Python a little. However, IDLE goes further than the command line tool and makes it possible to write applications with greater ease.

A vast number of other tools are available for you to use when writing Python applications. This book doesn't tell you much about them because IDLE performs every task needed and it comes with Python. However, as your skills increase, you might find that tools such as Komodo Edit (`http://www.activestate.com/komodo-edit/downloads`) are easier to work with than IDLE. You can find a great list of these tools at `https://wiki.python.org/moin/IntegratedDevelopmentEnvironments`.

Understanding the Integrated Development Environment (IDLE)

You can literally create any Python application you want using just a text editor. As long as the editor outputs pure text rather than formatted text as a word processor does, you can use it to write Python code. However, using a text editor isn't efficient or straightforward. To make the development process easier, developers have written Interactive Development Environments (IDEs). The IDE that comes with Python is IDLE. However, many other IDEs are capable of working with Python.

The feature set provided by IDEs varies. In fact, that's why there are so many of them on the market. IDLE provides a basic feature set that is shared by most IDEs out there. It provides the functionality required to

✔ Write Python code.

✔ Recognize and highlight keywords and certain types of special text.

✔ Perform both simple editing (such as cut, copy, and paste) and code-specific editing (such as showing the parentheses that surround an expression).

✔ Save and open Python files.

✔ Browse the Python path to make locating files easy.

✔ Browse and locate Python classes.

✔ Perform simple debugging tasks (removing errors from the code).

IDLE differs from the command-line version of Python in that you get a full-fledged GUI and you can accomplish many tasks much more easily through IDLE than through the command line. In addition, the command line doesn't really offer all the same features as IDLE. Yes, you can debug your application using the command line, but it's a difficult, error-prone process. Using IDLE is a whole lot easier.

Starting IDLE

You find IDLE in the Python 3.3 folder on your system as IDLE (Python GUI). When you click or double-click this entry (depending on your platform), you see the IDLE editor shown in Figure 4-1. The two lines of text contain information about the Python host and provide suggestions on the commands you can try. The precise information you see differs by platform. Your screenshots may differ from mine depending on the version of Python you use, the platform you use, how you have IDLE configured, and how you have your system configured.

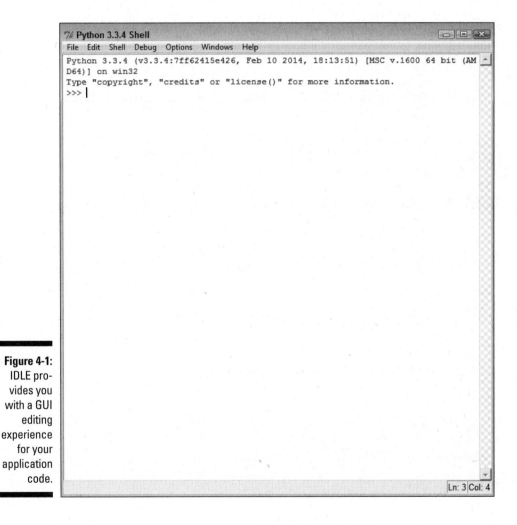

Figure 4-1:
IDLE provides you with a GUI editing experience for your application code.

Using standard commands

IDLE provides all the same commands as the command-line version of Python. It doesn't list them all because the assumption is that you'll use the GUI features of IDLE to make things easy. However, if you want, you can type **help()** and press Enter to enter help mode, even though this command isn't listed as one of the initial commands for IDLE as it is for the command-line version. Figure 4-2 shows the results.

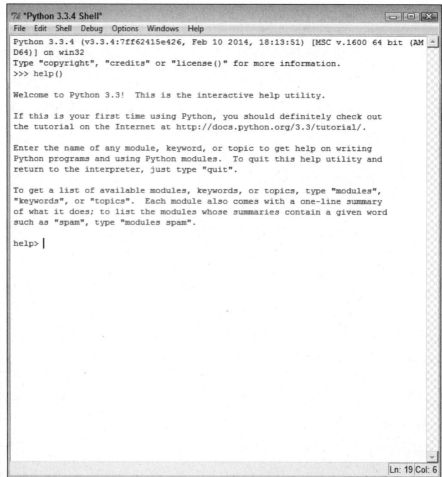

Figure 4-2: You can access all the same commands in IDLE that you can with the command line version.

Understanding color coding

The book doesn't show the color coding that you see when you type **help( )**, but you can see it in the editor. Color coding lets you see commands with greater ease and differentiate commands from other sorts of text. Press Enter to get out of help mode. As with the command-line version, you see descriptive text each time you perform an action.

Now, type **print('This is some text.')** and press Enter. You see the expected output, just as you normally would (see Figure 4-3). Notice the color coding, though. The `print()` command is in purple text to show that it's a command. The text within the `print()` command is green to show that it's data and not a command. The output is shown in blue. The color coding makes things a lot easier, which is just one of many reasons that using IDLE is easier than using the command line.

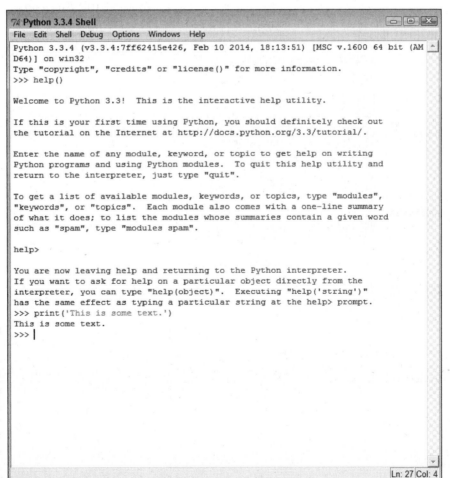

Figure 4-3:
With color coding, you can easily determine the use for each kind of text in an application.

```
7⋌ Python 3.3.4 Shell

File  Edit  Shell  Debug  Options  Windows  Help

Python 3.3.4 (v3.3.4:7ff62415e426, Feb 10 2014, 18:13:51) [MSC v.1600 64 bit (AM
D64)] on win32
Type "copyright", "credits" or "license()" for more information.
>>> help()

Welcome to Python 3.3!  This is the interactive help utility.

If this is your first time using Python, you should definitely check out
the tutorial on the Internet at http://docs.python.org/3.3/tutorial/.

Enter the name of any module, keyword, or topic to get help on writing
Python programs and using Python modules.  To quit this help utility and
return to the interpreter, just type "quit".

To get a list of available modules, keywords, or topics, type "modules",
"keywords", or "topics".  Each module also comes with a one-line summary
of what it does; to list the modules whose summaries contain a given word
such as "spam", type "modules spam".

help>

You are now leaving help and returning to the Python interpreter.
If you want to ask for help on a particular object directly from the
interpreter, you can type "help(object)".  Executing "help('string')"
has the same effect as typing a particular string at the help> prompt.
>>> print('This is some text.')
This is some text.
>>> |

                                                          Ln: 27 Col: 4
```

Getting GUI help

IDLE makes obtaining the help you need easy. Look at the Help menu and you see three entries for obtaining help:

- ✔ **About IDLE:** Provides you with the latest information about IDLE.

- ✔ **IDLE Help:** Shows you a text file containing information about working with the IDLE IDE. For example, this is where you find a list of the IDLE commands.

- ✔ **Python Docs:** Contains information required to work with Python commands and other elements.

Choose Help➪About IDLE to see the About IDLE dialog box shown in Figure 4-4. Near the middle of the dialog box, you see URLs for obtaining additional help. Each of the buttons displays a text file containing useful information, especially in the README and NEWS files. Click Close to exit this dialog box.

Figure 4-4:
The About IDLE dialog box contains useful information that you might not see otherwise.

Precisely what you see when you choose Help➪Python Docs depends on the platform you use. Figure 4-5 shows the Windows version of the dialog box. The Python Docs file contains information about how to work with and use Python to create applications. It even has a tutorial section in which you can find additional helpful tips after working your way through this book.

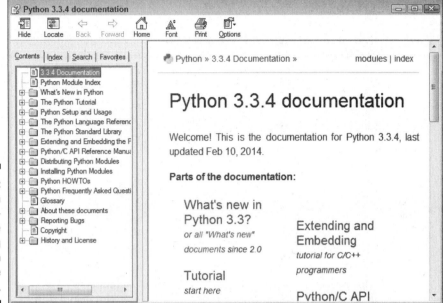

Figure 4-5:
Use Python
Docs to dis-
cover more
about using
Python
to create
applications.

Configuring IDLE

IDLE is basically a fancy text editor, when you think about it, so it's not sur-
prising that you can configure it to perform the task of editing text better.
Choose Options➪Configure IDLE to see the IDLE Preferences dialog box
shown in Figure 4-6. This is where you can choose things like what font IDLE
uses when displaying text. In the figure, you see the Font/Tabs tab, which lets
you choose the size and style font used for text, along with the number of
spaces used for indentation (see the "Understanding the Use of Indentation"
section of this chapter for details).

As previously mentioned, IDLE uses color coding to make reading and understanding the code easier. This tab lets you choose the colors used to perform
highlighting, as shown in Figure 4-7. Notice that you can save your selections
as a theme. You can create different themes for different needs. For example,
you may use one theme when you use your laptop or other computing device
in bright conditions and another theme in low light conditions.

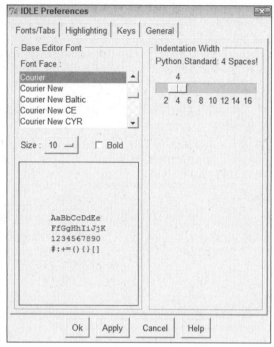

Figure 4-6:
Configure
IDLE to
meet your
particular
require-
ments.

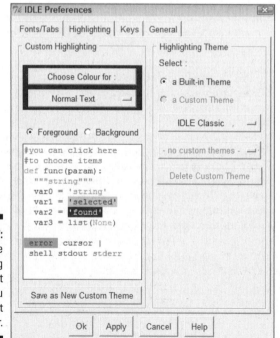

Figure 4-7:
Change the
highlighting
used for text
so that you
can see it
better.

Even though you won't see shortcut keys used very often in this book due to platform differences, IDLE does support them. The shortcut keys on your platform may differ from those shown in Figure 4-8. IDLE comes with built-in key sets for Windows, Mac, OS X, and Unix. You can choose any of these themes by clicking the small button next to the IDLE Classic Windows entry (see Figure 4-8). You can also create your own custom theme that's based on another application you use.

Figure 4-8:
Use shortcut keys that make the most sense to you as a developer.

The General tab, shown in Figure 4-9, controls how IDLE works. For example, you can tell IDLE to open a Python Shell window (so that you can experiment) or an Edit window (so that you can write an application). The default is to open a Python Shell window so that you can experiment with Python and try new techniques. You can also control whether IDLE prompts you to save files before running applications (always a good idea in case the application causes the system to freeze) and the size of the initial window when you create one. Paragraph formatting keeps your text from becoming too long to comfortably see in the window. The defaults you see normally work just fine, so there really isn't a good reason to change them.

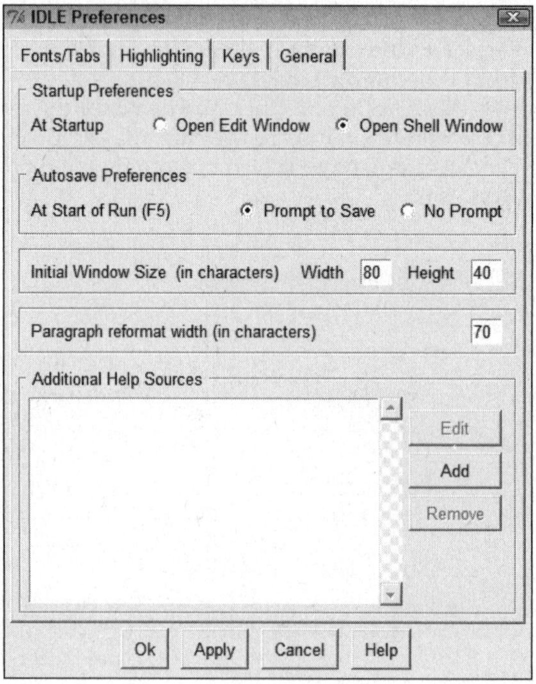

Figure 4-9:
The General
tab controls
the func-
tioning of
the IDLE
application.

The Additional Help Sources feature lets you create new help sources for IDLE to use. For example, you can create a link to an online source, such as Python's online documentation at `https://docs.python.org/release/3.3.4/`. To add a new source, click Add. You see the New Help Source dialog box, shown in Figure 4-10, where you can add the text that appears on the Help menu for this information source and the location of that source on a hard drive or online. When you finish adding the source, click OK and you'll see it added to the IDLE Help menu. There are also buttons on the General tab of the IDLE Preferences dialog box for editing and removing help sources.

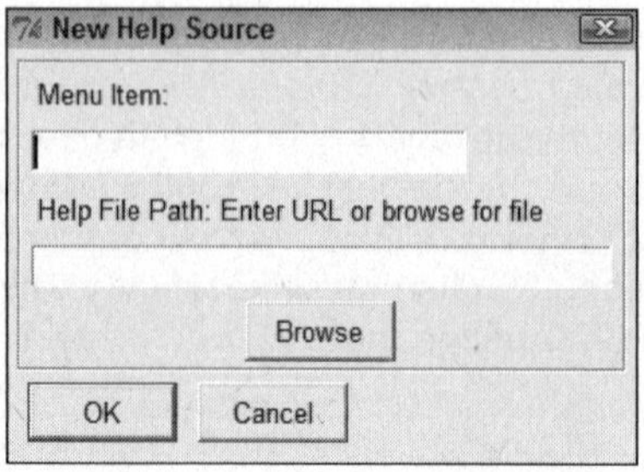

Figure 4-10:
Create
new help
sources as
needed to
make your
develop-
ment experi-
ence easier.

Creating the Application

It's time to create your first Python application. Your initial Python Shell window won't work for creating an application, so you can begin by creating a new Edit window for the application. You'll type the required commands and then save the file to disk.

Opening a new window

The initial Python Shell window is just fine for experimentation, but you need a nice, clean Edit window for typing your first application. The Python Shell window is interactive, which means that it gives you immediate feedback for any commands you type. The Edit window provides a static environment, where you type commands, save them, and then run them after you type enough commands to create an application. The two windows serve distinctly different purposes.

Choose File➪New File to create a new window. A new window like the one shown in Figure 4-11 opens. Notice that the title bar says Python 3.3.4 Untitled instead of Python 3.3.4 Shell. A Python Shell window will always have the word "Shell" in the title bar. The two windows also have some unique toolbar entries. For example, an Edit window includes the Run command, which you use later to test your application.

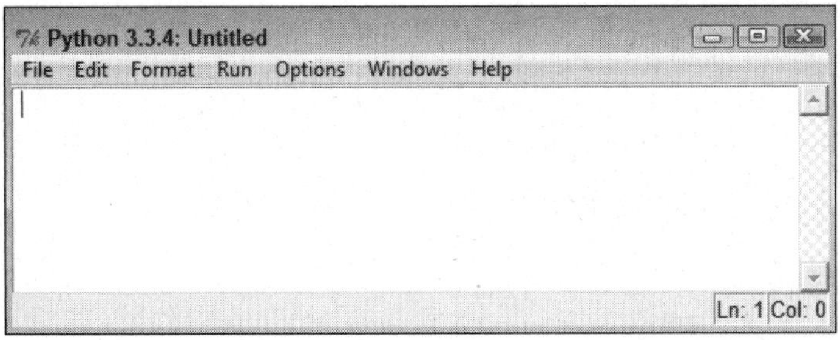

```
┌─────────────────────────────────────────────────────────────┐
│ ⁊⁄₄ Python 3.3.4: Untitled                        ─  □  ✕    │
│  File  Edit  Format  Run  Options  Windows  Help            │
│ │                                                        ▲   │
│                                                              │
│                                                              │
│                                                              │
│                                                              │
│                                                              │
│                                                         ▼    │
│                                              Ln: 1 Col: 0    │
└─────────────────────────────────────────────────────────────┘
```

Figure 4-11:
Use the Edit window to create applications.

Working with the Edit window is just like working with any other text editor. You have access to basic editing commands such as Copy, Cut, and Paste. Pressing Enter moves to the next line rather than executing a command as it would when working in the Python Shell window. That's because the Edit window is a static environment — one where you type commands and save them for later reuse.

The Edit window also provides special commands to format the text. The "Understanding the Use of Indentation" and "Adding Comments" sections of this chapter describe how to use the formatting features. What you need to know now is that these formatting commands act differently from those in a standard text editor because they help you control the appearance of code rather than of generic text. Many of the formatting features work automatically, so you don't need to worry about them now.

Finally, the Edit window provides access to commands that tell Python to perform the steps in the procedure you create one at a time. This process is called *running* the application. The "Running the Application" section of this chapter describes this process in greater detail.

Typing the command

As with the Python Shell window, you can simply type a command into the Edit window. To see how this works, type **print(**. Notice that the Edit window provides you with helpful information about the `print()` command, as shown in Figure 4-12. The information is a little terse, so you may not understand it now. As the book progresses, you learn more about the `print()` command and the help provided by the Edit window will make more sense. For now, the word `value` is the one that you need to focus on. The `print()` command needs a value before it can print anything and you'll encounter a host of different values as the book progresses.

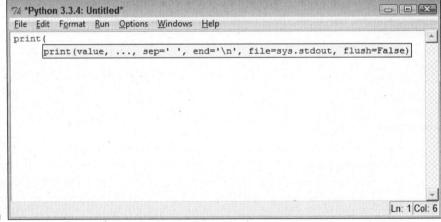

Figure 4-12: The Edit window provides helpful information about the commands you type.

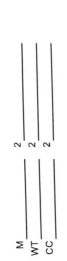

M ————————————— 2

WT ———————————— 2

CC ———————————— 2

Running the Application

Applications aren't much good if you can't run them. Python provides a variety of methods for running any application you create. This section explores the easiest method for running an application after you create it. You see additional methods in the "Loading and Running Existing Applications" section of the chapter. The important thing to remember is that Python provides an extremely flexible environment, so if one method of performing a task doesn't quite work, another method will almost certainly succeed.

To run this first application, choose Run⇨Run Module. You see a new copy of the Python Shell window opens and then the output of your application appears, as shown in Figure 4-16.

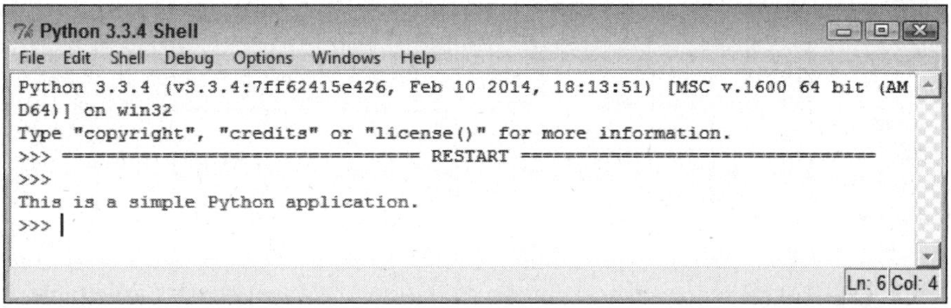

Figure 4-16:
The output
of the
example
application
appears in a
Python Shell
window.

```
7₄ Python 3.3.4 Shell                                          □ ▣ ▣
File   Edit   Shell   Debug   Options   Windows   Help
Python 3.3.4 (v3.3.4:7ff62415e426, Feb 10 2014, 18:13:51) [MSC v.1600 64 bit (AM
D64)] on win32
Type "copyright", "credits" or "license()" for more information.
>>> ============================= RESTART ================================
>>>
This is a simple Python application.
>>> |
                                                              Ln: 6 Col: 4
```

The top two lines of the output in Figure 4-16 should be familiar by now — they're the information that always appears when you start the shell. Next comes a

```
============================= RESTART ================================
```

message. You see this message every time you run the application. To see this for yourself, select the Edit window and choose Run⇨Run Module. The original Python Shell window is selected, another message appears, and you see the output from your application again, as shown in Figure 4-17.

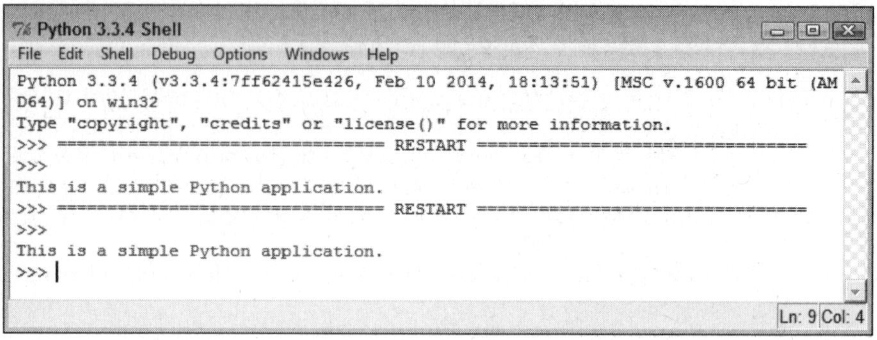

Figure 4-17:
The Python
Shell
window
displays
a Restart
message
each time
you run the
application.

```
7% Python 3.3.4 Shell                                              □  ▣  ✕
File  Edit  Shell  Debug  Options  Windows  Help
Python 3.3.4 (v3.3.4:7ff62415e426, Feb 10 2014, 18:13:51) [MSC v.1600 64 bit (AM
D64)] on win32
Type "copyright", "credits" or "license()" for more information.
>>> ========================== RESTART ==================================
>>>
This is a simple Python application.
>>> ========================== RESTART ==================================
>>>
This is a simple Python application.
>>> |
                                                                  Ln: 9 Col: 4
```

Understanding the Use of Indentation

As you work through the examples in this book, you see that certain lines
are indented. In fact, the examples also provide a fair amount of white space
(such as extra lines between lines of code). Python ignores any indentation
in your application. The main reason to add indentation is to provide visual
cues about your code. In the same way that indentation is used for book
outlines, indentation in code shows the relationships between various code
elements.

The various uses of indentation will become more familiar as you work your
way through the examples in the book. However, it's important to know at
the outset why indentation is used and how it gets put in place. So, it's time
for another example. The following steps help you create a new example that
uses indentation to make the relationship between application elements a lot
more apparent and easier to figure out later.

1. **Choose File⇨New File.**

   IDLE creates a new Edit window for you.

2. **Type** print("This is a really long line of text that will " +.

   You see the text displayed normally onscreen, just as you expect. The
   plus sign (+) tells Python that there is additional text to display. Adding
   text from multiple lines together into a single long piece of text is called
   concatenation. You learn more about using this feature later in the book,
   so you don't need to worry about it now.

3. **Press Enter.**

   The insertion point doesn't go back to the beginning of the line, as you
   might expect. Instead, it ends up directly under the first double quote,

as shown in Figure 4-18. This feature is called automatic indention and it's one of the features that differentiates a regular text editor from one designed to write code.

4. **Type** "appear on multiple lines in the source code file.") **and press Enter.**

   Notice that the insertion point goes back to the beginning of the line. When IDLE senses that you have reached the end of the code, it automatically outdents the text to its original position.

5. **Choose File⇨Save.**

   You see the Save As dialog box.

6. **Type** LongLine.py **in the File Name field and click Save to save it.**

7. **Choose Run⇨Run Module.**

   A new Python Shell window opens with the text displayed. Even though the text appears on multiple lines in the source code file, it appears on just one line in the output, as shown in Figure 4-19.

Figure 4-18: The Edit window automatically indents some types of text.

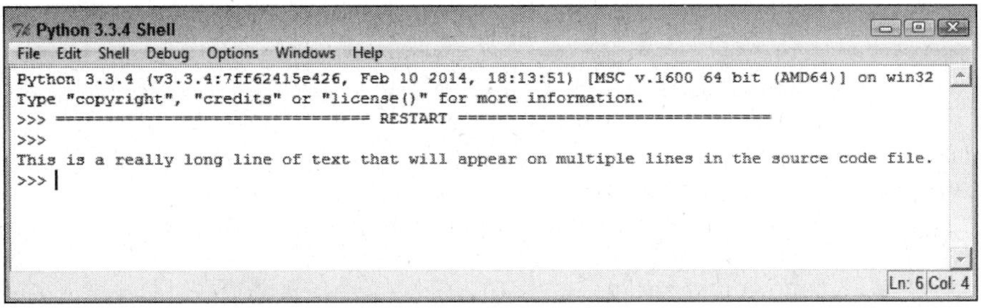

Figure 4-19: Use concatenation to make multiple lines of text appear on a single line in the output.

Adding Comments

People create notes for themselves all the time. When you need to buy groceries, you look through your cabinets, determine what you need, and write it down on a list. When you get to the store, you review your list to remember what you need. Using notes comes in handy for all sorts of needs, such as tracking the course of a conversation between business partners or remembering the essential points of a lecture. Humans need notes to jog their memories. Comments in source code are just another form of note. You add them to the code so that you can remember what task the code performs later. The following sections describe comments in more detail.

Understanding comments

Computers need some special way to determine that the text you're writing is a comment, not code to execute. Python provides two methods of defining text as a comment and not as code. The first method is the single-line comment. It uses the number sign (#), like this:

```
# This is a comment.
print("Hello from Python!") #This is also a comment.
```

A single-line comment can appear on a line by itself or it can appear after executable code. It appears on only one line. You typically use a single-line comment for short descriptive text, such as an explanation of a particular bit of code.

When you need to create a longer comment, you use a multiline comment. A multiline comment both starts and ends with three double quotes ("""), like this:

```
"""
    Application: Comments.py
    Written by: John
    Purpose: Shows how to use comments.
"""
```

Everything between the two sets of triple double quotes is considered a comment. You typically use multiline comments for longer explanations of who created an application, why it was created, and what tasks it performs. Of course, there aren't any hard rules on precisely how you use comments. The main goal is to tell the computer precisely what is and isn't a comment so that it doesn't become confused.

Even though single-line and multiline comments are both comments, the IDLE editor makes it easy to tell the difference between the two. When you're using the default color scheme, single-line comments show up in red text, while multiline comments show up in green text. Python doesn't care about the coloration; it's only there to help you as the developer.

Using comments to leave yourself reminders

A lot of people don't really understand comments — they don't quite know what to do with notes in code. Keep in mind that you might write a piece of code today and then not look at it for years. You need notes to jog your memory so that you remember what task the code performs and why you wrote it. In fact, here are some common reasons to use comments in your code:

✔ Reminding yourself about what the code does and why you wrote it

✔ Telling others how to maintain your code

✔ Making your code accessible to other developers

✔ Listing ideas for future updates

✔ Providing a list of documentation sources you used to write the code

✔ Maintaining a list of improvements you've made

You can use comments in a lot of other ways, too, but these are the most common ways. Look at the way comments are used in the examples in the book, especially as you get to later chapters where the code becomes more complex. As your code becomes more complex, you need to add more comments and make the comments pertinent to what you need to remember about it.

Using comments to keep code from executing

Developers also sometimes use the commenting feature to keep lines of code from executing (referred to as *commenting out*). You might need to do this in order to determine whether a line of code is causing your application to fail. In fact, it's such a common and useful way to work with code that a technique for adding this sort of comment is built right in to IDLE. Here's an example of how this feature works. Say that you have an application like the one shown in Figure 4-20 (found in the `Comments.py` file provided as part of the downloadable source code).

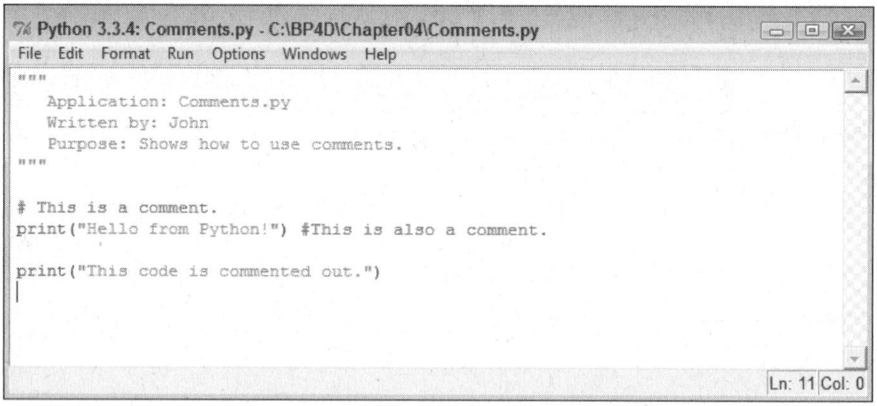

Figure 4-20:
Sometimes developers need to comment out lines of code.

You might want to comment out the line that reads `print("This code is commented out.")`. To make this happen, place the insertion point at the beginning of the line, or simply select the entire line, and choose Format⇨Comment Out Region. IDLE then adds a single-line comment to the code, as shown in Figure 4-21. Notice that this single-line comment uses two number signs (##) to differentiate it from a single-line comment you create by hand.

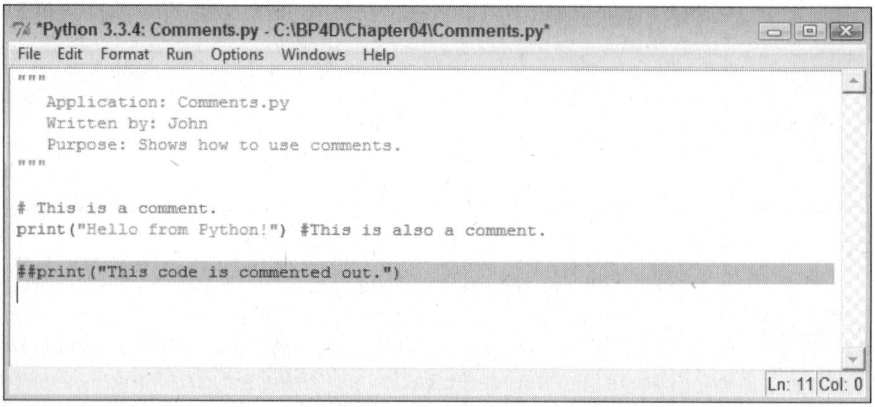

Figure 4-21:
Comment out any code you don't want Python to execute.

Of course, you don't know yet whether the commenting has worked. Save the file to disk and then choose Run⇨Run Module. You see a new Python Shell window open with just a single line of output, as shown in Figure 4-22. So, the first `print()` command, which isn't commented out, executes just fine, but the second one doesn't.

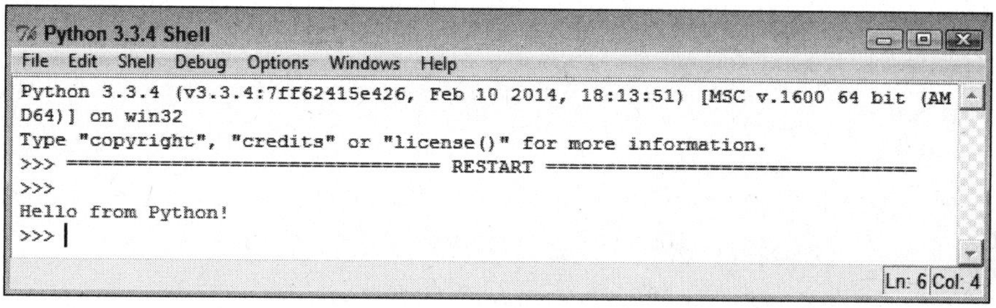

Figure 4-22: Commented out lines of code don't execute.

```
7⁄ Python 3.3.4 Shell
File  Edit  Shell  Debug  Options  Windows  Help
Python 3.3.4 (v3.3.4:7ff62415e426, Feb 10 2014, 18:13:51) [MSC v.1600 64 bit (AM
D64)] on win32
Type "copyright", "credits" or "license()" for more information.
>>> ============================== RESTART ==============================
>>>
Hello from Python!
>>>
                                                                    Ln: 6 Col: 4
```

To add the code back into the application, place the insertion point at the beginning of the line, or highlight the entire line, and choose Format⇨Uncomment Region. IDLE removes the comment that it added earlier. Save the file and then choose Run⇨Run Module to see the result. This time, you see both `print()` commands execute, as shown in Figure 4-23.

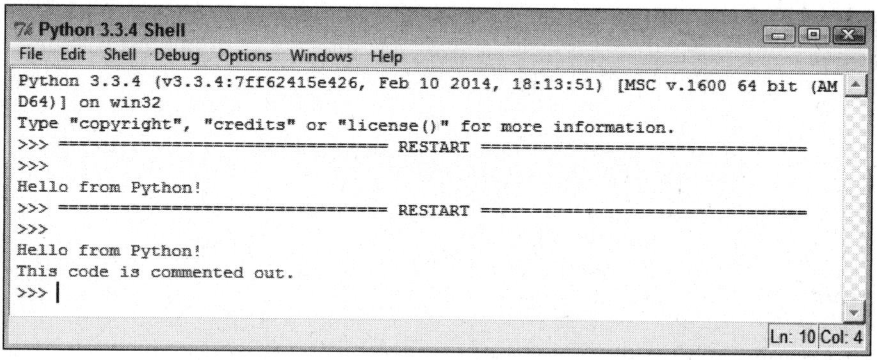

Figure 4-23: Both `print()` commands execute when neither is commented out.

```
7⁄ Python 3.3.4 Shell
File  Edit  Shell  Debug  Options  Windows  Help
Python 3.3.4 (v3.3.4:7ff62415e426, Feb 10 2014, 18:13:51) [MSC v.1600 64 bit (AM
D64)] on win32
Type "copyright", "credits" or "license()" for more information.
>>> ============================== RESTART ==============================
>>>
Hello from Python!
>>> ============================== RESTART ==============================
>>>
Hello from Python!
This code is commented out.
>>>
                                                                   Ln: 10 Col: 4
```

You can comment out multiple lines of code at once by highlighting all of the lines and choosing Format⇨Comment Out Region. Likewise, you can uncomment out multiple lines of code by highlighting all the lines and choosing Format⇨Uncomment Region. It isn't necessary to comment out or uncomment out one line at a time unless you have just one line of code to check.

Loading and Running Existing Applications

Running your application immediately after you write it is fun and interesting, but at some point you'll close IDLE and be left with a file on your disk. The file contains your application, but you need to know how to use that file to execute it. Python actually provides a considerable number of ways to achieve this task. The following sections describe just three of these approaches.

Using the command line or terminal window

The command line, or terminal window, provides the means to execute commands by typing them in. You can also create batch files to execute a number of commands as part of a batch process. In this case, you're looking at the native command environment provided by the platform you're using, rather than at the specialized Python command line. When working in this environment, you type commands to start Python and perform specific tasks. For example, if you want to execute FirstApp (described in the "Creating the Application" section of this chapter), you type **python FirstApp.py** and press Enter. Figure 4-24 shows typical results. You can execute any other application this way as well.

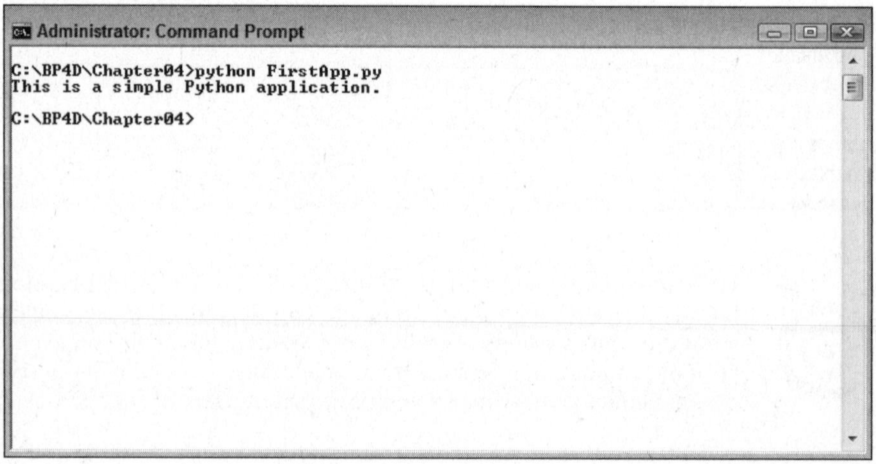

```
Administrator: Command Prompt

C:\BP4D\Chapter04>python FirstApp.py
This is a simple Python application.

C:\BP4D\Chapter04>
```

Figure 4-24: It's possible to execute an application directly at the command line.

Using the Edit window

Any time you're in IDLE, you can open an existing application in an Edit window and execute it, just as you have in previous sections of this chapter. To perform this task, load the file you saved earlier by choosing File⇨Open. You see an Open dialog box that looks similar to the Save As dialog box shown in Figure 4-14. Choose the folder containing the application in the Look In field and highlight it in the list provided. Click Open to open the file. At this point, you can choose Run⇨Run Module to run the application, just as you would normally.

Using the Python Shell window or Python command line

When you're in the IDLE Python Shell window or at the Python command line, you're in an environment where you can type commands and see them executed immediately. However, you need to know the right commands to perform specific tasks. In this case, the command is a little more complex than the print() command you've been using to date. If you want to execute FirstApp, you need a really odd-looking command like one of the two shown here:

```
exec(open("C:\\BP4D\\Chapter04\\FirstApp.py").read())
exec(open("C:/BP4D/Chapter04/FirstApp.py").read())
```

The preceding two commands are really the same one using a different type of slash. The command works equally well with forward slashes or backslashes. What this command says to do is this:

1. Open the FirstApp.py file located in the \BP4D\Chapter04 folder on the C drive (open() command).

2. Read the content of this file into the Python environment (read() command).

3. Execute the instructions found in the file after it's loaded (exec() command).

It's a little early for a command like this one, but you'll discover that you can create combined commands of all sorts later in the book. For now, just try the command to see that it works. Figure 4-25 shows typical results.

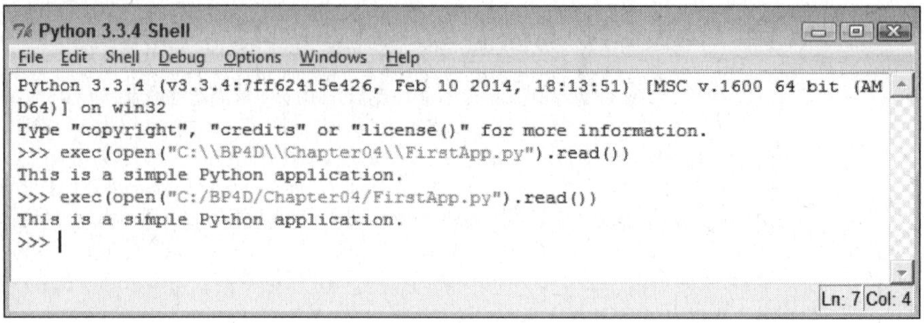

Figure 4-25:
Use forward
slashes or
backslashes
to define
the loca-
tion of your
application.

```
74 Python 3.3.4 Shell                                    _ □ ✕
File  Edit  Shell  Debug  Options  Windows  Help
Python 3.3.4 (v3.3.4:7ff62415e426, Feb 10 2014, 18:13:51) [MSC v.1600 64 bit (AM
D64)] on win32
Type "copyright", "credits" or "license()" for more information.
>>> exec(open("C:\\BP4D\\Chapter04\\FirstApp.py").read())
This is a simple Python application.
>>> exec(open("C:/BP4D/Chapter04/FirstApp.py").read())
This is a simple Python application.
>>>  |
                                                    Ln: 7 Col: 4
```

Closing IDLE

Eventually, you need to close IDLE when your session is finished. The commands for closing IDLE appear on the File menu, and there are actually two of
them (which seems a bit confusing):

- **Close:** Closes just the window that currently has focus. This means that
  if you're in a Python Shell window after running an application, just the
  Python Shell window closes and not the associated Edit window.

- **Exit:** Closes the current window and all associated windows. This means
  that if you're in a Python Shell window after running an application, both
  the Python Shell window and the associated Edit window close.

When you close a window, IDLE checks to ensure that you have saved any
content to disk. If you haven't saved the content, you see a dialog box asking
whether you want to save it.

The File➪Close and File➪Exit commands affect only the current session. For
example, if you open two separate Python files, you need to close each file
separately because each file is opened in a separate session.

Part II
Talking the Talk

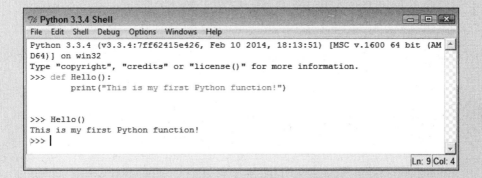

See an example of how you can combine functions and repetitive tasks at www.dummies.com/extras/beginningprogramming withpython.

In this part . . .

✔ See how to create variables to hold data.

✔ Create functions to make code easier to read.

✔ Tell your Python application to make a decision.

✔ Perform repeating tasks.

✔ Ensure that your application can deal with errors.

Chapter 5

Storing and Modifying Information

In This Chapter

▶ Understanding data storage

▶ Considering the kinds of data storage

▶ Adding dates and times to applications

Chapter 3 introduces you to CRUD, Create, Read, Update, and Delete — not that Chapter 3 contains cruddy material. This acronym provides an easy method to remember precisely what tasks all computer programs perform with information you want to manage. Of course, geeks use a special term for information — data, but either information or data works fine for this book.

In order to make information useful, you have to have some means of storing it permanently. Otherwise, every time you turned the computer off, all your information would be gone and the computer would provide limited value. In addition, Python must provide some rules for modifying information. The alternative is to have applications running amok, changing information in any and every conceivable manner. This chapter is about controlling information — defining how information is stored permanently and manipulated by applications you create.

Storing Information

An application requires fast access to information or else it will take a long time to complete tasks. As a result, applications store information in memory. However, memory is temporary. When you turn off the machine, the information must be stored in some permanent form, such as on your hard drive, a Universal Serial Bus (USB) flash drive, or a Secure Digital (SD) card. In addition, you must also consider the form of the information, such as whether it's a number or text. The following sections discuss the issue of storing information as part of an application in more detail.

Seeing variables as storage boxes

When working with applications, you store information in variables. A *variable* is a kind of storage box. Whenever you want to work with the information, you access it using the variable. If you have new information you want to store, you put it in a variable. Changing information means accessing the variable first and then storing the new value in the variable. Just as you store things in boxes in the real world, so you store things in variables (a kind of storage box) when working with applications.

Computers are actually pretty tidy. Each variable stores just one piece of information. Using this technique makes it easy to find the particular piece of information you need — unlike in your closet, where things from ancient Egypt could be hidden. Even though the examples you work with in previous chapters don't use variables, most applications rely heavily on variables to make working with information easier.

Using the right box to store the data

People tend to store things in the wrong sort of box. For example, you might find a pair of shoes in a garment bag and a supply of pens in a shoebox. However, Python likes to be neat. As a result, you find numbers stored in one sort of variable and text stored in an entirely different kind of variable. Yes, you use variables in both cases, but the variable is designed to store a particular kind of information. Using specialized variables makes it possible to work with the information inside in particular ways. You don't need to worry about the details just yet — just keep in mind that each kind of information is stored in a special kind of variable.

Python uses specialized variables to store information to make things easy for the programmer and to ensure that the information remains safe. However, computers don't actually know about information types. All that the computer knows about are 0s and 1s, which is the absence or presence of a voltage. At a higher level, computers do work with numbers, but that's the extent of what computers do. Numbers, letters, dates, times, and any other kind of information you can think about all come down to 0s and 1s in the computer system. For example, the letter *A* is actually stored as 01000001 or the number 65. The computer has no concept of the letter *A* or of a date such as 8/31/2014.

Defining the Essential Python Data Types

Every programming language defines variables that hold specific kinds of information, and Python is no exception. The specific kind of variable is called a *data type*. Knowing the data type of a variable is important because it tells you what kind of information you find inside. In addition, when you want to store information in a variable, you need a variable of the correct data type to do it. Python doesn't allow you to store text in a variable designed to hold numeric information. Doing so would damage the text and cause problems with the application. You can generally classify Python data types as numeric, string, and Boolean, although there really isn't any limit on just how you can view them. The following sections describe each of the standard Python data types within these classifications.

Putting information into variables

To place a value into any variable, you make an assignment using the assignment operator (=). Chapter 6 discusses the whole range of basic Python operators in more detail, but you need to know how to use this particular operator to some extent now. For example, to place the number 5 into a variable named myVar, you type **myVar = 5** and press Enter at the Python prompt. Even though Python doesn't provide any additional information to you, you can always type the variable name and press Enter to see the value it contains, as shown in Figure 5-1.

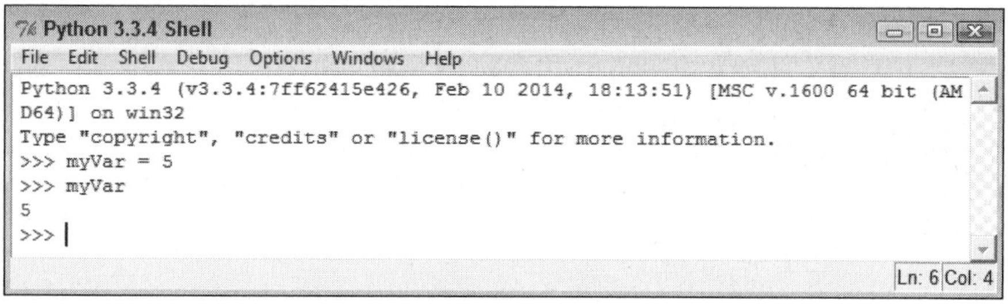

Figure 5-1:
Use the assignment operator to place information into a variable.

```
7⁄ Python 3.3.4 Shell
File  Edit  Shell  Debug  Options  Windows  Help
Python 3.3.4 (v3.3.4:7ff62415e426, Feb 10 2014, 18:13:51) [MSC v.1600 64 bit (AM
D64)] on win32
Type "copyright", "credits" or "license()" for more information.
>>> myVar = 5
>>> myVar
5
>>> |
                                                              Ln: 6 Col: 4
```

Understanding the numeric types

Humans tend to think about numbers in general terms. We view 1 and 1.0 as being the same number — one of them simply has a decimal point. However, as far as we're concerned, the two numbers are equal and we could easily use them interchangeably. Python views them as being different kinds of numbers because each form requires a different kind of processing. The following sections describe the integer, floating-point, and complex number classes of data types that Python supports.

Integers

Any whole number is an *integer*. For example, the value 1 is a whole number, so it's an integer. On the other hand, 1.0 isn't a whole number; it has a decimal part to it, so it's not an integer. Integers are represented by the int data type.

As with storage boxes, variables have capacity limits. Trying to stuff a value that's too large into a storage box results in an error. On most platforms, you can store numbers between –9,223,372,036,854,775,808 and 9,223,372,036,854,775,807 within an int (which is the maximum value that fits in a 64-bit variable). Even though that's a really large number, it isn't infinite.

When working with the int type, you have access to a number of interesting features. Many of them appear later in the book, but one feature is the ability to use different numeric bases:

- **Base 2:** Uses only 0 and 1 as numbers.
- **Base 8:** Uses the numbers 0 through 7.
- **Base 10:** Uses the usual numeric system.
- **Base 16:** Is also called *hex* and uses the numbers 0 through 9 and the letters A through F to create 16 different possible values.

To tell Python when to use bases other than base 10, you add a 0 and a special letter to the number. For example, 0b100 is the value one-zero-zero in base 2. Here are the letters you normally use:

- **b:** Base 2
- **o:** Base 8
- **x:** Base 16

It's also possible to convert numeric values to other bases using the bin(), oct(), and hex() commands. So, putting everything together, you can see how to convert between bases using the commands shown in Figure 5-2. Try the command shown in the figure yourself so that you can see how the various bases work. Using a different base actually makes things easier in many situations, and you'll encounter some of those situations later in the book. For now, all you really need to know is that integers support different numeric bases.

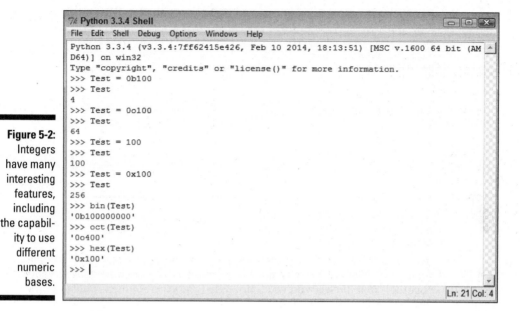

Figure 5-2:
Integers
have many
interesting
features,
including
the capabil-
ity to use
different
numeric
bases.

Floating-point values

Any number that includes a decimal portion is a floating-point value. For example, 1.0 has a decimal part, so it's a floating-point value. Many people get confused about whole numbers and floating-point numbers, but the difference is easy to remember. If you see a decimal in the number, then it's a floating-point value. Python stores floating-point values in the float data type.

Floating-point values have an advantage over integer values in that you can store immensely large or incredibly small values in them. As with integer variables, floating-point variables have a storage capacity. In their case, the maximum value that a variable can contain is $\pm 1.7976931348623157 \times 10^{308}$ and the minimum value that a variable can contain is $\pm 2.2250738585072014 \times 10^{-308}$ on most platforms.

When working with floating-point values, you can assign the information to the variable in a number of ways. The two most common methods are to provide the number directly and to use scientific notation. When using scientific notation, an *e* separates the number from its exponent. Figure 5-3 shows both methods of making an assignment. Notice that using a negative exponent results in a fractional value.

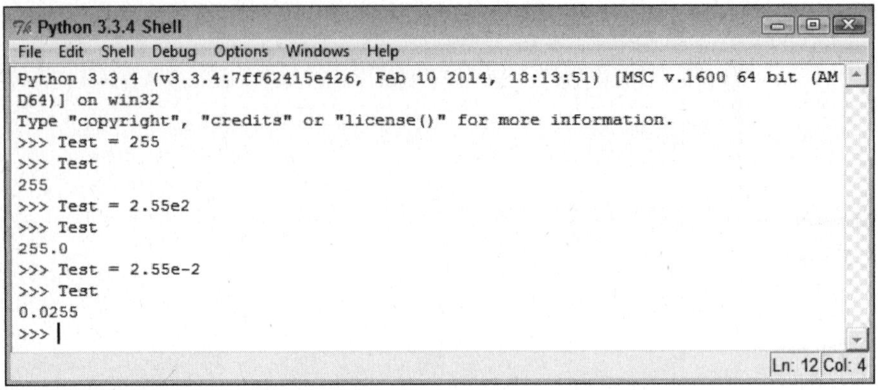

Figure 5-3:
Floating-
point values
provide
multiple
assignment
techniques.

```
7₄ Python 3.3.4 Shell
File  Edit  Shell  Debug  Options  Windows  Help
Python 3.3.4 (v3.3.4:7ff62415e426, Feb 10 2014, 18:13:51) [MSC v.1600 64 bit (AM
D64)] on win32
Type "copyright", "credits" or "license()" for more information.
>>> Test = 255
>>> Test
255
>>> Test = 2.55e2
>>> Test
255.0
>>> Test = 2.55e-2
>>> Test
0.0255
>>> |
                                                               Ln: 12 Col: 4
```

Complex numbers

You may or may not remember complex numbers from school. A *complex number* consists of a real number and an imaginary number that are paired together. Just in case you've completely forgotten about complex numbers, you can read about them at `http://www.mathsisfun.com/numbers/complex-numbers.html`. Real-world uses for complex numbers include:

✔ Electrical engineering

✔ Fluid dynamics

✔ Quantum mechanics

✔ Computer graphics

✔ Dynamic systems

Complex numbers have other uses, too, but this list should give you some ideas. In general, if you aren't involved in any of these disciplines, you probably won't ever encounter complex numbers. However, Python is one of the few languages that provides a built-in data type to support them. As you progress through the book, you find other ways in which Python lends itself especially well to science and engineering.

The imaginary part of a complex number always appears with a *j* after it. So, if you want to create a complex number with 3 as the real part and 4 as the imaginary part, you make an assignment like this:

```
myComplex = 3 + 4j
```

If you want to see the real part of the variable, you simply type **myComplex. real** at the Python prompt and press Enter. Likewise, if you want to see the imaginary part of the variable, you type **myComplex.imag** at the Python prompt and press Enter.

Understanding the need for multiple number types

A lot of new developers (and even some older ones) have a hard time understanding why there is a need for more than one numeric type. After all, humans can use just one kind of number. To understand the need for multiple number types, you have to understand a little about how a computer works with numbers.

An integer is stored in the computer as simply a series of bits that the computer reads directly. A value of 0100 in binary equates to a value of 4 in decimal. On the other hand, numbers that have decimal points are stored in an entirely different manner. Think back to all those classes you slept through on exponents in school — they actually come in handy sometimes. A floating-point number is stored as a sign bit (plus or minus), *mantissa* (the fractional part of the number), and *exponent* (the power of 2). (Some texts use the term *significand* in place of mantissa — the terms are interchangeable.) To obtain the floating-point value, you use the equation:

```
Value = Mantissa * 2^Exponent
```

At one time, computers all used different floating-point representations, but they all use the IEEE-754 standard now. You can read about this standard at `http://grouper. ieee.org/groups/754/`. A full explanation of precisely how floating-point numbers work is outside the scope of this book, but you can read a fairly understandable description at `http://www.cprogramming. com/tutorial/floating_point/ understanding_floating_point_ representation.html`. Nothing helps you understand a concept like playing with the values. You can find a really interesting floating-point number converter at `http://www. h-schmidt.net/FloatConverter/ IEEE754.html`, where you can click the individual bits (to turn them off or on) and see the floating-point number that results.

As you might imagine, floating-point numbers tend to consume more space in memory because of their complexity. In addition, they use an entirely different area of the processor — one that works more slowly than the part used for integer math. Finally, integers are precise, as contrasted to floating-point numbers, which can't precisely represent some numbers, so you get an approximation instead. However, floating-point variables can store much larger numbers. The bottom line is that decimals are unavoidable in the real world, so you need floating-point numbers, but using integers when you can reduces the amount of memory your application consumes and helps it work faster. There are many trade-offs in computer systems, and this one is unavoidable.

Understanding Boolean values

It may seem amazing, but computers always give you a straight answer! A computer will never provide "maybe" as output. Every answer you get is either True or False. In fact, there is an entire branch of mathematics called Boolean algebra that was originally defined by George Boole (a super-geek of his time) that computers rely upon to make decisions. Contrary to common belief, Boolean algebra has existed since 1854 — long before the time of computers.

Determining a variable's type

Sometimes you might want to know the variable type. Perhaps the type isn't obvious from the code or you've received the information from a source whose code isn't accessible. Whenever you want to see the type of a variable, use the `type()` method. For example, if you start by placing a value of 5 in `myInt` by typing **myInt = 5** and pressing Enter, you can find the type of `myInt` by typing **type(myInt)** and pressing Enter. The output will be `<class 'int'>`, which means that `myInt` contains an `int` value.

When using Boolean value in Python, you rely on the `bool` type. A variable of this type can contain only two values: `True` or `False`. You can assign a value by using the `True` or `False` keywords, or you can create an expression that defines a logical idea that equates to true or false. For example, you could say, `myBool = 1 > 2`, which would equate to `False` because 1 is most definitely not greater than 2. You see the `bool` type used extensively in the book, so don't worry about understanding this concept right now.

Understanding strings

Of all the data types, strings are the most easily understood by humans and not understood at all by computers. If you have read the previous chapters in this book, you have already seen strings used quite. For example, all the example code in Chapter 4 relies on strings. A *string* is simply any grouping of characters you place within double quotes. For example, `myString = "Python is a great language."` assigns a string of characters to `myString`.

The computer doesn't see letters at all. Every letter you use is represented by a number in memory. For example, the letter *A* is actually the number 65. To see this for yourself, type **ord("A")** at the Python prompt and press Enter. You see 65 as output. It's possible to convert any single letter to its numeric equivalent using the `ord()` command.

Because the computer doesn't really understand strings, but strings are so useful in writing applications, you sometimes need to convert a string to a number. You can use the `int()` and `float()` commands to perform this conversion. For example, if you type **myInt = int("123")** and press Enter at the Python prompt, you create an `int` named `myInt` that contains the value `123`. Figure 5-4 shows how you can perform this task and validate the content and type of `myInt`.

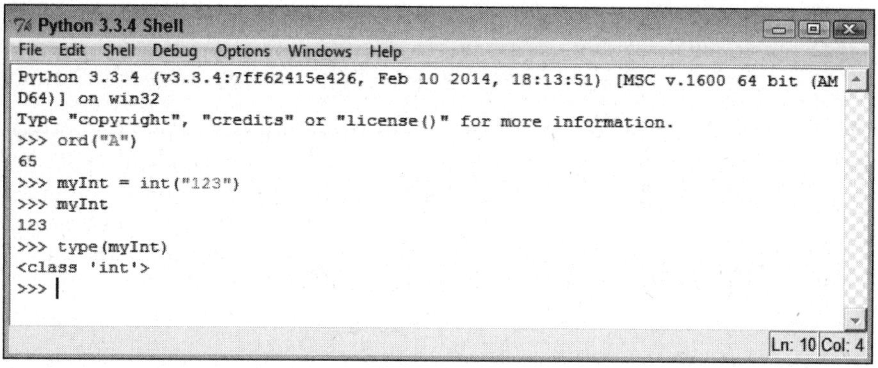

Figure 5-4:
Converting
a string to
a number
is easy
using the
`int()` and
`float()`
commands.

```
Python 3.3.4 Shell
File  Edit  Shell  Debug  Options  Windows  Help
Python 3.3.4 (v3.3.4:7ff62415e426, Feb 10 2014, 18:13:51) [MSC v.1600 64 bit (AM
D64)] on win32
Type "copyright", "credits" or "license()" for more information.
>>> ord("A")
65
>>> myInt = int("123")
>>> myInt
123
>>> type(myInt)
<class 'int'>
>>> |
                                                                       Ln: 10 Col: 4
```

You can convert numbers to a string as well by using the `str()` command.
For example, if you type **myStr = str(1234.56)** and press Enter, you create
a string containing the value `"1234.56"` and assign it to `myStr`. Figure 5-5
shows this type of conversion and the test you can perform on it. The point
is that you can go back and forth between strings and numbers with great
ease. Later chapters demonstrate how these conversions make a lot of seemingly impossible tasks quite doable.

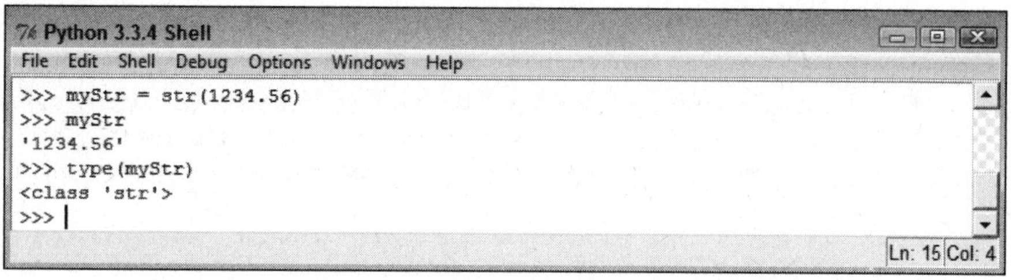

Figure 5-5:
It's possible
to convert
numbers to
strings as
well.

```
Python 3.3.4 Shell
File  Edit  Shell  Debug  Options  Windows  Help
>>> myStr = str(1234.56)
>>> myStr
'1234.56'
>>> type(myStr)
<class 'str'>
>>> |
                                                                       Ln: 15 Col: 4
```

Working with Dates and Times

Dates and times are items that most people work with quite a bit. Society
bases almost everything on the date and time that a task needs to be or
was completed. We make appointments and plan events for specific dates
and times. Most of our day revolves around the clock. Because of the time-
oriented nature of humans, it's a good idea to look at how Python deals with
interacting with dates and time (especially storing these values for later use).
As with everything else, computers understand only numbers — the date and
time don't really exist.

To work with dates and times, you need to perform a special task in Python.
When writing computer books, chicken-and-egg scenarios always arise, and
this is one of them. To use dates and times, you must issue a special `import`

datetime command. Technically, this act is called *importing a module,* and you learn more about it in Chapter 10. Don't worry how the command works right now — just use it whenever you want to do something with date and time.

Computers do have clocks inside them, but the clocks are for the humans using the computer. Yes, some software also depends on the clock, but again, the emphasis is on human needs rather than anything the computer might require. To get the current time, you can simply type **datetime.datetime. now()** and press Enter. You see the full date and time information as found on your computer's clock (see Figure 5-6).

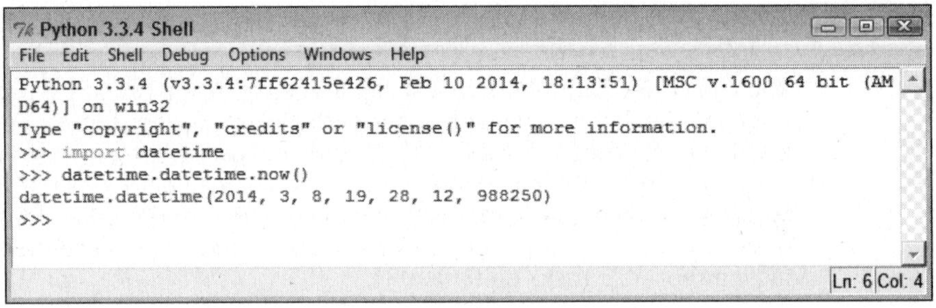

Figure 5-6:
Get the current date and time using the now() command.

```
74 Python 3.3.4 Shell                                              _ □ ×
File  Edit  Shell  Debug  Options  Windows  Help
Python 3.3.4 (v3.3.4:7ff62415e426, Feb 10 2014, 18:13:51) [MSC v.1600 64 bit (AM
D64)] on win32
Type "copyright", "credits" or "license()" for more information.
>>> import datetime
>>> datetime.datetime.now()
datetime.datetime(2014, 3, 8, 19, 28, 12, 988250)
>>>
                                                              Ln: 6 Col: 4
```

You may have noticed that the date and time are a little hard to read in the existing format. Say that you want to get just the current date, in a readable format. It's time to combine a few things you discovered in previous sections to accomplish that task. Type **str(datetime.datetime.now().date())** and press Enter. Figure 5-7 shows that you now have something a little more usable.

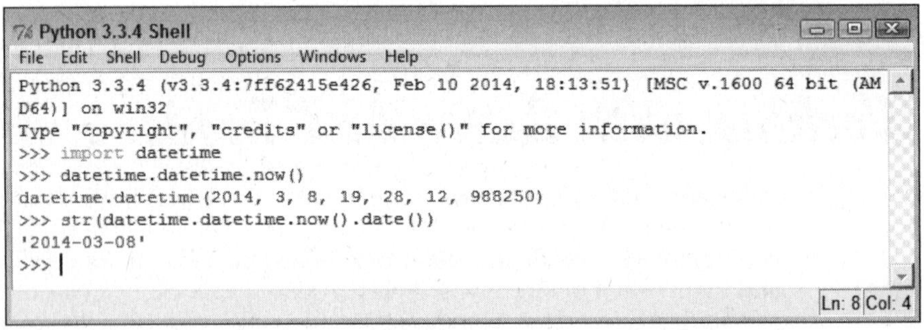

Figure 5-7:
Make the date and time more readable using the str() command.

```
74 Python 3.3.4 Shell                                              _ □ ×
File  Edit  Shell  Debug  Options  Windows  Help
Python 3.3.4 (v3.3.4:7ff62415e426, Feb 10 2014, 18:13:51) [MSC v.1600 64 bit (AM
D64)] on win32
Type "copyright", "credits" or "license()" for more information.
>>> import datetime
>>> datetime.datetime.now()
datetime.datetime(2014, 3, 8, 19, 28, 12, 988250)
>>> str(datetime.datetime.now().date())
'2014-03-08'
>>> |
                                                              Ln: 8 Col: 4
```

Interestingly enough, Python also has a time() command, which you can use to obtain the current time. You can obtain separate values for each of the components that make up date and time using the day, month, year, hour, minute, second, and microsecond values. Later chapters help you understand how to use these various date and time features to keep application users informed about the current date and time on their system.

Chapter 6

Managing Information

In This Chapter

▶ Understanding the Python view of data

▶ Using operators to assign, modify, and compare data

▶ Organizing code using functions

▶ Interacting with the user

*W*hether you use the term *information* or *data* to refer to the content that applications manage, the fact is that you must provide some means of working with it or your application really doesn't have a purpose. Throughout the rest of the book, you see *information* and *data* used interchangeably because they really are the same thing, and in real-world situations, you'll encounter them both, so getting used to both is a good idea. No matter which term you use, you need some means of assigning data to variables, modifying the content of those variables to achieve specific goals, and comparing the result you receive with desired results. This chapter addresses all three requirements so that you can start to control data within your applications.

It's also essential to start working through methods of keeping your code understandable. Yes, you could write your application as a really long procedure, but trying to understand such a procedure is incredibly hard, and you'd find yourself repeating some steps because they must be done more than once. Functions are one way for you to package code so that it's easier to understand and reuse as needed.

Applications also need to interact with the user. Yes, some perfectly usable applications are out there that don't really interact with the user, but they're extremely rare and don't really do much, for the most part. In order to provide a useful service, most applications interact with the user to discover how the user wants to manage data. You get an overview of this process in this chapter. Of course, you visit the topic of user interaction quite often throughout the book because it's an important topic.

Controlling How Python Views Data

As discussed in Chapter 5, all data on your computer is stored as 0s and 1s. The computer doesn't understand the concept of letters, Boolean values, dates, times, or any other kind of information except numbers. In addition, a computer's capability to work with numbers is both inflexible and relatively simplistic. When you work with a string in Python, you're depending on Python to translate the concept of a string into a form the computer can understand. The storage containers that your application creates and uses in the form of variables tell Python how to treat the 0s and 1s that the computer has stored. So, it's important to understand that the Python view of data isn't the same as your view of data or the computer's view of data — Python acts as an intermediary to make your applications functional.

To manage data within an application, the application must control the way in which Python views the data. The use of operators, packaging methods such as functions, and the introduction of user input all help applications control data. All these techniques rely, in part, on making comparisons. Determining what to do next means understanding what state the data is in now as compared to some other state. If the variable contains the name John now, but you really want it to contain Mary instead, then you first need to know that it does in fact contain John. Only then can you make the decision to change the content of the variable to Mary.

Making comparisons

Python's main method for making comparisons is through the use of operators. In fact, operators play a major role in manipulating data as well. The upcoming "Working with Operators" section discusses how operators work and how you can use them in applications to control data in various ways. Later chapters use operators extensively as you discover techniques for creating applications that can make decisions, perform tasks repetitively, and interact with the user in interesting ways. However, the basic idea behind operators is that they help applications perform various types of comparisons.

In some cases, you use some fancy methods for performing comparisons in an application. For example, you can compare the output of two functions (as described in the "Comparing function output" section, later in this chapter). With Python, you can perform comparisons at a number of levels so that you can manage data without a problem in your application. Using these techniques hides detail so that you can focus on the point of the comparison and define how to react to that comparison rather than become mired in detail.

Your choice of techniques for performing comparisons affects the manner in which Python views the data and determines the sorts of things you can do to manage the data after the comparison is made. All this functionality might seem absurdly complex at the moment, but the important point to remember is that applications require comparisons in order to interact with data correctly.

Understanding how computers make comparisons

Computers don't understand packaging, such as functions, or any of the other structures that you create with Python. All this packaging is for your benefit, not the computer's. However, computers do directly support the concept of operators. Most Python operators have a direct corollary with a command that the computer understands directly. For example, when you ask whether one number is greater than another number, the computer can actually perform this computation directly, using an operator. (The upcoming section explains operators in detail.)

Some comparisons aren't direct. Computers work only with numbers. So, when you ask Python to compare two strings, what Python actually does is compare the numeric value of each character in the string. For example, the letter *A* is actually the number 65 in the computer. A lowercase letter *a* has a different numeric value — 97. As a result, even though you might see ABC as being equal to abc, the computer doesn't agree — it sees them as different because the numeric values of their individual letters are different.

Working with Operators

Operators are the basis for both control and management of data within applications. You use operators to define how one piece of data is compared to another and to modify the information within a single variable. In fact, operators are essential to performing any sort of math-related task and to assigning data to variables in the first place.

When using an operator, you must supply either a variable or an expression. You already know that a variable is a kind of storage box used to hold data. An *expression* is an equation or formula that provides a description of a mathematical concept. In most cases, the result of evaluating an expression is a Boolean (true or false) value. The following sections describe operators in detail because you use them everywhere throughout the rest of the book.

Understanding Python's one ternary operator

A ternary operator requires three elements. Python supports just one such operator, and you use it to determine the truth value of an expression. This operator takes the following form:

```
TrueValue if Expression else
    FalseValue
```

When the `Expression` is true, the operator outputs `TrueValue`. When the expression is false, it outputs `FalseValue`. As an example, if you type

```
"Hello" if True else
    "Goodbye"
```

the operator outputs a response of `'Hello'`. However, if you type

```
"Hello" if False else
    "Goodbye"
```

the operator outputs a response of `'Goodbye'`. This is a handy operator for times when you need to make a quick decision and don't want to write a lot of code to do it.

One of the advantages of using Python is that it normally has more than one way to do things. Python has an alternative form of this ternary operator — an even shorter shortcut. It takes the following form:

```
(FalseValue, TrueValue)
    [Expression]
```

As before, when `Expression` is true, the operator outputs `TrueValue`; otherwise, it outputs `FalseValue`. Notice that the `TrueValue` and `FalseValue` elements are reversed in this case. An example of this version is

```
("Hello", "Goodbye") [True]
```

In this case, the output of the operator is `'Goodbye'` because that's the value in the `TrueValue` position. Of the two forms, the first is a little clearer, while the second is shorter.

Defining the operators

An *operator* accepts one or more inputs in the form of variables or expressions, performs a task (such as comparison or addition), and then provides an output consistent with that task. Operators are classified partially by their effect and partially by the number of elements they require. For example, a unary operator works with a single variable or expression; a binary operator requires two.

The elements provided as input to an operator are called *operands*. The operand on the left side of the operator is called the left operand, while the operand on the right side of the operator is called the right operand. The following list shows the categories of operators that you use within Python:

- Unary
- Arithmetic
- Relational

> ✔ Logical
>
> ✔ Bitwise
>
> ✔ Assignment
>
> ✔ Membership
>
> ✔ Identity

Each of these categories performs a specific task. For example, the arithmetic operators perform math-based tasks, while relational operators perform comparisons. The following sections describe the operators based on the category in which they appear.

Unary

Unary operators require a single variable or expression as input. You often use these operators as part of a decision-making process. For example, you might want to find something that isn't like something else. Table 6-1 shows the unary operators.

Table 6-1	Python Unary Operators	
Operator	**Description**	**Example**
~	Inverts the bits in a number so that all the 0 bits become 1 bits and vice versa.	~4 results in a value of –5
–	Negates the original value so that positive becomes negative and vice versa.	–(–4) results in 4 and –4 results in –4
+	Is provided purely for the sake of completeness. This operator returns the same value that you provide as input.	+4 results in a value of 4

Arithmetic

Computers are known for their capability to perform complex math. However, the complex tasks that computers perform are often based on much simpler math tasks, such as addition. Python provides access to libraries that help you perform complex math tasks, but you can always create your own libraries of math functions using the simple operators found in Table 6-2.

Table 6-2	Python Arithmetic Operators	
Operator	*Description*	*Example*
+	Adds two values together	5 + 2 = 7
–	Subtracts the right operand from the left operand	5 – 2 = 3
*	Multiplies the right operand by the left operand	5 * 2 = 10
/	Divides the left operand by the right operand	5 / 2 = 2.5
%	Divides the left operand by the right operand and returns the remainder	5 % 2 = 1
**	Calculates the exponential value of the right operand by the left operand	5 ** 2 = 25
//	Performs integer division, in which the left operand is divided by the right operand and only the whole number is returned (also called floor division)	5 // 2 = 2

Relational

The relational operators compare one value to another and tell you when the relationship you've provided is true. For example, 1 is less than 2, but 1 is never greater than 2. The truth value of relations is often used to make decisions in your applications to ensure that the condition for performing a specific task is met. Table 6-3 describes the relational operators.

Table 6-3	Python Relational Operators	
Operator	*Description*	*Example*
==	Determines whether two values are equal. Notice that the relational operator uses two equals signs. A mistake many developers make is using just one equals sign, which results in one value being assigned to another.	1 == 2 is False
!=	Determines whether two values are not equal. Some older versions of Python allowed you to use the <> operator in place of the != operator. Using the <> operator results in an error in current versions of Python.	1 != 2 is True
>	Verifies that the left operand value is greater than the right operand value.	1 > 2 is False

Operator	Description	Example
<	Verifies that the left operand value is less than the right operand value.	1 < 2 is True
>=	Verifies that the left operand value is greater than or equal to the right operand value.	1 >= 2 is False
<=	Verifies that the left operand value is less than or equal to the right operand value.	1 <= 2 is True

Logical

The logical operators combine the true or false value of variables or expressions so that you can determine their resultant truth value. You use the logical operators to create Boolean expressions that help determine whether to perform tasks. Table 6-4 describes the logical operators.

Table 6-4	Python Logical Operators	
Operator	**Description**	**Example**
and	Determines whether both operands are true.	True and True is True
		True and False is False
		False and True is False
		False and False is False
or	Determines when one of two operands is true.	True or True is True
		True or False is True
		False or True is True
		False or False is False
not	Negates the truth value of a single operand. A true value becomes false and a false value becomes true.	not True is False
		not False is True

Bitwise

The bitwise operators interact with the individual bits in a number. For example, the number 6 is actually 0b0110 in binary.

If your binary is a little rusty, you can use the handy Binary to Decimal to Hexadecimal Converter at `http://www.mathsisfun.com/binary-decimal-hexadecimal-converter.html`. You need to enable JavaScript to make the site work.

A bitwise operator would interact with each bit within the number in a specific way. When working with a logical bitwise operator, a value of 0 counts as false and a value of 1 counts as true. Table 6-5 describes the bitwise operators.

Table 6-5	Python Bitwise Operators	
Operator	*Description*	*Example*
& (And)	Determines whether both individual bits within two operators are true and sets the resulting bit to true when they are.	0b1100 & 0b0110 = 0b0100
| (Or)	Determines whether either of the individual bits within two operators is true and sets the resulting bit to true when one of them is.	0b1100 | 0b0110 = 0b1110
^ (Exclusive or)	Determines whether just one of the individual bits within two operators is true and sets the resulting bit to true when one is. When both bits are true or both bits are false, the result is false.	0b1100 ^ 0b0110 = 0b1010
~ (One's complement)	Calculates the one's complement value of a number.	~0b1100 = −0b1101 ~0b0110 = −0b0111
<< (Left shift)	Shifts the bits in the left operand left by the value of the right operand. All new bits are set to 0 and all bits that flow off the end are lost.	0b00110011 << 2 = 0b11001100
>> (Right shift)	Shifts the bits in the left operand right by the value of the right operand. All new bits are set to 0 and all bits that flow off the end are lost.	0b00110011 >> 2 = 0b00001100

Assignment

The assignment operators place data within a variable. The simple assignment operator appears in previous chapters of the book, but Python offers a number of other interesting assignment operators that you can use. These other assignment operators can perform mathematical tasks during the assignment process, which makes it possible to combine assignment with a math operation. Table 6-6 describes the assignment operators. For this particular table, the initial value of MyVar in the Example column is 5.

Table 6-6	Python Assignment Operators	
Operator	*Description*	*Example*
=	Assigns the value found in the right operand to the left operand.	MyVar = 2 results in MyVar containing 2
+=	Adds the value found in the right operand to the value found in the left operand and places the result in the left operand.	MyVar += 2 results in MyVar containing 7
-=	Subtracts the value found in the right operand from the value found in the left operand and places the result in the left operand.	MyVar -= 2 results in MyVar containing 3
*=	Multiplies the value found in the right operand by the value found in the left operand and places the result in the left operand.	MyVar *= 2 results in MyVar containing 10
/=	Divides the value found in the left operand by the value found in the right operand and places the result in the left operand.	MyVar /= 2 results in MyVar containing 2.5
%=	Divides the value found in the left operand by the value found in the right operand and places the remainder in the left operand.	MyVar %= 2 results in MyVar containing 1
**=	Determines the exponential value found in the left operand when raised to the power of the value found in the right operand and places the result in the left operand.	MyVar **= 2 results in MyVar containing 25
//=	Divides the value found in the left operand by the value found in the right operand and places the integer (whole number) result in the left operand.	MyVar //= 2 results in MyVar containing 2

Membership

The membership operators detect the appearance of a value within a list or sequence and then output the truth value of that appearance. Think of the membership operators as you would a search routine for a database. You enter a value that you think should appear in the database, and the search routine finds it for you or reports that the value doesn't exist in the database. Table 6-7 describes the membership operators.

Table 6-7	Python Membership Operators	
Operator	*Description*	*Example*
In	Determines whether the value in the left operand appears in the sequence found in the right operand.	"Hello" in "Hello Goodbye" is True
not in	Determines whether the value in the left operand is missing from the sequence found in the right operand.	"Hello" not in "Hello Goodbye" is False

Identity

The identity operators determine whether a value or expression is of a certain class or type. You use identity operators to ensure that you're actually working with the sort of information that you think you are. Using the identity operators can help you avoid errors in your application or determine the sort of processing a value requires. Table 6-8 describes the identity operators.

Table 6-8	Python Identity Operators	
Operator	*Description*	*Example*
Is	Evaluates to true when the type of the value or expression in the right operand points to the same type in the left operand.	type(2) is int is True
is not	Evaluates to true when the type of the value or expression in the right operand points to a different type than the value or expression in the left operand.	type(2) is not int is False

Understanding operator precedence

When you create simple statements that contain just one operator, the order of determining the output of that operator is also simple. However, when you start working with multiple operators, it becomes necessary to determine which operator to evaluate first. For example, it's important to know whether 1 + 2 * 3 evaluates to 7 (where the multiplication is done first) or 9 (where the addition is done first). An order of operator precedence tells you that the answer is 7 unless you use parentheses to override the default order. In this case, (1 + 2) * 3 would evaluate to 9 because the parentheses have a higher order of precedence than multiplication does. Table 6-9 defines the order of operator precedence for Python.

Table 6-9	Python Operator Precedence
Operator	*Description*
( )	You use parentheses to group expressions and to override the default precedence so that you can force an operation of lower precedence (such as addition) to take precedence over an operation of higher precedence (such as multiplication).
**	Exponentiation raises the value of the left operand to the power of the right operand.
~ + -	Unary operators interact with a single variable or expression.
* / % //	Multiply, divide, modulo, and floor division.
+ -	Addition and subtraction.
>> <<	Right and left bitwise shift.
&	Bitwise AND.
^ |	Bitwise exclusive OR and standard OR.
<= < > >=	Comparison operators.
== !=	Equality operators.
= %= /= //= -= += *= **=	Assignment operators.
Is is not	Identity operators.
In not in	Membership operators.
not or and	Logical operators.

Creating and Using Functions

To manage information properly, you need to organize the tools used to perform the required tasks. Each line of code that you create performs a specific task, and you combine these lines of code to achieve a desired result. Sometimes you need to repeat the instructions with different data, and in some cases your code becomes so long that it's hard to keep track of what each part does. Functions serve as organization tools that keep your code neat and tidy. In addition, functions make it easy to reuse the instructions you've created as needed with different data. This section of the chapter tells you all about functions. More important, in this section you start creating your first serious applications in the same way that professional developers do.

Viewing functions as code packages

You go to your closet, open the door, and everything spills out. In fact, it's an avalanche, and you're lucky that you've survived. That bowling ball in the top shelf could have done some severe damage! However, you're armed with storage boxes and soon you have everything in the closet in neatly organized boxes. The shoes go in one box, games in another, and old cards and letters in yet another. After you're done, you can find anything you want in the closet without fear of injury. Functions are just like that — they take messy code and place it in packages that make it easy to see what you have and understand how it works.

Commentaries abound on just what functions are and why they're necessary, but when you boil down all that text, it comes down to a single idea: Functions provide a means of packaging code to make it easy to find and access. If you can think of functions as organizers, you find that working with them is much easier. For example, you can avoid the problem that many developers have of stuffing the wrong items in a function. All your functions will have a single purpose, just like those storage boxes in the closet.

Understanding code reusability

You go to your closet, take out pants and shirt, remove the labels, and put them on. At the end of the day, you take everything off and throw it in the trash. Hmmm . . . That really isn't what most people do. Most people take the clothes off, wash them, and then put them back into the closet for reuse. Functions are reusable, too. No one wants to keep repeating the same task; it becomes monotonous and boring. When you create a function, you define a package of code that you can use over and over to perform the same task. All you need to do is tell the computer to perform a specific task by telling it which function to use. The computer faithfully executes each instruction in the function absolutely every time you ask it to do so.

When you work with functions, the code that needs services from the function is named the *caller,* and it calls upon the function to perform tasks for it. Much of the information you see about functions refers to the caller. The caller must supply information to the function, and the function returns information to the caller.

At one time, computer programs didn't include the concept of code reusability. As a result, developers had to keep reinventing the same code. It didn't take long for someone to come up with the idea of functions, though, and the concept has evolved over the years until functions have become quite flexible. You can make functions do anything you want. Code reusability is a necessary part of applications to

✔ Reduce development time

✔ Reduce programmer error

✔ Increase application reliability

✔ Allow entire groups to benefit from the work of one programmer

✔ Make code easier to understand

✔ Improve application efficiency

In fact, functions do a whole list of things for applications in the form of reusability. As you work through the examples in this book, you see how reusability makes your life significantly easier. If not for reusability, you'd still be programming by plugging 0s and 1s into the computer by hand.

Defining a function

Creating a function doesn't require much work. Python tends to make things fast and easy for you. The following steps show you the process of creating a function that you can later access:

1. **Open a Python Shell window.**

   You see the familiar Python prompt.

2. **Type** def Hello(): **and press Enter.**

This step tells Python to define a function named Hello. The parentheses are important because they define any requirements for using the function. (There aren't any requirements in this case.) The colon at the end tells Python that you're done defining the way in which people will access the function. Notice that the insertion pointer is now indented, as shown in Figure 6-1. This indentation is a reminder that you must give the function a task to perform.

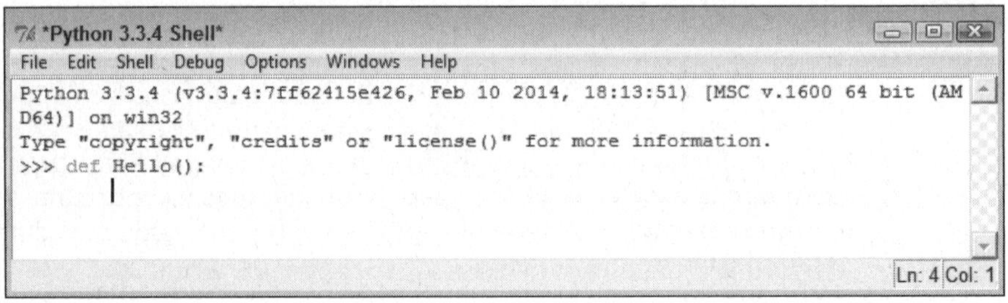

Figure 6-1:
Define
the name
of your
function.

```
7⁄ *Python 3.3.4 Shell*                                    _ □ ×
File  Edit  Shell  Debug  Options  Windows  Help
Python 3.3.4 (v3.3.4:7ff62415e426, Feb 10 2014, 18:13:51) [MSC v.1600 64 bit (AM
D64)] on win32
Type "copyright", "credits" or "license()" for more information.
>>> def Hello():
        |
                                                          Ln: 4 Col: 1
```

3. **Type** print("This is my first Python function!") **and press Enter.**

You should notice two things, as shown in Figure 6-2. First, the insertion pointer is still indented because IDLE is waiting for you to provide the next step in the function. Second, Python hasn't executed the print() function because it's part of a function and is not in the main part of the window.

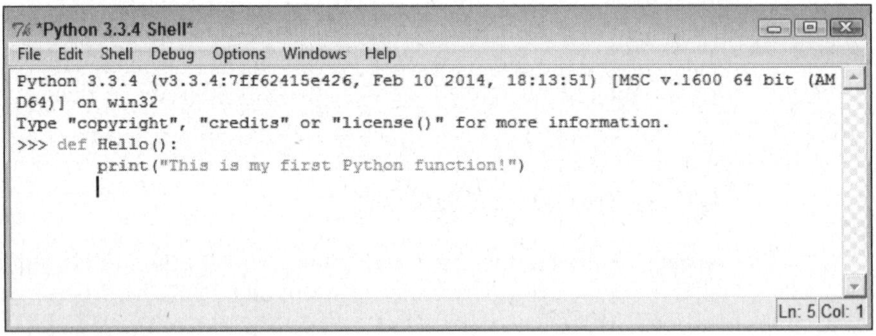

Figure 6-2:
IDLE is
waiting for
your next
instruction.

```
7⁄ *Python 3.3.4 Shell*                                    _ □ ×
File  Edit  Shell  Debug  Options  Windows  Help
Python 3.3.4 (v3.3.4:7ff62415e426, Feb 10 2014, 18:13:51) [MSC v.1600 64 bit (AM
D64)] on win32
Type "copyright", "credits" or "license()" for more information.
>>> def Hello():
        print("This is my first Python function!")
        |
                                                          Ln: 5 Col: 1
```

4. **Press Enter.**

The function is now complete. You can tell because the insertion point is now to the left side, as shown in Figure 6-3. In addition, the Python prompt (>>>) has returned.

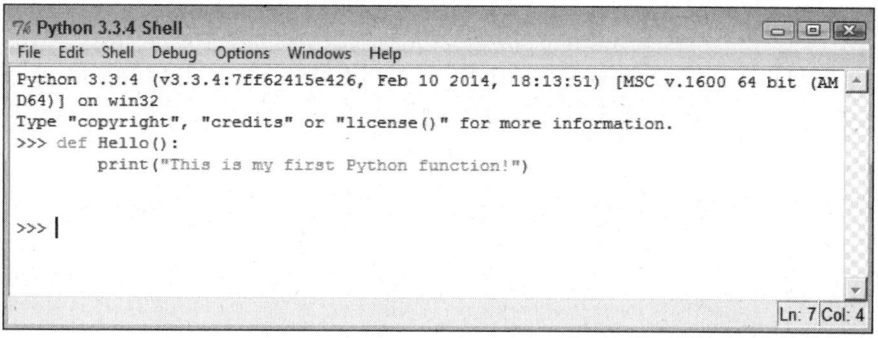

Figure 6-3:
The function is complete, and IDLE waits for you to provide another instruction.

```
7₄ Python 3.3.4 Shell                                          ▢ ▢ ✕
File  Edit  Shell  Debug  Options  Windows  Help
Python 3.3.4 (v3.3.4:7ff62415e426, Feb 10 2014, 18:13:51) [MSC v.1600 64 bit (AM
D64)] on win32
Type "copyright", "credits" or "license()" for more information.
>>> def Hello():
        print("This is my first Python function!")

>>> |

                                                          Ln: 7 Col: 4
```

Even though this is a really simple function, it demonstrates the pattern you use when creating any Python function. You define a name, provide any requirements for using the function (none in this case), and provide a series of steps for using the function. A function ends when an extra line is added (you press Enter twice).

Working with functions in the Edit window is the same as working with them in the Python Shell window, except that you can save the Edit window content to disk. This example also appears with the downloadable source code as `FirstFunction.py`. Try loading the file into an Edit window using the same technique you use in the "Using the Edit window" section of Chapter 4.

Accessing functions

After you define a function, you probably want to use it to perform useful work. Of course, this means knowing how to access the function. In the previous section, you create a new function named `Hello()`. To access this function, you type **Hello()** and press Enter. Figure 6-4 shows the output you see when you execute this function.

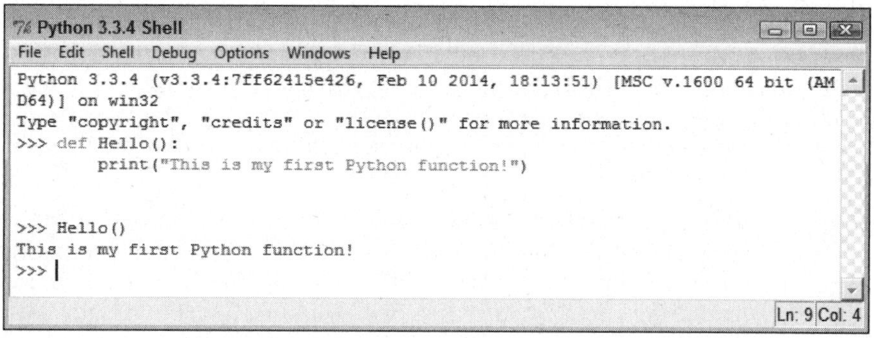

Figure 6-4:
Whenever you type the function's name, you get the output the function provides.

```
7₄ Python 3.3.4 Shell                                          ▢ ▢ ✕
File  Edit  Shell  Debug  Options  Windows  Help
Python 3.3.4 (v3.3.4:7ff62415e426, Feb 10 2014, 18:13:51) [MSC v.1600 64 bit (AM
D64)] on win32
Type "copyright", "credits" or "license()" for more information.
>>> def Hello():
        print("This is my first Python function!")


>>> Hello()
This is my first Python function!
>>> |

                                                          Ln: 9 Col: 4
```

Every function you create will provide a similar pattern of usage. You type the function name, an open parenthesis, any required input, and a close parenthesis; then you press Enter. In this case, you have no input, so all you type is **Hello( )**. As the chapter progresses, you see other examples for which input is required.

Sending information to functions

The `FirstFunction.py` example is nice because you don't have to keep typing that long string every time you want to say `Hello()`. However, it's also quite limited because you can use it to say only one thing. Functions should be flexible and allow you to do more than just one thing. Otherwise, you end up writing a lot of functions that vary by the data they use rather than the functionality they provide. Using arguments helps you create functions that are flexible and can use a wealth of data.

Understanding arguments

The term *argument* doesn't mean that you're going to have a fight with the function; it means that you supply information to the function to use in processing a request. Perhaps a better word for it would be input, but the term *input* has been used for so many other purposes that developers decided to use something a bit different: argument. Although the purpose of an argument might not be clear from its name, understanding what it does is relatively straightforward. An argument makes it possible for you to send data to the function so that the function can use it when performing a task. Using arguments makes your function more flexible.

The `Hello()` function is currently inflexible because it prints just one string. Adding an argument to the function can make it a lot more flexible because you can send strings to the function to say anything you want. To see how arguments work, create a new function in the Python Shell window (or open the `Arguments01.py` file of the downloadable source; see the Introduction for the URL). This version of `Hello()`, `Hello2()`, requires an argument:

```
def Hello2( Greeting ):
    print(Greeting)
```

Notice that the parentheses are no longer empty. They contain a word, `Greeting`, which is the argument for `Hello2()`. The `Greeting` argument is actually a variable that you can pass to `print()` in order to see it onscreen.

Sending required arguments

You have a new function, `Hello2()`. This function requires that you provide an argument to use it. At least, that's what you've heard so far. Type **Hello2()** and press Enter in the Python Shell window. You see an error message, as shown in Figure 6-5, telling you that `Hello2()` requires an argument.

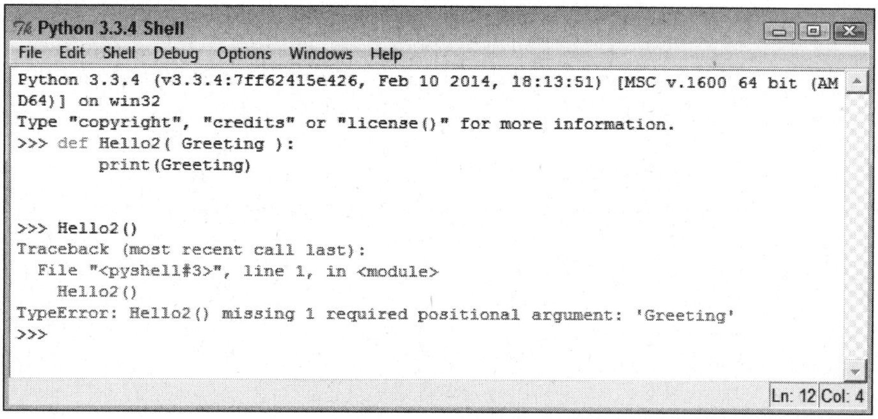

Figure 6-5:
You must
supply an
argument
or you get
an error
message.

Not only does Python tell you that the argument is missing, it tells you the name of the argument as well. Creating a function the way you have done so far means that you must supply an argument. Type **Hello2("This is an interesting function.")** and press Enter. This time, you see the expected output. However, you still don't know whether `Hello2()` is flexible enough to print multiple messages. Type **Hello2("Another message...")** and press Enter. You see the expected output again, as shown in Figure 6-6, so `Hello2()` is indeed an improvement over `Hello()`.

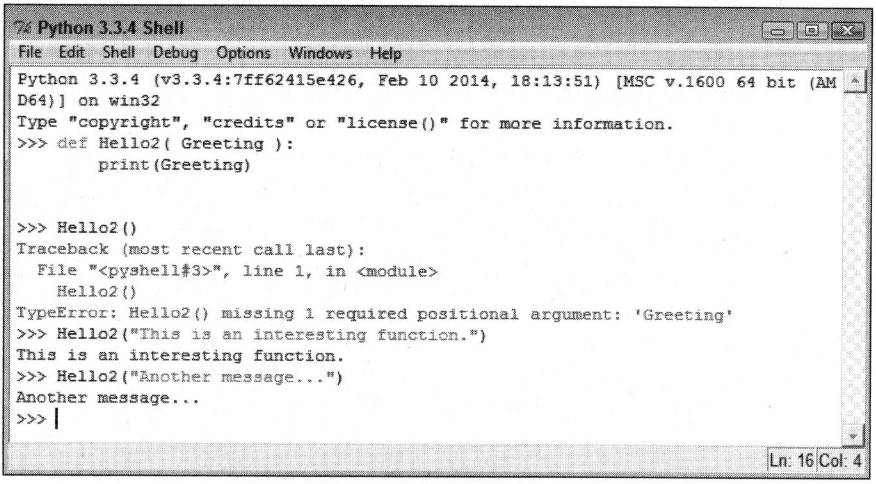

Figure 6-6:
Use
Hello2()
to print any
message
you desire.

You might easily to assume that Greeting will accept only a string from the tests you have performed so far. **Type Hello2(1234)**, press Enter, and you see 1234 as the output. Likewise, type **Hello2(5 + 5)** and press Enter. This time you see the result of the expression, which is 10.

Sending arguments by keyword

As your functions become more complex and the methods to use them do as well, you may want to provide a little more control over precisely how you call the function and provide arguments to it. Up until now, you have *positional arguments,* which means that you have supplied values in the order in which they appear in the argument list for the function definition. However, Python also has a method for sending arguments by keyword. In this case, you supply the name of the argument followed by an equals sign (=) and the argument value. To see how this works, open a Python Shell window and type the following function (which is also found in the Arguments02.py file):

```
def AddIt(Value1, Value2):
    print(Value1, " + ", Value2, " = ", (Value1 + Value2))
```

Notice that the print() function argument includes a list of items to print and that those items are separated by commas. In addition, the arguments are of different types. Python makes it easy to mix and match arguments in this manner.

Time to test AddIt(). Of course, you want to try the function using positional arguments first, so type **AddIt(2, 3)** and press Enter. You see the expected output of 2 + 3 = 5. Now type **AddIt(Value2 = 3, Value1 = 2)** and press Enter. Again, you receive the output 2 + 3 = 5 even though the position of the arguments has been reversed.

Giving function arguments a default value

Whether you make the call using positional arguments or keyword arguments, the functions to this point have required that you supply a value. Sometimes a function can use default values when a common value is available. Default values make the function easier to use and less likely to cause errors when a developer doesn't provide an input. To create a default value, you simply follow the argument name with an equals sign and the default value. To see how this works, open a Python Shell window and type the following function (which you can also find in the Arguments03.py file):

```
def Hello3(Greeting = "No Value Supplied"):
    print(Greeting)
```

This is yet another version of the original `Hello()` and updated `Hello2()` functions, but `Hello3()` automatically compensates for individuals who don't supply a value. When someone tries to call `Hello3()` without an argument, it doesn't raise an error. Type **Hello3()** and press Enter to see for yourself. Type **Hello3("This is a string.")** to see a normal response. Lest you think the function is now unable to use other kinds of data, type **Hello3(5)** and press Enter; then **Hello3(2 + 7)** and press Enter. Figure 6-7 shows the output from all these tests.

```
7⁄₄ Python 3.3.4 Shell                                              □ ▣ ▣
File  Edit  Shell  Debug  Options  Windows  Help
Python 3.3.4 (v3.3.4:7ff62415e426, Feb 10 2014, 18:13:51) [MSC v.1600 64 bit (AM
D64)] on win32
Type "copyright", "credits" or "license()" for more information.
>>> def Hello3(Greeting = "No Value Supplied"):
        print(Greeting)


>>> Hello3()
No Value Supplied
>>> Hello3("This is a string.")
This is a string.
>>> Hello3(5)
5
>>> Hello3(2 + 7)
9
>>> |
                                                            Ln: 15 Col: 4
```

Figure 6-7: Supply default arguments when possible to make your functions easier to use.

Creating functions with a variable number of arguments

In most cases, you know precisely how many arguments to provide with your function. It pays to work toward this goal whenever you can because functions with a fixed number of arguments are easier to troubleshoot later. However, sometimes you simply can't determine how many arguments the function will receive at the outset. For example, when you create a Python application that works at the command line, the user might provide no arguments, the maximum number of arguments (assuming there is one), or any number of arguments in between.

Fortunately, Python provides a technique for sending a variable number of arguments to a function. You simply create an argument that has an asterisk in front of it, such as `*VarArgs`. The usual technique is to provide a second argument that contains the number of arguments passed as an input. Here is an example (also found in the `VarArgs.py` file) of a function that can print a variable number of elements. (Don't worry too much if you don't understand it completely now — you haven't seen some of these techniques used before.)

```
def Hello4(ArgCount, *VarArgs):
    print("You passed ", ArgCount, " arguments.")
    for Arg in VarArgs:
        print(Arg)
```

This example uses something called a `for` loop. You meet this structure in Chapter 8. For now, all you really need to know is that it takes the arguments out of `VarArgs` one at a time, places the individual argument into `Arg`, and then prints `Arg` using `print()`. What should interest you most is seeing how a variable number of arguments can work.

After you type the function into a new Python Shell window, type **Hello4(1, "A Test String.")** and press Enter. You should see the number of arguments and the test string as output — nothing too exiting there. However, now type **Hello4(3, "One", "Two", "Three")** and press Enter. As shown in Figure 6-8, the function handles the variable number of arguments without any problem at all.

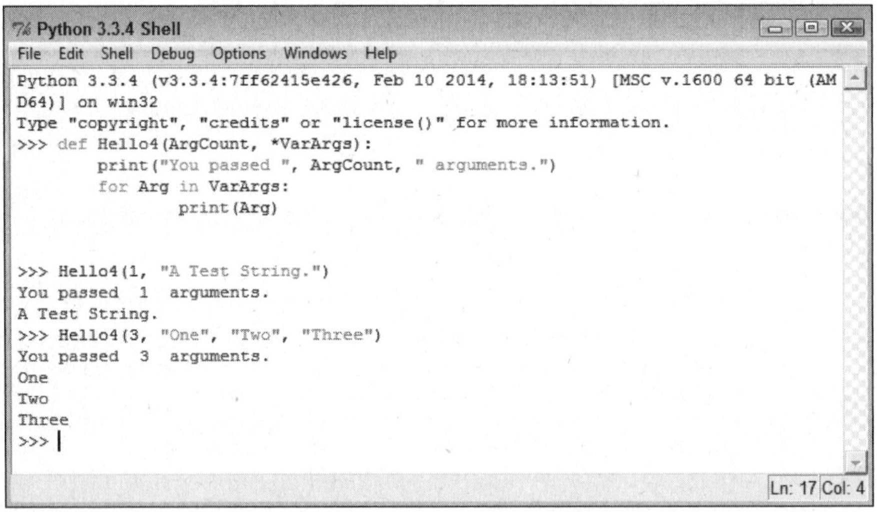

Figure 6-8:
Variable argument functions can make your applications more flexible.

```
7% Python 3.3.4 Shell
File  Edit  Shell  Debug  Options  Windows  Help
Python 3.3.4 (v3.3.4:7ff62415e426, Feb 10 2014, 18:13:51) [MSC v.1600 64 bit (AM
D64)] on win32
Type "copyright", "credits" or "license()" for more information.
>>> def Hello4(ArgCount, *VarArgs):
        print("You passed ", ArgCount, " arguments.")
        for Arg in VarArgs:
                print(Arg)

>>> Hello4(1, "A Test String.")
You passed  1  arguments.
A Test String.
>>> Hello4(3, "One", "Two", "Three")
You passed  3  arguments.
One
Two
Three
>>> |
                                                    Ln: 17 Col: 4
```

Returning information from functions

Functions can display data directly or they can return the data to the caller so that the caller can do something more with it. In some cases, a function displays data directly as well as returns data to the caller, but it's more common for a function to either display the data directly or to return it to the caller.

Just how functions work depends on the kind of task the function is supposed to perform. For example, a function that performs a math-related task is more likely to return the data to the caller than certain other functions.

To return data to a caller, a function needs to include the keyword `return`, followed by the data to return. You have no limit on what you can return to a caller. Here are some types of data that you commonly see returned by a function to a caller:

- ✔ **Values:** Any value is acceptable. You can return numbers, such as 1 or 2.5; strings, such as "Hello There!"; or Boolean values, such as True or False.

- ✔ **Variables:** The content of any variable works just as well as a direct value. The caller receives whatever data is stored in the variable.

- ✔ **Expressions:** Many developers use expressions as a shortcut. For example, you can simply return A + B rather than perform the calculation, place the result in a variable, and then return the variable to the caller. Using the expression is faster and accomplishes the same task.

- ✔ **Results from other functions:** You can actually return data from another function as part of the return of your function.

It's time to see how return values work. Open a Python Shell window and type the following code (or open the `ReturnValue.py` file instead):

```
def DoAdd(Value1, Value2):
    return Value1 + Value2
```

This function accepts two values as input and then returns the sum of those two values. Yes, you could probably perform this task without using a function, but this is how many functions start. To test this function, type **print("The sum of 3 + 4 is ", DoAdd(3, 4))** and press Enter. You see the expected output shown in Figure 6-9.

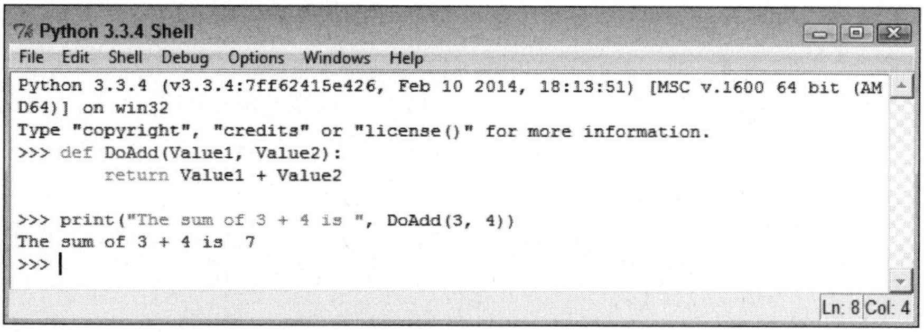

Figure 6-9:
Return values can make your functions even more useful.

```
74 Python 3.3.4 Shell
File  Edit  Shell  Debug  Options  Windows  Help
Python 3.3.4 (v3.3.4:7ff62415e426, Feb 10 2014, 18:13:51) [MSC v.1600 64 bit (AM
D64)] on win32
Type "copyright", "credits" or "license()" for more information.
>>> def DoAdd(Value1, Value2):
        return Value1 + Value2

>>> print("The sum of 3 + 4 is ", DoAdd(3, 4))
The sum of 3 + 4 is  7
>>> |
                                                            Ln: 8 Col: 4
```

Comparing function output

You use functions with return values in a number of ways. For example, the previous section of this chapter shows how you can use functions to provide input for another function. You use functions to perform all sorts of tasks. One of the ways to use functions is for comparison purposes. You can actually create expressions from them that define a logical output.

To see how this might work, use the DoAdd() function from the previous section. Type **print("3 + 4 equals 2 + 5 is ", (DoAdd(3, 4) == DoAdd(2, 5)))** and press Enter. You see the truth value of the statement that 3 + 4 equals 2 + 5, as shown in Figure 6-10. The point is that functions need not provide just one use or that you view them in just one way. Functions can make your code quite versatile and flexible.

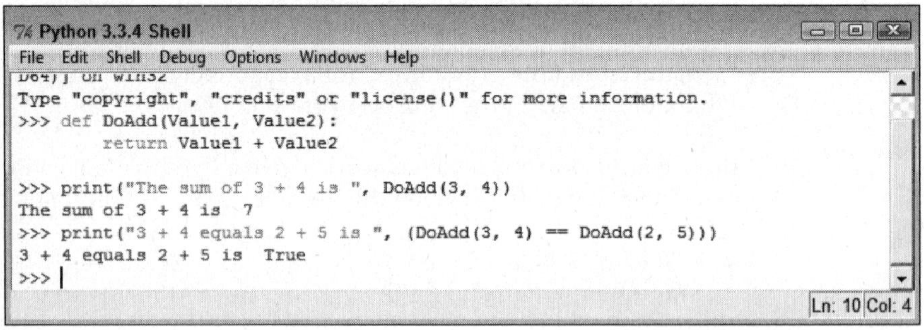

Figure 6-10:
Use your
functions to
perform a
wide variety
of tasks.

```
76 Python 3.3.4 Shell
File  Edit  Shell  Debug  Options  Windows  Help
DoA)] on win32
Type "copyright", "credits" or "license()" for more information.
>>> def DoAdd(Value1, Value2):
        return Value1 + Value2

>>> print("The sum of 3 + 4 is ", DoAdd(3, 4))
The sum of 3 + 4 is  7
>>> print("3 + 4 equals 2 + 5 is ", (DoAdd(3, 4) == DoAdd(2, 5)))
3 + 4 equals 2 + 5 is  True
>>>
                                                          Ln: 10 Col: 4
```

Getting User Input

Very few applications exist in their own world — that is, apart from the user. In fact, most applications interact with users in a major way because computers are designed to serve user needs. To interact with a user, an application must provide some means of obtaining user input. Fortunately, the most commonly used technique for obtaining input is also relatively easy to implement. You simply use the input() function to do it.

The input() function always outputs a string. Even if a user types a number, the output from the input() function is a string. This means that if you are expecting a number, you need to convert it after receiving the input. The input() function also lets you provide a string prompt. This prompt is displayed to tell the user what to provide in the way of information.

The Input01.py file contains an example of using the input() function in a simple way. Here's the code for that example:

```
Name = input("Tell me your name: ")
print("Hello ", Name)
```

In this case, the input() function asks the user for a name. After the user types a name and presses Enter, the example outputs a customized greeting to the user. Try running this example at the command prompt or the Python Shell window. Figure 6-11 shows typical results when you input John as the username.

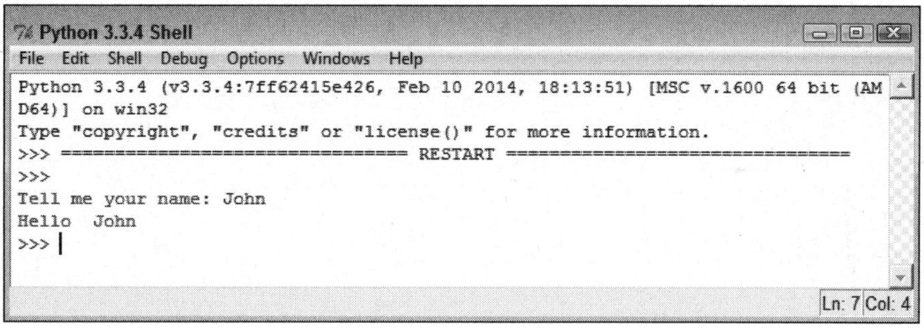

Figure 6-11:
Provide a
username
and see a
greeting as
output.

```
74 Python 3.3.4 Shell
File  Edit  Shell  Debug  Options  Windows  Help
Python 3.3.4 (v3.3.4:7ff62415e426, Feb 10 2014, 18:13:51) [MSC v.1600 64 bit (AM
D64)] on win32
Type "copyright", "credits" or "license()" for more information.
>>> ================================ RESTART ================================
>>>
Tell me your name: John
Hello  John
>>>
                                                                    Ln: 7 Col: 4
```

You can use input() for other kinds of data; all you need is the correct conversion function. For example, the code in the Input02.py file provides one technique for performing such a conversion, as shown here:

```
ANumber = float(input("Type a number: "))
print("You typed: ", ANumber)
```

When you run this example, the application asks for a numeric input. The call to float() converts the input to a number. After the conversion, print() outputs the result. When you run the example using a value such as 5.5, you obtain the desired result.

It's important to understand that data conversion isn't without risk. If you attempt to type something other than a number, you get an error message, as shown in Figure 6-12. Chapter 9 helps you understand how to detect and fix errors before they cause a system crash.

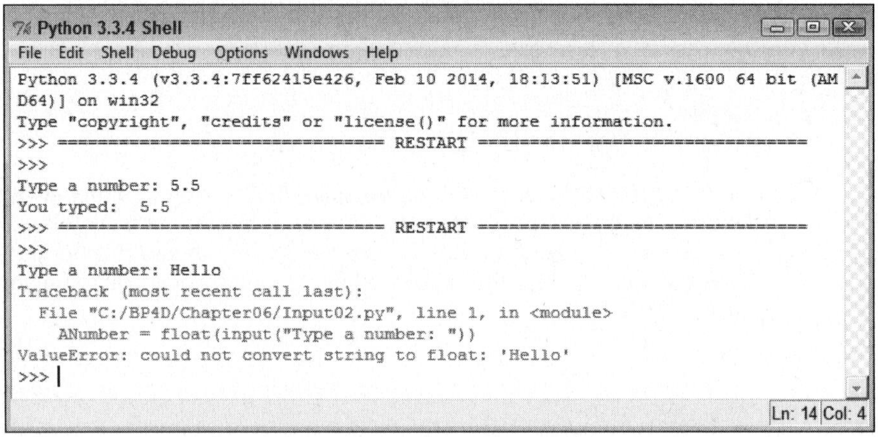

Figure 6-12:
Data conversion changes the input type to whatever you need, but could cause errors.

```
7 Python 3.3.4 Shell                                                      — □ ✕
File  Edit  Shell  Debug  Options  Windows  Help
Python 3.3.4 (v3.3.4:7ff62415e426, Feb 10 2014, 18:13:51) [MSC v.1600 64 bit (AM
D64)] on win32
Type "copyright", "credits" or "license()" for more information.
>>> ================================ RESTART ================================
>>>
Type a number: 5.5
You typed:  5.5
>>> ================================ RESTART ================================
>>>
Type a number: Hello
Traceback (most recent call last):
  File "C:/BP4D/Chapter06/Input02.py", line 1, in <module>
    ANumber = float(input("Type a number: "))
ValueError: could not convert string to float: 'Hello'
>>> |
                                                              Ln: 14 Col: 4
```

Chapter 7

Making Decisions

In This Chapter

▶ Using the `if` statement to make simple decisions

▶ Performing more advanced decision making with the `if...else` statement

▶ Creating multiple decision levels by nesting statements

The ability to make a decision, to take one path or another, is an essential element of performing useful work. Math gives the computer the capability to obtain useful information. Decisions make it possible to do something with the information after it's obtained. Without the capability to make decisions, a computer would be useless. So any language you use will include the capability to make decisions in some manner. This chapter explores the techniques that Python uses to make decisions.

Think through the process you use when making a decision. You obtain the actual value of something, compare it to a desired value, and then act accordingly. For example, when you see a signal light and see that it's red, you compare the red light to the desired green light, decide that the light isn't green, and then stop. Most people don't take time to consider the process they use because they use it so many times every day. Decision making comes naturally to humans, but computers must perform the following tasks every time:

1. Obtain the actual or current value of something.

2. Compare the actual or current value to a desired value.

3. Perform an action that corresponds to the desired outcome of the comparison.

Making Simple Decisions Using the if Statement

The if statement is the easiest method for making a decision in Python. It simply states that if something is true, Python should perform the steps that follow. The following sections tell you how you can use the if statement to make decisions of various sorts in Python. You may be surprised at what this simple statement can do for you.

Understanding the if statement

You use if statements regularly in everyday life. For example, you may say to yourself, "If it's Wednesday, I'll eat tuna salad for lunch." The Python if statement is a little less verbose, but it follows precisely the same pattern. Say you create a variable, TestMe, and place a value of 6 in it, like this:

```
TestMe = 6
```

You can then ask the computer to check for a value of 6 in TestMe, like this:

```
if TestMe == 6:
    print("TestMe does equal 6!")
```

Every Python if statement begins, oddly enough, with the word *if*. When Python sees if, it knows that you want it to make a decision. After the word *if* comes a condition. A *condition* simply states what sort of comparison you want Python to make. In this case, you want Python to determine whether TestMe contains the value 6.

Notice that the condition uses the relational equality operator, ==, and not the assignment operator, =. A common mistake that developers make is to use the assignment operator rather than the equality operator. You can see a list of relational operators in Chapter 6.

The condition always ends with a colon (:). If you don't provide a colon, Python doesn't know that the condition has ended and will continue to look for additional conditions on which to base its decision. After the colon come any tasks you want Python to perform. In this case, Python prints a statement saying that TestMe is equal to 6.

Using the if statement in an application

It's possible to use the if statement in a number of ways in Python. However, you immediately need to know about three common ways to use it:

- ✔ Use a single condition to execute a single statement when the condition is true.

- ✔ Use a single condition to execute multiple statements when the condition is true.

- ✔ Combine multiple conditions into a single decision and execute one or more statements when the combined condition is true.

The following sections explore these three possibilities and provide you with examples of their use. You see additional examples of how to use the if statement throughout the book because it's such an important method of making decisions.

Working with relational operators

A *relational operator* determines how a value on the left side of an expression compares to the value on the right side of an expression. After it makes the determination, it outputs a value of true or false that reflects the truth value of the expression. For example, 6 == 6 is true, while 5 == 6 is false. Table 6-3 contains a listing of the relational operators. The following steps show how to create and use an if statement. This example also appears with the downloadable source code as SimpleIf1.py.

1. **Open a Python Shell window.**

   You see the familiar Python prompt.

2. **Type** TestMe = 6 **and press Enter.**

   This step assigns a value of 6 to TestMe. Notice that it uses the assignment operator and not the equality operator.

3. **Type** if TestMe == 6: **and press Enter.**

   This step creates an if statement that tests the value of TestMe using the equality operator. You should notice two features of the Python Shell at this point:

   - The word *if* is highlighted in a different color than the rest of the statement.

   - The next line is automatically indented.

4. Type print("TestMe does equal 6!") **and press Enter.**

Notice that Python doesn't execute the if statement yet. It does indent the next line. The word *print* appears in a special color because it's a function name. In addition, the text appears in another color to show you that it's a string value. Color coding makes it much easier to see how Python works.

5. Press Enter.

The Python Shell outdents this next line and executes the if statement, as shown in Figure 7-1. Notice that the output is in yet another color. Because TestMe contains a value of 6, the if statement works as expected.

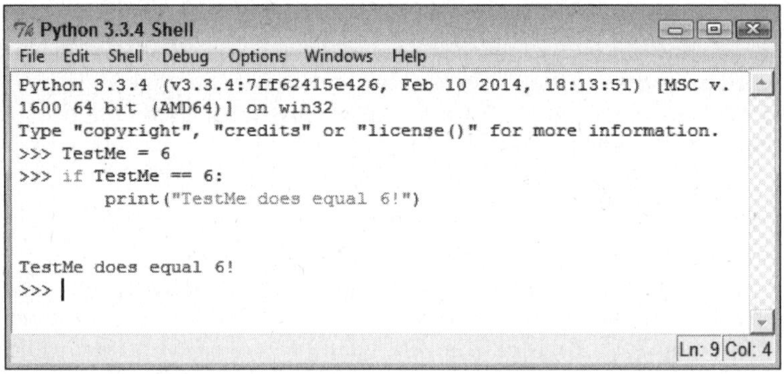

Figure 7-1:
Simple if
statements
can help
your appli-
cation know
what to do
in certain
conditions.

```
74 Python 3.3.4 Shell                                    [ - ] [ □ ] [ X ]
File   Edit   Shell   Debug   Options   Windows   Help
Python 3.3.4 (v3.3.4:7ff62415e426, Feb 10 2014, 18:13:51) [MSC v.
1600 64 bit (AMD64)] on win32
Type "copyright", "credits" or "license()" for more information.
>>> TestMe = 6
>>> if TestMe == 6:
        print("TestMe does equal 6!")


TestMe does equal 6!
>>> |
                                                          Ln: 9 Col: 4
```

Performing multiple tasks

Sometimes you want to perform more than one task after making a decision. Python relies on indentation to determine when to stop executing tasks as part of an if statement. As long as the next line is indented, it's part of the if statement. When the next line is outdented, it becomes the first line of code outside the if block. A *code block* consists of a statement and the tasks associated with that statement. The same term is used no matter what kind of statement you're working with, but in this case, you're working with an if statement that is part of a code block. This example also appears with the downloadable source code as SimpleIf2.py.

1. Open a Python Shell window.

You see the familiar Python prompt.

2. Type the following code into the window — pressing Enter after each line:

```
TestMe = 6
if TestMe == 6:
    print("TestMe does equal 6!")
    print("All done!")
```

Notice that the shell continues to indent lines as long as you continue to type code. Each line you type is part of the current `if` statement code block.

When working in the shell, you create a block by typing one line of code after another. If you press Enter twice in a row without entering any text, the code block is ended, and Python executes the entire code block at one time.

3. **Press Enter.**

Python executes the entire code block. You see the output shown in Figure 7-2.

Figure 7-2: A code block can contain multiple lines of code — one for each task.

```
Python 3.3.4 Shell
File  Edit  Shell  Debug  Options  Windows  Help
Python 3.3.4 (v3.3.4:7ff62415e426, Feb 10 2014, 18:13:51) [MSC v.
1600 64 bit (AMD64)] on win32
Type "copyright", "credits" or "license()" for more information.
>>> TestMe = 6
>>> if TestMe == 6:
        print("TestMe does equal 6!")
        print("All done!")


TestMe does equal 6!
All done!
>>>
                                                              Ln: 11 Col: 4
```

Making multiple comparisons using logical operators

So far, the examples have all shown a single comparison. Real life often requires that you make multiple comparisons to account for multiple requirements. For example, when baking cookies, if the timer has gone off and the edges are brown, it's time to take the cookies out of the oven.

In order to make multiple comparisons, you create multiple conditions using relational operators and combine them using logical operators (see Table 6-4). A *logical operator* describes how to combine conditions. For example, you might say $x == 6$ and $y == 7$ as two conditions for performing one or more tasks. The and keyword is a logical operator that states that both conditions must be true.

One of the most common uses for making multiple comparisons to determine when a value is within a certain range. In fact, *range checking,* the act of determining whether data is between two values, is an important part of making your application secure and user friendly. The following steps help you see how to perform this task. In this case, you create a file so that you can run the application multiple times. This example also appears with the downloadable source code as `SimpleIf3.py`.

1. **Open a Python File window.**

   You see an editor in which you can type the example code.

2. **Type the following code into the window — pressing Enter after each line:**

   ```
   Value = int(input("Type a number between 1 and 10: "))

   if (Value > 0) and (Value <= 10):
       print("You typed: ", Value)
   ```

   The example begins by obtaining an input value. You have no idea what the user has typed other than that it's a value of some sort. The use of the `int()` function means that the user must type a whole number (one without a decimal portion). Otherwise, the application will raise an *exception* (an error indication; Chapter 9 describes exceptions). This first check ensures that the input is at least of the correct type.

   The `if` statement contains two conditions. The first states that `Value` must be greater than 0. You could also present this condition as `Value >= 1`. The second condition states that `Value` must be less than or equal to 10. Only when `Value` meets both of these conditions will the `if` statement succeed and print the value the user typed.

3. **Choose Run➪Run Module.**

   You see a Python Shell window open with a prompt to type a number between 1 and 10.

4. **Type 5 and press Enter.**

   The application determines that the number is in the right range and outputs the message shown in Figure 7-3.

5. **Repeat Steps 3 and 4, but type 22 instead of 5.**

   The application doesn't output anything because the number is in the wrong range. Whenever you type a value that's outside the programmed range, the statements that are part of the `if` block aren't executed.

6. **Repeat Steps 3 and 4, but type 5.5 instead of 5.**

   Python displays the error message shown in Figure 7-4. Even though you may think of 5.5 and 5 as both being numbers, Python sees the first number as a floating-point value and the second as an integer.

7. Repeat Steps 3 and 4, but type Hello **instead of 5.**

Python displays about the same error message as before. Python doesn't differentiate between types of wrong input. It only knows that the input type is incorrect and therefore unusable.

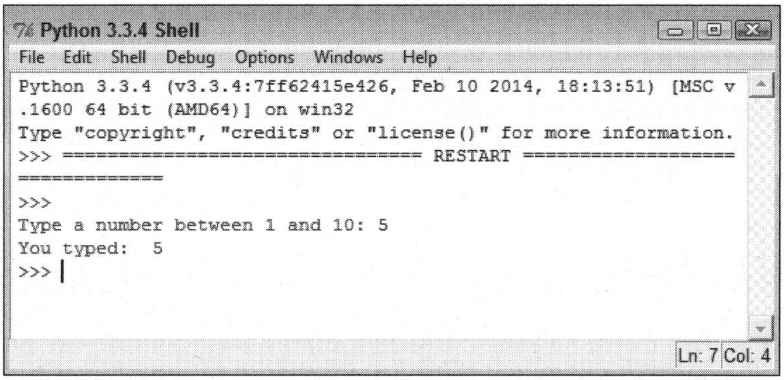

Figure 7-3:
The application verifies the value is in the right range and outputs a message.

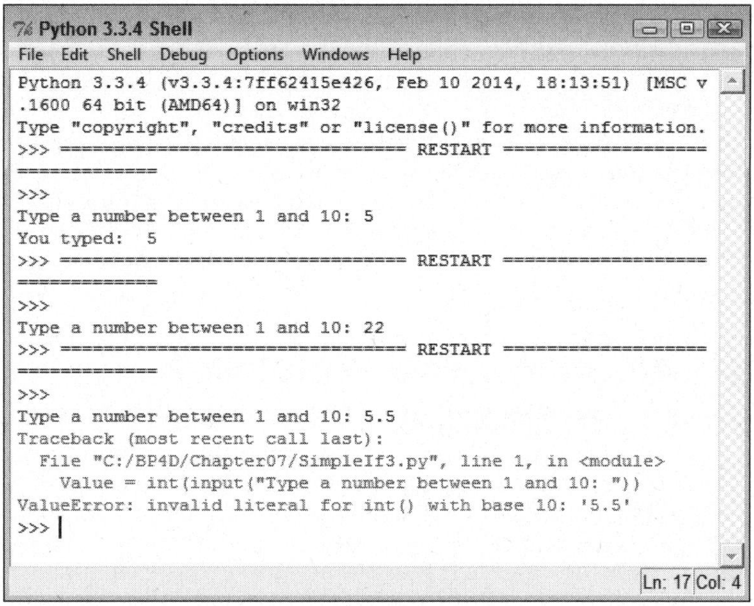

```
7% Python 3.3.4 Shell

File  Edit  Shell  Debug  Options  Windows  Help

Python 3.3.4 (v3.3.4:7ff62415e426, Feb 10 2014, 18:13:51) [MSC v
.1600 64 bit (AMD64)] on win32
Type "copyright", "credits" or "license()" for more information.
>>> ================================ RESTART ====================
=============
>>>
Type a number between 1 and 10: 5
You typed:   5
>>> |

                                                        Ln: 7 Col: 4
```

Figure 7-4:
Typing the wrong type of information results in an error message.

```
7% Python 3.3.4 Shell

File  Edit  Shell  Debug  Options  Windows  Help

Python 3.3.4 (v3.3.4:7ff62415e426, Feb 10 2014, 18:13:51) [MSC v
.1600 64 bit (AMD64)] on win32
Type "copyright", "credits" or "license()" for more information.
>>> ================================ RESTART ====================
=============
>>>
Type a number between 1 and 10: 5
You typed:   5
>>> ================================ RESTART ====================
=============
>>>
Type a number between 1 and 10: 22
>>> ================================ RESTART ====================
=============
>>>
Type a number between 1 and 10: 5.5
Traceback (most recent call last):
  File "C:/BP4D/Chapter07/SimpleIf3.py", line 1, in <module>
    Value = int(input("Type a number between 1 and 10: "))
ValueError: invalid literal for int() with base 10: '5.5'
>>> |

                                                        Ln: 17 Col: 4
```

The best applications use various kinds of range checking to ensure that the application behaves in a predictable manner. The more predictable an application becomes, the less the user thinks about the application and the more time the user spends on performing useful work. Productive users tend to be a lot happier than those who constantly fight with their applications.

Choosing Alternatives Using the if...else Statement

Many of the decisions you make in an application fall into a category of choosing one of two options based on conditions. For example, when looking at a signal light, you choose one of two options: press on the brake to stop or press the accelerator to continue. The option you choose depends on the conditions. A green light signals that you can continue on through the light; a red light tells you to stop. The following sections describe how Python makes it possible to choose between two alternatives.

Understanding the if...else statement

With Python, you choose one of two alternatives using the `else` clause of the `if` statement. A *clause* is an addition to a code block that modifies the way in which it works. Most code blocks support multiple clauses. In this case, the `else` clause enables you to perform an alternative task, which increases the usefulness of the `if` statement. Most developers refer to the form of the `if` statement that has the `else` clause included as the `if...else` statement, with the ellipsis implying that something happens between `if` and `else`.

Sometimes developers encounter problems with the `if...else` statement because they forget that the `else` clause always executes when the conditions for the `if` statement aren't met. It's important to think about the consequences of always executing a set of tasks when the conditions are false. Sometimes doing so can lead to unintended consequences.

Using the if...else statement in an application

The `SimpleIf3.py` example is a little less helpful than it could be when the user enters a value that's outside the intended range. Even entering data of the wrong type produces an error message, but entering the correct type of data outside the range tells the user nothing. In this example, you discover the means for correcting this problem by using an `else` clause. The following steps demonstrate just one reason to provide an alternative action when the condition for an `if` statement is false. This example also appears with the downloadable source code as `IfElse.py`.

1. **Open a Python File window.**

   You see an editor in which you can type the example code.

2. **Type the following code into the window — pressing Enter after each line:**

```
Value = int(input("Type a number between 1 and 10: "))

if (Value > 0) and (Value <= 10):
    print("You typed: ", Value)
else:
    print("The value you typed is incorrect!")
```

   As before, the example obtains input from the user and then determines whether that input is in the correct range. However, in this case, the `else` clause provides an alternative output message when the user enters data outside the desired range.

   Notice that the `else` clause ends with a colon, just as the `if` statement does. Most clauses that you use with Python statements have a colon associated with them so that Python knows when the clause has ended. If you receive a coding error for your application, make sure that you check for the presence of the colon as needed.

3. **Choose Run⇨Run Module.**

   You see a Python Shell window open with a prompt to type a number between 1 and 10.

4. **Type 5 and press Enter.**

   The application determines that the number is in the right range and outputs the message shown previously in Figure 7-3.

5. **Repeat Steps 3 and 4, but type 22 instead of 5.**

   This time the application outputs the error message shown in Figure 7-5. The user now knows that the input is outside the desired range and knows to try entering it again.

Using the if...elif statement in an application

You go to a restaurant and look at the menu. The restaurant offers eggs, pancakes, waffles, and oatmeal for breakfast. After you choose one of the items, the server brings it to you. Creating a menu selection requires something like an `if...else` statement, but with a little extra oomph. In this case, you use the `elif` clause to create another set of conditions. The `elif` clause is a combination of the `else` clause and a separate `if` statement. The following steps describe how to use the `if...elif` statement to create a menu. This example also appears with the downloadable source code as `IfElif.py`.

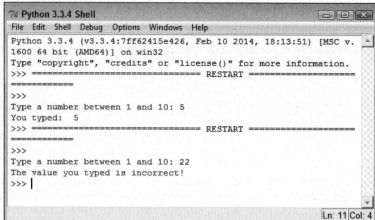

Figure 7-5:
It's always
a good idea
to provide
feedback
for incorrect
input.

1. **Open a Python File window.**

   You see an editor in which you can type the example code.

2. **Type the following code into the window — pressing Enter after each line:**

```python
print("1. Red")
print("2. Orange")
print("3. Yellow")
print("4. Green")
print("5. Blue")
print("6. Purple")

Choice = int(input("Select your favorite color: "))

if (Choice == 1):
   print("You chose Red!")
elif (Choice == 2):
   print("You chose Orange!")
elif (Choice == 3):
   print("You chose Yellow!")
elif (Choice == 4):
   print("You chose Green!")
elif (Choice == 5):
   print("You chose Blue!")
elif (Choice == 6):
   print("You chose Purple!")
else:
   print("You made an invalid choice!")
```

   The example begins by displaying a menu. The user sees a list of choices for the application. It then asks the user to make a selection, which it places inside `Choice`. The use of the `int()` function ensures that the user can't type anything other than a number.

After the user makes a choice, the application looks for it in the list of potential values. In each case, `Choice` is compared against a particular value to create a condition for that value. When the user types 1, the application outputs the message `"You chose Red!"`. If none of the options is correct, the `else` clause is executed by default to tell the user that the input choice is invalid.

3. **Choose Run⇨Run Module.**

   You see a Python Shell window open with the menu displayed. The application asks you to select your favorite color.

4. **Type** 1 **and press Enter.**

   The application displays the appropriate output message, as shown in Figure 7-6.

5. **Repeat Steps 3 and 4, but type** 5 **instead of 1.**

   The application displays a different output message — the one associated with the requested color.

6. **Repeat Steps 3 and 4, but type** 8 **instead of 1.**

   The application tells you that you made an invalid choice.

7. **Repeat Steps 3 and 4, but type** Red **instead of 1.**

   The application displays the expected error message, as shown in Figure 7-7. Any application you create should be able to detect errors and incorrect inputs. Chapter 9 shows you how to handle errors so that they're user friendly.

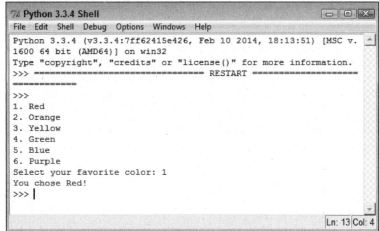

Figure 7-6:
Menus let you choose one option from a list of options.

Figure 7-7:
Every
application
you create
should
include
some means
of detecting
errant input.

No switch statement?

If you've worked with other languages, you might notice that Python lacks a switch statement (if you haven't, there is no need to worry about it with Python). Developers commonly use the switch statement in other languages to create menu-based applications. The `if...elif` statement is generally used for the same purpose in Python.

However, the `if...elif` statement doesn't provide quite the same functionality as a switch statement because it doesn't enforce the use of a single variable for comparison purposes. As a result, some developers rely on Python's dictionary functionality to stand in for the switch statement. Chapter 13 describes how to work with dictionaries.

Using Nested Decision Statements

The decision-making process often happens in levels. For example, when you go to the restaurant and choose eggs for breakfast, you have made a first-level decision. Now the server asks you what type of toast you want with your eggs. The server wouldn't ask this question if you had ordered pancakes, so the selection of toast becomes a second-level decision. When the breakfast arrives, you decide whether you want to use jelly on your toast. This is a third-level decision. If you had selected a kind of toast that doesn't work well with jelly, you might not have had to make this decision at all. This process of making decisions in levels, with each level reliant on the decision made at the previous level, is called *nesting*. Developers often use nesting techniques to create applications that can make complex decisions based on various inputs. The following sections describe several kinds of nesting you can use within Python to make complex decisions.

Using multiple if or if...else statements

The most commonly used multiple selection technique is a combination of `if` and `if...else` statements. This form of selection is often called a *selection tree* because of its resemblance to the branches of a tree. In this case, you follow a particular path to obtain a desired result. The example in this section also appears with the downloadable source code as `MultipleIfElse.py`.

1. **Open a Python File window.**

   You see an editor where you can type the example code.

2. **Type the following code into the window — pressing Enter after each line:**

```python
One = int(input("Type a number between 1 and 10: "))
Two = int(input("Type a number between 1 and 10: "))

if (One >= 1) and (One <= 10):
    if (Two >= 1) and (Two <= 10):
        print("Your secret number is: ", One * Two)
    else:
        print("Incorrect second value!")
else:
    print("Incorrect first value!")
```

   This is simply an extension of the `IfElse.py` example you see in the "Using the if...else statement in an application" section of the chapter. However, notice that the indentation is different. The second `if...else` statement is indented within the first `if...else` statement. The indentation tells Python that this is a second-level statement.

3. **Choose Run⇨Run Module.**

   You see a Python Shell window open with a prompt to type a number between 1 and 10.

4. **Type 5 and press Enter.**

   The shell asks for another number between 1 and 10.

5. **Type 2 and press Enter.**

   You see the combination of the two numbers as output, as shown in Figure 7-8.

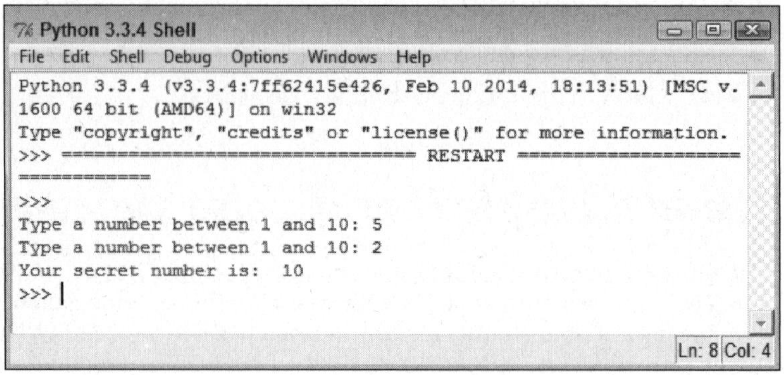

Figure 7-8:
Adding mul-
tiple levels
lets you per-
form tasks
with greater
complexity.

```
76 Python 3.3.4 Shell                                         □ □ ▣
File  Edit  Shell  Debug  Options  Windows  Help
Python 3.3.4 (v3.3.4:7ff62415e426, Feb 10 2014, 18:13:51) [MSC v.
1600 64 bit (AMD64)] on win32
Type "copyright", "credits" or "license()" for more information.
>>> ================================ RESTART ====================
============
>>>
Type a number between 1 and 10: 5
Type a number between 1 and 10: 2
Your secret number is:  10
>>> |
                                                         Ln: 8 Col: 4
```

This example has the same input features as the `IfElse.py` example. For example, if you attempt to provide a value that's outside the requested range, you see an error message. The error message is tailored for either the first or second input value so that the user knows which value was incorrect.

Providing specific error messages is always useful because users tend to become confused and frustrated otherwise. In addition, a specific error message helps you find errors in your application much faster.

Combining other types of decisions

It's possible to use any combination of `if`, `if...else`, and `if...elif` statements to produce a desired outcome. You can nest the code blocks as many levels deep as needed to perform the required checks. For example, Listing 7-1 shows what you might accomplish for a breakfast menu. This example also appears with the downloadable source code as `MultipleIfElif.py`.

Listing 7-1:   Creating a Breakfast Menu

```
print("1. Eggs")
print("2. Pancakes")
print("3. Waffles")
print("4. Oatmeal")
MainChoice = int(input("Choose a breakfast item: "))

if (MainChoice == 2):
   Meal = "Pancakes"
elif (MainChoice == 3):
   Meal = "Waffles"

if (MainChoice == 1):
   print("1. Wheat Toast")
   print("2. Sour Dough")
   print("3. Rye Toast")
   print("4. Pancakes")
   Bread = int(input("Choose a type of bread: "))

   if (Bread == 1):
      print("You chose eggs with wheat toast.")
   elif (Bread == 2):
      print("You chose eggs with sour dough.")
   elif (Bread == 3):
      print("You chose eggs with rye toast.")
   elif (Bread == 4):
      print("You chose eggs with pancakes.")
   else:
      print("We have eggs, but not that kind of bread.")

elif (MainChoice == 2) or (MainChoice == 3):
   print("1. Syrup")
   print("2. Strawberries")
   print("3. Powdered Sugar")
   Topping = int(input("Choose a topping: "))

   if (Topping == 1):
      print ("You chose " + Meal + " with syrup.")
   elif (Topping == 2):
      print ("You chose " + Meal + " with strawberries.")
   elif (Topping == 3):
      print ("You chose " + Meal + " with powdered
           sugar.")
   else:
      print ("We have " + Meal + ", but not that
           topping.")

elif (MainChoice == 4):
   print("You chose oatmeal.")

else:
   print("We don't serve that breakfast item!")
```

This example has some interesting features. For one thing, you might assume that an `if...elif` statement always requires an `else` clause. This example shows a situation that doesn't require such a clause. You use an `if...elif` statement to ensure that `Meal` contains the correct value, but you have no other options to consider.

The selection technique is the same as you saw for the previous examples. A user enters a number in the correct range to obtain a desired result. Three of the selections require a secondary choice, so you see the menu for that choice. For example, when ordering eggs, it isn't necessary to choose a topping, but you do want a topping for pancakes or waffles.

Notice that this example also combines variables and text in a specific way. Because a topping can apply equally to waffles or pancakes, you need some method for defining precisely which meal is being served as part of the output. The `Meal` variable that the application defines earlier is used as part of the output after the topping choice is made.

The best way to understand this example is to play with it. Try various menu combinations to see how the application works. For example, Figure 7-9 shows what happens when you choose a waffle breakfast with a strawberry topping.

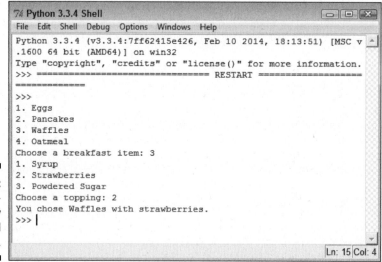

Figure 7-9:
Many applications rely on multilevel menus.

```
7. Python 3.3.4 Shell
File  Edit  Shell  Debug  Options  Windows  Help
Python 3.3.4 (v3.3.4:7ff62415e426, Feb 10 2014, 18:13:51) [MSC v
.1600 64 bit (AMD64)] on win32
Type "copyright", "credits" or "license()" for more information.
>>> ================================ RESTART ====================
==============
>>>
1. Eggs
2. Pancakes
3. Waffles
4. Oatmeal
Choose a breakfast item: 3
1. Syrup
2. Strawberries
3. Powdered Sugar
Choose a topping: 2
You chose Waffles with strawberries.
>>> |
                                                          Ln: 15 Col: 4
```

Chapter 8

Performing Repetitive Tasks

● ●

In This Chapter

▶ Performing a task a specific number of times

▶ Performing a task until completion

▶ Placing one task loop within another

● ●

*A*ll the examples in the book so far have performed a series of steps just one time and then stopped. However, the real world doesn't work this way. Many of the tasks that humans perform are repetitious. For example, the doctor might state that you need to exercise more and tell you to do 100 push-ups each day. If you just do one push-up, you won't get much benefit from the exercise and you definitely won't be following the doctor's orders. Of course, because you know precisely how many push-ups to do, you can perform the task a specific number of times. Python allows the same sort of repetition using the `for` statement.

Unfortunately, you don't always know how many times to perform a task. For example, consider needing to check a stack of coins for one of extreme rarity. Taking just the first coin from the top, examining it, and deciding that it either is or isn't the rare coin doesn't complete the task. Instead, you must examine each coin in turn, looking for the rare coin. Your stack may contain more than one. Only after you have looked at every coin in the stack can you say that the task is complete. However, because you don't know how many coins are in the stack, you don't know how many times to perform the task at the outset. You only know the task is done when the stack is gone. Python performs this kind of repetition using the `while` statement.

Most programming languages call any sort of repeating sequence of events a *loop*. The idea is to picture the repetition as a circle, with the code going round and round executing tasks until the loop ends. Loops are an essential part of application elements such as menus. In fact, writing most modern applications without using loops would be impossible.

In some cases, you must create loops within loops. For example, to create a multiplication table, you use a loop within a loop. The inner loop calculates the column values and the outer loop moves between rows. You see such an example later in the chapter, so don't worry too much about understanding precisely how such things work right now.

Processing Data Using the for Statement

The first looping code block that most developers encounter is the `for` statement. It's hard to imagine creating a conventional programming language that lacks such a statement. In this case, the loop executes a fixed number of times, and you know the number of times it will execute before the loop even begins. Because everything about a `for` loop is known at the outset, `for` loops tend to be the easiest kind of loop to use. However, in order to use one, you need to know how many times to execute the loop. The following sections describe the `for` loop in greater detail.

Understanding the for statement

A `for` loop begins with a `for` statement. The `for` statement describes how to perform the loop. The Python `for` loop works through a sequence of some type. It doesn't matter whether the sequence is a series of letters in a string or items within a collection. You can even specify a range of values to use by specifying the `range()` function. Here's a simple `for` statement.

```
for Letter in "Howdy!":
```

The statement begins with the keyword `for`. The next item is a variable that holds a single element of a sequence. In this case, the variable name is `Letter`. The `in` keyword tells Python that the sequence comes next. In this case, the sequence is the string `"Howdy"`. The `for` statement always ends with a colon, just as the decision-making statements described in Chapter 7 do.

Indented under the `for` statement are the tasks you want performed within the `for` loop. Python considers every following indented statement part of the code block that composes the `for` loop. Again, the `for` loop works just like the decision-making statements in Chapter 7.

Creating a basic for loop

The best way to see how a `for` loop actually works is to create one. In this case, the example uses a string for the sequence. The `for` loop processes each of the characters in the string in turn until it runs out of characters. This example also appears with the downloadable source code as `SimpleFor.py`.

1. **Open a Python File window.**

   You see an editor in which you can type the example code.

2. **Type the following code into the window — pressing Enter after each line:**

   ```
   LetterNum = 1

   for Letter in "Howdy!":
       print("Letter ", LetterNum, " is ", Letter)
       LetterNum+=1
   ```

   The example begins by creating a variable, `LetterNum`, to track the number of letters that have been processed. Every time the loop completes, `LetterNum` is updated by 1.

   The `for` statement works through the sequence of letters in the string `"Howdy!"`. It places each letter, in turn, in `Letter`. The code that follows displays the current `LetterNum` value and its associated character found in `Letter`.

3. **Choose Run⇨Run Module.**

   A Python Shell window opens. The application displays the letter sequence along with the letter number, as shown in Figure 8-1.

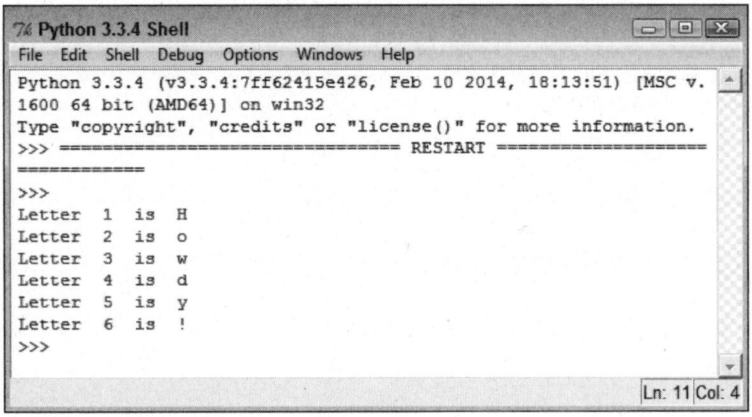

Figure 8-1: Use the `for` loop to process the characters in a string one at a time.

```
7⅘ Python 3.3.4 Shell
File  Edit  Shell  Debug  Options  Windows  Help
Python 3.3.4 (v3.3.4:7ff62415e426, Feb 10 2014, 18:13:51) [MSC v.
1600 64 bit (AMD64)] on win32
Type "copyright", "credits" or "license()" for more information.
>>> ================================ RESTART ====================
============
>>>
Letter   1  is   H
Letter   2  is   o
Letter   3  is   w
Letter   4  is   d
Letter   5  is   y
Letter   6  is   !
>>>
                                                        Ln: 11 Col: 4
```

Controlling execution with the break statement

Life is often about exceptions to the rule. For example, you might want an assembly line to produce a number of clocks. However, at some point, the assembly line runs out of a needed part. If the part isn't available, the assembly line must stop in the middle of the processing cycle. The count hasn't completed, but the line must be stopped anyway until the missing part is restocked.

Interruptions also occur in computers. You might be streaming data from an online source when a network glitch occurs and breaks the connection; the stream temporarily runs dry, so the application runs out of things to do even though the set number of tasks isn't completed.

The break clause makes breaking out of a loop possible. However, you don't simply place the break clause in your code — you surround it with an if statement that defines the condition for issuing a break. The statement might say something like this: If the stream runs dry, then break out of the loop.

In this example, you see what happens when the count reaches a certain level when processing a string. The example is a little contrived in the interest of keeping things simple, but it reflects what could happen in the real world when a data element is too long to process (possibly indicating an error condition). This example also appears with the downloadable source code as ForBreak.py.

1. **Open a Python File window.**

   You see an editor where you can type the example code.

2. **Type the following code into the window — pressing Enter after each line:**

```
Value = input("Type less than 6 characters: ")
LetterNum = 1

for Letter in Value:
    print("Letter ", LetterNum, " is ", Letter)
    LetterNum+=1
    if LetterNum > 6:
        print("The string is too long!")
        break
```

This example builds on the one found in the previous section. However, it lets the user provide a variable-length string. When the string is longer than six characters, the application stops processing it.

The `if` statement contains the conditional code. When `LetterNum` is greater than 6, it means that the string is too long. Notice the second level of indentation used for the `if` statement. In this case, the user sees an error message stating that the string is too long, and then the code executes a `break` to end the loop.

3. **Choose Run⇨Run Module.**

   You see a Python Shell window open with a prompt asking for input.

4. **Type** Hello **and press Enter.**

   The application lists each character in the string, as shown in Figure 8-2.

5. **Perform Steps 3 and 4 again, but type** I am too long. **instead of Hello.**

   The application displays the expected error message and stops processing the string at character 6, as shown in Figure 8-3.

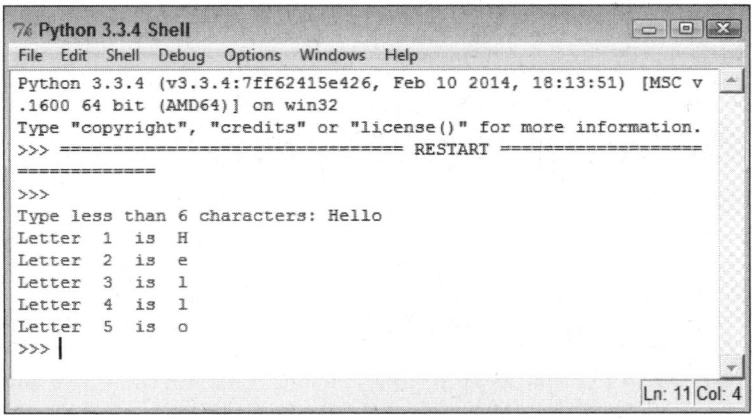

```
76 Python 3.3.4 Shell                                    [ - ][ □ ][ X ]
 File  Edit  Shell  Debug  Options  Windows  Help
 Python 3.3.4 (v3.3.4:7ff62415e426, Feb 10 2014, 18:13:51) [MSC v
 .1600 64 bit (AMD64)] on win32
 Type "copyright", "credits" or "license()" for more information.
 >>> ================================ RESTART ====================
 ==============
 >>>
 Type less than 6 characters: Hello
 Letter   1   is   H
 Letter   2   is   e
 Letter   3   is   l
 Letter   4   is   l
 Letter   5   is   o
 >>> |
                                                          Ln: 11 Col: 4
```

Figure 8-2: A short string is successfully processed by the application.

This example adds *length checking* to your repertoire of application data error checks. Chapter 7 shows how to perform range checks, which ensure that a value meets specific limits. The length check is necessary to ensure that data, especially strings, aren't going to overrun the size of data fields. In addition, a small input size makes it harder for intruders to perform certain types of hacks on your system, which makes your system more secure.

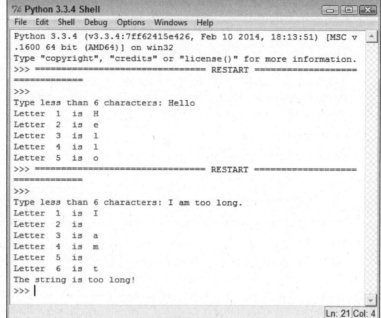

Figure 8-3:
Long strings
are trun-
cated to
ensure that
they remain
a certain
size.

Controlling execution with the continue statement

Sometimes you want to check every element in a sequence, but don't want to process certain elements. For example, you might decide that you want to process all the information for every car in a database except brown cars. Perhaps you simply don't need the information about that particular color of car. The `break` clause simply ends the loop, so you can't use it in this situation. Otherwise, you won't see the remaining elements in the sequence.

The `break` clause alternative that many developers use is the `continue` clause. As with the `break` clause, the `continue` clause appears as part of an `if` statement. However, processing continues with the next element in the sequence rather than ending completely.

The following steps help you see how the `continue` clause differs from the `break` clause. In this case, the code refuses to process the letter *w*, but will process every other letter in the alphabet. This example also appears with the downloadable source code as `ForContinue.py`.

1. **Open a Python File window.**

   You see an editor in which you can type the example code.

2. **Type the following code into the window — pressing Enter after each line:**

   ```
   LetterNum = 1

   for Letter in "Howdy!":
       if Letter == "w":
           continue
           print("Encountered w, not processed.")
       print("Letter ", LetterNum, " is ", Letter)
       LetterNum+=1
   ```

   This example is based on the one found in the "Creating a basic for loop" section, earlier in this chapter. However, this example adds an `if` statement with the `continue` clause in the `if` code block. Notice the `print()` function that is part of the `if` code block. You never see this string printed because the current loop iteration ends immediately.

3. **Choose Run➪Run Module.**

   You see a Python Shell window open. The application displays the letter sequence along with the letter number, as shown in Figure 8-4. However, notice the effect of the `continue` clause — the letter *w* isn't processed.

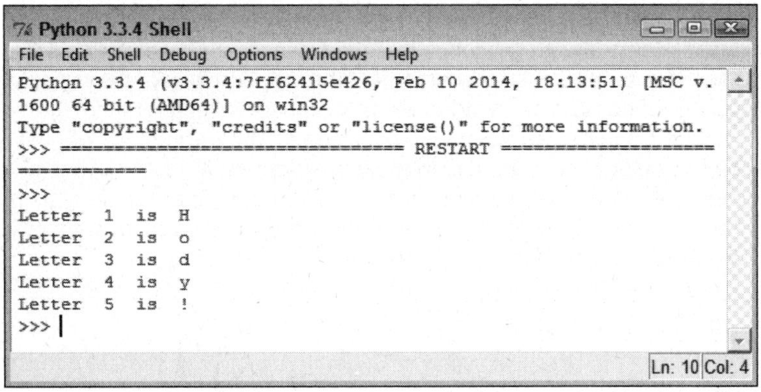

Figure 8-4:
Use the
`continue`
clause
to avoid
processing
specific
elements.

```
7⁄ Python 3.3.4 Shell                              _ □ ✕
File  Edit  Shell  Debug  Options  Windows  Help
Python 3.3.4 (v3.3.4:7ff62415e426, Feb 10 2014, 18:13:51) [MSC v.
1600 64 bit (AMD64)] on win32
Type "copyright", "credits" or "license()" for more information.
>>> ================================ RESTART ====================
============
>>>
Letter  1  is  H
Letter  2  is  o
Letter  3  is  d
Letter  4  is  y
Letter  5  is  !
>>> |
                                               Ln: 10 Col: 4
```

Controlling execution with the pass clause

The Python language includes something not commonly found in other languages: a second sort of continue clause. The pass clause works almost the same way as the continue clause does, except that it allows completion of the code in the if code block in which it appears. The following steps use an example that is precisely the same as the one found in the previous section, "Controlling execution with the continue statement," except that it uses a pass clause instead. This example also appears with the downloadable source code as ForPass.py.

1. **Open a Python File window.**

   You see an editor in which you can type the example code.

2. **Type the following code into the window — pressing Enter after each line:**

```
LetterNum = 1

for Letter in "Howdy!":
    if Letter == "w":
        pass
        print("Encountered w, not processed.")
    print("Letter ", LetterNum, " is ", Letter)
    LetterNum+=1
```

3. **Choose Run⇨Run Module.**

   You see a Python Shell window open. The application displays the letter sequence along with the letter number, as shown in Figure 8-5. However, notice the effect of the pass clause — the letter *w* isn't processed. In addition, the example displays the string that wasn't displayed for the continue clause example.

The continue clause makes it possible to silently bypass specific elements in a sequence and to avoid executing any additional code for that element. Use the pass clause when you need to perform some sort of post processing on the element, such as logging the element in an error log, displaying a message to the user, or handling the problem element in some other way. The continue and pass clauses both do the same thing, but they're used in distinctly different situations.

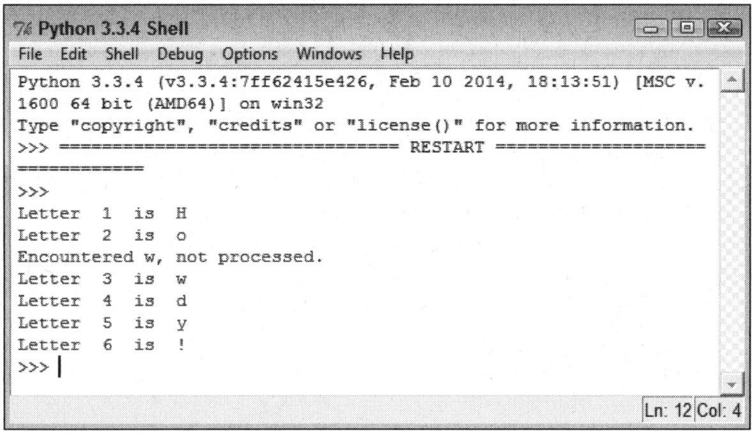

Figure 8-5: Using the `pass` clause allows for post processing of an unwanted input.

```
7 Python 3.3.4 Shell
File  Edit  Shell  Debug  Options  Windows  Help
Python 3.3.4 (v3.3.4:7ff62415e426, Feb 10 2014, 18:13:51) [MSC v.
1600 64 bit (AMD64)] on win32
Type "copyright", "credits" or "license()" for more information.
>>> ================================ RESTART ====================
============
>>>
Letter  1  is  H
Letter  2  is  o
Encountered w, not processed.
Letter  3  is  w
Letter  4  is  d
Letter  5  is  y
Letter  6  is  !
>>> |
                                                          Ln: 12 Col: 4
```

Controlling execution with the else statement

Python has another loop clause that you won't find with other languages: `else`. The `else` clause makes executing code possible even if you have no elements to process in a sequence. For example, you might need to convey to the user that there simply isn't anything to do. In fact, that's what the following example does. This example also appears with the downloadable source code as `ForElse.py`.

1. **Open a Python File window.**

   You see an editor in which you can type the example code.

2. **Type the following code into the window — pressing Enter after each line:**

```python
Value = input("Type less than 6 characters: ")
LetterNum = 1

for Letter in Value:
    print("Letter ", LetterNum, " is ", Letter)
    LetterNum+=1
else:
    print("The string is blank.")
```

This example is based on the one found in the "Creating a basic for loop" section, earlier in the chapter. However, when a user presses Enter without typing something, the `else` clause is executed.

3. **Choose Run⇨Run Module.**

   You see a Python Shell window open and a prompt asking for input.

4. **Type** Hello **and press Enter.**

   The application lists each character in the string, as shown in Figure 8-2.

5. **Repeat Steps 3 and 4. However, simply press Enter instead of entering any sort of text.**

   You see the alternative message shown in Figure 8-6 that tells you the string is blank.

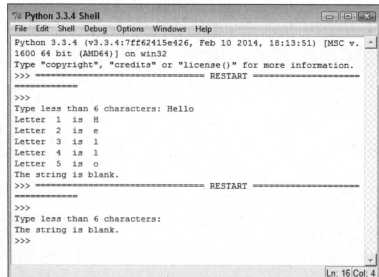

Figure 8-6:
The `else` clause makes it possible to perform tasks based on an empty sequence.

It's easy to misuse the `else` clause because an empty sequence doesn't always signify a simple lack of input. An empty sequence could also signal an application error or other conditions that need to be handled differently from a simple omission of data. Make sure you understand how the application works with data to ensure that the `else` clause doesn't end up hiding potential error conditions, rather than making them visible so that they can be fixed.

Processing Data Using the while Statement

You use the `while` statement for situations when you're not sure how much data the application will have to process. Instead of instructing Python to process a static number of items, you use the `while` statement to tell Python to continue processing items until it runs out of items. This kind of loop is useful when you need to perform tasks such as downloading files of unknown size or streaming data from a source such as a radio station. Any situation in which you can't define at the outset how much data the application will process is a good candidate for the `while` statement that is described more fully in the sections that follow.

Understanding the while statement

The `while` statement works with a condition rather than a sequence. The condition states that the `while` statement should perform a task until the condition is no longer true. For example, imagine a deli with a number of customers standing in front of the counter. The salesperson continues to service customers until no more customers are left in line. The line could (and probably will) grow as the other customers are handled, so it's impossible to know at the outset how many customers will be served. All the salesperson knows is that continuing to serve customers until no more are left is important. Here is how a `while` statement might look:

```
while Sum < 5:
```

The statement begins with the `while` keyword. It then adds a condition. In this case, a variable, `Sum`, must be less than 5 for the loop to continue. Nothing specifies the current value of `Sum`, nor does the code define how the value of `Sum` will change. The only thing that is known when Python executes the statement is that `Sum` must be less than 5 for the loop to continue performing tasks. The statement ends with a colon and the tasks are indented below the statement.

Because the `while` statement doesn't perform a series of tasks a set number of times, creating an *endless loop* is possible, meaning that the loop never ends. For example, say that `Sum` is set to 0 when the loop begins, and the ending condition is that `Sum` must be less than 5. If the value of `Sum` never increases, the loop will continue executing forever (or at least until the computer is shut down). Endless loops can cause all sorts of bizarre problems on systems, such as slowdowns and even computer freezes, so it's best to avoid them. You must always provide a method for the loop to end when using a `while` loop (contrasted with the `for` loop, in which the end of the sequence determines the end of the loop). So, when working with the `while` statement, you must perform three tasks:

1. Create the environment for the condition (such as setting `Sum` to `0`).

2. State the condition within the `while` statement (such as `Sum < 5`).

3. Update the condition as needed to ensure that the loop eventually ends (such as adding `Sum+=1` to the `while` code block).

As with the `for` statement, you can modify the default behavior of the `while` statement. In fact, you have access to the same four clauses to modify the `while` statement behavior:

✔ `break`: Ends the current loop.

✔ `continue`: Immediately ends processing of the current element.

✔ `pass`: Ends processing of the current element after completing the statements in the `if` block.

✔ `else`: Provides an alternative processing technique when conditions aren't met for the loop.

Using the while statement in an application

You can use the `while` statement in many ways, but this first example is straightforward. It simply displays a count based on the starting and ending condition of a variable named `Sum`. The following steps help you create and test the example code. This example also appears with the downloadable source code as `SimpleWhile.py`.

1. **Open a Python File window.**

   You see an editor in which you can type the example code.

2. **Type the following code into the window — pressing Enter after each line:**

```
Sum = 0

while Sum < 5:
    print(Sum)
    Sum+=1
```

The example code demonstrates the three tasks you must perform when working with a `while` loop in a straightforward manner. It begins by setting Sum to 0, which is the first step of setting the condition environment. The condition itself appears as part of the `while` statement. The end of the `while` code block accomplishes the third step. Of course, the code displays the current value of Sum before it updates the value of Sum.

A `while` statement provides flexibility that you don't get with a `for` statement. This example shows a relatively straightforward way to update Sum. However, you can use any update method required to meet the goals of the application. Nothing says that you have to update Sum in a specific manner. In addition, the condition can be as complex as you want it to be. For example, you can track the current value of three or four variables if so desired. Of course, the more complex you make the condition, the more likely it is that you'll create an endless loop, so you have a practical limit as to how complex you should make the `while` loop condition.

3. **Choose Run⇨Run Module.**

   Python executes the `while` loop and displays the numeric sequence shown in Figure 8-7.

Figure 8-7: The simple `while` loop displays a sequence of numbers.

```
7⁄ Python 3.3.4 Shell
File  Edit  Shell  Debug  Options  Windows  Help
Python 3.3.4 (v3.3.4:7ff62415e426, Feb 10 2014, 18:13:51) [MSC v.
1600 64 bit (AMD64)] on win32
Type "copyright", "credits" or "license()" for more information.
>>> ================================ RESTART ====================
============
>>>
0
1
2
3
4
>>> |
                                                          Ln: 10 Col: 4
```

Nesting Loop Statements

In some cases, you can use either a `for` loop or a `while` loop to achieve the same effect. The manners work differently, but the effect is the same. In this example, you create a multiplication table generator by nesting a `while` loop within a `for` loop. Because you want the output to look nice, you use a little formatting as well (Chapter 11 provides you with detailed instruction in this regard). This example also appears with the downloadable source code as `ForElse.py`.

1. **Open a Python File window.**

   You see an editor in which you can type the example code.

2. **Type the following code into the window — pressing Enter after each line:**

```python
X = 1
Y = 1

print ('{:>4}'.format(' '), end= ' ')

for X in range(1, 11):
    print('{:>4}'.format(X), end=' ')

print()

for X in range(1,11):
    print('{:>4}'.format(X), end=' ')
    while Y <= 10:
        print('{:>4}'.format(X * Y), end=' ')
        Y+=1
    print()
    Y=1
```

This example begins by creating two variables, X and Y, to hold the row and column value of the table. X is the row variable and Y is the column variable.

To make the table readable, this example must create a heading at the top and another along the side. When users see a 1 at the top and a 1 at the side, and follow these values to where they intersect in the table, they can see the value of the two numbers when multiplied.

The first `print()` statement adds a space (because nothing appears in the corner of the table; see Figure 8-8 to more easily follow this discussion). All the formatting statement says is to create a space 4 characters wide and place a space within it. The `{:>4}` part of the code determines the size of the column. The `format(' ')` function determines what appears in that space. The end attribute of the `print()` statement changes the ending character from a carriage return to a simple space.

The first `for` loop displays the numbers 1 through 10 at the top of the table. The `range()` function creates the sequence of numbers for you. When using the `range()` function, you specify the starting value, which is 1 in this case, and one more than the ending value, which is 11 in this case.

At this point, the cursor is sitting at the end of the heading row. To move it to the next line, the code issues a print() call with no other information.

Even though the next bit of code looks quite complex, you can figure it out if you look at it a line at a time. The multiplication table shows the values from 1 * 1 to 10 * 10, so you need ten rows and ten columns to display the information. The for statement tells Python to create ten rows.

Look again at Figure 8-8 to note the row heading. The first print() call displays the row heading value. Of course, you have to format this information, and the code uses a space of four characters that end with a space, rather than a carriage return, in order to continue printing information in that row.

The while loop comes next. This loop prints the columns in an individual row. The column values are the multiplied values of X * Y. Again, the output is formatted to take up four spaces. The while loop ends when Y is updated to the next value using Y+=1.

Now you're back into the for loop. The print() statement ends the current row. In addition, Y must be reset to 1 so that it's ready for the beginning of the next row, which begins with 1.

3. **Choose Run⇨Run Module.**

   You see the multiplication table shown in Figure 8-8.

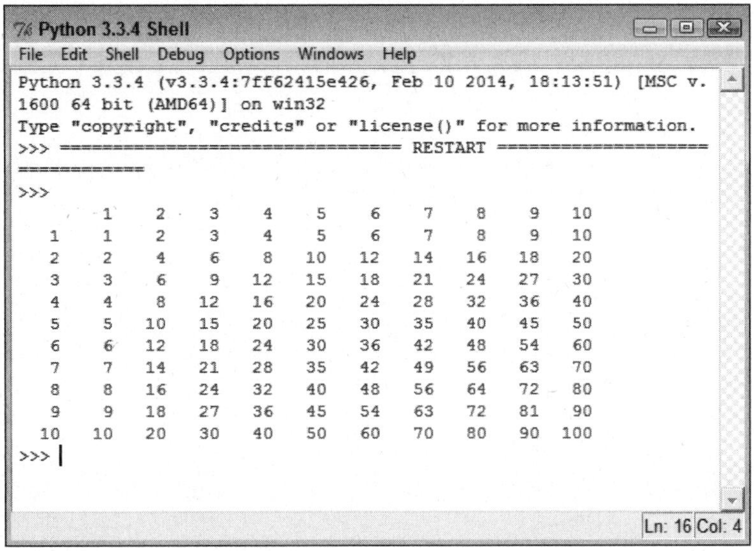

Figure 8-8: The multiplication table is pleasing to the eye thanks to its formatting.

Chapter 9

Dealing with Errors

In This Chapter

▶ Defining problems in communication with Python

▶ Understanding error sources

▶ Handling error conditions

▶ Specifying that an error has occurred

▶ Developing your own error indicators

▶ Performing tasks even after an error occurs

*M*ost application code of any complexity has errors in it. When your application suddenly freezes for no apparent reason, that's an error. Seeing one of those obscure message dialog boxes is another kind of error. However, errors can occur that don't provide you with any sort of notification. An application might perform the wrong computation on a series of numbers you provide, resulting in incorrect output that you may never know about unless someone tells you that something is wrong or you check for the issue yourself. Errors need not be consistent, either. You may see them on some occasions and not on others. For example, an error can occur only when the weather is bad or the network is overloaded. In short, errors occur in all sorts of situations and for all sorts of reasons. This chapter tells you about all sorts of errors and what to do when your application encounters them.

It shouldn't surprise you that errors occur — applications are written by humans, and humans make mistakes. Most developers call application errors *exceptions,* meaning that they're the exception to the rule. Because exceptions do occur in applications, you need to detect and do something about them whenever possible. The act of detecting and processing an exception is called *error handling* or *exception handling.* In order to properly detect errors, you need to know about error sources and why errors occur in the first place. When you do detect the error, you must process it by *catching* the exception. Catching an exception means examining it and possibly doing something about it. So, another part of this chapter is about discovering how to perform exception handling in your own application.

Sometimes your code detects an error in the application. When this happens, you need to *raise* or *throw* an exception. You see both terms used for the same thing, which simply means that your code encountered an error it couldn't handle, so it passed the error information onto another piece of code to *handle* (interpret, process, and, with luck, fix the exception). In some cases, you use custom error message objects to pass on the information. Even though Python has a wealth of generic message objects that cover most situations, some situations are special. For example, you might want to provide special support for a database application, and Python won't normally cover that contingency with a generic message object. It's important to know when to handle exceptions locally, when to send them to the code that called your code, and when to create special exceptions so that every part of the application knows how to handle the exception — all topics covered by this chapter.

There are also times when you must ensure that your application handles an exception gracefully, even if that means shutting the application down. Fortunately, Python provides the `finally` clause, which always executes, even when an exception occurs. You can place code to close files or perform other essential tasks in the code block associated with this clause. Even though you won't perform this task all the time, it's the last topic discussed in the chapter.

Knowing Why Python Doesn't Understand You

Developers often get frustrated with programming languages and computers because they seemingly go out of their way to cause communication problems. Of course, programming languages and computers are both inanimate — there is no desire for anything on the part of either. Programming languages and computers also don't think; they accept whatever the developer has to say quite literally. Therein lies the problem.

Neither Python nor the computer will "know what you mean" when you type instructions as code. Both follow whatever instructions you provide to the letter and literally as you provide them. You may not have meant to tell Python to delete a data file unless some absurd condition occurred. However, if you don't make the conditions clear, Python will delete the file whether the condition exists or not. When an error of this sort happens, people commonly say that the application has a *bug* in it. Bugs are simply coding errors that you can remove using a debugger. (A *debugger* is a special kind of tool that lets you stop or pause application execution, examine the content of variables, and generally dissect the application to see what makes it tick.)

Errors occur in many cases when the developer makes assumptions that simply aren't true. Of course, this includes assumptions about the application user, who probably doesn't care about the extreme level of care you took when crafting your application. The user will enter bad data. Again, Python won't know or care that the data is bad and will process it even when your intent was to disallow the bad input. Python doesn't understand the concepts of good or bad data; it simply processes incoming data according to any rules you set, which means that you must set rules to protect users from themselves.

Python isn't proactive or creative — those qualities exist only in the developer. When a network error occurs or the user does something unexpected, Python doesn't create a solution to fix the problem. It only processes code. If you don't provide code to handle the error, the application is likely to fail and crash ungracefully — possibly taking all of the user's data with it. Of course, the developer can't anticipate every potential error situation, either, which is why most complex applications have errors in them — errors of omission, in this case.

Some developers out there think they can create bulletproof code, despite the absurdity of thinking that such code is even possible. Smart developers assume that some number of bugs will get through the code-screening process, that nature and users will continue to perform unexpected actions, and that even the smartest developer can't anticipate every possible error condition. Always assume that your application is subject to errors that will cause exceptions; that way, you'll have the mindset required to actually make your application more reliable.

Considering the Sources of Errors

You might be able to divine the potential sources of error in your application by reading tea leaves, but that's hardly an efficient way to do things. Errors actually fall into well-defined categories that help you predict (to some degree) when and where they'll occur. By thinking about these categories as you work through your application, you're far more likely to discover potential errors sources before they occur and cause potential damage. The two principle categories are

- Errors that occur at a specific time
- Errors that are of a specific type

The following sections discuss these two categories in greater detail. The overall concept is that you need to think about error classifications in order to start finding and fixing potential errors in your application before they become a problem.

Classifying when errors occur

Errors occur at specific times. The two major time frames are

- Compile time
- Runtime

No matter when an error occurs, it causes your application to misbehave. The following sections describe each time frame.

Compile time

A compile time error occurs when you ask Python to run the application. Before Python can run the application, it must interpret the code and put it into a form that the computer can understand. A computer relies on machine code that is specific to that processor and architecture. If the instructions you write are malformed or lack needed information, Python can't perform the required conversion. It presents an error that you must fix before the application can run.

Fortunately, compile-time errors are the easiest to spot and fix. Because the application won't run with a compile-time error in place, user never sees this error category. You fix this sort of error as you write your code.

The appearance of a compile-time error should tell you that other typos or omissions could exist in the code. It always pays to check the surrounding code to ensure that no other potential problems exist that might not show up as part of the compile cycle.

Runtime

A runtime error occurs after Python compiles the code you write and the computer begins to execute it. Runtime errors come in several different types, and some are harder to find than others. You know you have a runtime error when the application suddenly stops running and displays an exception dialog box or when the user complains about erroneous output (or at least instability).

Not all runtime errors produce an exception. Some runtime errors cause instability (the application freezes), errant output, or data damage. Runtime errors can affect other applications or create unforeseen damage to the platform on which the application is running. In short, runtime errors can cause you quite a bit of grief, depending on precisely the kind of error you're dealing with at the time.

Many runtime errors are caused by errant code. For example, you can misspell the name of a variable, preventing Python from placing information in the correct variable during execution. Leaving out an optional but necessary argument when calling a method can also cause problems. These are examples of *errors of commission,* which are specific errors associated with your code. In general, you can find these kinds of errors using a debugger or by simply reading your code line by line to check for errors.

Runtime errors can also be caused by external sources not associated with your code. For example, the user can input incorrect information that the application isn't expecting, causing an exception. A network error can make a required resource inaccessible. Sometimes even the computer hardware has a glitch that causes a nonrepeatable application error. These are all examples of *errors of omission,* from which the application might recover if your application has error-trapping code in place. It's important that you consider both kinds of runtime errors — errors of commission and omission — when building your application.

Distinguishing error types

You can distinguish errors by type, that is, by how they're made. Knowing the error types helps you understand where to look in an application for potential problems. Exceptions work like many other things in life. For example, you know that electronic devices don't work without power. So, when you try to turn your television on and it doesn't do anything, you might look to ensure that the power cord is firmly seated in the socket.

Understanding the error types helps you locate errors faster, earlier, and more consistently, resulting in fewer misdiagnoses. The best developers know that fixing errors while an application is in development is always easier than fixing it when the application is in production because users are inherently impatient and want errors fixed immediately and correctly. In addition, fixing an error earlier in the development cycle is always easier than fixing it when the application nears completion because less code exists to review.

The trick is to know where to look. With this in mind, Python (and most other programming languages) breaks errors into the following types:

- ✔ Syntactical
- ✔ Semantic
- ✔ Logical

The following sections examine each of these error types in more detail. I've arranged the sections in order of difficulty, starting with the easiest to find. A syntactical error is generally the easiest; a logical error is generally the hardest.

Syntactical

Whenever you make a typo of some sort, you create a syntactical error. Some Python syntactical errors are quite easy to find because the application simply doesn't run. The interpreter may even point out the error for you by highlighting the errant code and displaying an error message. However, some syntactical errors are quite hard to find. Python is case sensitive, so you may use the wrong case for a variable in one place and find that the variable isn't quite working as you thought it would. Finding the one place where you used the wrong capitalization can be quite challenging.

Most syntactical errors occur at compile time and the interpreter points them out for you. Fixing the error is made easy because the interpreter generally tells you what to fix, and with considerable accuracy. Even when the interpreter doesn't find the problem, syntactical errors prevent the application from running correctly, so any errors the interpreter doesn't find show up during the testing phase. Few syntactical errors should make it into production as long as you perform adequate application testing.

Semantic

When you create a loop that executes one too many times, you don't generally receive any sort of error information from the application. The application will happily run because it thinks that it's doing everything correctly, but that one additional loop can cause all sorts of data errors. When you create an error of this sort in your code, it's called a *semantic error*.

Semantic errors occur because the meaning behind a series of steps used to perform a task is wrong — the result is incorrect even though the code apparently runs precisely as it should. Semantic errors are tough to find, and you sometimes need some sort of debugger to find them. (Chapter 19 provides a discussion of tools that you can use with Python to perform tasks such as debugging applications. You can also find blog posts about debugging on my blog at http://blog.johnmuellerbooks.com.)

Logical

Some developers don't create a division between semantic and logical errors, but they are different. A semantic error occurs when the code is essentially correct but the implementation is wrong (such as having a loop execute once too often). Logical errors occur when the developer's thinking is faulty. In many cases, this sort of error happens when the developer uses a relational or logical operator incorrectly. However, logical errors can happen in all sorts of other ways, too. For example, a developer might think that data is always stored on the local hard drive, which means that the application may behave in an unusual manner when it attempts to load data from a network drive instead.

Logical errors are quite hard to fix because the problem isn't with the actual code, yet the code itself is incorrectly defined. The thought process that went into creating the code is faulty; therefore, the developer who created the error is less likely to find it. Smart developers use a second pair of eyes to help spot logical errors. Having a formal application specification also helps because the logic behind the tasks the application performs is usually given a formal review.

Catching Exceptions

Generally speaking, a user should never see an exception dialog box. Your application should always catch the exception and handle it before the user sees it. Of course, the real world is different — users do see unexpected exceptions from time to time. However, catching every potential exception is still the goal when developing an application. The following sections describe how to catch exceptions and handle them.

Understanding the built-in exceptions

Python comes with a host of built-in exceptions — far more than you might think possible. You can see a list of these exceptions at `https://docs.python.org/3.3/library/exceptions.html`. The documentation breaks the exception list down into categories. Here is a brief overview of the Python exception categories that you work with regularly:

✔ **Base classes:** The base classes provide the essential building blocks (such as the `Exception` exception) for other exceptions. However, you might actually see some of these exceptions, such as the `ArithmeticError` exception, when working with an application.

✔ **Concrete exceptions:** Applications can experience hard errors — errors that are hard to overcome because there really isn't a good way to handle them or they signal an event that the application must handle. For example, when a system runs out of memory, Python generates a `MemoryError` exception. Recovering

from this error is hard because it isn't always possible to release memory from other uses. When the user presses an interrupt key (such as Ctrl+C or Delete), Python generates a `KeyboardInterrupt` exception. The application must handle this exception before proceeding with any other tasks.

✔ **OS exceptions:** The operating system can generate errors that Python then passes them along to your application. For example, if your application tries to open a file that doesn't exist, the operating system generates a `FileNotFoundError` exception.

✔ **Warnings:** Python tries to warn you about unexpected events or actions that could result in errors later. For example, if you try to inappropriately use a resource, such as an icon, Python generates a `ResourceWarning` exception. It's important to remember that this particular category is a warning and not an actual error: Ignoring it can cause you woe later, but you can ignore it.

Basic exception handling

To handle exceptions, you must tell Python that you want to do so and then provide code to perform the handling tasks. You have a number of ways in which you can perform this task. The following sections start with the simplest method first and then move on to more complex methods that offer added flexibility.

Handling a single exception

In Chapter 7, the IfElse.py and other examples have a terrible habit of spitting out exceptions when the user inputs unexpected values. Part of the solution is to provide range checking. However, range checking doesn't overcome the problem of a user typing text such as Hello in place of an expected numeric value. Exception handling provides a more complex solution to the problem, as described in the following steps. This example also appears with the downloadable source code as BasicException1.py.

1. **Open a Python File window.**

   You see an editor in which you can type the example code.

2. **Type the following code into the window — pressing Enter after each line:**

   ```
   try:
       Value = int(input("Type a number between 1 and 10:
           "))
   except ValueError:
       print("You must type a number between 1 and 10!")
   else:

       if (Value > 0) and (Value <= 10):
           print("You typed: ", Value)
       else:
           print("The value you typed is incorrect!")
   ```

   The code within the try block has its exceptions handled. In this case, handling the exception means getting input from the user using the int(input()) calls. If an exception occurs outside this block, the code doesn't handle it. With reliability in mind, the temptation might be to enclose all the executable code in a try block so that every exception would be handled. However, you want to make your exception handling small and specific to make locating the problem easier.

The `except` block looks for a specific exception in this case: `ValueError`. When the user creates a `ValueError` exception by typing Hello instead of a numeric value, this particular exception block is executed. If the user were to generate some other exception, this `except` block wouldn't handle it.

The `else` block contains all the code that is executed when the `try` block code is successful (doesn't generate an exception). The remainder of the code is in this block because you don't want to execute it unless the user does provide valid input. When the user provides a whole number as input, the code can then range check it to ensure that it's correct.

3. **Choose Run⇨Run Module.**

   You see a Python Shell window open. The application asks you to type a number between 1 and 10.

4. **Type** Hello **and press Enter.**

   The application displays an error message, as shown in Figure 9-1.

Figure 9-1:
Typing
the wrong
input type
generates
an error
instead
of an
exception.

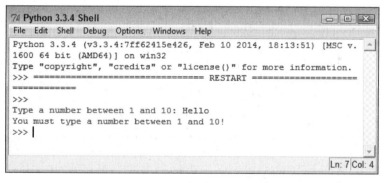

```
Python 3.3.4 Shell
File   Edit   Shell   Debug   Options   Windows   Help
Python 3.3.4 (v3.3.4:7ff62415e426, Feb 10 2014, 18:13:51) [MSC v.
1600 64 bit (AMD64)] on win32
Type "copyright", "credits" or "license()" for more information.
>>> ================================ RESTART ====================
============
>>>
Type a number between 1 and 10: Hello
You must type a number between 1 and 10!
>>> |
                                                          Ln: 7 Col: 4
```

5. **Perform Steps 3 and 4 again, but type** 5.5 **instead of Hello.**

   The application generates the same error message, as shown in Figure 9-1.

6. **Perform Steps 3 and 4 again, but type** 22 **instead of Hello.**

   The application outputs the expected range error message, as shown in Figure 9-2. Exception handling doesn't weed out range errors. You must still check for them separately.

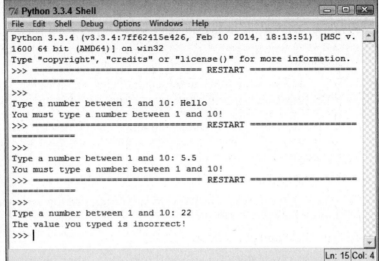

Figure 9-2:
Exception
handling
doesn't
ensure that
the value is
in the cor-
rect range.

7. **Perform Steps 3 and 4 again, but type** 7 **instead of Hello.**

   This time, the application finally reports that you've provided a correct value of 7. Even though it seems like a lot of work to perform this level of checking, you can't really be certain that your application is working correctly without it.

8. **Perform Steps 3 and 4 again, but press Ctrl+C, Cmd+C, or the alterna-tive for your platform instead of typing anything.**

   The application generates a KeyboardInterrupt exception, as shown in Figure 9-3. Because this exception isn't handled, it's still a problem for the user. You see several techniques for fixing this problem later in the chapter.

Using the except clause without an exception

You can create an exception handling block in Python that's generic because it doesn't look for a specific exception. In most cases, you want to provide a specific exception when performing exception handling for these reasons:

✔ To avoid hiding an exception you didn't consider when designing the application

✔ To ensure that others know precisely which exceptions your application will handle

✔ To handle the exceptions correctly using specific code for that exception

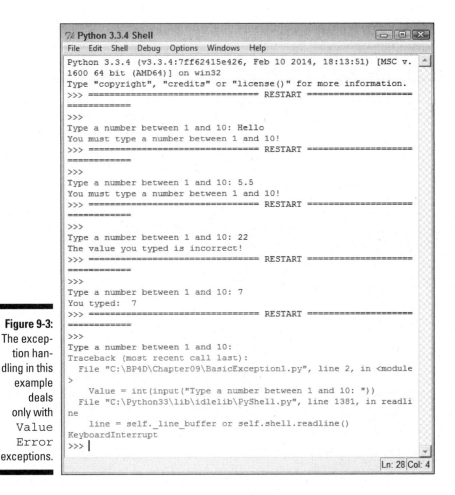

Figure 9-3:
The excep-
tion han-
dling in this
example
deals
only with
Value
Error
exceptions.

However, sometimes you may need a generic exception-handling capability, such as when you're working with third-party libraries or interacting with an external service. The following steps demonstrate how to use an `except` clause without a specific exception attached to it. This example also appears with the downloadable source code as `BasicException2.py`.

1. Open a Python File window.

   You see an editor in which you can type the example code.

2. Type the following code into the window — pressing Enter after each line:

```
try:
    Value = int(input("Type a number between 1 and 10:
        "))
except:
    print("You must type a number between 1 and 10!")
else:

    if (Value > 0) and (Value <= 10):
        print("You typed: ", Value)
    else:
        print("The value you typed is incorrect!")
```

The only difference between this example and the previous example is that the `except` clause doesn't have the `ValueError` exception specifically associated with it. The result is that this `except` clause will also catch any other exception that occurs.

3. Choose Run⇨Run Module.

You see a Python Shell window open. The application asks you to type a number between 1 and 10.

4. Type Hello **and press Enter.**

The application displays an error message (refer to Figure 9-1).

5. Perform Steps 3 and 4 again, but type 5.5 **instead of Hello.**

The application generates the same error message (again, refer to Figure 9-1).

6. Perform Steps 3 and 4 again, but type 22 **instead of Hello.**

The application outputs the expected range error message (refer to Figure 9-2). Exception handling doesn't weed out range errors. You must still check for them separately.

7. Perform Steps 3 and 4 again, but type 7 **instead of Hello.**

This time, the application finally reports that you've provided a correct value of 7. Even though it seems like a lot of work to perform this level of checking, you can't really be certain that your application is working correctly without it.

8. Perform Steps 3 and 4 again, but press Ctrl+C, Cmd+C, or the alternative for your platform instead of typing anything.

You see the error message that's usually associated with input error, as shown in Figure 9-4. The error message is incorrect, which might confuse users. However, the plus side is that the application didn't crash, which means that you won't lose any data and the application can recover. Using generic exception handling does have some advantages, but you must use it carefully.

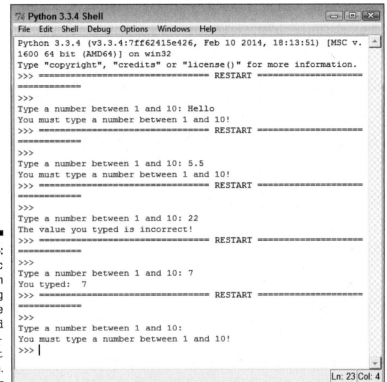

Figure 9-4:
Generic exception handling traps the Keyboard Inter- rupt exception.

Working with exception arguments

Most exceptions don't provide arguments (a list of values that you can check for additional information). The exception either occurs or it doesn't. However, a few exceptions do provide arguments, and you see them used later in the book. The arguments tell you more about the exception and pro- vide details that you need to correct it.

For the sake of completeness, this chapter includes a simple example that generates an exception with an argument. You can safely skip the remainder of this section if desired because the information is covered in more detail later in the book. This example also appears with the downloadable source code as ExceptionWithArguments.py.

1. **Open a Python File window.**

   You see an editor in which you can type the example code.

2. **Type the following code into the window — pressing Enter after each line:**

```python
import sys

try:
    File = open('myfile.txt')
except IOError as e:
    print("Error opening file!\r\n" +
        "Error Number: {0}\r\n".format(e.errno) +
        "Error Text: {0}".format(e.strerror))
else:
    print("File opened as expected.")
    File.close();
```

   This example uses some advanced features. The `import` statement obtains code from another file. Chapter 10 tells you how to use this Python feature.

   The `open()` function opens a file and provides access to the file through the `File` variable. Chapter 15 tells you how file access works. Given that `myfile.txt` doesn't exist in the application directory, the operating system can't open it and will tell Python that the file doesn't exist.

   Trying to open a nonexistent file generates an `IOError` exception. This particular exception provides access to two arguments:

   - `errno`: Provides the operating system error number as an integer

   - `strerror`: Contains the error information as a human-readable string

   The `as` clause places the exception information into a variable, `e`, that you can access as needed for additional information. The `except` block contains a `print()` call that formats the error information into an easily read error message.

   If you should decide to create the `myfile.txt` file, the `else` clause executes. In this case, you see a message stating that the file opened normally. The code then closes the file without doing anything with it.

3. **Choose Run⇨Run Module.**

   You see a Python Shell window open. The application displays the Error opening file information, as shown in Figure 9-5.

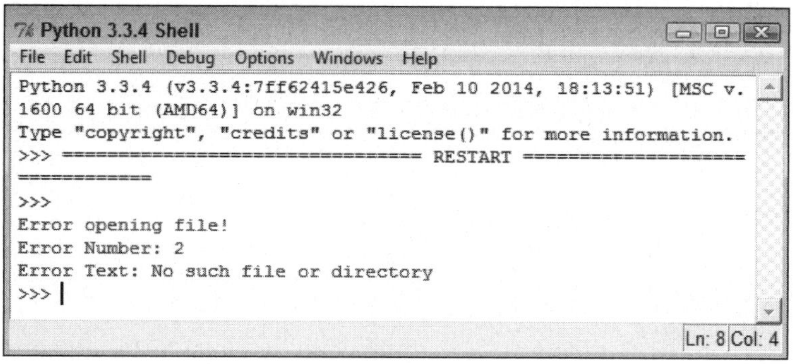

Figure 9-5:
Attempting
to open a
nonexistent
file never
works.

```
7⁄ Python 3.3.4 Shell                                    □ □ ⊠
File  Edit  Shell  Debug  Options  Windows  Help
Python 3.3.4 (v3.3.4:7ff62415e426, Feb 10 2014, 18:13:51) [MSC v.
1600 64 bit (AMD64)] on win32
Type "copyright", "credits" or "license()" for more information.
>>> =============================== RESTART ====================
============
>>>
Error opening file!
Error Number: 2
Error Text: No such file or directory
>>> |
                                                    Ln: 8 Col: 4
```

TECHNICAL STUFF

Obtaining a list of exception arguments

The list of arguments supplied with exceptions varies by exception and by what the sender provides. It isn't always easy to figure out what you can hope to obtain in the way of additional information. One way to handle the problem is to simply print everything using code like this (this example
also appears with the downloadable source code as `GetExceptionArguments1.py`):

```python
import sys

try:
    File = open('myfile.txt')
except IOError as e:
    for Arg in e.args:
        print(Arg)
else:
    print("File opened as expected.")
    File.close();
```

The `args` property always contains a list of the exception arguments in string format. You can
use a simple `for` loop to print each of the arguments. The only problem with this approach is that
you're missing the argument names, so you know the output information (which is obvious in this
case), but you don't know what to call it.

A more complex method of dealing with the issue is to print both the names and the contents of the
arguments. The following code displays both the names and the values of each of the arguments
(this example also appears with the downloadable source as `GetExceptionArguments2.py`):

```python
import sys

try:
    File = open('myfile.txt')
```

(continued)

(continued)

```
    except IOError as e:
        for Entry in dir(e):
            if (not Entry.startswith("_")):
                try:
                    print(Entry, " = ", e.__getattribute__(Entry))
                except AttributeError:
                    print("Attribute ", Entry, " not accessible.")
    else:
        print("File opened as expected.")
        File.close();
```

In this case, you begin by getting a listing of the attributes associated with the error argument object using the `dir()` function. The output of the `dir()` function is a list of strings containing the names of the attributes that you can print. Only those arguments that don't start with an underscore (_) contain useful information about the exception. However, even some of those entries are inaccessible, so you must encase the output code in a second `try...except` block (see the "Nested exception handling" section, later in the chapter, for details).

The attribute name is easy because it's contained in `Entry`. To obtain the value associated with that attribute, you must use the `__getattribute__()` function and supply the name of the attribute you want. When you run this code, you see both the name and the value of each of the attributes supplied with a particular error argument object. In this case, the actual output is as follows:

```
args    =  (2, 'No such file or directory')
Attribute  characters_written  not accessible.
errno   =  2
filename    =  myfile.txt
strerror    =  No such file or directory
winerror    =  None
with_traceback  =  <built-in method with_traceback of
    FileNotFoundError object at 0x0000000003416DC8>
```

Handling multiple exceptions with a single except clause

Most applications can generate multiple exceptions for a single line of code. This fact demonstrated earlier in the chapter with the `BasicException1.py` example. How you handle the multiple exceptions depends on your goals for the application, the types of exceptions, and the relative skill of your users. Sometimes when working with a less skilled user, it's simply easier to say that the application experienced a nonrecoverable error and then log the details into a log file in the application directory or a central location.

Using a single `except` clause to handle multiple exceptions works only when a common source of action fulfills the needs of all the exception types. Otherwise, you need to handle each exception individually. The following steps show how to handle multiple exceptions using a single `except` clause. This example also appears with the downloadable source code as `MultipleException1.py`.

1. **Open a Python File window.**

   You see an editor in which you can type the example code.

2. **Type the following code into the window — pressing Enter after each line:**

```
try:
    Value = int(input("Type a number between 1 and 10:
        "))
except (ValueError, KeyboardInterrupt):
    print("You must type a number between 1 and 10!")
else:

    if (Value > 0) and (Value <= 10):
        print("You typed: ", Value)
    else:
        print("The value you typed is incorrect!")
```

This code is very much like the `BasicException1.py`. However, notice that the `except` clause now sports both a `ValueError` and a `KeyboardInterrupt` exception. In addition, these exceptions appear within parentheses and are separated by commas.

3. **Choose Run⇨Run Module.**

   You see a Python Shell window open. The application asks you to type a number between 1 and 10.

4. **Type Hello and press Enter.**

   The application displays an error message (refer to Figure 9-1).

5. **Perform Steps 3 and 4 again, but type 22 instead of Hello.**

   The application outputs the expected range error message (refer to Figure 9-2).

6. **Perform Steps 3 and 4 again, but press Ctrl+C, Cmd+C, or the alternative for your platform instead of typing anything.**

   You see the error message that's usually associated with error input (refer to Figure 9-1).

7. **Perform Steps 3 and 4 again, but type 7 instead of Hello.**

   This time, the application finally reports that you've provided a correct value of 7.

Handling multiple exceptions with multiple except clauses

When working with multiple exceptions, it's usually a good idea to place each exception in its own `except` clause. This approach allows you to provide custom handling for each exception and makes it easier for the user to know precisely what went wrong. Of course, this approach is also a lot more work.

The following steps demonstrate how to perform exception handling using multiple `except` clauses. This example also appears with the downloadable source code as `MultipleException2.py`.

1. **Open a Python File window.**

   You see an editor in which you can type the example code.

2. **Type the following code into the window — pressing Enter after each line:**

   ```python
   try:
       Value = int(input("Type a number between 1 and 10:
           "))
   except ValueError:
       print("You must type a number between 1 and 10!")
   except KeyboardInterrupt:
       print("You pressed Ctrl+C!")
   else:

       if (Value > 0) and (Value <= 10):
           print("You typed: ", Value)
       else:
           print("The value you typed is incorrect!")
   ```

   Notice the use of multiple `except` clauses in this case. Each `except` clause handles a different exception. You can use a combination of techniques, with some `except` clauses handling just one exception and other `except` clauses handling multiple exceptions. Python lets you use the approach that works best for the error-handling situation.

3. **Choose Run⇨Run Module.**

   You see a Python Shell window open. The application asks you to type a number between 1 and 10.

4. **Type Hello and press Enter.**

   The application displays an error message (refer to Figure 9-1).

5. **Perform Steps 3 and 4 again, but type 22 instead of Hello.**

   The application outputs the expected range error message (refer to Figure 9-2).

6. **Perform Steps 3 and 4 again, but press Ctrl+C, Cmd+C, or the alternative for your platform instead of typing anything.**

   The application outputs a specific message that tells the user what went wrong, as shown in Figure 9-6.

7. **Perform Steps 3 and 4 again, but type 7 instead of Hello.**

   This time, the application finally reports that you've provided a correct value of 7.

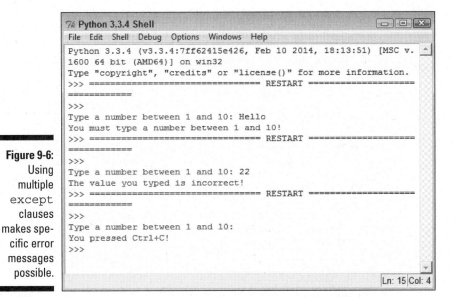

```
Python 3.3.4 Shell
File  Edit  Shell  Debug  Options  Windows  Help
Python 3.3.4 (v3.3.4:7ff62415e426, Feb 10 2014, 18:13:51) [MSC v.
1600 64 bit (AMD64)] on win32
Type "copyright", "credits" or "license()" for more information.
>>> ================================ RESTART ====================
============
>>>
Type a number between 1 and 10: Hello
You must type a number between 1 and 10!
>>> ================================ RESTART ====================
============
>>>
Type a number between 1 and 10: 22
The value you typed is incorrect!
>>> ================================ RESTART ====================
============
>>>
Type a number between 1 and 10:
You pressed Ctrl+C!
>>>
                                                          Ln: 15 Col: 4
```

Figure 9-6:
Using
multiple
except
clauses
makes spe-
cific error
messages
possible.

Handling more specific to less specific exceptions

One strategy for handling exceptions is to provide specific except clauses for all known exceptions and generic except clauses to handle unknown exceptions. You can see the exception hierarchy that Python uses at https://docs.python.org/3.3/library/exceptions. html#exception-hierarchy. When viewing this chart, BaseException is the uppermost exception. Most exceptions are derived from Exception. When working through math errors, you can use the generic ArithmeticError or a more specific ZeroDivisionError exception.

Python evaluates except clauses in the order in which they appear in the source code file. The first clause is examined first, the second clause is examined second, and so on. The following steps help you examine an example that demonstrates the importance of using the correct exception order. In this case, you perform tasks that result in math errors. This example also appears with the downloadable source code as MultipleException3.py.

1. **Open a Python File window.**

   You see an editor in which you can type the example code.

2. **Type the following code into the window — pressing Enter after each line:**

```python
try:
    Value1 = int(input("Type the first number: "))
    Value2 = int(input("Type the second number: "))
    Output = Value1 / Value2
except ValueError:
    print("You must type a whole number!")
except KeyboardInterrupt:
    print("You pressed Ctrl+C!")
except ArithmeticError:
    print("An undefined math error occurred.")
except ZeroDivisionError:
    print("Attempted to divide by zero!")
else:
    print(Output)
```

   The code begins by obtaining two inputs: `Value1` and `Value2`. The first two `except` clauses handle unexpected input. The second two `except` clauses handle math exceptions, such as dividing by zero. If everything goes well with the application, the `else` clause executes, which prints the result of the operation.

3. **Choose Run⇨Run Module.**

   You see a Python Shell window open. The application asks you to type the first number.

4. **Type Hello and press Enter.**

   As expected, Python displays the `ValueError` exception message. However, it always pays to check for potential problems.

5. **Choose Run⇨Run Module again.**

   You see a Python Shell window open. The application asks you to type the first number.

6. **Type 8 and press Enter.**

   The application asks you to enter the second number.

7. Type 0 **and press Enter.**

You see the error message for the `ArithmeticError` exception, as shown in Figure 9-7. What you should actually see is the `ZeroDivisionError` exception because it's more specific than the `ArithmeticError` exception.

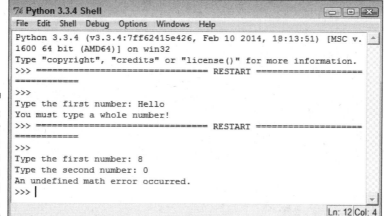

Figure 9-7: The order in which Python processes exceptions is important.

```
Python 3.3.4 Shell                                                    □ ▣ ✖

File  Edit  Shell  Debug  Options  Windows  Help

Python 3.3.4 (v3.3.4:7ff62415e426, Feb 10 2014, 18:13:51) [MSC v.
1600 64 bit (AMD64)] on win32
Type "copyright", "credits" or "license()" for more information.
>>> =============================== RESTART ====================
============
>>>
Type the first number: Hello
You must type a whole number!
>>> =============================== RESTART ====================
============
>>>
Type the first number: 8
Type the second number: 0
An undefined math error occurred.
>>> |
                                                            Ln: 12 Col: 4
```

8. Reverse the order of the two exceptions so that they look like this:

```
except ZeroDivisionError:
    print("Attempted to divide by zero!")
except ArithmeticError:
    print("An undefined math error occurred.")
```

9. Perform Steps 5 through 7 again.

This time, you see the `ZeroDivisionError` exception message because the exceptions appear in the correct order.

10. Perform Steps 5 through 7 again, but type 2 **for the second number instead of 0.**

This time, the application finally reports an output value of 4.0, as shown in Figure 9-8.

Notice that the output shown in Figure 9-8 is a floating-point value. Division results in a floating-point value unless you specify that you want an integer output by using the floor division operator (//).

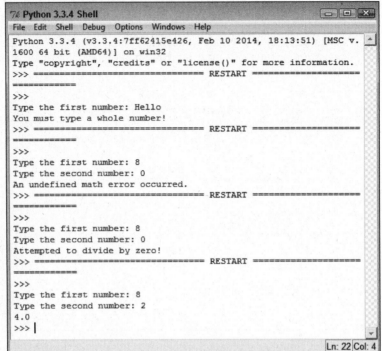

Figure 9-8:
Providing
usable input
results in
a usable
output.

Nested exception handling

Sometimes you need to place one exception-handling routine within another in a process called *nesting*. When you nest exception-handling routines, Python tries to find an exception handler in the nested level first and then moves to the outer layers. You can nest exception-handling routines as deeply as needed to make your code safe.

One of the more common reasons to use a dual layer of exception-handling code is when you want to obtain input from a user and need to place the input code in a loop to ensure that you actually get the required information. The following steps demonstrate how this sort of code might work. This example also appears with the downloadable source code as `MultipleException4.py`.

1. Open a Python File window.

You see an editor in which you can type the example code.

2. **Type the following code into the window — pressing Enter after each line:**

```
TryAgain = True

while TryAgain:

    try:
        Value = int(input("Type a whole number. "))
    except ValueError:
        print("You must type a whole number!")

        try:
            DoOver = input("Try again (y/n)? ")
        except:
            print("OK, see you next time!")
            TryAgain = False
        else:
            if (str.upper(DoOver) == "N"):
                TryAgain = False

    except KeyboardInterrupt:
        print("You pressed Ctrl+C!")
        print("See you next time!")
        TryAgain = False
    else:
        print(Value)
        TryAgain = False
```

The code begins by creating an input loop. Using loops for this type of purpose is actually quite common in applications because you don't want the application to end every time an input error is made. This is a simplified loop, and normally you create a separate function to hold the code.

When the loop starts, the application asks the user to type a whole number. It can be any integer value. If the user types any non-integer value or presses Ctrl+C, Cmd+C, or another interrupt key combination, the exception-handling code takes over. Otherwise, the application prints the value that the user supplied and sets TryAgain to False, which causes the loop to end.

A ValueError exception can occur when the user makes a mistake. Because you don't know why the user input the wrong value, you have to ask if the user wants to try again. Of course, getting more input from the user could generate another exception. The inner try . . . except code block handles this secondary input.

Notice the use of the str.upper() function when getting character input from the user. This function makes it possible to receive y or Y as input and accept them both. Whenever you ask the user for character input, it's a good idea to convert lowercase characters to uppercase so that you can perform a single comparison (reducing the potential for error).

The `KeyboardInterrupt` exception displays two messages and then exits automatically by setting `TryAgain` to `False`. The `KeyboardInterrupt` occurs only when the user presses a specific key combination designed to end the application. The user is unlikely to want to continue using the application at this point.

3. **Choose Run⇨Run Module.**

   You see a Python Shell window open. The application asks the user to input a whole number.

4. **Type** Hello **and press Enter.**

   The application displays an error message and asks whether you want to try again.

5. **Type** Y **and press Enter.**

   The application asks you to input a whole number again, as shown in Figure 9-9.

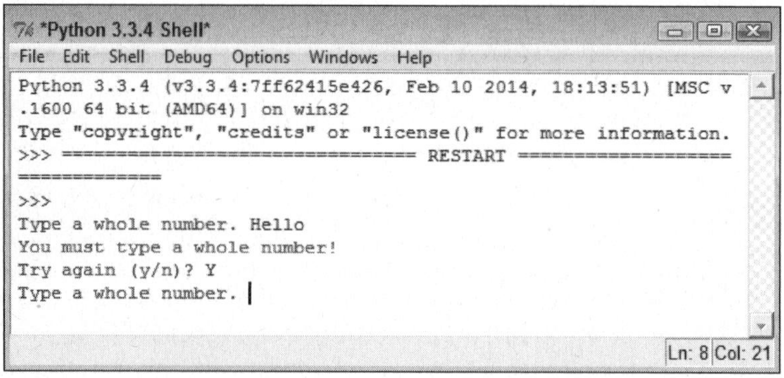

Figure 9-9:
Using a loop means that the application can recover from the error.

```
7⁄ *Python 3.3.4 Shell*                                    _ ▢ ✕
File  Edit  Shell  Debug  Options  Windows  Help
Python 3.3.4 (v3.3.4:7ff62415e426, Feb 10 2014, 18:13:51) [MSC v
.1600 64 bit (AMD64)] on win32
Type "copyright", "credits" or "license()" for more information.
>>> ================================ RESTART ====================
==============
>>>
Type a whole number. Hello
You must type a whole number!
Try again (y/n)? Y
Type a whole number. |
                                                      Ln: 8 Col: 21
```

6. **Type** 5.5 **and press Enter.**

   The application again displays the error message and asks whether you want to try again.

7. **Press Ctrl+C, Cmd+C, or another key combination to interrupt the application.**

   The application ends, as shown in Figure 9-10. Notice that the message is the one from the inner exception. The application never gets to the outer exception because the inner exception handler provides generic exception handling.

8. **Choose Run⇨Run Module.**

   You see a Python Shell window open. The application asks the user to input a whole number.

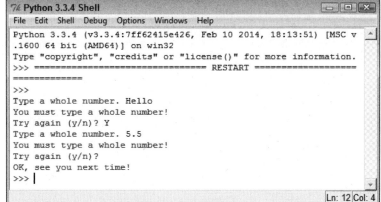

Figure 9-10:
The inner exception handler provides secondary input support.

9. **Press Ctrl+C, Cmd+C, or another key combination to interrupt the application.**

The application ends, as shown in Figure 9-11. Notice that the message is the one from the outer exception. In Steps 7 and 9, the user ends the application by pressing an interrupt key. However, the application uses two different exception handlers to address the problem.

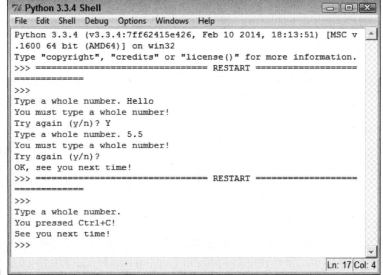

Figure 9-11:
The outer exception handler provides primary input support.

Raising Exceptions

So far, the examples in this chapter have reacted to exceptions. Something happens and the application provides error-handling support for that event. However, situations arise for which you may not know how to handle an error event during the application design process. Perhaps you can't even handle the error at a particular level and need to pass it up to some other level to handle. In short, in some situations, your application must generate an exception. This act is called *raising* (or sometimes *throwing*) the exception. The following sections describe common scenarios in which you raise exceptions in specific ways.

Raising exceptions during exceptional conditions

The example in this section demonstrates how you raise a simple exception — that it doesn't require anything special. The following steps simply create the exception and then handle it immediately. This example also appears with the downloadable source code as `RaiseException1.py`.

1. **Open a Python File window.**

   You see an editor in which you can type the example code.

2. **Type the following code into the window — pressing Enter after each line:**

   ```
   try:
       raise ValueError
   except ValueError:
       print("ValueError Exception!")
   ```

   You wouldn't ever actually create code that looks like this, but it shows you how raising an exception works at its most basic level. In this case, the `raise` call appears within a `try . . . except` block. A basic raise call simply provides the name of the exception to raise (or throw). You can also provide arguments as part of the output to provide additional information.

   Notice that this `try . . . except` block lacks an `else` clause because there is nothing to do after the call. Although you rarely use a `try . . . except` block in this manner, you can. You may encounter situations like this one sometimes and need to remember that adding the `else` clause is purely optional. On the other hand, you must add at least one `except` clause.

3. Choose Run⇨Run Module.

You see a Python Shell window open. The application displays the expected exception text, as shown in Figure 9-12.

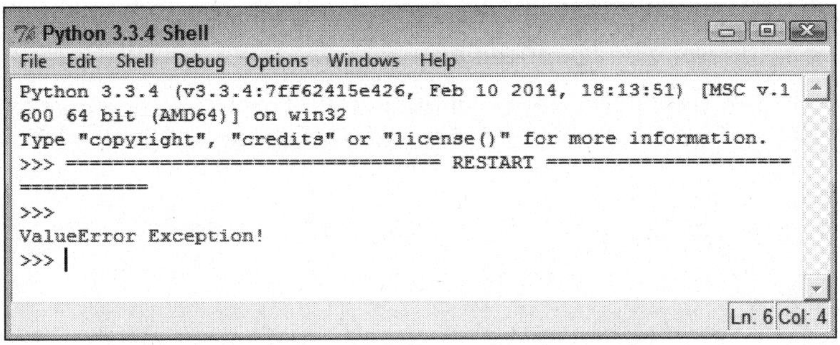

Figure 9-12:
Raising
an excep-
tion only
requires
a call to
raise.

```
7⁄ Python 3.3.4 Shell
File  Edit  Shell  Debug  Options  Windows  Help
Python 3.3.4 (v3.3.4:7ff62415e426, Feb 10 2014, 18:13:51) [MSC v.1
600 64 bit (AMD64)] on win32
Type "copyright", "credits" or "license()" for more information.
>>> ================================ RESTART ======================
===========
>>>
ValueError Exception!
>>> |
                                                        Ln: 6 Col: 4
```

Passing error information to the caller

Python provides exceptionally flexible error handling in that you can pass information to the *caller* (the code that is calling your code) no matter which exception you use. Of course, the caller may not know that the information is available, which leads to a lot of discussion on the topic. If you're working with someone else's code and don't know whether additional information is available, you can always use the technique described in the "Obtaining a list of exception arguments" sidebar earlier in this chapter to find it.

You may have wondered whether you could provide better information when working with a `ValueError` exception than with an exception provided natively by Python. The following steps show that you can modify the output so that it does include helpful information. This example also appears with the downloadable source code as `RaiseException2.py`.

1. Open a Python File window.

You see an editor in which you can type the example code.

2. Type the following code into the window — pressing Enter after each line:

```
try:
    Ex = ValueError()
    Ex.strerror = "Value must be within 1 and 10."
    raise Ex
except ValueError as e:
    print("ValueError Exception!", e.strerror)
```

The ValueError exception normally doesn't provide an attribute named strerror (a common name for string error), but you can add it simply by assigning a value to it as shown. When the example raises the exception, the except clause handles it as usual but obtains access to the attributes using e. You can then access the e.strerror member to obtain the added information.

3. Choose Run⇨Run Module.

You see a Python Shell window open. The application displays an expanded ValueError exception, as shown in Figure 9-13.

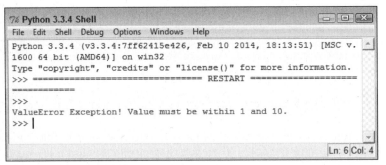

Figure 9-13:
It's possible to add error information to any exception.

Creating and Using Custom Exceptions

Python provides a wealth of standard exceptions that you should use whenever possible. These exceptions are incredibly flexible, and you can even modify them as needed (within reason) to meet specific needs. For example, the "Passing error information to the caller" section of this chapter demonstrates how to modify a ValueError exception to allow for additional data. However, sometimes you simply must create a custom exception because none of the standard exceptions will work. Perhaps the exception name just doesn't tell the viewer the purpose that the exception serves. You may need a custom exception for specialized database work or when working with a service.

The example in this section is going to seem a little complicated for now because you haven't worked with classes before. Chapter 14 introduces you to classes and helps you understand how they work. If you want to skip this section until after you read Chapter 14, you can do so without any problem.

The example in this section shows a quick method for creating your own exceptions. To perform this task, you must create a class that uses an existing exception as a starting point. To make things a little easier, this example creates an exception that builds upon the functionality provided by the ValueError exception. The advantage of using this approach rather than the one shown in the "Passing error information to the caller" section, the preceding section in this chapter, is that this approach tells anyone who follows you precisely what the addition to the ValueError exception is; additionally, it makes the modified exception easier to use. This example also appears with the downloadable source code as CustomException.py.

1. **Open a Python File window.**

   You see an editor in which you can type the example code.

2. **Type the following code into the window — pressing Enter after each line:**

```
class CustomValueError(ValueError):
    def __init__(self, arg):
        self.strerror = arg
        self.args = {arg}

try:
    raise CustomValueError("Value must be within 1 and
        10.")
except CustomValueError as e:
    print("CustomValueError Exception!", e.strerror)
```

This example essentially replicates the functionality of the example in the "Passing error information to the caller" section of the chapter. However, it places the same error in both strerror and args so that the developer has access to either (as would normally happen).

The code begins by creating the CustomValueError class that uses the ValueError exception class as a starting point. The __init__() function provides the means for creating a new instance of that class. Think of the class as a blueprint and the instance as the building created from the blueprint.

Notice that the strerror attribute has the value assigned directly to it, but args receives it as an array. The args member normally contains an array of all the exception values, so this is standard procedure, even when args contains just one value as it does now.

The code for using the exception is considerably easier than modifying ValueError directly. All you do is call raise with the name of the exception and the arguments you want to pass, all on one line.

3. Choose Run⇨Run Module.

You see a Python Shell window open. The application displays the letter sequence, along with the letter number, as shown in Figure 9-14.

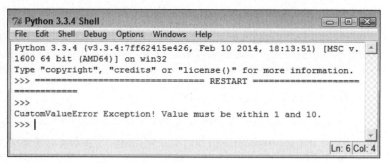

Figure 9-14:
Custom
exceptions
can make
your code
easier to
read.

Using the finally Clause

Normally you want to handle any exception that occurs in a way that doesn't cause the application to crash. However, sometimes you can't do anything to fix the problem, and the application is most definitely going to crash. At this point, your goal is to cause the application to crash gracefully, which means closing files so that the user doesn't lose data and performing other tasks of that nature. Anything you can do to keep damage to data and the system to a minimum is an essential part of handling data for a crashing application.

The `finally` clause is part of the crashing-application strategy. You use this clause to perform any required last-minute tasks. Normally, the `finally` clause is quite short and uses only calls that are likely to succeed without further problem. It's essential to close the files, log the user off, and perform other required tasks, and then let the application crash before something terrible happens (such as a total system failure). With this necessity in mind, the following steps show a simple example of using the `finally` clause. This example also appears with the downloadable source code as `ExceptionWithFinally.py`.

1. Open a Python File window.

You see an editor in which you can type the example code.

2. **Type the following code into the window — pressing Enter after each line:**

```
import sys

try:
    raise ValueError
    print("Raising an exception.")
except ValueError:
    print("ValueError Exception!")
    sys.exit()
finally:
    print("Taking care of last minute details.")

print("This code will never execute.")
```

In this example, the code raises a `ValueError` exception. The `except` clause executes as normal when this happens. The call to `sys.exit()` means that the application exits after the exception is handled. Perhaps the application can't recover in this particular instance, but the application normally ends, which is why the final `print()` function call won't ever execute.

The `finally` clause code always executes. It doesn't matter whether the exception happens or not. The code you place in this block needs to be common code that you always want to execute. For example, when working with a file, you place the code to close the file into this block to ensure that the data isn't damaged by remaining in memory rather than going to disk.

3. **Choose Run⇨Run Module.**

You see a Python Shell window open. The application displays the `except` clause message and the `finally` clause message, as shown in Figure 9-15. The `sys.exit()` call prevents any other code from executing.

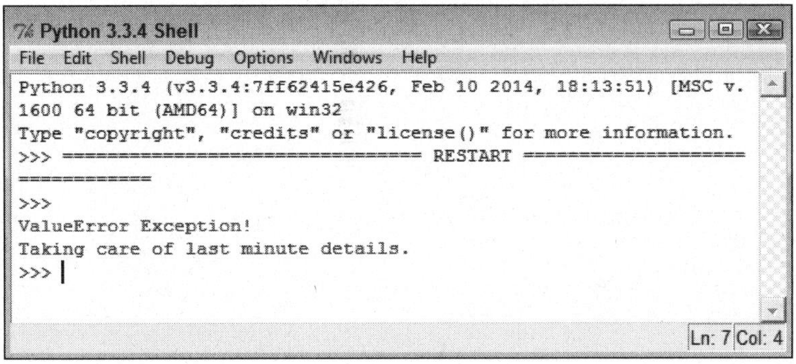

Figure 9-15: Use the `finally` clause to ensure specific actions take place before the application ends.

```
74 Python 3.3.4 Shell
File  Edit  Shell  Debug  Options  Windows  Help
Python 3.3.4 (v3.3.4:7ff62415e426, Feb 10 2014, 18:13:51) [MSC v.
1600 64 bit (AMD64)] on win32
Type "copyright", "credits" or "license()" for more information.
>>> ================================ RESTART ====================
============
>>>
ValueError Exception!
Taking care of last minute details.
>>> |
                                                            Ln: 7 Col: 4
```

4. **Comment out the `raise ValueError` call by preceding it with two pound signs, like this:**

```
##raise ValueError
```

Removing the exception will demonstrate how the `finally` clause actually works.

5. **Save the file to disk to ensure that Python sees the change.**

6. **Choose Run⇨Run Module.**

You see a Python Shell window open. The application displays a series of messages, including the `finally` clause message, as shown in Figure 9-16. This part of the example shows that the `finally` clause always executes, so you need to use it carefully.

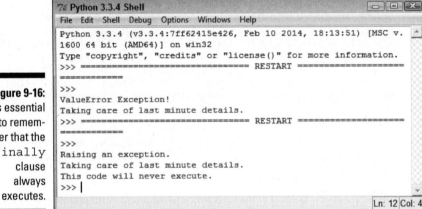

Figure 9-16:
It's essential to remember that the `finally` clause always executes.

Part III
Performing Common Tasks

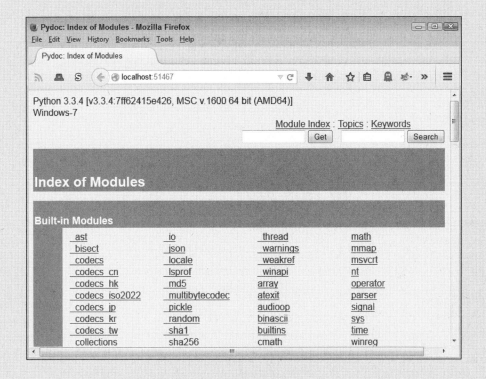

See an example of how you can named arguments in format strings at
www.dummies.com/extras/beginningprogrammingwithpython.

In this part . . .

✔ Gain access to Python modules.

✔ Slice and dice strings to meet your output needs.

✔ Create lists of objects you want to manage.

✔ Use collections to organize data efficiently.

✔ Develop classes to make code reusable.

Chapter 10

Interacting with Modules

● ●

In This Chapter

▶ Organizing your code

▶ Adding code from outside sources to your application

▶ Locating code libraries on disk

▶ Looking at the library code

▶ Obtaining and reading the Python library documentation

● ●

*T*he examples in this book are small, but the functionality of the resulting applications is extremely limited as well. Even tiny real-world applications contain thousands of lines of code. In fact, applications that contain millions of lines of code are somewhat common. Imagine trying to work with a file large enough to contain millions of lines of code — you'd never find anything. In short, you need some method to organize code into small pieces that are easier to manage, much like the examples in this book. The Python solution is to place code in separate code groupings called *modules*. Commonly used modules that contain source code for generic needs are called *libraries*.

Modules are contained in separate files. In order to use the module, you must tell Python to grab the file and read it into the current application. The process of obtaining code found in external files is called *importing*. You import a module or library to use the code it contains. A few examples in the book have already shown the import statement in use, but this chapter explains the import statement in detail so that you know how to use it.

As part of the initial setup, Python created a pointer to the general-purpose libraries that it uses. That's why you can simply add an import statement with the name of the library and Python can find it. However, it pays to know how to locate the files on disk in case you ever need to update them or you want to add your own modules and libraries to the list of files that Python can use.

The library code is self-contained and well documented (at least in most cases it is). Some developers might feel that they never need to look at the library code, and they're right to some degree — you never have to look at the library code in order to use it. You might want to view the library code, though, to ensure that you understand how the code works. In addition, the library code can teach you new programming techniques that you might not otherwise discover. So, viewing the library code is optional, but it can be helpful.

The one thing you do need to know how to do is obtain and use the Python library documentation. This chapter shows you how to obtain and use the library documentation as part of the application-creation process.

Creating Code Groupings

It's important to group like pieces of code together to make the code easier to use, modify, and understand. As an application grows, managing the code found in a single file becomes harder and harder. At some point, the code becomes impossible to manage because the file has become too large for anyone to work with.

The term *code* is used broadly in this particular case. Code groupings can include:

✔ Classes

✔ Functions

✔ Variables

✔ Runnable code

The collection of classes, functions, variables, and runnable code within a module is known as *attributes*. A module has attributes that you access by that attribute's name. Later sections in this chapter discuss precisely how module access works.

The runnable code can actually be written in a language other than Python. For example, it's somewhat common to find modules that are written in C/C++ instead of Python. The reason that some developers use runnable code is to make the Python application faster, less resource intensive, and better able to use a particular platform's resources. However, using runnable code comes with the downside of making your application less portable (able to run on other platforms) unless you have runnable code modules for each platform that you want to support. In addition, dual-language applications can be harder to maintain because you must have developers who can speak each of the computer languages used in the application.

The most common way to create a module is to define a separate file containing the code you want to group separately from the rest of the application. For example, you might want to create a print routine that an application uses in a number of places. The print routine isn't designed to work on its own but is part of the application as a whole. You want to separate it because the application uses it in numerous places and you could potentially use the same code in another application. The ability to reuse code ranks high on the list of reasons to create modules.

To make things easier to understand, the examples in this chapter use a common module. The module doesn't do anything too amazing, but it demonstrates the principles of working with modules. Open a Python File window and create a new file named `MyLibrary.py`. Type the code found in Listing 10-1 and save it to disk. (This module also appears with the downloadable source code as `MyLibrary.py`.)

Listing 10-1:   A Simple Demonstration Module

```
def SayHello(Name):
    print("Hello ", Name)
    return

def SayGoodbye(Name):
    print("Goodbye ", Name)
    return
```

The example code contains two simple functions named `SayHello()` and `SayGoodbye()`. In both cases, you supply a `Name` to print and the function prints it onscreen along with a greeting for you. At that point, the function returns control to the caller. Obviously, you normally create more complicated functions, but these functions work well for the purposes of this chapter.

Importing Modules

In order to use a module, you must import it. Python places the module code inline with the rest of your application in memory — as if you had created one huge file. Neither file is changed on disk — they're still separate, but the way Python views the code is different.

You have two ways to import modules. Each technique is used in specific circumstances:

- ✔ `import`: You use the `import` statement when you want to import an entire module. This is the most common method that developers use to import modules because it saves time and requires only one line of code. However, this approach also uses more memory resources than does the approach of selectively importing the attributes you need, which the next paragraph describes.

- ✔ `from...import`: You use the `from...import` statement when you want to selectively import individual module attributes. This method saves resources, but at the cost of complexity. In addition, if you try to use an attribute that you didn't import, Python registers an error. Yes, the module still contains the attribute, but Python can't see it because you didn't import it.

Now that you have a better idea of how to import modules, it's time to look at them in detail. The following sections help you work through importing modules using the two techniques available in Python.

Changing the current Python directory

The directory that Python is using to access code affects which modules you can load. The Python library files are always included in the list of locations that Python can access, but Python knows nothing of the directory you use to hold your source code unless you tell it to look there. The easiest method for accomplishing this task is to change the current Python directory to point to your code folder using these steps:

1. **Open the Python Shell.**

   You see the Python Shell window appear.

2. **Type** import os **and press Enter.**

This action imports the Python os library. You need to import this library to change the directory (the location Python sees on disk) to the working directory for this book.

3. **Type** os.chdir("C:\BP4D\Chapter10") **and press Enter.**

You need to use the directory that contains the downloadable source or your own project files on your local hard drive. The book uses the default book directory described in Chapter 4. Python can now use the downloadable source code directory to access modules that you create for this chapter.

Using the import statement

The `import` statement is the most common method for importing a module into Python. This approach is fast and ensures that the entire module is ready for use. The following steps get you started using the `import` statement.

1. **Open the Python Shell.**

   You see the Python Shell window appear.

2. **Change directories to the downloadable source code directory.**

   See the instructions found in the "Changing the current Python directory" sidebar.

3. **Type** import MyLibrary **and press Enter.**

   Python imports the contents of the `MyLibrary.py` file that you created in the "Creating Code Groupings" section of the chapter. The entire library is now ready for use.

   It's important to know that Python also creates a cache of the module in the __pycache__ subdirectory. If you look into your source code directory after you import `MyLibrary` for the first time, you see the new __pycache__ directory. If you want to make changes to your module, you must delete this directory. Otherwise, Python will continue to use the unchanged cache file instead of your updated source code file.

4. **Type** dir(MyLibrary) **and press Enter.**

   You see a listing of the module contents, which includes the `SayHello()` and `SayGoodbye()` functions, as shown in Figure 10-1. (A discussion of the other entries appears in the "Viewing the Module Content" section of the chapter.)

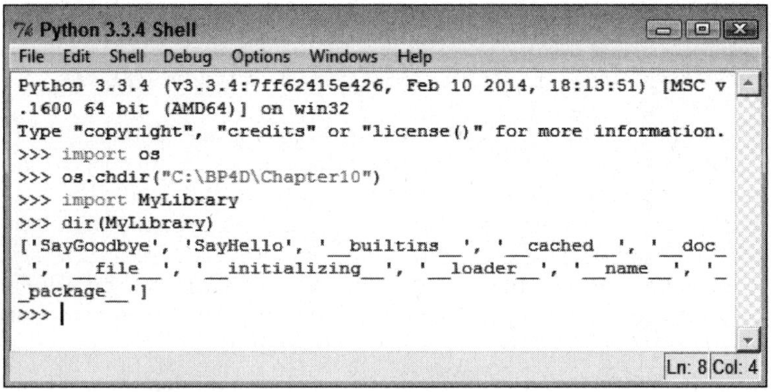

Figure 10-1:
A directory listing shows that Python imports both functions from the module.

```
Python 3.3.4 Shell
File  Edit  Shell  Debug  Options  Windows  Help
Python 3.3.4 (v3.3.4:7ff62415e426, Feb 10 2014, 18:13:51) [MSC v
.1600 64 bit (AMD64)] on win32
Type "copyright", "credits" or "license()" for more information.
>>> import os
>>> os.chdir("C:\BP4D\Chapter10")
>>> import MyLibrary
>>> dir(MyLibrary)
['SayGoodbye', 'SayHello', '__builtins__', '__cached__', '__doc_
_', '__file__', '__initializing__', '__loader__', '__name__', '_
_package__']
>>>
                                                        Ln: 8 Col: 4
```

5. **Type** MyLibrary.SayHello("Josh") **and press Enter.**

The `SayHello()` function outputs the expected text, as shown in Figure 10-2.

Figure 10-2:
The `Say Hello()` function outputs the expected greeting.

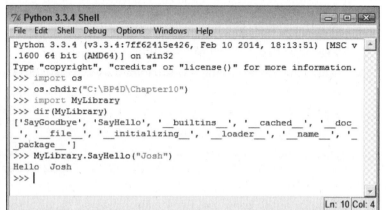

```
7⁄₆ Python 3.3.4 Shell                                        ⊟ ⊡ ✕
File  Edit  Shell  Debug  Options  Windows  Help
Python 3.3.4 (v3.3.4:7ff62415e426, Feb 10 2014, 18:13:51) [MSC v
.1600 64 bit (AMD64)] on win32
Type "copyright", "credits" or "license()" for more information.
>>> import os
>>> os.chdir("C:\BP4D\Chapter10")
>>> import MyLibrary
>>> dir(MyLibrary)
['SayGoodbye', 'SayHello', '__builtins__', '__cached__', '__doc_
_', '__file__', '__initializing__', '__loader__', '__name__', '__
_package__']
>>> MyLibrary.SayHello("Josh")
Hello  Josh
>>> |
                                                        Ln: 10 Col: 4
```

Notice that you must precede the attribute name, which is the `Say Hello()` function in this case, with the module name, which is `MyLibrary`. The two elements are separated by a period. Every call to a module that you import follows the same pattern.

6. **Type** MyLibrary.SayGoodbye("Sally") **and press Enter.**

The `SayGoodbye( )` function outputs the expected text.

7. **Close the Python Shell.**

The Python Shell window closes.

Using the from...import statement

The `from...import` statement has the advantage of importing only the attributes you need from a module. This difference means that the module uses less memory and other system resources than using the `import` statement does. In addition, the `from...import` statement makes the module a little easier to use because some commands, such as `dir()`, show less information, or only the information that you actually need. The point is that you get only what you want and not anything else. The following steps demonstrate using the `from...import` statement.

1. **Open the Python Shell.**

   You see the Python Shell window appear.

2. **Change directories to the downloadable source code directory.**

   See the instructions found in the "Changing the current Python directory" sidebar.

3. **Type** from MyLibrary import SayHello **and press Enter.**

   Python imports the SayHello() function that you create in the "Creating Code Groupings" section, earlier in the chapter. Only this specific function is now ready for use.

   You can still import the entire module, should you want to do so. The two techniques for accomplishing the task are to create a list of modules to import (the names can be separated by commas, such as from MyLibrary import SayHello, SayGoodbye) or to use the asterisk (*) in place of a specific attribute name. The asterisk acts as a wildcard character that imports everything.

4. **Type** dir(MyLibrary) **and press Enter.**

   Python displays an error message, as shown in Figure 10-3. Python imports only the attributes that you specifically request. This means that the MyLibrary module isn't in memory — only the attributes that you requested are in memory.

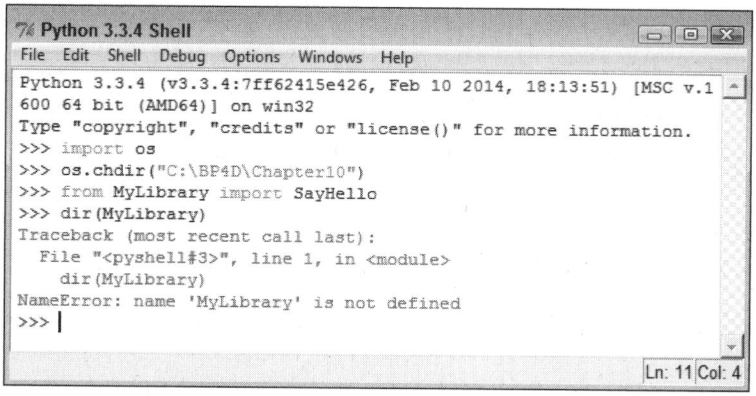

Figure 10-3:
The
from...
import
statement
imports only
the items
that you
specifically
request.

```
7% Python 3.3.4 Shell                                    □ □ ▨
File  Edit  Shell  Debug  Options  Windows  Help
Python 3.3.4 (v3.3.4:7ff62415e426, Feb 10 2014, 18:13:51) [MSC v.1
600 64 bit (AMD64)] on win32
Type "copyright", "credits" or "license()" for more information.
>>> import os
>>> os.chdir("C:\BP4D\Chapter10")
>>> from MyLibrary import SayHello
>>> dir(MyLibrary)
Traceback (most recent call last):
  File "<pyshell#3>", line 1, in <module>
    dir(MyLibrary)
NameError: name 'MyLibrary' is not defined
>>> |
                                                    Ln: 11 Col: 4
```

5. **Type** dir(SayHello) **and press Enter.**

   You see a listing of attributes that are associated with the SayHello() function, as shown in Figure 10-4. It isn't important to know how these attributes work just now, but you'll use some of them later in the book.

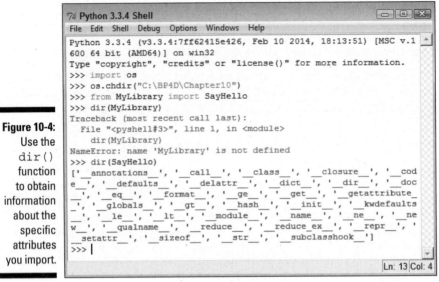

Figure 10-4:
Use the
`dir()`
function
to obtain
information
about the
specific
attributes
you import.

6. **Type** SayHello("Angie") **and press Enter.**

The `SayHello()` function outputs the expected text, as shown in Figure 10-5.

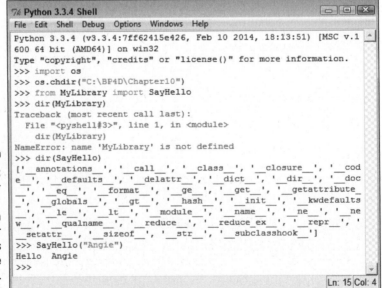

Figure 10-5:
The `Say
Hello()`
function
no longer
requires
the module
name.

When you import attributes using the `from...import` statement, you don't need to precede the attribute name with a module name. This feature makes the attribute easier to access.

Using the `from...import` statement can also cause problems. If two attributes have the same name, you can import only one of them. The `import` statement prevents name collisions, which is important when you have a large number of attributes to import. In sum, you must exercise care when using the `from...import` statement.

7. Type SayGoodbye("Harold") **and press Enter.**

You imported only the `SayHello()` function, so Python knows nothing about `SayGoodbye()` and displays an error message. The selective nature of the `from...import` statement can cause problems when you assume that an attribute is present when it really isn't.

8. Close the Python Shell.

The Python Shell window closes.

Finding Modules on Disk

In order to use the code in a module, Python must be able to locate the module and load it into memory. The location information is stored as paths within Python. Whenever you request that Python import a module, Python looks at all the files in its list of paths to find it. The path information comes from three sources:

- ✔ **Environment variables:** Chapter 3 tells you about Python environment variables, such as PYTHONPATH, that tell Python where to find modules on disk.

- ✔ **Current directory:** Earlier in this chapter, you discover that you can change the current Python directory so that it can locate any modules used by your application.

- ✔ **Default directories:** Even when you don't define any environment variables and the current directory doesn't yield any usable modules, Python can still find its own libraries in the set of default directories that are included as part of its own path information.

It's helpful to know the current path information because the lack of a path can cause your application to fail. The following steps demonstrate how you can obtain path information:

1. Open the Python Shell.

You see the Python Shell window appear.

2. **Type** import sys **and press Enter.**

3. **Type** for p in sys.path: **and press Enter.**

   Python automatically indents the next line for you. The sys.path attribute always contains a listing of default paths.

4. **Type** print(p) **and press Enter twice.**

   You see a listing of the path information, as shown in Figure 10-6. Your listing may be different from the one shown in Figure 10-6, depending on your platform, the version of Python you have installed, and the Python features you have installed.

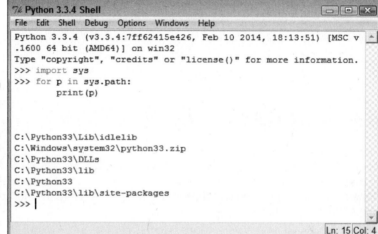

Figure 10-6:
The sys.
path
attribute
contains a
listing of the
individual
paths for
your system.

The sys.path attribute is reliable but may not always contain every path that Python can see. If you don't see a needed path, you can always check in another place that Python looks for information. The following steps show how to perform this task:

1. **Type** import os **and press Enter.**

2. **Type** os.environ['PYTHONPATH'].split(os.pathsep) **and press Enter.**

   When you have a PYTHONPATH environment variable defined, you see a list of paths, as shown in Figure 10-7. However, if you don't have the environment variable defined, you see an error message instead.

   Notice that both the sys.path and the os.environ['PYTHONPATH'] attributes contain the C:\BP4D\Chapter10 entry in this case. The sys.path attribute doesn't include the split() function, which is why the example uses a `for` loop with it. However, the `os.environ['PYTHONPATH']` attribute does include the `split()` function, so you can use it to create a list of individual paths.

You must provide `split()` with a value to look for in splitting a list of items. The `os.pathsep` *constant* (a variable that has one, unchangeable, defined value) defines the path separator for the current platform so that you can use the same code on any platform that supports Python.

3. **Close the Python Shell.**

   The Python Shell window closes.

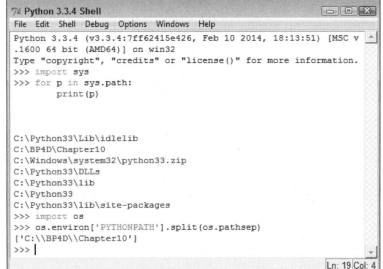

Figure 10-7:
You must request information about environment variables separately.

You can also add and remove items from `sys.path`. For example, if you want to add Chapter 9 to the list of modules, you type **`sys.path.append("C:\\BP4D\\Chapter09")`** and press Enter in the Python Shell window. When you list the `sys.path` contents again, you see that the new entry is added. Likewise, when you want to remove an entry, such as Chapter 9, you type **`sys.path.remove("C:\\BP4D\\Chapter09")`** and press Enter.

Viewing the Module Content

Python gives you several different ways to view module content. The method that most developers use is to work with the `dir()` function, which tells you about the attributes that the module provides.

Look at Figure 10-1, earlier in the chapter. In addition to the `SayGoodbye()` and `SayHello()` function entries discussed previously, the list has other entries. These attributes are automatically generated by Python for you. These attributes perform the following tasks or contain the following information:

- ✔ `__builtins__`: Contains a listing of all the built-in attributes that are accessible from the module. Python adds these attributes automatically for you.

- ✔ `__cached__`: Tells you the name and location of the cached file that is associated with the module. The location information (path) is relative to the current Python directory.

- ✔ `__doc__`: Outputs help information for the module, assuming that you've actually filled it in. For example, if you type `os.__doc__` and press Enter, Python will output the help information associated with the os library.

- ✔ `__file__`: Tells you the name and location of the module. The location information (path) is relative to the current Python directory.

- ✔ `__initializing__`: Determines whether the module is in the process of initializing itself. Normally this attribute returns a value of `False`. This attribute is useful when you need to wait until one module is done loading before you import another module that depends on it.

- ✔ `__loader__`: Outputs the loader information for this module. The *loader* is a piece of software that gets the module and puts it into memory so that Python can use it. This is one attribute you rarely (if ever) use.

- ✔ `__name__`: Tells you just the name of the module.

- ✔ `__package__`: This attribute is used internally by the import system to make it easier to load and manage modules. You don't need to worry about this particular attribute.

It may surprise you to find that you can drill down even further into the attributes. Type **dir(MyLibrary.SayHello)** and press Enter. You see the entries shown in Figure 10-8.

Some of these entries, such as `__name__`, also appeared in the module listing. However, you might be curious about some of the other entries. For example, you might want to know what `__sizeof__` is all about. One way to get additional information is to type **help("__sizeof__")** and press Enter. You see some scanty (but useful) help information, as shown in Figure 10-9.

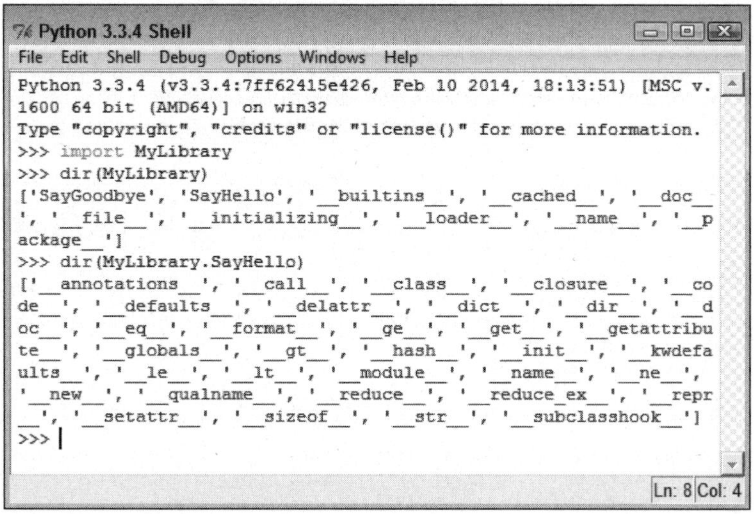

Figure 10-8:
Drill down
as far as
needed to
understand
the modules
that you use
in Python.

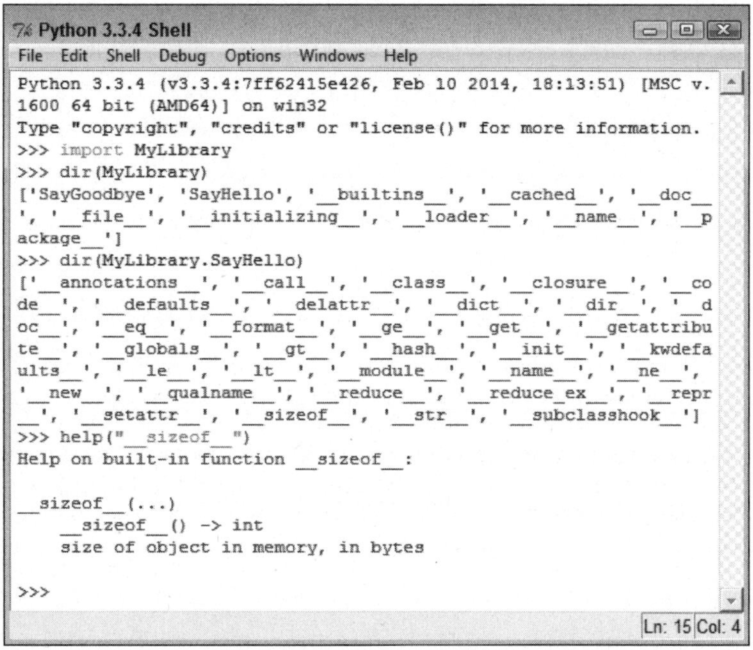

Figure 10-9:
Try getting
some help
information
about the
attribute
you want to
know about.

Python isn't going to blow up if you try the attribute. Even if the shell does experience problems, you can always start a new one. So, another way to check out a module is to simply try the attributes. For example, if you type **MyLibrary.SayHello.__sizeof__()** and press Enter, you see the size of the SayHello() function in bytes, as shown in Figure 10-10.

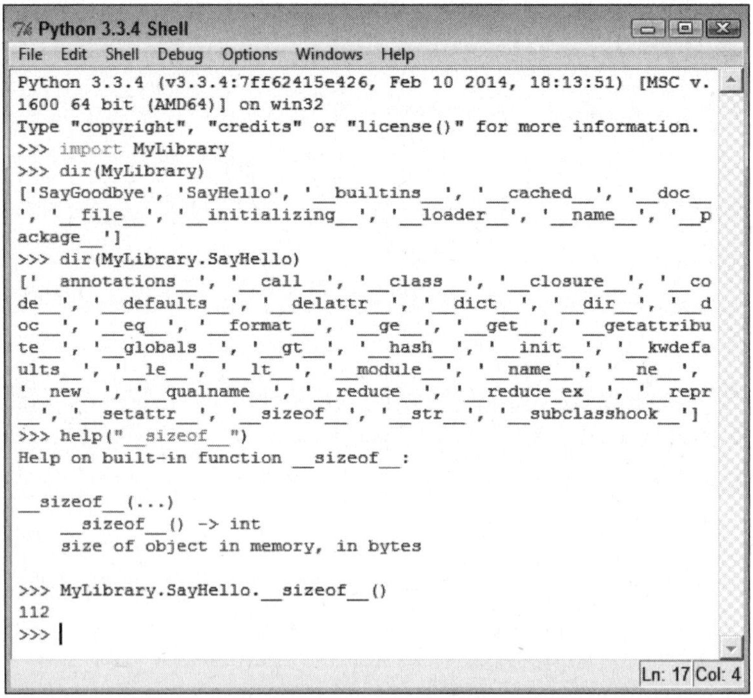

Figure 10-10:
Using the attributes will help you get a better feel for how they work.

```
7% Python 3.3.4 Shell                                        ▭ ▫ ✕
File  Edit  Shell  Debug  Options  Windows  Help
Python 3.3.4 (v3.3.4:7ff62415e426, Feb 10 2014, 18:13:51) [MSC v.
1600 64 bit (AMD64)] on win32
Type "copyright", "credits" or "license()" for more information.
>>> import MyLibrary
>>> dir(MyLibrary)
['SayGoodbye', 'SayHello', '__builtins__', '__cached__', '__doc__
', '__file__', '__initializing__', '__loader__', '__name__', '__p
ackage__']
>>> dir(MyLibrary.SayHello)
['__annotations__', '__call__', '__class__', '__closure__', '__co
de__', '__defaults__', '__delattr__', '__dict__', '__dir__', '__d
oc__', '__eq__', '__format__', '__ge__', '__get__', '__getattribu
te__', '__globals__', '__gt__', '__hash__', '__init__', '__kwdefa
ults__', '__le__', '__lt__', '__module__', '__name__', '__ne__',
'__new__', '__qualname__', '__reduce__', '__reduce_ex__', '__repr
__', '__setattr__', '__sizeof__', '__str__', '__subclasshook__']
>>> help("__sizeof__")
Help on built-in function __sizeof__:

__sizeof__(...)
    __sizeof__() -> int
    size of object in memory, in bytes

>>> MyLibrary.SayHello.__sizeof__()
112
>>> |
                                                    Ln: 17 Col: 4
```

Unlike many other programming languages, Python also makes the source code for its native language libraries available. For example, when you look into the \Python33\Lib directory, you see a listing of .py files that you can open in IDLE with no problem at all. Try opening the os.py library that you use for various tasks in this chapter, and you see the content shown in Figure 10-11.

```
7/6 Python 3.3.4: os.py - C:\Python33\Lib\os.py                          [ - ] [ □ ] [ x ]
File  Edit  Format  Run  Options  Windows  Help
r"""OS routines for Mac, NT, or Posix depending on what system we're on.

This exports:
  - all functions from posix, nt, os2, or ce, e.g. unlink, stat, etc.
  - os.path is either posixpath or ntpath
  - os.name is either 'posix', 'nt', 'os2' or 'ce'.
  - os.curdir is a string representing the current directory ('.' or ':')
  - os.pardir is a string representing the parent directory ('..' or '::')
  - os.sep is the (or a most common) pathname separator ('/' or ':' or '\\')
  - os.extsep is the extension separator (always '.')
  - os.altsep is the alternate pathname separator (None or '/')
  - os.pathsep is the component separator used in $PATH etc
  - os.linesep is the line separator in text files ('\r' or '\n' or '\r\n')
  - os.defpath is the default search path for executables
  - os.devnull is the file path of the null device ('/dev/null', etc.)

Programs that import and use 'os' stand a better chance of being
portable between different platforms.  Of course, they must then
only use functions that are defined by all platforms (e.g., unlink
and opendir), and leave all pathname manipulation to os.path
(e.g., split and join).
"""

#'

import sys, errno
import stat as st

_names = sys.builtin_module_names

# Note:  more names are added to __all__ later.
__all__ = ["altsep", "curdir", "pardir", "sep", "pathsep", "linesep",
           "defpath", "name", "path", "devnull", "SEEK_SET", "SEEK_CUR",
           "SEEK_END", "fsencode", "fsdecode", "get_exec_path", "fdopen",
           "popen", "extsep"]

def _exists(name):
    return name in globals()

def _get_exports_list(module):
                                                              Ln: 1 Col: 0
```

Figure 10-11:
Directly
viewing
module
code can
help in
understand-
ing it.

Viewing the content directly can help you discover new programming techniques and better understand how the library works. The more time you
spend working with Python, the better you'll become at using it to build interesting applications.

Make sure that you just look at the library code and don't accidentally change
it. If you accidentally change the code, your applications can stop working.
Worse yet, you can introduce subtle bugs into your application that will
appear only on your system and nowhere else. Always exercise care when
working with library code.

Using the Python Module Documentation

You can use the doc() function whenever needed to get quick help. However, you have a better way to study the modules and libraries located in the Python path — the Python Module Documentation. This feature often appears as Module Docs in the Python folder on your system. It's also referred to as pydoc. Whatever you call it, the Python Module Documentation makes life a lot easier for developers. The following sections describe how to work with this feature.

Opening the pydoc application

Pydoc is just another Python application. It actually appears in the \Python33\Lib directory of your system as pydoc.py. As with any other .py file, you can open this one with IDLE and study how it works. You can start it using the Module Docs shortcut that appears in the Python folder on your system or by using a command at the command prompt.

The application creates a localized server that works with your browser to display information about the Python modules and libraries. So, when you start this application, you see a command (terminal) window open like the one shown in Figure 10-12.

Accessing pydoc on Windows

The Windows installation of Python has a problem. When you click Module Docs, nothing happens. Of course, this is a bit disconcerting because users are apt to feel that something is wrong with their systems or with Python itself. It turns out that the shortcut is faulty. To overcome this problem, you must create a new shortcut using the following steps:

1. **Right-click the Desktop and choose New⇨ Shortcut from the context menu.**

   You see the Create Shortcut wizard.

2. **Type** C:\Python33\python.exe C:\Python33\ Lib\pydoc.py -b **and click Next.**

   This command line starts a copy of the pydoc server so that you can access module information.

3. **Type** pydoc **and click Finish.**

   Windows creates a new shortcut for you. This shortcut allows you to access the module help information that currently doesn't work with Python 3.3.4 on Windows.

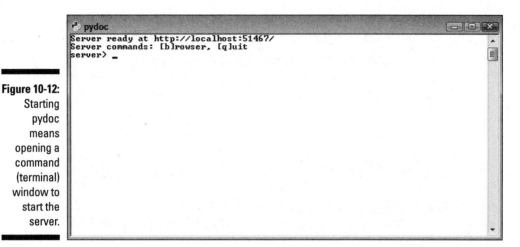

Figure 10-12:
Starting
pydoc
means
opening a
command
(terminal)
window to
start the
server.

As with any server, your system may prompt you for permissions. For example, you may see a warning from your firewall telling you that pydoc is attempting to access the local system. You need to give pydoc permission to work with the system so that you can see the information it provides. Any virus detection that you have installed may need permission to let pydoc continue as well. Some platforms, such as Windows, may require an elevation in privileges to run pydoc.

Normally, the server automatically opens a new browser window for you, as shown in Figure 10-13. This window contains links to the various modules that are contained on your system, including any custom modules you create and include in the Python path. To see information about any module, you can simply click its link.

The command prompt provides you with two commands to control the server. You simply type the letter associated with the command and press Enter to activate it. Here are the two commands:

✔ b: Starts a new copy of the default browser with the index page loaded.

✔ q: Stops the server.

When you're done browsing the help information, make sure that you stop the server by typing q and pressing Enter at the command prompt. Stopping the server frees any resources it uses and closes any holes you made in your firewall to accommodate pydoc.

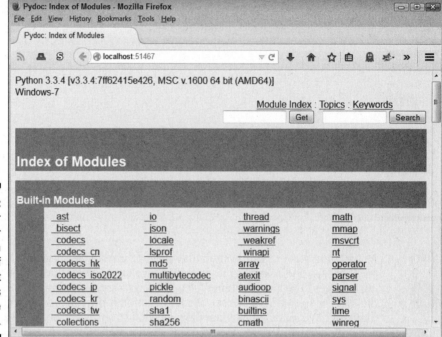

Figure 10-13:
Your
browser
displays a
number of
links that
appear as
part of the
Index page.

Using the quick-access links

Refer back to Figure 10-13. Near the top of the page, you see three links. These links provide quick access to the site features. The browser always begins at the Module Index. If you need to return to this page, simply click the Module Index link.

The Topics link takes you to the page shown in Figure 10-14. This page contains links for essential Python topics. For example, if you want to know more about Boolean values, click the BOOLEAN link. The page you see next describes how Boolean values work in Python. At the bottom of the page are related links that lead to pages that contain additional helpful information.

The Keywords link takes you to the page shown in Figure 10-15. What you see is a list of the keywords that Python supports. For example, if you want to know more about creating `for` loops, you click the for link.

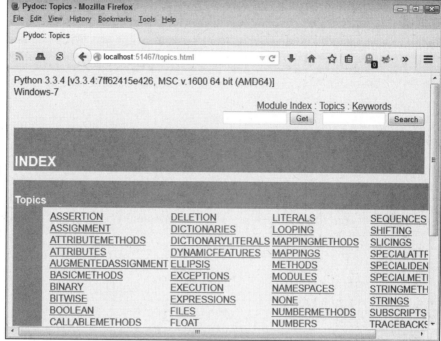

Figure 10-14:
The Topics
page tells
you about
essential
Python
topics, such
as how
Boolean
values work.

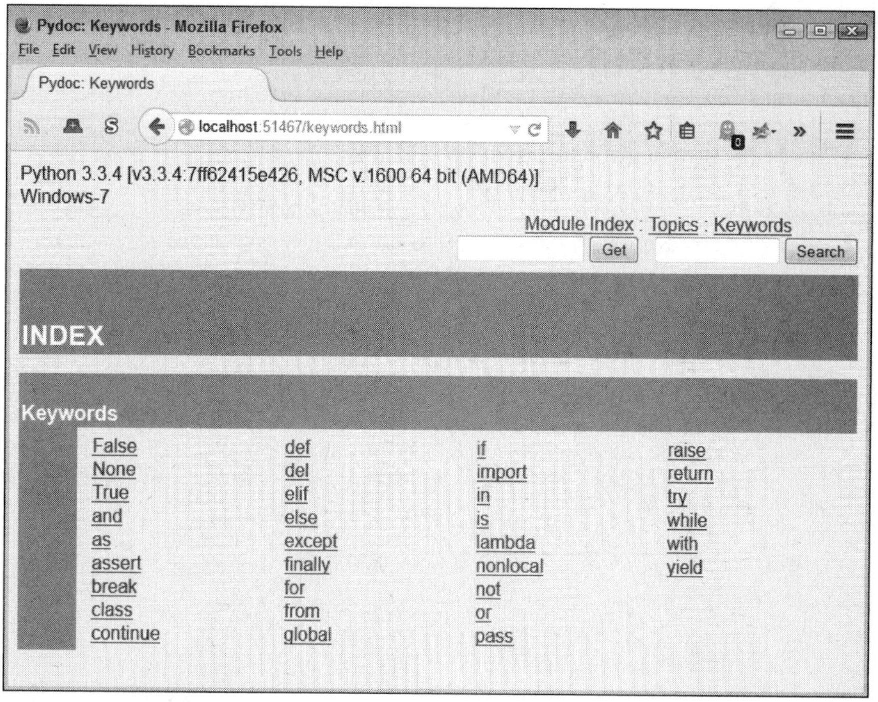

Figure 10-15:
The
Keywords
page
contains
a listing of
keywords
that Python
supports.

Typing a search term

The pages also include two text boxes near the top. The first has a Get button next to it and the second has a Search button next to it. When you type a search term in the first text box and click Get, you see the documentation for that particular module or attribute. Figure 10-16 shows what you see when you type **print** and click Get.

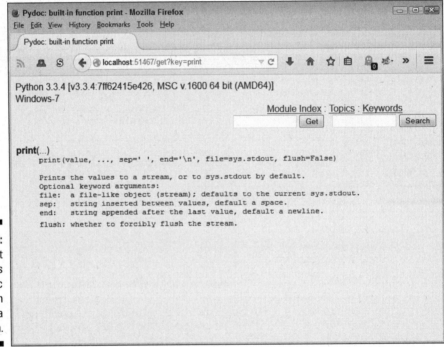

Figure 10-16:
Using Get obtains specific information about a search term.

When you type a search term in the second text box and click Search, you see all the topics that could relate to that search term. Figure 10-17 shows typical results when you type **print** and click Search. In this case, you click a link, such as calendar, to see additional information.

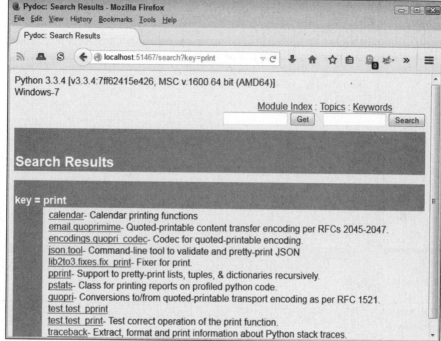

Python 3.3.4 [v3.3.4:7ff62415e426, MSC v.1600 64 bit (AMD64)]
Windows-7

Module Index : Topics : Keywords

Get   Search

Search Results

key = print

    calendar- Calendar printing functions
    email.quoprimime- Quoted-printable content transfer encoding per RFCs 2045-2047.
    encodings.quopri_codec- Codec for quoted-printable encoding.
    json.tool- Command-line tool to validate and pretty-print JSON
    lib2to3.fixes.fix_print- Fixer for print.
    pprint- Support to pretty-print lists, tuples, & dictionaries recursively.
    pstats- Class for printing reports on profiled python code.
    quopri- Conversions to/from quoted-printable transport encoding as per RFC 1521.
    test.test_pprint
    test.test_print- Test correct operation of the print function.
    traceback- Extract, format and print information about Python stack traces.

Figure 10-17:
Using
Search
obtains a
list of topics
about a
search term.

Viewing the results

The results you get when you view a page depends on the topic. Some topics
are brief, such as the one shown in Figure 10-16 for print. However, other
topics are extensive. For example, if you were to click the calendar link in
Figure 10-17, you would see a significant amount of information, as shown in
Figure 10-18.

In this particular case, you see related module information, error information,
functions, data, and all sorts of additional information about the calendar
printing functions. The amount of information you see depends partly on the
complexity of the topic and partly on the amount of information the developer provided with the module. For example, if you were to select MyLibrary
from the Module Index page, you would see only a list of functions and no
documentation at all.

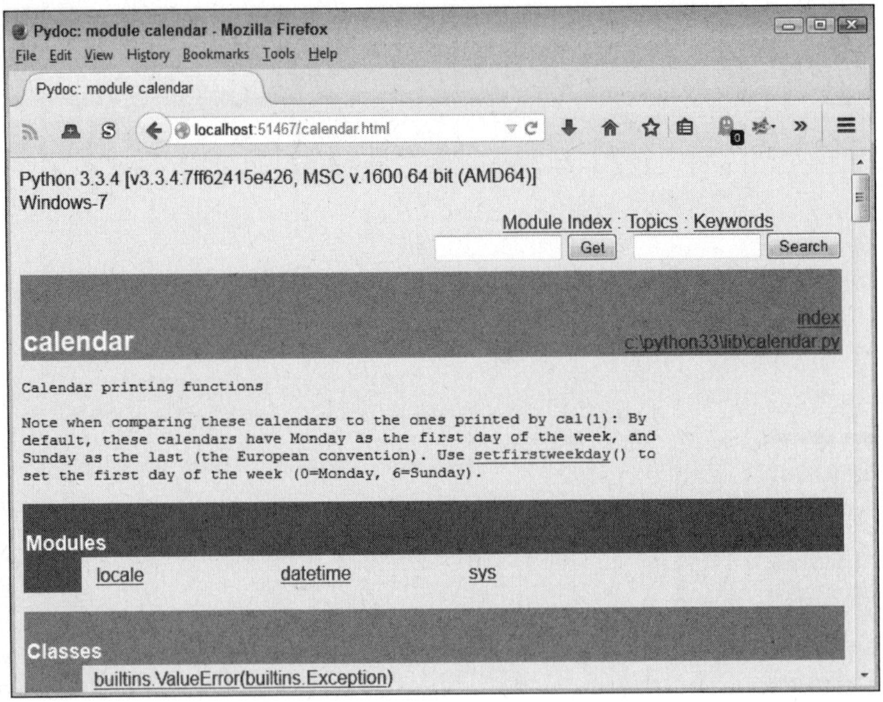

Figure 10-18: Some pages contain extensive information.

Chapter 11

Working with Strings

In This Chapter

▶ Considering the string difference

▶ Using special characters in strings

▶ Working with single characters

▶ Performing string-specific tasks

▶ Finding what you need in a string

▶ Modifying the appearance of string output

*Y*our computer doesn't understand strings. It's a basic fact. Computers understand numbers, not letters. When you see a string on the computer screen, the computer actually sees a series of numbers. However, humans understand strings quite well, so applications need to be able to work with them. Fortunately, Python makes working with strings relatively easy. It translates the string you understand into the numbers the computer understands, and vice versa.

In order to make strings useful, you need to be able to manipulate them. Of course, that means taking strings apart and using just the pieces you need or searching the string for specific information. This chapter describes how you can build strings using Python, dissect them as needed, and use just the parts you want after you find what's required. String manipulation is an important part of applications because humans depend on computers performing that sort of work for them (even though the computer has no idea of what a string is).

After you have the string you want, you need to present it to the user in an eye-pleasing manner. The computer doesn't really care how it presents the string, so often you get the information, but it lacks pizzazz. In fact, it may be downright difficult to read. Knowing how to format strings so that they look nice onscreen is important because users need to see information in a form they understand. By the time you complete this chapter, you know how to create, manipulate, and format strings so that the user sees precisely the right information.

Understanding That Strings Are Different

Most aspiring developers (and even a few who have written code for a long time) really have a hard time understanding that computers truly do only understand 0s and 1s. Even larger numbers are made up of 0s and 1s. Comparisons take place with 0s and 1s. Data is moved using 0s and 1s. In short, strings don't exist for the computer (and numbers just barely exist). Although grouping 0s and 1s to make numbers is relatively easy, strings are a lot harder because now you're talking about information that the computer must manipulate as numbers but present as characters.

There are no strings in computer science. Strings are made up of characters, and individual characters are actually numeric values. When you work with strings in Python, what you're really doing is creating an assembly of characters that the computer sees as numeric values. That's why the following sections are so important. They help you understand why strings are so special. Understanding this material will save you a lot of headaches later.

Defining a character using numbers

To create a character, you must first define a relationship between that character and a number. More important, everyone must agree that when a certain number appears in an application and is viewed as a character by that application, the number is translated into a specific character. One of the most common ways to perform this task is to use the American Standard Code for Information Interchange (ASCII). Python uses ASCII to translate the number 65 to the letter *A*. The chart at http://www.asciitable.com/ shows the various numeric values and their character equivalents.

Every character you use must have a different numeric value assigned to it. The letter *A* uses a value of 65. To create a lowercase *a*, you must assign a different number, which is 97. The computer views *A* and *a* as completely different characters, even though people view them as uppercase and lowercase versions of the same character.

The numeric values used in this chapter are in decimal. However, the computer still views them as 0s and 1s. For example, the letter *A* is really the value 01000001 and the letter *a* is really the value 01100001. When you see an *A* onscreen, the computer sees a binary value instead.

Having just one character set to deal with would be nice. However, not every-one could agree on a single set of numeric values to equate with specific characters. Part of the problem is that ASCII doesn't support characters used by other languages; also, it lacks the capability to translate special characters into an onscreen presentation. In fact, character sets abound. You can see a number of them at `http://www.i18nguy.com/unicode/codepages.html`. Click one of the character set entries to see how it assigns specific numeric values to each character. Most characters sets do use ASCII as a starting point.

Using characters to create strings

Python doesn't make you jump through hoops to create strings. However, the term *string* should actually give you a good idea of what happens. Think about beads or anything else you might string. You place one bead at a time onto the string. Eventually you end up with some type of ornamentation — perhaps a necklace or tree garland. The point is that these items are made up of individual beads.

The same concept used for necklaces made of beads holds true for strings in computers. When you see a sentence, you understand that the sentence is made up of individual characters that are strung together by the program-ming language you use. The language creates a structure that holds the indi-vidual characters together. So, the language, not the computer, knows that so many numbers in a row (each number being represented as a character) defines a string such as a sentence.

You may wonder why it's important to even know how Python works with characters. The reason is that many of the functions and special features that Python provides work with individual characters, and it's important to know that Python sees the individual characters. Even though you see a sentence, Python sees a specific number of characters.

Unlike most programming languages, strings can use either single quotes or double quotes. For example, "Hello There!" with double quotes is a string, as is 'Hello There!' with single quotes. Python also supports triple double and single quotes that let you create strings spanning multiple lines. The following steps help you create an example that demonstrates some of the string features that Python provides. This example also appears with the downloadable source code as `BasicString.py`.

1. **Open a Python File window.**

   You see an editor in which you can type the example code.

2. **Type the following code into the window — pressing Enter after each line:**

```
print('Hello There (Single Quote)!')
print("Hello There (Double Quote)!")
print("""This is a multiple line
string using triple double quotes.
You can also use triple single quotes.""")
```

Each of the three `print()` function calls demonstrates a different principle in working with strings. It's equally acceptable to enclose the string in either single or double quotes. When you use a triple quote (either single or double), the text can appear on multiple lines.

3. **Choose Run⇨Run Module.**

You see a Python Shell window open. The application outputs the text. Notice that the multiline text appears on three lines (see Figure 11-1), just as it does in the source code file, so this is a kind of formatting. You can use multiline formatting to ensure that the text breaks where you want it to onscreen.

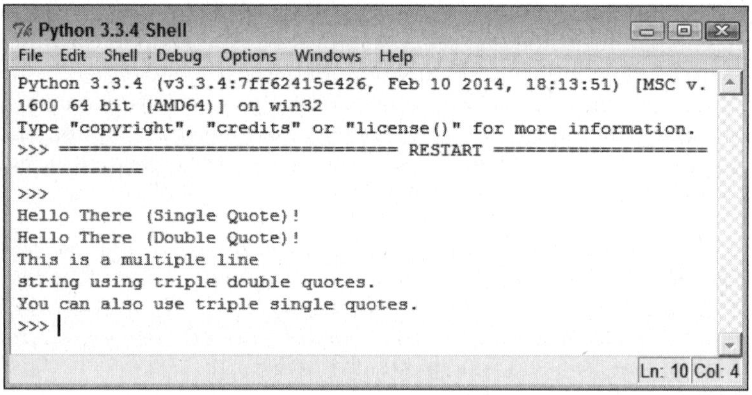

Figure 11-1:
Strings consist of individual characters that are linked together.

```
Python 3.3.4 Shell
File  Edit  Shell  Debug  Options  Windows  Help
Python 3.3.4 (v3.3.4:7ff62415e426, Feb 10 2014, 18:13:51) [MSC v.
1600 64 bit (AMD64)] on win32
Type "copyright", "credits" or "license()" for more information.
>>> ================================ RESTART ====================
============
>>>
Hello There (Single Quote)!
Hello There (Double Quote)!
This is a multiple line
string using triple double quotes.
You can also use triple single quotes.
>>> |
                                                        Ln: 10 Col: 4
```

Creating Stings with Special Characters

Some strings include special characters. These characters are different from the alphanumeric and punctuation characters that you're used to using. In fact, they fall into these categories:

✔ **Control:** An application requires some means of determining that a particular character isn't meant to be displayed but rather to control the display. All the control movements are based on the *insertion pointer,* the line you see when you type text on the screen. For example, you don't see a tab character. The tab character provides a space between two elements, and the size of that space is controlled by a tab stop. Likewise, when you want to go to the next line, you use a carriage return (which returns the insertion pointer to the beginning of the line) and linefeed (which places the insertion pointer on the next line) combination.

✔ **Accented:** Characters that have accents, such as the acute (´), grave (`), circumflex (^), umlaut or diaeresis (¨), tilde (~), or ring (°), represent special spoken sounds, in most cases. You must use special characters to create alphabetical characters with these accents included.

✔ **Drawing:** It's possible to create rudimentary art with some characters. You can see examples of the box-drawing characters at `http://jrgraphix. net/r/Unicode/2500-257F`. Some people actually create art using ASCII characters as well (`http://www.asciiworld.com/`).

✔ **Typographical:** A number of typographical characters, such as the pilcrow (¶),are used when displaying certain kinds of text onscreen, especially when the application acts as an editor.

✔ **Other:** Depending on the character set you use, the selection of characters is nearly endless. You can find a character for just about any need. The point is that you need some means of telling Python how to present these special characters.

A common need when working with strings, even strings from simple console applications, is control characters. With this in mind, Python provides escape sequences that you use to define control characters directly (and a special escape sequence for other characters).

An *escape sequence* literally escapes the common meaning of a letter, such as *a,* and gives it a new meaning (such as the ASCII bell or beep). The combination of the backslash (\) and a letter (such as *a*) is commonly viewed as a single letter by developers — an *escape character* or *escape code.* Table 11-1 provides an overview of these escape sequences.

Table 11-1	Python Escape Sequences
Escape Sequence	*Meaning*
\newline	Ignored
\\	Backslash (\)
\'	Single quote (')
\"	Double quote (")

(continued)

Table 11-1 *(continued)*

Escape Sequence	Meaning
\a	ASCII Bell (BEL)
\b	ASCII Backspace (BS)
\f	ASCII Formfeed (FF)
\n	ASCII Linefeed (LF)
\r	ASCII Carriage Return (CR)
\t	ASCII Horizontal Tab (TAB)
\u*hhhh*	Unicode character (a specific kind of character set with broad appeal across the world) with a hexadecimal value that replaces *hhhh*
\v	ASCII Vertical Tab (VT)
ooo	ASCII character with octal numeric value that replaces *ooo*
\x*hh*	ASCII character with hexadecimal value that replaces *hh*

The best way to see how the escape sequences work is to try them. The following steps help you create an example that tests various escape sequences so that you can see them in action. This example also appears with the downloadable source code as `SpecialCharacters.py`.

1. **Open a Python File window.**

   You see an editor in which you can type the example code.

2. **Type the following code into the window — pressing Enter after each line:**

   ```
   print("Part of this text\r\nis on the next line.")
   print("This is an A with a grave accent: \xC0.")
   print("This is a drawing character: \u2562.")
   print("This is a pilcrow: \266.")
   print("This is a division sign: \xF7.")
   ```

   The example code uses various techniques to achieve the same end — to create a special character. Of course, you use control characters directly, as shown in the first line. Many special letters are accessible using a hexadecimal number that has two digits (as in the second and fifth lines). However, some require that you rely on Unicode numbers (which always require four digits), as shown in the third line. Octal values use three digits and have no special character associated with them, as shown in the fourth line.

3. Choose Run⇨Run Module.

You see a Python Shell window open. The application outputs the expected text and special characters, as shown in Figure 11-2.

The Python shell uses a standard character set across platforms, so the Python Shell should use the same special characters no matter which platform you test. However, when creating your application, make sure to test it on various platforms to see how the application will react. A character set on one platform may use different numbers for special characters than another platform does. In addition, user selection of character sets could have an impact on how special characters displayed by your application appear. Always make sure that you test special character usage completely.

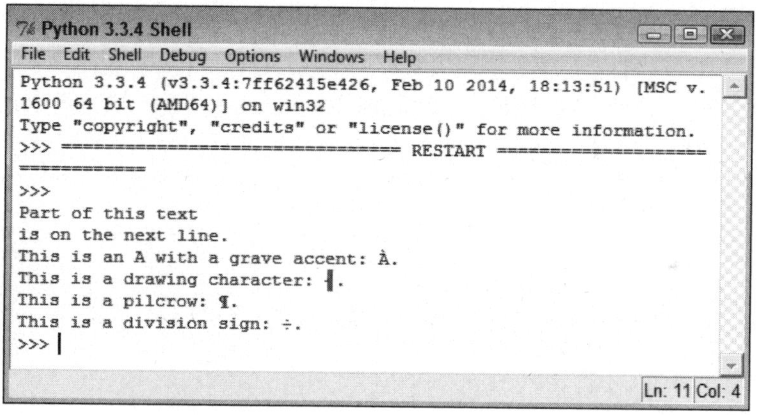

Figure 11-2:
Use special
characters
as needed
to present
special
information
or to format
the output.

```
7/6 Python 3.3.4 Shell
File  Edit  Shell  Debug  Options  Windows  Help
Python 3.3.4 (v3.3.4:7ff62415e426, Feb 10 2014, 18:13:51) [MSC v.
1600 64 bit (AMD64)] on win32
Type "copyright", "credits" or "license()" for more information.
>>> ================================ RESTART =====================
=============
>>>
Part of this text
is on the next line.
This is an A with a grave accent: À.
This is a drawing character: ▮.
This is a pilcrow: ¶.
This is a division sign: ÷.
>>> |
                                                            Ln: 11 Col: 4
```

Selecting Individual Characters

Earlier in the chapter, you discover that strings are made up of individual characters. They are, in fact, just like beads on a necklace — with each bead being an individual element of the whole string.

Python makes it possible to access individual characters in a string. This is an important feature because you can use it to create new strings that contain only part of the original. In addition, you can combine strings to create new results. The secret to this feature is the square bracket. You place a square bracket with a number in it after the name of the variable. Here's an example:

```
MyString = "Hello World"
print(MyString[0])
```

In this case, the output of the code is the letter *H*. Python strings are zero-based, which means they start with the number *0* and proceed from there. For example, if you were to type `print(MyString[1])`, the output would be the letter *e*.

You can also obtain a range of characters from a string. Simply provide the beginning and ending letter count separated by a colon in the square brackets. For example, `print(MyString[6:11])` would output the word World. The output would begin with letter 7 and end with letter 12 (remember that the index is zero based).

The following steps demonstrate some basic tasks that you can perform using Python's character-selection technique. This example also appears with the downloadable source code as `Characters.py`.

1. **Open a Python File window.**

   You see an editor in which you can type the example code.

2. **Type the following code into the window — pressing Enter after each line.**

   ```
   String1 = "Hello World"
   String2 = "Python is Fun!"

   print(String1[0])
   print(String1[0:5])
   print(String1[:5])
   print(String1[6:])

   String3 = String1[:6] + String2[:6]
   print(String3)

   print(String2[:7]*5)
   ```

The example begins by creating two strings. It then demonstrates various methods for using the index on the first string. Notice that you can leave out the beginning or ending number in a range if you want to work with the remainder of that string.

The next step is to combine two substrings. In this case, the code combines the beginning of `String1` with the beginning of `String2` to create `String3`.

The use of the + sign to combine two strings is called *concatenation*. It's one of the handier operators to remember when you're working with strings in an application.

The final step is to use a Python feature called *repetition*. You use repetition to make a number of copies of a string or substring.

3. Choose Run⇨Run Module.

You see a Python Shell window open. The applications outputs a series of substrings and string combinations, as shown in Figure 11-3.

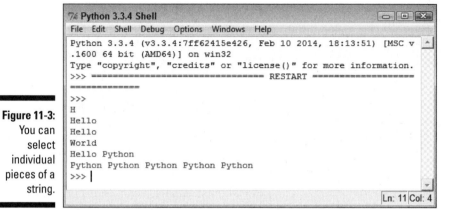

Figure 11-3:
You can select individual pieces of a string.

Slicing and Dicing Strings

Working with ranges of characters provides some degree of flexibility, but it doesn't provide you with the capability to actually manipulate the string content or discover anything about it. For example, you might want to change the characters to uppercase or determine whether the string contains all letters. Fortunately, Python has functions that help you perform tasks of this sort. Here are the most commonly used functions:

- ✔ capitalize(): Capitalizes the first letter of a string.

- ✔ center(*width, fillchar=" "*): Centers a string so that it fits within the number of spaces specified by *width*. If you supply a character for *fillchar*, the function uses that character. Otherwise, center() uses spaces to create a string of the desired width.

- ✔ expandtabs(*tabsize=8*): Expands tabs in a string by replacing the tab with the number of spaces specified by *tabsize*. The function defaults to 8 spaces per tab when *tabsize* isn't provided.

- ✔ isalnum(): Returns True when the string has at least one character and all characters are alphanumeric (letters or numbers).

- ✔ isalpha(): Returns True when the string has at least one character and all characters are alphabetic (letters only).

- ✔ isdecimal(): Returns True when a Unicode string contains only decimal characters.

- ✔ isdigit(): Returns True when a string contains only digits (numbers and not letters).

- ✔ islower(): Returns True when a string has at least one alphabetic character and all alphabetic characters are in lowercase.

- ✔ isnumeric(): Returns True when a Unicode string contains only numeric characters.

- ✔ isspace(): Returns True when a string contains only whitespace characters (which includes spaces, tabs, carriage returns, linefeeds, form feeds, and vertical tabs, but not the backspace).

- ✔ istitle(): Returns True when a string is cased for use as a title, such as *Hello World*. However, the function requires that even little words have the title case. For example, *Follow a Star* returns False, even though it's properly cased, but *Follow A Star* returns True.

- ✔ isupper(): Returns True when a string has at least one alphabetic character and all alphabetic characters are in uppercase.

- ✔ join(*seq*): Creates a string in which the base string is separated in turn by each character in *seq* in a repetitive fashion. For example, if you start with MyString = "Hello" and type print(MyString.join("!*!")), the output is !Hello*Hello!.

- ✔ len(*string*): Obtains the length of *string*.

- ✔ ljust(*width, fillchar=" "*): Left justifies a string so that it fits within the number of spaces specified by *width*. If you supply a character for *fillchar*, the function uses that character. Otherwise, ljust() uses spaces to create a string of the desired width.

- ✔ lower(): Converts all uppercase letters in a string to lowercase letters.

- ✔ lstrip(): Removes all leading whitespace characters in a string.

- ✔ max(*str*): Returns the character that has the maximum numeric value in *str*. For example, *a* would have a larger numeric value than *A*.

- ✔ min(*str*): Returns the character that has the minimum numeric value in *str*. For example, *A* would have a smaller numeric value than *a*.

- ✔ rjust(*width, fillchar=" "*): Right justifies a string so that it fits within the number of spaces specified by *width*. If you supply a character for *fillchar*, the function uses that character. Otherwise, rjust() uses spaces to create a string of the desired width.

- ✔ rstrip(): Removes all trailing whitespace characters in a string.

- ✔ split(*str=" ", num=string.count(str)*): Splits a string into substrings using the delimiter specified by *str* (when supplied). The default is to use a space as a delimiter. Consequently, if your string contains *A Fine Day*, the output would be three substrings consisting of *A*, *Fine*, and *Day*. You use *num* to define the number of substrings to return. The default is to return every substring that the function can produce.

✔ splitlines(*num=string.count('\n')*): Splits a string that contains newline (\n) characters into individual strings. Each break occurs at the newline character. The output has the newline characters removed. You can use *num* to specify the number of strings to return.

✔ strip(): Removes all leading and trailing whitespace characters in a string.

✔ swapcase(): Inverts the case for each alphabetic character in a string.

✔ title(): Returns a string in which the initial letter in each word is in uppercase and all remaining letters in the word are in lowercase.

✔ upper(): Converts all lowercase letters in a string to uppercase letters.

✔ zfill (*width*): Returns a string that is left-padded with zeros so that the resulting string is the size of *width*. This function is designed for use with strings containing numeric values. It retains the original sign information (if any) supplied with the number.

Playing with these functions a bit can help you understand them better. The following steps create an example that demonstrates some of the tasks you can perform using these functions. This example also appears with the downloadable source code as Functions.py.

1. **Open a Python File window.**

   You see an editor in which you can type the example code.

2. **Type the following code into the window — pressing Enter after each line:**

```python
MyString = "  Hello World  "

print(MyString.upper())

print(MyString.strip())
print(MyString.center(21, "*"))
print(MyString.strip().center(21, "*"))

print(MyString.isdigit())
print(MyString.istitle())

print(max(MyString))

print(MyString.split())
print(MyString.split()[0])
```

The code begins by creating MyString, which includes spaces before and after the text so that you can see how space-related functions work. The initial task is to convert all the characters to uppercase.

Removing extra space is a common task in application development. The strip() function performs this task well. The center() function lets you add padding to both the left and right side of a string so that it consumes a desired amount of space. When you combine the strip() and center() functions, the output is different from when you use the center() function alone.

You can combine functions to produce a desired result. Python executes each of the functions one at a time from left to right. The order in which the functions appear will affect the output, and developers commonly make the mistake of putting the functions in the wrong order. If your output is different from what you expected, try changing the function order.

Some functions work on the string as an input rather than on the string instance. The max() function falls into this category. If you had typed MyString.max(), Python would have displayed an error. The bulleted list that appears earlier in this section shows which functions require this sort of string input.

When working with functions that produce a list as an output, you can access an individual member by providing an index to it. The example shows how to use split() to split the string into substrings. It then shows how to access just the first substring in the list. You find out more about working with lists in Chapter 12.

3. **Choose Run⇨Run Module.**

   You see a Python Shell window open. The application outputs a number of modified strings, as shown in Figure 11-4.

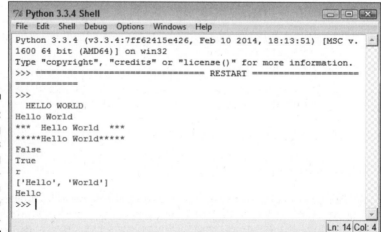

Figure 11-4: Using functions makes string manipulation a lot more flexible.

Locating a Value in a String

There are times when you need to locate specific information in a string. For example, you may want to know whether a string contains the word Hello in it. One of the essential purposes behind creating and maintaining data is to be able to search it later to locate specific bits of information. Strings are no different — they're most useful when you can find what you need quickly and without any problems. Python provides a number of functions for searching strings. Here are the most commonly used functions:

- ✔ `count(str, beg= 0, end=len(string))`: Counts how many times *str* occurs in a string. You can limit the search by specifying a beginning index using *beg* or an ending index using *end*.

- ✔ `endswith(suffix, beg=0, end=len(string))`: Returns True when a string ends with the characters specified by *suffix*. You can limit the check by specifying a beginning index using *beg* or an ending index using *end*.

- ✔ `find(str, beg=0, end=len(string))`: Determines whether *str* occurs in a string and outputs the index of the location. You can limit the search by specifying a beginning index using *beg* or a ending index using *end*.

- ✔ `index(str, beg=0, end=len(string))`: Provides the same functionality as `find()`, but raises an exception when *str* isn't found.

- ✔ `replace(old, new [, max])`: Replaces all occurrences of the character sequence specified by *old* in a string with the character sequence specified by *new*. You can limit the number of replacements by specifying a value for *max*.

- ✔ `rfind(str, beg=0, end=len(string))`: Provides the same functionality as `find()`, but searches backward from the end of the string instead of the beginning.

- ✔ `rindex(str, beg=0, end=len(string))`: Provides the same functionality as `index()`, but searches backward from the end of the string instead of the beginning.

- ✔ `startswith(prefix, beg=0, end=len(string))`: Returns True when a string begins with the characters specified by *prefix*. You can limit the check by specifying a beginning index using *beg* or an ending index using *end*.

Finding the data that you need is an essential programming task — one that is required no matter what kind of application you create. The following steps help you create an example that demonstrates the use of search functionality within strings. This example also appears with the downloadable source code as `SearchString.py`.

1. **Open a Python File window.**

   You see an editor in which you can type the example code.

2. **Type the following code into the window — pressing Enter after each line:**

   ```python
   SearchMe = "The apple is red and the berry is blue!"

   print(SearchMe.find("is"))
   print(SearchMe.rfind("is"))

   print(SearchMe.count("is"))

   print(SearchMe.startswith("The"))
   print(SearchMe.endswith("The"))

   print(SearchMe.replace("apple", "car")
        .replace("berry", "truck"))
   ```

   The example begins by creating `SearchMe`, a string with two instances of the word *is*. The two instances are important because they demonstrate how searches differ depending on where you start. When using `find()`, the example starts from the beginning of the string. By contrast, `rfind()` starts from the end of the string.

   Of course, you won't always know how many times a certain set of characters appears in a string. The `count()` function lets you determine this value.

   Depending on the kind of data you work with, sometimes the data is heavily formatted and you can use a particular pattern to your advantage. For example, you can determine whether a particular string (or substring) ends or begins with a specific sequence of characters. You could just as easily use this technique to look for a part number.

   The final bit of code replaces *apple* with *car* and *berry* with *truck*. Notice the technique used to place the code on two lines. In some cases, your code will need to appear on multiple lines to make it more readable.

3. **Choose Run⇨Run Module.**

   You see a Python Shell window open. The application displays the output shown in Figure 11-5. Notice especially that the searches returned different indexes based on where they started in the string. Using the correct function when performing searches is essential to ensure that you get the results you expected.

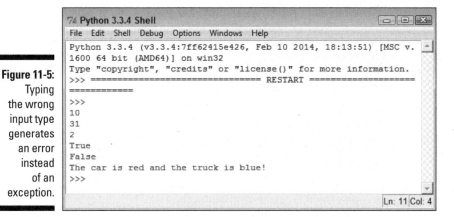

Figure 11-5:
Typing
the wrong
input type
generates
an error
instead
of an
exception.

Formatting Strings

You can format strings in a number of ways using Python. The main emphasis of formatting is to present the string in a form that is both pleasing to the user and easy to understand. Formatting doesn't mean adding special fonts or effects in this case, but refers merely to the presentation of the data. For example, the user might want a fixed-point number rather than a decimal number as output.

You have quite a few ways to format strings and you see a number of them as the book progresses. However, the focus of most formatting is the `format()` function. You create a formatting specification as part of the string and then use the `format()` function to add data to that string. A format specification may be as simple as two curly brackets { } that specify a placeholder for data. You can number the placeholder to create special effects. For example, {0} would contain the first data element in a string. When the data elements are numbered, you can even repeat them so that the same data appears more than once in the string.

The formatting specification follows a colon. When you want to create just a formatting specification, the curly brackets contain just the colon and whatever formatting you want to use. For example, {:f} would create a fixed-point number as output. If you want to number the entries, the number that precedes the colon: {0:f} creates a fixed-point number output for data element one. The formatting specification follows this form, with the italicized elements serving as placeholders here:

```
[[fill]align] [sign] [#] [0] [width] [,] [.precision] [type]
```

The specification at `https://docs.python.org/3/library/string.html` provides you with the in-depth details, but here's an overview of what the various entries mean:

- **fill:** Defines the fill character used when displaying data that is too small to fit within the assigned space.

- **align:** Specifies the alignment of data within the display space. You can use these alignments:

  - <: Left aligned

  - >: Right aligned

  - ^: Centered

  - =: Justified

- **sign:** Determines the use of signs for the output:

  - +: Positive numbers have a plus sign and negative numbers have a minus sign.

  - -: Negative numbers have a minus sign.

  - <space>: Positive numbers are preceded by a space and negative numbers have a minus sign.

- **#:** Specifies that the output should use the alternative display format for numbers. For example, hexadecimal numbers will have a 0x prefix added to them.

- **0:** Specifies that the output should be sign aware and padded with zeros as needed to provide consistent output.

- **width:** Determines the full width of the data field (even if the data won't fit in the space provided).

- **,:** Specifies that numeric data should have commas as a thousands separator.

- **.precision:** Determines the number of characters after the decimal point.

- **type:** Specifies the output type, even if the input type doesn't match. The types are split into three groups:

  - *String:* Use an s or nothing at all to specify a string.

  - *Integer:* The integer types are as follows: b (binary); c (character); d (decimal); o (octal); x (hexadecimal with lowercase letters); X (hexadecimal with uppercase letters); and n (locale-sensitive decimal that uses the appropriate characters for the thousands separator).

- *Floating point:* The floating-point types are as follows: e (exponent using a lowercase e as a separator); E (exponent using an uppercase E as a separator); f (lowercase fixed point); F (uppercase fixed point); g (lowercase general format); G (uppercase general format); n (local-sensitive general format that uses the appropriate characters for the decimal and thousands separators); and % (percentage).

The formatting specification elements must appear in the correct order or Python won't know what to do with them. If you specify the alignment before the fill character, Python displays an error message rather than performing the required formatting. The following steps help you see how the formatting specification works and demonstrate the order you need to follow in using the various formatting specification criteria. This example also appears with the downloadable source code as `Formatted.py`.

1. **Open a Python File window.**

   You see an editor in which you can type the example code.

2. **Type the following code into the window — pressing Enter after each line:**

```
Formatted = "{:d}"
print(Formatted.format(7000))

Formatted = "{:,d}"
print(Formatted.format(7000))

Formatted = "{:^15,d}"
print(Formatted.format(7000))

Formatted = "{:*^15,d}"
print(Formatted.format(7000))

Formatted = "{:*^15.2f}"
print(Formatted.format(7000))

Formatted = "{:*>15X}"
print(Formatted.format(7000))

Formatted = "{:*<#15x}"
print(Formatted.format(7000))

Formatted = "A {0} {1} and a {0} {2}."
print(Formatted.format("blue", "car", "truck"))
```

The example starts simply with a field formatted as a decimal value. It then adds a thousands separator to the output. The next step is to make the field wider than needed to hold the data and to center the data within the field. Finally, the field has an asterisk added to pad the output.

Of course, there are other data types in the example. The next step is to display the same data in fixed-point format. The example also shows the output in both uppercase and lowercase hexadecimal format. The uppercase output is right aligned and the lowercase output is left aligned.

Finally, the example shows how you can use numbered fields to your advantage. In this case, it creates an interesting string output that repeats one of the input values.

3. Choose Run⇨Run Module.

You see a Python Shell window open. The application outputs data in various forms, as shown in Figure 11-6.

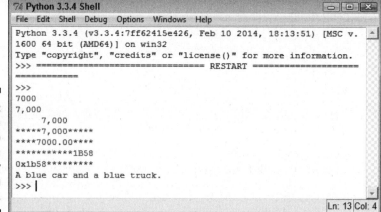

Figure 11-6: Use formatting to present data in precisely the form you want.

```
74 Python 3.3.4 Shell                              □ □ ▣
File  Edit  Shell  Debug  Options  Windows  Help
Python 3.3.4 (v3.3.4:7ff62415e426, Feb 10 2014, 18:13:51) [MSC v.
1600 64 bit (AMD64)] on win32
Type "copyright", "credits" or "license()" for more information.
>>> ================================ RESTART ====================
=============
>>>
7000
7,000
      7,000
*****7,000*****
****7000.00****
***********1B58
0x1b58*********
A blue car and a blue truck.
>>> |
                                              Ln: 13 Col: 4
```

Chapter 12

Managing Lists

• •

In This Chapter

▶ Defining why lists are important

▶ Generating lists

▶ Looking through lists

▶ Working with list items sequentially

▶ Changing list content

▶ Locating specific information in lists

▶ Putting list items in order

▶ Using the Counter object to your advantage

• •

A lot of people lose sight of the fact that most programming techniques are based on the real world. Part of the reason is that programmers often use terms that other people don't to describe these real-world objects. For example, most people would call a place to store something a box or a cupboard — but programmers insist on using the term *variable*. Lists are different. Everyone makes lists and uses them in various ways to perform an abundance of tasks. In fact, you're probably surrounded by lists of various sorts where you're sitting right now as you read this book. So, this chapter is about something you already use quite a lot. The only difference is that you need to think of lists in the same way Python does.

You may read that lists are hard to work with. The reason that some people find working with lists difficult is that they're not used to actually thinking about the lists they create. When you create a list, you simply write items down in whatever order makes sense to you. Sometimes you rewrite the list when you're done to put it in a specific order. In other cases, you use your finger as a guide when going down the list to make looking through it easier. The point is that everything you normally do with lists is also doable within Python. The difference is that you must now actually think about what you're doing in order to make Python understand what you want done.

Lists are incredibly important in Python. This chapter introduces you to the concepts used to create, manage, search, and print lists (among other tasks). When you complete the chapter, you can use lists to make your Python applications more robust, faster, and more flexible. In fact, you'll wonder how you ever got along without using lists in the past. The important thing to keep in mind is that you have already used lists most of your life. There really isn't any difference now except that you must now think about the actions that you normally take for granted when managing your own lists.

Organizing Information in an Application

People create lists to organize information and make it easier to access and change. You use lists in Python for the same reason. In many situations, you really do need some sort of organizational aid to hold data. For example, you might want to create a single place to look for days of the week or months of the year. The names of these items would appear in a list, much as they would if you needed to commit them to paper in the real world. The following sections describe lists and how they work in more detail.

Defining organization using lists

The Python specification defines a list as a kind of sequence. *Sequences* simply provide some means of allowing multiple data items to exist together in a single storage unit, but as separate entities. Think about one of those large mail holders you see in apartment buildings. A single mail holder contains a number of small mailboxes, each of which can contain mail. Python supports other kinds of sequences as well (Chapter 13 discusses a number of these sequences):

- Tuples
- Dictionaries
- Stacks
- Queues
- Deques

Of all the sequences, lists are the easiest to understand and are the most directly related to a real-world object. Working with lists helps you become better able to work with other kinds of sequences that provide greater functionality and improved flexibility. The point is that the data is stored in a list much as you would write it on a piece of paper — one item comes after another, as shown in Figure 12-1. The list has a beginning, a middle, and an end. As shown in the figure, the items are numbered. (Even if you might not normally number them in real life, Python always numbers the items for you.)

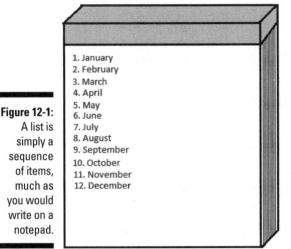

Figure 12-1:
A list is
simply a
sequence
of items,
much as
you would
write on a
notepad.

1. January
2. February
3. March
4. April
5. May
6. June
7. July
8. August
9. September
10. October
11. November
12. December

Understanding how computers view lists

The computer doesn't view lists in the same way that you do. It doesn't have an internal notepad and use a pen to write on it. A computer has memory. The computer stores each item in a list in a separate memory location, as shown in Figure 12-2. The memory is contiguous, so as you add new items, they're added to the next location in memory.

Figure 12-2:
Each item
added to a
list takes the
next position
in memory.

January	February	March	...	October	November	December

In many respects, the computer uses something like a mailbox to hold your list. The list as a whole is the mail holder. As you add items, the computer places it in the next mailbox within the mail holder.

Just as the mailboxes are numbered in a mail holder, the memory slots used for a list are numbered. The numbers begin with 0, not with 1 as you might expect. Each mailbox receives the next number in line. A mail holder with the months of the year would contain 12 mailboxes. The mailboxes would be numbered from 0 to 11 (not 12, as you might think). It's essential to get the numbering scheme down as quickly as possible because even experienced developers get into trouble by using 1 and not 0 as a starting point at times.

Depending on what sort of information you place in each mailbox, the mailboxes need not be of the same size. Python lets you store a string in one mailbox, an integer in another, and a floating-point value in another. The computer doesn't know what kind of information is stored in each mailbox and it doesn't care. All the computer sees is one long list of numbers that could be anything. Python performs all the work required to treat the data elements according to the right type and to ensure that when you request item five, you actually get item five.

In general, it's good practice to create lists of like items to make the data easier to manage. When creating a list of all integers, for example, rather than of mixed data, you can make assumptions about the information and don't have to spend nearly as much time checking it. However, in some situations, you might need to mix data. Many other programming languages require that lists have just one type of data, but Python offers the flexibility of using mixed data sorts. Just remember that using mixed data in a list means that you must determine the data type when retrieving the information in order to work with the data correctly. Treating a string as an integer would cause problems in your application.

Creating Lists

As in real life, before you can do anything with a list, you must create it. As previously stated, Python lists can mix types. However, it's always a best practice to restrict a list to a single type when you can. The following steps demonstrate how to create Python lists.

1. **Open a Python Shell window.**

   You see the familiar Python prompt.

2. **Type** List1 = ["One", 1, "Two", True] **and press Enter.**

   Python creates a list named `List1` for you. This list contains two string values (One and Two), an integer value (1), and a Boolean value (True). Of course, you can't actually see anything because Python processes the command without saying anything.

Notice that each data type that you type is a different color. When you use the default color scheme, Python displays strings in green, numbers in black, and Boolean values in orange. The color of an entry is a cue that tells you whether you have typed the entry correctly, which helps reduce errors when creating a list.

3. Type print(List1) **and press Enter.**

You see the content of the list as a whole, as shown in Figure 12-3. Notice that the string entries appear in single quotes, even though you typed them using double quotes. Strings can appear in either single quotes or double quotes in Python.

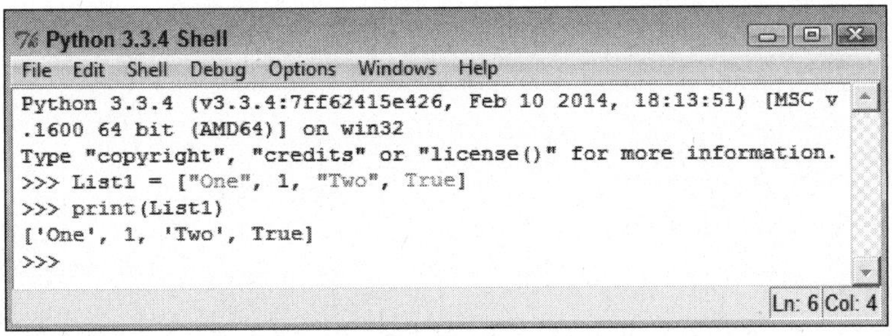

Figure 12-3: Python displays the content of List1.

```
7% Python 3.3.4 Shell
File  Edit  Shell  Debug  Options  Windows  Help
Python 3.3.4 (v3.3.4:7ff62415e426, Feb 10 2014, 18:13:51) [MSC v
.1600 64 bit (AMD64)] on win32
Type "copyright", "credits" or "license()" for more information.
>>> List1 = ["One", 1, "Two", True]
>>> print(List1)
['One', 1, 'Two', True]
>>>
                                                        Ln: 6 Col: 4
```

4. Type dir(List1) **and press Enter.**

Python displays a list of actions that you can perform using lists, as shown in Figure 12-4. Notice that the output is actually a list. So, you're using a list to determine what you can do with another list.

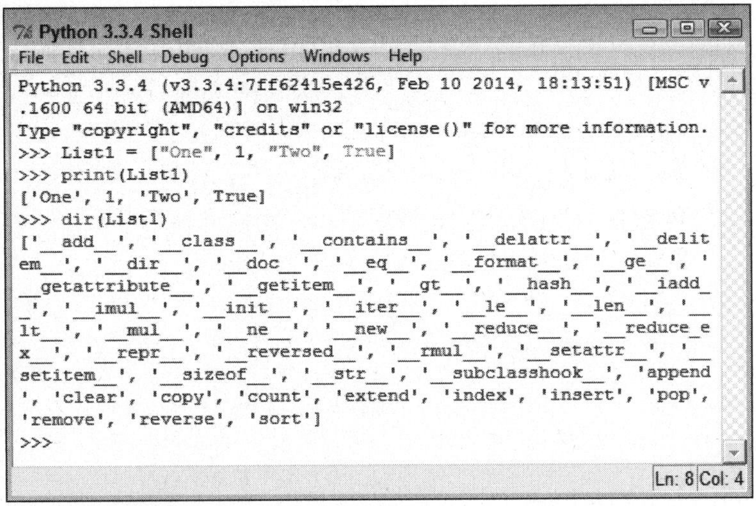

Figure 12-4: Python provides a listing of the actions you can perform using a list.

```
7% Python 3.3.4 Shell
File  Edit  Shell  Debug  Options  Windows  Help
Python 3.3.4 (v3.3.4:7ff62415e426, Feb 10 2014, 18:13:51) [MSC v
.1600 64 bit (AMD64)] on win32
Type "copyright", "credits" or "license()" for more information.
>>> List1 = ["One", 1, "Two", True]
>>> print(List1)
['One', 1, 'Two', True]
>>> dir(List1)
['__add__', '__class__', '__contains__', '__delattr__', '__delit
em__', '__dir__', '__doc__', '__eq__', '__format__', '__ge__', '
__getattribute__', '__getitem__', '__gt__', '__hash__', '__iadd_
_', '__imul__', '__init__', '__iter__', '__le__', '__len__', '__
lt__', '__mul__', '__ne__', '__new__', '__reduce__', '__reduce_e
x__', '__repr__', '__reversed__', '__rmul__', '__setattr__', '__
setitem__', '__sizeof__', '__str__', '__subclasshook__', 'append
', 'clear', 'copy', 'count', 'extend', 'index', 'insert', 'pop',
'remove', 'reverse', 'sort']
>>>
                                                        Ln: 8 Col: 4
```

As you start working with objects of greater complexity, you need to remember that the `dir()` command always shows what tasks you can perform using that object. The actions that appear without underscores are the main actions that you can perform using a list. These actions are the following:

- append
- clear
- copy
- count
- extend
- index
- insert
- pop
- remove
- reverse
- sort

5. **Close the Python Shell window.**

Accessing Lists

After you create a list, you want to access the information it contains. An object isn't particularly useful if you can't at least access the information it contains. The previous section shows how to use the `print()` and `dir()` functions to interact with a list, but there are other ways to perform the task, as described in the following steps.

1. **Open a Python Shell window.**

   You see the familiar Python prompt.

2. **Type** List1 = ["One", 1, "Two", True] **and press Enter.**

   Python creates a list named `List1` for you.

3. Type **List1[1] and press Enter.**

You see the value 1 as output, as shown in Figure 12-5. The use of a number within a set of square brackets is called an index. Python always uses zero-based indexes, so asking for the element at index 1 means getting the second element in the list.

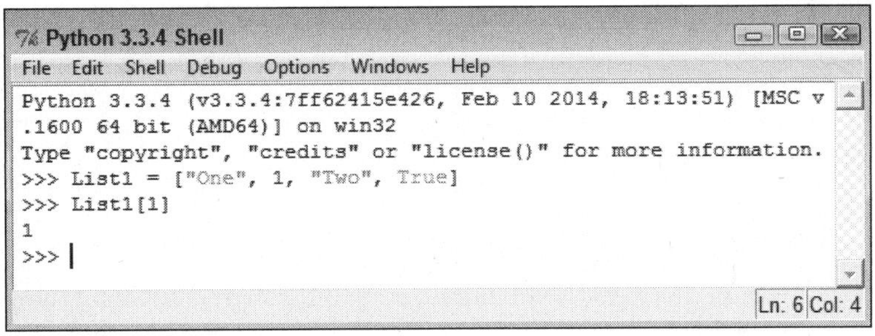

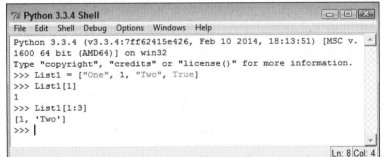

Figure 12-5:
Make sure
to use
the cor-
rect index
number.

4. Type List1[1:3] **and press Enter.**

You see a range of values that includes two elements, as shown in Figure 12-6. When typing a range, the end of the range is always one greater than the number of elements returned. In this case, that means that you get elements 1 and 2, not elements 1 through 3 as you might expect.

Figure 12-6:
Ranges
return mul-
tiple values.

5. Type List1[1:] **and press Enter.**

You see all the elements, starting from element 1 to the end of the list, as shown in Figure 12-7. A range can have a blank ending number, which simply means to print the rest of the list.

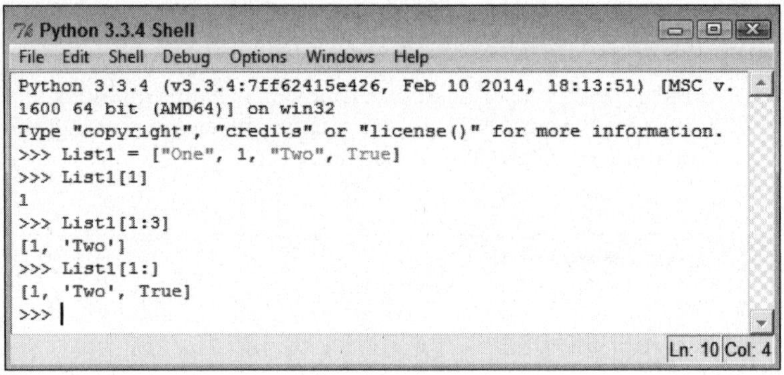

Figure 12-7:
Leaving the ending number of a range blank prints the rest of the list.

```
74 Python 3.3.4 Shell
File  Edit  Shell  Debug  Options  Windows  Help
Python 3.3.4 (v3.3.4:7ff62415e426, Feb 10 2014, 18:13:51) [MSC v.
1600 64 bit (AMD64)] on win32
Type "copyright", "credits" or "license()" for more information.
>>> List1 = ["One", 1, "Two", True]
>>> List1[1]
1
>>> List1[1:3]
[1, 'Two']
>>> List1[1:]
[1, 'Two', True]
>>> |
                                                          Ln: 10 Col: 4
```

6. **Type** List1[:3] **and press Enter.**

   Python displays the elements from 0 through 2. Leaving the start of a range blank means that you want to start with element 0, as shown in Figure 12-8.

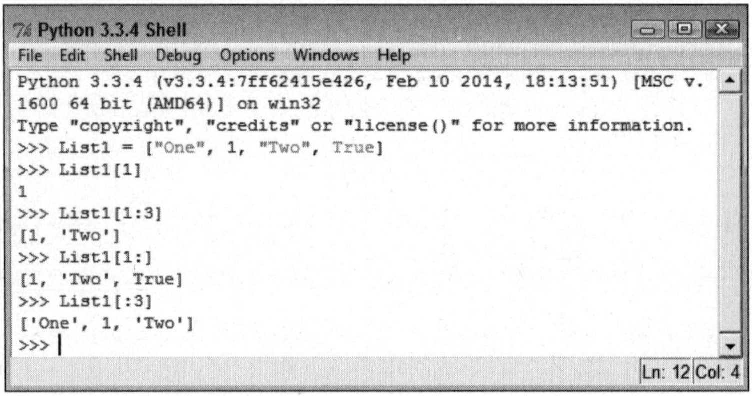

Figure 12-8:
Leaving the beginning number of a range blank prints from element 0.

```
74 Python 3.3.4 Shell
File  Edit  Shell  Debug  Options  Windows  Help
Python 3.3.4 (v3.3.4:7ff62415e426, Feb 10 2014, 18:13:51) [MSC v.
1600 64 bit (AMD64)] on win32
Type "copyright", "credits" or "license()" for more information.
>>> List1 = ["One", 1, "Two", True]
>>> List1[1]
1
>>> List1[1:3]
[1, 'Two']
>>> List1[1:]
[1, 'Two', True]
>>> List1[:3]
['One', 1, 'Two']
>>> |
                                                          Ln: 12 Col: 4
```

7. **Close the Python Shell window.**

Even though it's really confusing to do so, you can use negative indexes with Python. Instead of working from the left, Python will work from the right and backward. For example, if you have List1 = ["One", 1, "Two", True] and type List1[-2], you get Two as output. Likewise, typing List[-3] results in an output of 1. The rightmost element is element -1 in this case.

Looping through Lists

To automate the processing of list elements, you need some way to loop through the list. The easiest way to perform this task is to rely on a `for` statement, as described in the following steps. This example also appears with the downloadable source code as `ListLoop.py`.

1. **Open a Python File window.**

   You see an editor in which you can type the example code.

2. **Type the following code into the window — pressing Enter after each line:**

   ```
   List1 = [0, 1, 2, 3, 4, 5]

   for Item in List1:
       print(Item)
   ```

   The example begins by creating a list consisting of numeric values. It then uses a `for` loop to obtain each element in turn and print it onscreen.

3. **Choose Run⇨Run Module.**

   You see a Python Shell window open. The output shows the individual values in the list, one on each line, as shown in Figure 12-9.

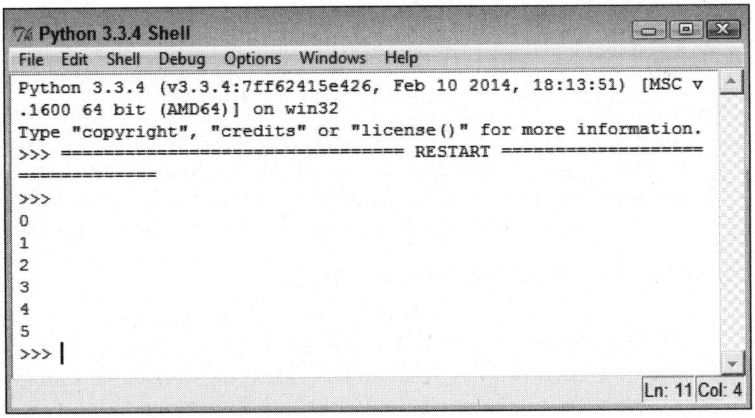

Figure 12-9:
A loop
makes it
easy to
obtain a
copy of
each item
and process
it as needed.

```
Python 3.3.4 Shell

File  Edit  Shell  Debug  Options  Windows  Help
Python 3.3.4 (v3.3.4:7ff62415e426, Feb 10 2014, 18:13:51) [MSC v
.1600 64 bit (AMD64)] on win32
Type "copyright", "credits" or "license()" for more information.
>>> ================================ RESTART ====================
==============
>>>
0
1
2
3
4
5
>>> |
                                                         Ln: 11 Col: 4
```

Modifying Lists

You can modify the content of a list as needed. Modifying a list means to change a particular entry, add a new entry, or remove an existing entry. To perform these tasks, you must sometimes read an entry. The concept of modification is found within the acronym CRUD, which stands for Create, Read, Update, and Delete. Here are the list functions associated with CRUD:

- ✔ append(): Adds a new entry to the end of the list.

- ✔ clear(): Removes all entries from the list.

- ✔ copy(): Creates a copy of the current list and places it in a new list.

- ✔ extend(): Adds items from an existing list and into the current list.

- ✔ insert(): Adds a new entry to the position specified in the list.

- ✔ pop(): Removes an entry from the end of the list.

- ✔ remove(): Removes an entry from the specified position in the list.

The following steps show how to perform modification tasks with lists. This is a hands-on exercise. As the book progresses, you see these same functions used within application code. The purpose of this exercise is to help you gain a feel for how lists work.

1. **Open a Python Shell window.**

    You see the familiar Python prompt.

2. **Type List1 = [] and press Enter.**

    Python creates a list named List1 for you.

    Notice that the square brackets are empty. List1 doesn't contain any entries. You can create empty lists that you fill with information later. In fact, this is precisely how many lists start because you usually don't know what information they will contain until the user interacts with the list.

3. **Type len(List1) and press Enter.**

    The len() function outputs 0, as shown in Figure 12-10. When creating an application, you can check for an empty list using the len() function. If a list is empty, you can't perform tasks such as removing elements from it because there is nothing to remove.

4. **Type List1.append(1) and press Enter.**

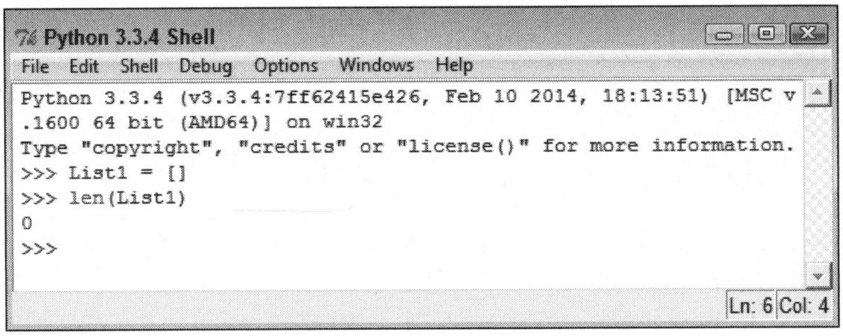

Figure 12-10:
Check for empty lists as needed in your application.

5. **Type** len(List1) **and press Enter.**

The len() function now reports a length of 1.

6. **Type** List1[0] **and press Enter.**

You see the value stored in element 0 of List1, as shown in Figure 12-11.

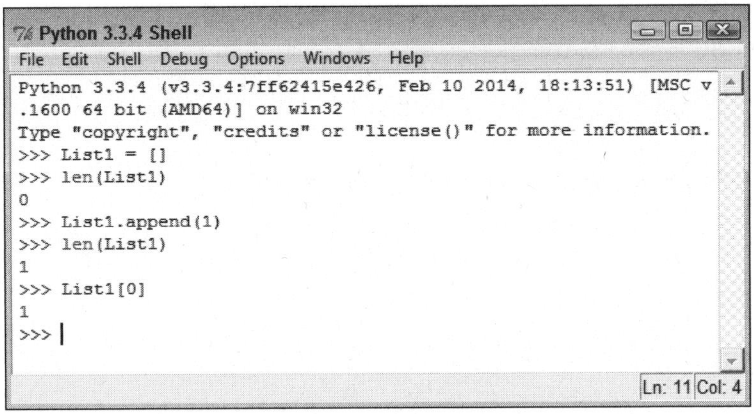

Figure 12-11:
Appending an element changes the list length and stores the value at the end of the list.

7. **Type** List1.insert(0, 2) **and press Enter.**

The insert() function requires two arguments. The first argument is the index of the insertion, which is element 0 in this case. The second argument is the object you want inserted at that point, which is 2 in this case.

8. **Type** List1 **and press Enter.**

Python has added another element to List1. However, using the insert() function lets you add the new element before the first element, as shown in Figure 12-12.

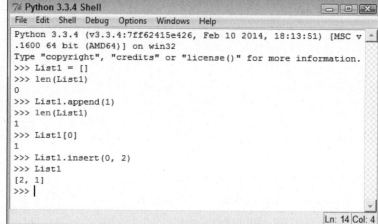

Figure 12-12: Inserting provides flexibility in deciding where to add an element.

```
7½ Python 3.3.4 Shell                                    ▢ ▣ ✖
File  Edit  Shell  Debug  Options  Windows  Help
Python 3.3.4 (v3.3.4:7ff62415e426, Feb 10 2014, 18:13:51) [MSC v
.1600 64 bit (AMD64)] on win32
Type "copyright", "credits" or "license()" for more information.
>>> List1 = []
>>> len(List1)
0
>>> List1.append(1)
>>> len(List1)
1
>>> List1[0]
1
>>> List1.insert(0, 2)
>>> List1
[2, 1]
>>> |
                                                  Ln: 14 Col: 4
```

9. **Type** List2 = List1.copy() **and press Enter.**

   The new list, List2, is a precise copy of List1. Copying is often used to create a temporary version of an existing list so that a user can make temporary modifications to it rather than to the original list. When the user is done, the application can either delete the temporary list or copy it to the original list.

10. **Type** List1.extend(List2) **and press Enter.**

    Python copies all the elements in List2 to the end of List1. Extending is commonly used to consolidate two lists.

11. **Type** List1 **and press Enter.**

    You see that the copy and extend processes have worked. List1 now contains the values 2, 1, 2, and 1, as shown in Figure 12-13.

12. **Type** List1.pop() **and press Enter.**

    Python displays a value of 1, as shown in Figure 12-14. The 1 was stored at the end of the list, and pop() always removes values from the end.

13. **Type** List1.remove(1) **and press Enter.**

    This time, Python removes the item at element 1. Unlike the pop() function, the remove() function doesn't display the value of the item it removed.

14. **Type** List1.clear() **and press Enter.**

    Using clear() means that the list shouldn't contain any elements now.

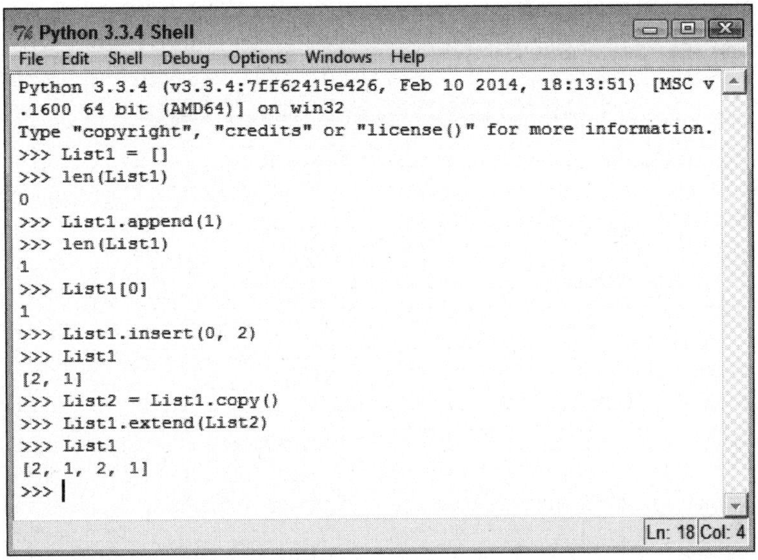

Figure 12-13:
Copying and
extending
provide
methods for
moving a
lot of data
around
quickly.

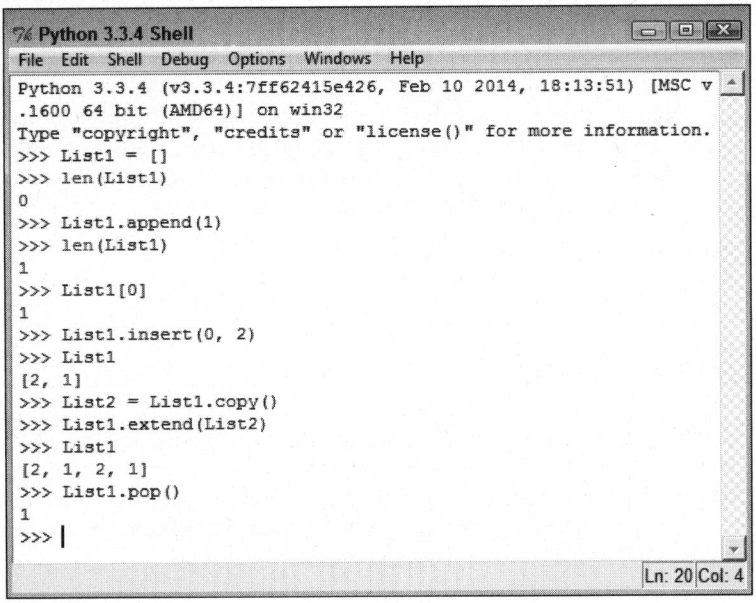

```
7% Python 3.3.4 Shell
File  Edit  Shell  Debug  Options  Windows  Help
Python 3.3.4 (v3.3.4:7ff62415e426, Feb 10 2014, 18:13:51) [MSC v
.1600 64 bit (AMD64)] on win32
Type "copyright", "credits" or "license()" for more information.
>>> List1 = []
>>> len(List1)
0
>>> List1.append(1)
>>> len(List1)
1
>>> List1[0]
1
>>> List1.insert(0, 2)
>>> List1
[2, 1]
>>> List2 = List1.copy()
>>> List1.extend(List2)
>>> List1
[2, 1, 2, 1]
>>> |
                                                    Ln: 18 Col: 4
```

Figure 12-14:
Use pop()
to remove
elements
from the end
of a list.

```
7% Python 3.3.4 Shell
File  Edit  Shell  Debug  Options  Windows  Help
Python 3.3.4 (v3.3.4:7ff62415e426, Feb 10 2014, 18:13:51) [MSC v
.1600 64 bit (AMD64)] on win32
Type "copyright", "credits" or "license()" for more information.
>>> List1 = []
>>> len(List1)
0
>>> List1.append(1)
>>> len(List1)
1
>>> List1[0]
1
>>> List1.insert(0, 2)
>>> List1
[2, 1]
>>> List2 = List1.copy()
>>> List1.extend(List2)
>>> List1
[2, 1, 2, 1]
>>> List1.pop()
1
>>> |
                                                    Ln: 20 Col: 4
```

Using operators with lists

Lists can also rely on operators to perform certain tasks. For example, if you want to create a list that contains four copies of the word *Hello*, you could use `MyList = ["Hello"] * 4` to fill it. A list allows repetition as needed. The multiplication operator (*) tells Python how many times to repeat a given item. It's essential to remember that every repeated element is separate, so what `MyList` contains is `['Hello', 'Hello', 'Hello', 'Hello']`.

You can also use concatenation to fill a list. For example, using `MyList = ["Hello"] + ["World"] + ["!"] * 4` creates six elements in `MyList`. The first element is Hello, followed by World and ending with four elements with one exclamation mark (!) in each element.

The membership operator (`in`) also works with lists. This chapter uses a straightforward and easy-to-understand method of searching lists (the recommended approach). However, you can use the membership operator to make things shorter and simpler by using `"Hello" in MyList`. Assuming that you have your list filled with `['Hello', 'World', '!', '!', '!', '!']`, the output of this statement is `True`.

15. Type len(List1) **and press Enter.**

You see that the output is 0. `List1` is definitely empty. At this point, you've tried all the modification methods that Python provides for lists. Work with `List1` some more using these various functions until you feel comfortable making changes to the list.

16. Close the Python Shell window.

Searching Lists

Modifying a list isn't very easy when you don't know what the list contains. The ability to search a list is essential if you want to make maintenance tasks easier. The following steps help you create an application that demonstrates the ability to search a list for specific values. This example also appears with the downloadable source code as `SearchList.py`.

1. Open a Python File window.

You see an editor in which you can type the example code.

2. Type the following code into the window — pressing Enter after each line:

```
Colors = ["Red", "Orange", "Yellow", "Green", "Blue"]

ColorSelect = ""

while str.upper(ColorSelect) != "QUIT":
    ColorSelect = input("Please type a color name: ")
    if (Colors.count(ColorSelect) >= 1):
        print("The color exists in the list!")
    elif (str.upper(ColorSelect) != "QUIT"):
        print("The list doesn't contain the color.")
```

The example begins by creating a list named `Colors` that contains color names. It also creates a variable named `ColorSelect` to hold the name of the color that the user wants to find. The application then enters a loop where the user is asked for a color name that is placed in `ColorSelect`. As long as this variable doesn't contain the word QUIT, the application continues a loop that requests input.

Whenever the user inputs a color name, the application asks the list to count the number of occurrences of that color. When the value is equal to or greater than one, the list does contain the color and an appropriate message appears onscreen. On the other hand, when the list doesn't contain the requested color, an alternative message appears onscreen.

Notice how this example uses an `elif` clause to check whether `ColorSelect` contains the word QUIT. This technique of including an `elif` clause ensures that the application doesn't output a message when the user wants to quit the application. You need to use similar techniques when you create your applications to avoid potential user confusion or even data loss (when the application performs a task the user didn't actually request).

3. Choose Run➪Run Module.

You see a Python Shell window open. The application asks you to type a color name.

4. Type Blue **and press Enter.**

You see a message telling you that the color does exist in the list, as shown in Figure 12-15.

5. Type Purple **and press Enter.**

You see a message telling you that the color doesn't exist, as shown in Figure 12-16.

6. Type Quit **and press Enter.**

The application ends. Notice that the application displays neither a success nor a failure message.

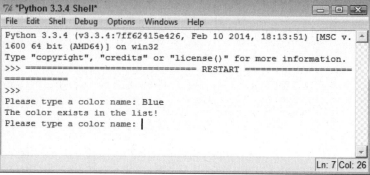

Figure 12-15:
Colors that
exist in the
list receive
the success
message.

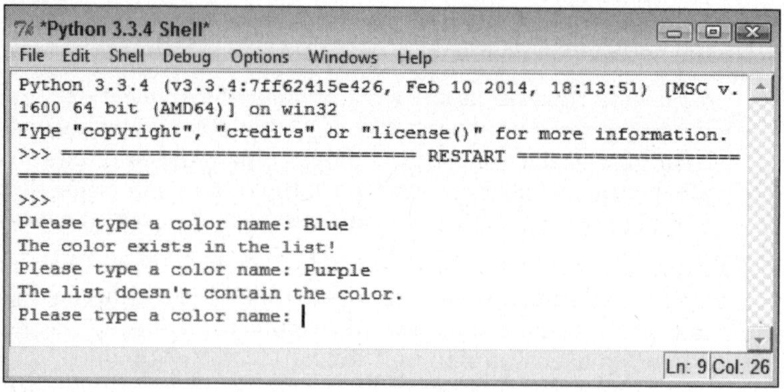

Figure 12-16:
Entering a
color that
doesn't exist
results in
a failure
message.

Sorting Lists

The computer can locate information in a list no matter what order it appears in. It's a fact, though, that longer lists are easier to search when you put them in sorted order. However, the main reason to put a list in sorted order is to make it easier for the human user to actually see the information the list contains. People work better with sorted information.

This example begins with an unsorted list. It then sorts the list and outputs it to the display. The following steps demonstrate how to perform this task. This example also appears with the downloadable source code as SortList.py.

1. **Open a Python File window.**

   You see an editor in which you can type the example code.

2. **Type the following code into the window — pressing Enter after each line:**

```python
Colors = ["Red", "Orange", "Yellow", "Green", "Blue"]

for Item in Colors:
    print(Item, end=" ")

print()

Colors.sort()

for Item in Colors:
    print(Item, end=" ")

print()
```

The example begins by creating an array of colors. The colors are currently in unsorted order. The example then prints the colors in the order in which they appear. Notice the use of the end=" " argument for the print() function to ensure that all color entries remain on one line (making them easier to compare).

Sorting the list is as easy as calling the sort() function. After the example calls the sort() function, it prints the list again so that you can see the result.

3. **Choose Run⇨Run Module.**

   You see a Python Shell window open. The application outputs both the unsorted and sorted lists, as shown in Figure 12-17.

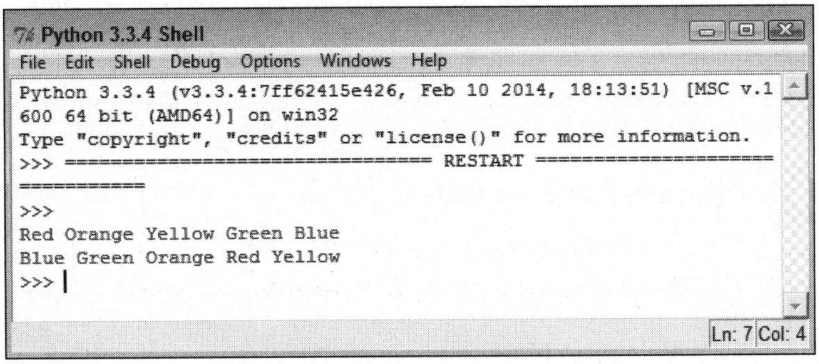

Figure 12-17:
Sorting a list is as easy as calling the sort() function.

```
7/6 Python 3.3.4 Shell                                          [_][□][✕]
File  Edit  Shell  Debug  Options  Windows  Help
Python 3.3.4 (v3.3.4:7ff62415e426, Feb 10 2014, 18:13:51) [MSC v.1 ▲
600 64 bit (AMD64)] on win32
Type "copyright", "credits" or "license()" for more information.
>>> ================================ RESTART ======================
===========
>>>
Red Orange Yellow Green Blue
Blue Green Orange Red Yellow
>>> |
                                                          Ln: 7 Col: 4
```

You may need to sort items in reverse order at times. To accomplish this task, you use the `reverse()` function. The function must appear on a separate line. So the previous example would look like this if you wanted to sort the colors in reverse order:

```
Colors = ["Red", "Orange", "Yellow", "Green", "Blue"]

for Item in Colors:
    print(Item, end=" ")

print()

Colors.sort()
Colors.reverse()

for Item in Colors:
    print(Item, end=" ")

print()
```

Working with the Counter Object

Sometimes you have a data source and you simply need to know how often things happen (such as the appearance of a certain item in the list). When you have a short list, you can simply count the items. However, when you have a really long list, it's nearly impossible to get an accurate count. For example, consider what it would take if you had a really long novel like *War and Peace* in a list and wanted to know the frequency of the words the novel used. The task would be impossible without a computer.

The `Counter` object lets you count items quickly. In addition, it's incredibly easy to use. This book shows the `Counter` object in use a number of times, but this chapter shows how to use it specifically with lists. The example in this section creates a list with repetitive elements and then counts how many times those elements actually appear. This example also appears with the downloadable source code as `UseCounterWithList.py`.

1. **Open a Python File window.**

   You see an editor in which you can type the example code.

2. **Type the following code into the window — pressing Enter after each line:**

```
from collections import Counter

MyList = [1, 2, 3, 4, 1, 2, 3, 1, 2, 1, 5]
ListCount = Counter(MyList)

print(ListCount)

for ThisItem in ListCount.items():
    print("Item: ", ThisItem[0],
          " Appears: ", ThisItem[1])

print("The value 1 appears {0} times."
      .format(ListCount.get(1)))
```

In order to use the `Counter` object, you must import it from `collections`. Of course, if you work with other collection types in your application, you can import the entire `collections` module by typing **import collections** instead.

The example begins by creating a list, `MyList`, with repetitive numeric elements. You can easily see that some elements appear more than once. The example places the list into a new `Counter` object, `ListCount`. You can create `Counter` objects in all sorts of ways, but this is the most convenient method when working with a list.

The `Counter` object and the list aren't actually connected in any way. When the list content changes, you must re-create the `Counter` object because it won't automatically see the change. An alternative to re-creating the counter is to call the `clear()` method first and then call the `update()` method to fill the Counter object with the new data.

The application prints `ListCount` in various ways. The first output is the `Counter` as it appears without any manipulation. The second output prints the individual unique elements in `MyList` along with the number of times each element appears. To obtain both the element and the number of times it appears, you must use the `items()` function as shown. Finally, the example demonstrates how to obtain an individual count from the list using the `get()` function.

3. **Choose Run⇨Run Module.**

   A Python Shell window opens, and you see the results of using the `Counter` object, as shown in Figure 12-18.

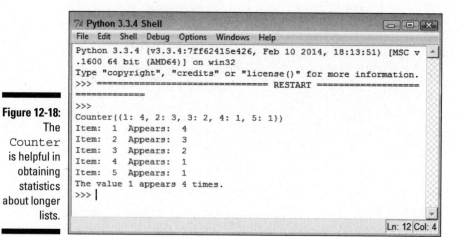

Figure 12-18:
The
Counter
is helpful in
obtaining
statistics
about longer
lists.

Notice that the information is actually stored in the Counter as a key and value pair. Chapter 13 discusses this topic in greater detail. All you really need to know for now is that the element found in MyList becomes a key in ListCount that identifies the unique element name. The value contains the number of times that that element appears within MyList.

Chapter 13

Collecting All Sorts of Data

● ●

In This Chapter

▶ Defining a collection

▶ Using tuples

▶ Using dictionaries

▶ Developing stacks using lists

▶ Using the `queue` module

▶ Using the `deque` module

● ●

*P*eople collect all sorts of things. The CDs stacked near your entertainment center, the plates that are part of a series, baseball cards, and even the pens from every restaurant you've ever visited are all collections. The collections you encounter when you write applications are the same as the collections in the real world. A *collection* is simply a grouping of like items in one place and usually organized into some easily understood form.

This chapter is about collections of various sorts. The central idea behind every collection is to create an environment in which the collection is properly managed and lets you easily locate precisely what you want at any given time. A set of bookshelves works great for storing books, DVDs, and other sorts of flat items. However, you probably put your pen collection in a holder or even a display case. The difference in storage locations doesn't change the fact that both house collections. The same is true with computer collections. Yes, there are differences between a stack and a `queue`, but the main idea is to provide the means to manage data properly and make it easy to access when needed.

Understanding Collections

In Chapter 12, you're introduced to sequences. A *sequence* is a succession of values that are bound together in a container. The simplest sequence is a string, which is a succession of characters. Next comes the list described in Chapter 12, which is a succession of objects. Even though a string and a list are both sequences, they have significant differences. For example, when working with a string, you set all the characters to lowercase — something you can't do with a list. On the other hand, lists let you append new items, which is something a string doesn't support. Collections are simply another kind of sequence, albeit a more complex sequence than you find in either a string or list.

No matter which sequence you use, they all support two functions: `index()` and `count()`. The `index()` function always returns the position of a specified item in the sequence. For example, you can return the position of a character in a string or the position of an object in a list. The `count()` function returns the number of times a specific item appears in the list. Again, the kind of specific item depends upon the kind of sequence.

You can use collections to create database-like structures using Python. Each collection type has a different purpose, and you use the various types in specific ways. The important idea to remember is that collections are simply another kind of sequence. As with every other kind of sequence, collections always support the `index()` and `count()` functions as part of their base functionality.

Python is designed to be extensible. However, it does rely on a base set of collections that you can use to create most application types. This chapter describes the most common collections:

- **Tuple:** A tuple is a collection used to create complex list-like sequences. An advantage of tuples is that you can nest the content of a tuple. This feature lets you create structures that can hold employee records or x-y coordinate pairs.

- **Dictionary:** As with the real dictionaries, you create key/value pairs when using the dictionary collection (think of a word and its associated definition). A dictionary provides incredibly fast search times and makes ordering data significantly easier.

- **Stack:** Most programming languages support stacks directly. However, Python doesn't support the stack, although there's a work-around for that. A stack is a first in/first out (FIFO) sequence. Think of a pile of pancakes: You can add new pancakes to the top and also take them off of the top. A stack is an important collection that you can simulate in Python using a list, which is precisely what this chapter does.

- **queue:** A `queue` is a last in/first out (LIFO) collection. You use it to track items that need to be processed in some way. Think of a `queue` as a line at the bank. You go into the line, wait your turn, and are eventually called to talk with a teller.

- **deque:** A double-ended `queue` (deque) is a `queue`-like structure that lets you add or remove items from either end, but not from the middle. You can use a deque as a `queue` or a stack or any other kind of collection to which you're adding and from which you're removing items in an orderly manner (in contrast to lists, tuples, and dictionaries, which allow randomized access and management).

Working with Tuples

As previously mentioned, a tuple is a collection used to create complex lists, in which you can embed one tuple within another. This embedding lets you create hierarchies with tuples. A hierarchy could be something as simple as the directory listing of your hard drive or an organizational chart for your company. The idea is that you can create complex data structures using a tuple.

Tuples are immutable, which means you can't change them. You can create a new tuple with the same name and modify it in some way, but you can't modify an existing tuple. Lists are mutable, which means that you can change them. So, a tuple can seem at first to be at a disadvantage, but immutability has all sorts of advantages, such as being more secure as well as faster. In addition, immutable objects are easier to use with multiple processors.

The two biggest differences between a tuple and a list are that a tuple is immutable and allows you to embed one tuple inside another. The following steps demonstrate how you can interact with a tuple in Python.

1. **Open a Python Shell window.**

   You see the familiar Python prompt.

2. **Type** MyTuple = ("Red", "Blue", "Green") **and press Enter.**

   Python creates a tuple containing three strings.

3. **Type** MyTuple **and press Enter.**

   You see the content of MyTuple, which is three strings, as shown in Figure 13-1. Notice that the entries use single quotes, even though you used double quotes to create the tuple. In addition, notice that a tuple uses parentheses rather than square brackets, as lists do.

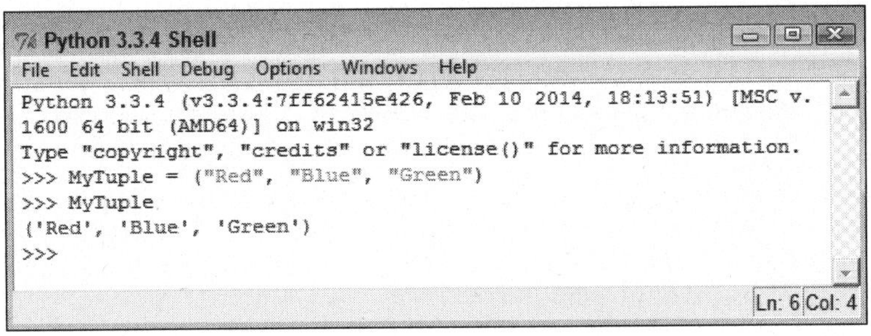

Figure 13-1: Tuples use parentheses, not square brackets.

```
Python 3.3.4 Shell
File  Edit  Shell  Debug  Options  Windows  Help
Python 3.3.4 (v3.3.4:7ff62415e426, Feb 10 2014, 18:13:51) [MSC v.
1600 64 bit (AMD64)] on win32
Type "copyright", "credits" or "license()" for more information.
>>> MyTuple = ("Red", "Blue", "Green")
>>> MyTuple
('Red', 'Blue', 'Green')
>>>
                                                          Ln: 6 Col: 4
```

4. Type dir(MyTuple) **and press Enter.**

Python presents a list of functions that you can use with tuples, as shown in Figure 13-2. Notice that the list of functions appears significantly smaller than the list of functions provided with lists in Chapter 12. The count() and index() functions are present.

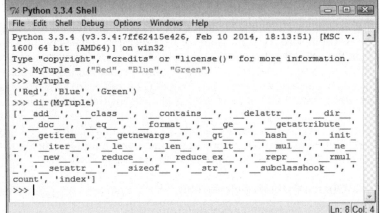

Figure 13-2:
Fewer
functions
seem to be
available
for use with
tuples.

```
Python 3.3.4 Shell
File  Edit  Shell  Debug  Options  Windows  Help
Python 3.3.4 (v3.3.4:7ff62415e426, Feb 10 2014, 18:13:51) [MSC v.
1600 64 bit (AMD64)] on win32
Type "copyright", "credits" or "license()" for more information.
>>> MyTuple = ("Red", "Blue", "Green")
>>> MyTuple
('Red', 'Blue', 'Green')
>>> dir(MyTuple)
['__add__', '__class__', '__contains__', '__delattr__', '__dir__'
, '__doc__', '__eq__', '__format__', '__ge__', '__getattribute__'
, '__getitem__', '__getnewargs__', '__gt__', '__hash__', '__init_
_', '__iter__', '__le__', '__len__', '__lt__', '__mul__', '__ne_
_', '__new__', '__reduce__', '__reduce_ex__', '__repr__', '__rmul_
_', '__setattr__', '__sizeof__', '__str__', '__subclasshook__', '
count', 'index']
>>> |
                                                          Ln: 8 Col: 4
```

However, appearances can be deceiving. For example, you can add new items using the __add__() function. When working with Python objects, look at all the entries before you make a decision as to functionality.

5. Type MyTuple = MyTuple.__add__(("Purple",)) **and press Enter.**

This code adds a new tuple to MyTuple and places the result in a new copy of MyTuple. The old copy of MyTuple is destroyed after the call.

The __add__() function accepts only tuples as input. This means that you must enclose the addition in parentheses. In addition, when creating a tuple with a single entry, you must add a comma after the entry, as shown in the example. This is an odd Python rule that you need to keep in mind or you'll see an error message similar to this one:

```
TypeError: can only concatenate tuple (not "str") to
   tuple
```

6. Type MyTuple **and press Enter.**

The addition to MyTuple appears at the end of the list, as shown in Figure 13-3. Notice that it appears at the same level as the other entries.

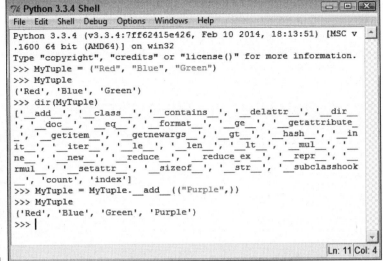

Figure 13-3:
This new
copy of
MyTuple
contains an
additional
entry.

7. **Type** MyTuple = MyTuple.__add__(("Yellow", ("Orange", "Black"))) **and press Enter.**

   This step adds three entries: Yellow, Orange, and Black. However, Orange and Black are added as a tuple within the main tuple, which creates a hierarchy. These two entries are actually treated as a single entry within the main tuple.

   You can replace the __add__() function with the concatenation operator. For example, if you want to add Magenta to the front of the tuple list, you type MyTuple = ("Magenta",) + MyTuple.

8. **Type** MyTuple[4] **and press Enter.**

   Python displays a single member of MyTuple, Orange. Tuples use indexes to access individual members, just as lists do. You can also specify a range when needed. Anything you can do with a list index you can also do with a tuple index.

9. **Type** MyTuple[5] **and press Enter.**

   You see a tuple that contains Orange and Black. Of course, you might not want to use both members in tuple form.

   Tuples do contain hierarchies on a regular basis. You can detect when an index has returned another tuple, rather than a value, by testing for type. For example, in this case, you could detect that the sixth item (index 5) contains a tuple by typing type(MyTuple[5]) == tuple. The output would be True in this case.

10. **Type** MyTuple[5][0] **and press Enter.**

    At this point, you see Orange as output. Figure 13-4 shows the results of the previous three commands so that you can see the progression of index usage. The indexes always appear in order of their level in the hierarchy.

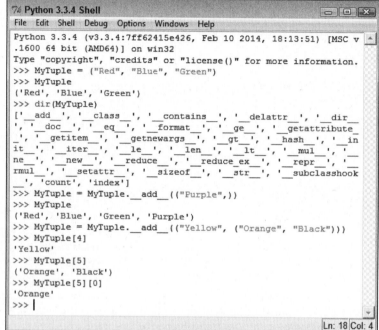

Figure 13-4:
Use indexes to gain access to the individual tuple members.

TIP

Using a combination of indexes and the __add__() function (or the concatenation operator, +), you can create flexible applications that rely on tuples. For example, you can remove an element from a tuple by making it equal to a range of values. If you wanted to remove the tuple containing Orange and Black, you type MyTuple = MyTuple[0:5].

Working with Dictionaries

A Python dictionary works just the same as its real-world counterpart — you create a key and value pair. It's just like the word and definition in a diction-ary. As with lists, dictionaries are mutable, which means that you can change them as needed. The main reason to use a dictionary is to make information lookup faster. The key is always short and unique so that the computer doesn't spend a lot of time looking for the information you need.

The following sections demonstrate how to create and use a dictionary. When you know how to work with dictionaries, you use that knowledge to make up for deficiencies in the Python language. Most languages include the concept of a switch statement, which is essentially a menu of choices from which one choice is selected. Python doesn't include this option, so you must normally rely on `if...elif` statements to perform the task. (Such statements work, but they aren't as clear as they could be.)

Creating and using a dictionary

Creating and using a `dictionary` is much like working with a `list`, except that you must now define a key and value pair. Here are the special rules for creating a key:

- ✔ **The key must be unique.** When you enter a duplicate key, the information found in the second entry wins — the first entry is simply replaced with the second.

- ✔ **The key must be immutable.** This rule means that you can use strings, numbers, or tuples for the key. You can't, however, use a list for a key.

You have no restrictions on the values you provide. A value can be any Python object, so you can use a `dictionary` to access an employee record or other complex data. The following steps help you understand how to use dictionaries better.

1. **Open a Python Shell window.**

   You see the familiar Python prompt.

2. **Type** Colors = {"Sam": "Blue", "Amy": "Red", "Sarah": "Yellow"} **and press Enter.**

   Python creates a `dictionary` containing three entries with people's favorite colors. Notice how you create the key and value pair. The key comes first, followed by a colon and then the value. Each entry is separated by a comma.

3. **Type** Colors **and press Enter.**

   You see the key and value pairs, as shown in Figure 13-5. However, notice that the entries are sorted in key order. A dictionary automatically keeps the keys sorted to make access faster, which means that you get fast search times even when working with a large data set. The downside is that creating the dictionary takes longer than using something like a list because the computer is busy sorting the entries.

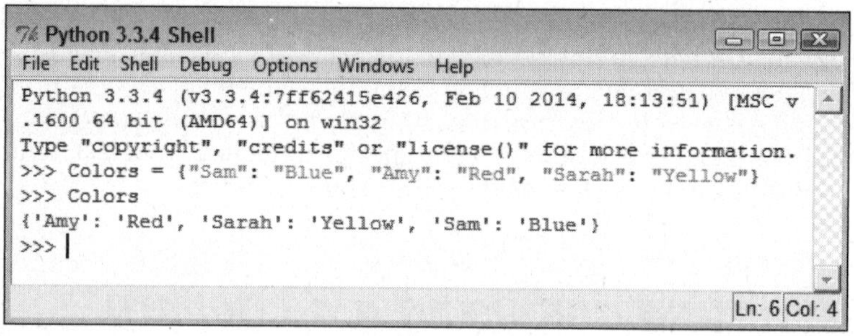

Figure 13-5:
A diction-
ary places
entries in
sorted order.

```
74 Python 3.3.4 Shell                                    [_][口][X]
File  Edit  Shell  Debug  Options  Windows  Help
Python 3.3.4 (v3.3.4:7ff62415e426, Feb 10 2014, 18:13:51) [MSC v
.1600 64 bit (AMD64)] on win32
Type "copyright", "credits" or "license()" for more information.
>>> Colors = {"Sam": "Blue", "Amy": "Red", "Sarah": "Yellow"}
>>> Colors
{'Amy': 'Red', 'Sarah': 'Yellow', 'Sam': 'Blue'}
>>> |
                                                     Ln: 6  Col: 4
```

Figure 13-5: A dictionary places entries in sorted order.

  4. **Type** Colors["Sarah"] **and press Enter.**

     You see the color associated with Sarah, Yellow, as shown in Figure 13-6. Using a string as a key, rather than using a numeric index, makes the code easier to read and makes it self-documenting to an extent. By making your code more readable, dictionaries save you considerable time in the long run (which is why they're so popular). However, the convenience of a dictionary comes at the cost of additional creation time and a higher use of resources, so you have trade-offs to consider.

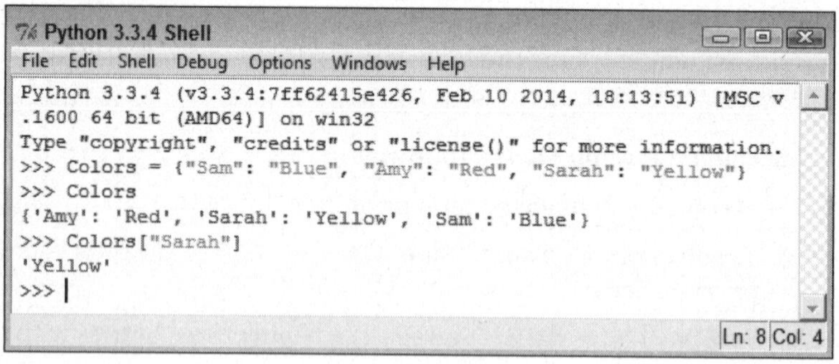

Figure 13-6: Dictionaries make value access easy and self-documenting.

```
74 Python 3.3.4 Shell                                    [_][口][X]
File  Edit  Shell  Debug  Options  Windows  Help
Python 3.3.4 (v3.3.4:7ff62415e426, Feb 10 2014, 18:13:51) [MSC v
.1600 64 bit (AMD64)] on win32
Type "copyright", "credits" or "license()" for more information.
>>> Colors = {"Sam": "Blue", "Amy": "Red", "Sarah": "Yellow"}
>>> Colors
{'Amy': 'Red', 'Sarah': 'Yellow', 'Sam': 'Blue'}
>>> Colors["Sarah"]
'Yellow'
>>> |
                                                     Ln: 8  Col: 4
```

  5. **Type** Colors.keys() **and press Enter.**

     The dictionary presents a list of the keys it contains, as shown in Figure 13-7. You can use these keys to automate access to the dictionary.

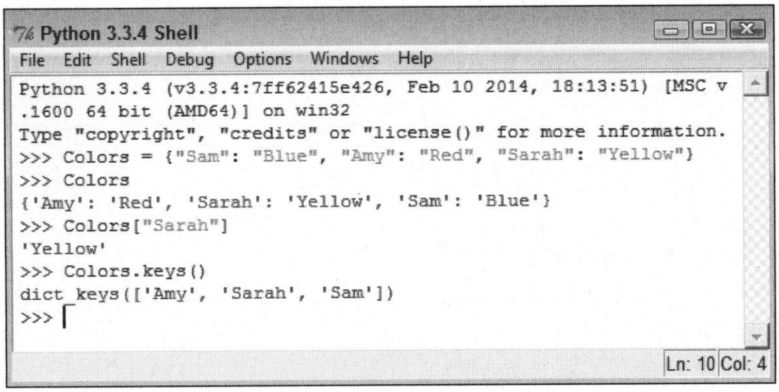

Figure 13-7:
You can ask
a dictionary
for a list of
keys.

```
74 Python 3.3.4 Shell
File  Edit  Shell  Debug  Options  Windows  Help
Python 3.3.4 (v3.3.4:7ff62415e426, Feb 10 2014, 18:13:51) [MSC v
.1600 64 bit (AMD64)] on win32
Type "copyright", "credits" or "license()" for more information.
>>> Colors = {"Sam": "Blue", "Amy": "Red", "Sarah": "Yellow"}
>>> Colors
{'Amy': 'Red', 'Sarah': 'Yellow', 'Sam': 'Blue'}
>>> Colors["Sarah"]
'Yellow'
>>> Colors.keys()
dict_keys(['Amy', 'Sarah', 'Sam'])
>>>
                                                          Ln: 10 Col: 4
```

6. **Type the following code (pressing Enter after each line and pressing Enter twice after the last line):**

```
for Item in Colors.keys():
    print("{0} likes the color {1}."
        .format(Item, Colors[Item]))
```

The example code outputs a listing of each of the user names and the user's favorite color, as shown in Figure 13-8. Using dictionaries can make creating useful output a lot easier. The use of a meaningful key means that the key can easily be part of the output.

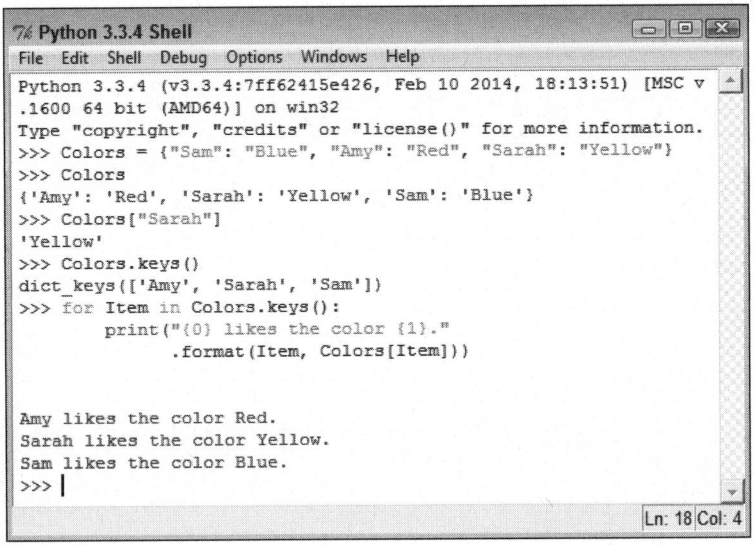

Figure 13-8:
You can
create
useful keys
to output
information
with greater
ease.

```
74 Python 3.3.4 Shell
File  Edit  Shell  Debug  Options  Windows  Help
Python 3.3.4 (v3.3.4:7ff62415e426, Feb 10 2014, 18:13:51) [MSC v
.1600 64 bit (AMD64)] on win32
Type "copyright", "credits" or "license()" for more information.
>>> Colors = {"Sam": "Blue", "Amy": "Red", "Sarah": "Yellow"}
>>> Colors
{'Amy': 'Red', 'Sarah': 'Yellow', 'Sam': 'Blue'}
>>> Colors["Sarah"]
'Yellow'
>>> Colors.keys()
dict_keys(['Amy', 'Sarah', 'Sam'])
>>> for Item in Colors.keys():
        print("{0} likes the color {1}."
                .format(Item, Colors[Item]))

Amy likes the color Red.
Sarah likes the color Yellow.
Sam likes the color Blue.
>>>
                                                          Ln: 18 Col: 4
```

7. Type Colors["Sarah"] = "Purple" **and press Enter.**

The `dictionary` content is updated so that Sarah now likes Purple instead of Yellow.

8. Type Colors.update({"Harry": "Orange"}) **and press Enter.**

A new entry is added to the `dictionary`.

9. Place your cursor at the end of the third line of the code you typed in Step 6 and press Enter.

The editor creates a copy of the code for you. This is a time-saving technique that you can use in the Python Shell when you experiment while using code that takes a while to type. Even though you have to type it the first time, you have no good reason to type it the second time.

10. Press Enter twice.

You see the updated output in Figure 13-9. Notice that Harry is added in sorted order. In addition, Sarah's entry is changed to the color Purple.

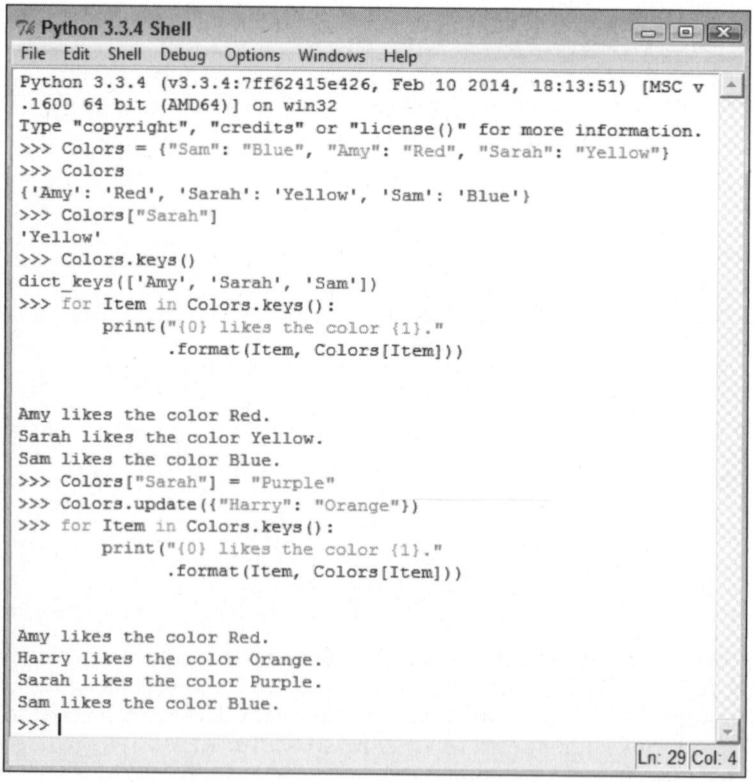

```
7% Python 3.3.4 Shell                                    □ □ ✕
File  Edit  Shell  Debug  Options  Windows  Help
Python 3.3.4 (v3.3.4:7ff62415e426, Feb 10 2014, 18:13:51) [MSC v
.1600 64 bit (AMD64)] on win32
Type "copyright", "credits" or "license()" for more information.
>>> Colors = {"Sam": "Blue", "Amy": "Red", "Sarah": "Yellow"}
>>> Colors
{'Amy': 'Red', 'Sarah': 'Yellow', 'Sam': 'Blue'}
>>> Colors["Sarah"]
'Yellow'
>>> Colors.keys()
dict_keys(['Amy', 'Sarah', 'Sam'])
>>> for Item in Colors.keys():
        print("{0} likes the color {1}."
              .format(Item, Colors[Item]))


Amy likes the color Red.
Sarah likes the color Yellow.
Sam likes the color Blue.
>>> Colors["Sarah"] = "Purple"
>>> Colors.update({"Harry": "Orange"})
>>> for Item in Colors.keys():
        print("{0} likes the color {1}."
              .format(Item, Colors[Item]))


Amy likes the color Red.
Harry likes the color Orange.
Sarah likes the color Purple.
Sam likes the color Blue.
>>> |

                                                    Ln: 29 Col: 4
```

Figure 13-9:
Dictionaries are easy to modify.

11. **Type** del Colors["Sam"] **and press Enter.**

    Python removes Sam's entry from the `dictionary`.

12. **Repeat Steps 9 and 10.**

    You verify that Sam's entry is actually gone.

13. **Type** len(Colors) **and press Enter.**

    The output value of 3 verifies that the `dictionary` contains only three entries now, rather than 4.

14. **Type** Colors.clear() **and press Enter.**

15. **Type** len(Colors) **and press Enter.**

    Python reports that `Colors` has 0 entries, so the dictionary is now empty.

16. **Close the Python Shell window.**

Replacing the switch statement with a dictionary

Most programming languages provide some sort of switch statement. A switch statement provides for elegant menu type selections. The user has a number of options but is allowed to choose only one of them. The program takes some course of action based on the user selection. Here is some representative code (it won't execute) of a `switch` statement you might find in another language:

```
switch(n)
{
   case 0:
      print("You selected blue.");
      break;
   case 1:
      print("You selected yellow.");
      break;
   case 2:
      print("You selected green.");
      break;
}
```

The application normally presents a menu-type interface, obtains the number of the selection from the user, and then chooses the correct course of action from the `switch` statement. It's straightforward and much neater than using a series of `if` statements to accomplish the same task.

Unfortunately, Python doesn't come with a switch statement. The best you can hope to do is use an `if...elif` statement for the task. However, by using a `dictionary`, you can simulate the use of a switch statement. The following steps help you create an example that will demonstrate the required technique. This example also appears with the downloadable source code as `PythonSwitch.py`.

1. **Open a Python File window.**

   You see an editor in which you can type the example code.

2. **Type the following code into the window — pressing Enter after each line:**

```
def PrintBlue():
    print("You chose blue!\r\n")

def PrintRed():
    print("You chose red!\r\n")

def PrintOrange():
    print("You chose orange!\r\n")

def PrintYellow():
    print("You chose yellow!\r\n")
```

   Before the code can do anything for you, you must define the tasks. Each of these functions defines a task associated with selecting a color option onscreen. Only one of them gets called at any given time.

3. **Type the following code into the window — pressing Enter after each line:**

```
ColorSelect = {
    0: PrintBlue,
    1: PrintRed,
    2: PrintOrange,
    3: PrintYellow
}
```

   This code is the `dictionary`. Each key is like the case part of the switch statement. The values specify what to do. In other words, this is the switch structure. The functions that you created earlier are the action part of the switch — the part that goes between the case statement and the break clause.

4. **Type the following code into the window — pressing Enter after each line:**

```
Selection = 0

while (Selection != 4):
    print("0. Blue")
    print("1. Red")
    print("2. Orange")
    print("3. Yellow")
    print("4. Quit")

    Selection = int(input("Select a color option: "))

    if (Selection >= 0) and (Selection < 4):
        ColorSelect[Selection]()
```

Finally, you see the user interface part of the example. The code begins by creating an input variable, `Selection`. It then goes into a loop until the user enters a value of 4.

During each loop, the application displays a list of options and then waits for user input. When the user does provide input, the application performs a range check on it. Any value between 0 and 3 selects one of the functions defined earlier using the `dictionary` as the switching mechanism.

5. **Choose Run⇨Run Module.**

You see a Python Shell window open. The application displays a menu like the one shown in Figure 13-10.

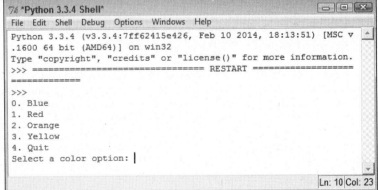

Figure 13-10: The application begins by displaying the menu.

6. Type 0 **and press Enter.**

The application tells you that you selected blue and then displays the menu again, as shown in Figure 13-11.

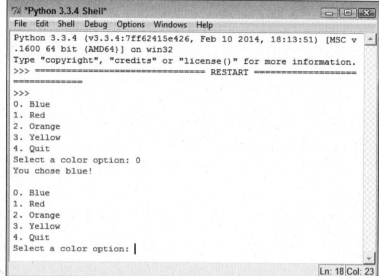

Figure 13-11:
After displaying your selection, the application displays the menu again.

7. Type 4 **and press Enter.**

The application ends.

Creating Stacks Using Lists

A stack is a handy programming structure because you can use it to save an application execution environment (the state of variables and other attributes of the application environment at any given time) or as a means of determining an order of execution. Unfortunately, Python doesn't provide a stack as a collection. However, it does provide lists, and you can use a `list` as a perfectly acceptable stack. The following steps help you create an example of using a `list` as a stack. This example also appears with the downloadable source code as `ListStack.py`.

1. **Open a Python File window.**

   You see an editor in which you can type the example code.

2. **Type the following code into the window — pressing Enter after each line:**

```python
MyStack = []
StackSize = 3

def DisplayStack():
    print("Stack currently contains:")
    for Item in MyStack:
        print(Item)

def Push(Value):
    if len(MyStack) < StackSize:
        MyStack.append(Value)
    else:
        print("Stack is full!")

def Pop():
    if len(MyStack) > 0:
        MyStack.pop()
    else:
        print("Stack is empty.")

Push(1)
Push(2)
Push(3)
DisplayStack()
input("Press any key when ready...")

Push(4)
DisplayStack()
input("Press any key when ready...")

Pop()
DisplayStack()
input("Press any key when ready...")

Pop()
Pop()
Pop()
DisplayStack()
```

In this example, the application creates a `list` and a variable to determine the maximum stack size. Stacks normally have a specific size range. This is admittedly a really small stack, but it serves well for the example's needs.

Stacks work by pushing a value onto the top of the stack and popping values back off the top of the stack. The `Push()` and `Pop()` functions perform these two tasks. The code adds `DisplayStack()` to make it easier to see the stack content as needed.

The remaining code *exercises the stack* (demonstrates its functionality) by pushing values onto it and then removing them. There are four main exercise sections that test stack functionality.

3. Choose Run⇨Run Module.

You see a Python Shell window open. The application fills the stack with information and then displays it onscreen, as shown in Figure 13-12. In this case, 3 is at the top of the stack because it's the last value added.

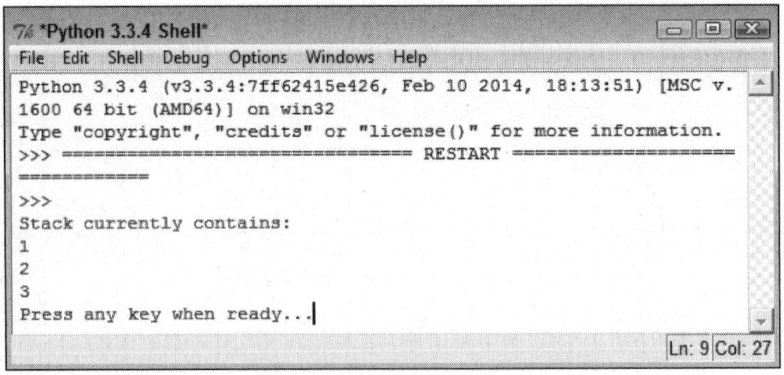

```
7¼ *Python 3.3.4 Shell*
File  Edit  Shell  Debug  Options  Windows  Help
Python 3.3.4 (v3.3.4:7ff62415e426, Feb 10 2014, 18:13:51) [MSC v.
1600 64 bit (AMD64)] on win32
Type "copyright", "credits" or "license()" for more information.
>>> ================================ RESTART =====================
=============
>>>
Stack currently contains:
1
2
3
Press any key when ready...|
                                                      Ln: 9 Col: 27
```

Figure 13-12:
A stack pushes values one on top of the other.

4. Press Enter.

The application attempts to push another value onto the stack. However, the stack is full, so the task fails, as shown in Figure 13-13.

5. Press Enter.

The application pops a value from the top of the stack. Remember that 3 is the top of the stack, so that's the value that is missing in Figure 13-14.

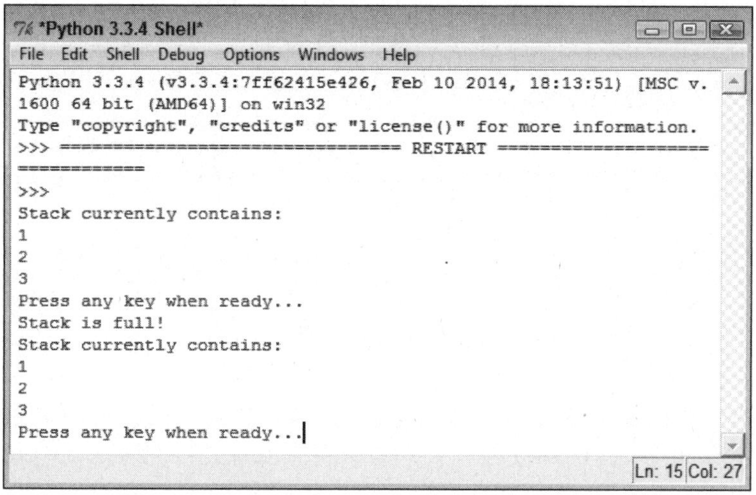

Figure 13-13:
When the stack is full, it can't accept any more values.

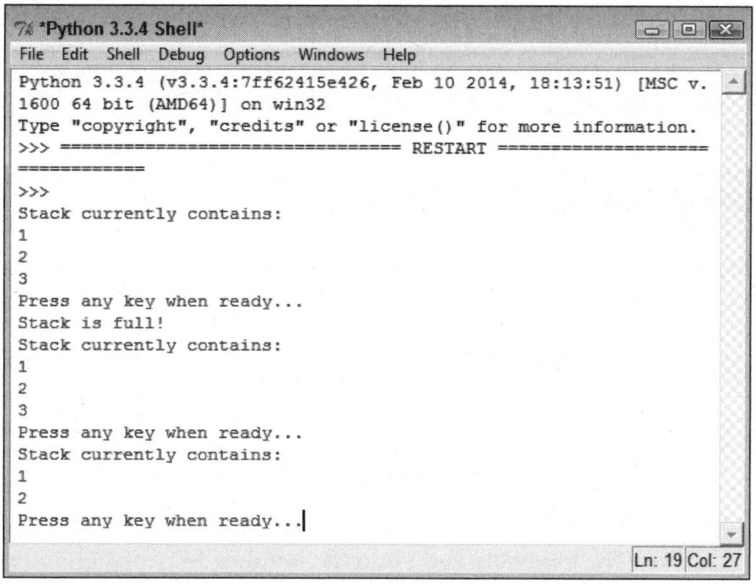

```
74 *Python 3.3.4 Shell*                          [ _ ][ □ ][ ✕ ]
File  Edit  Shell  Debug  Options  Windows  Help
Python 3.3.4 (v3.3.4:7ff62415e426, Feb 10 2014, 18:13:51) [MSC v.
1600 64 bit (AMD64)] on win32
Type "copyright", "credits" or "license()" for more information.
>>> =============================== RESTART ====================
=============
>>>
Stack currently contains:
1
2
3
Press any key when ready...
Stack is full!
Stack currently contains:
1
2
3
Press any key when ready...|
                                              Ln: 15 Col: 27
```

Figure 13-14:
Popping a value means removing it from the top of the stack.

```
74 *Python 3.3.4 Shell*                          [ _ ][ □ ][ ✕ ]
File  Edit  Shell  Debug  Options  Windows  Help
Python 3.3.4 (v3.3.4:7ff62415e426, Feb 10 2014, 18:13:51) [MSC v.
1600 64 bit (AMD64)] on win32
Type "copyright", "credits" or "license()" for more information.
>>> =============================== RESTART ====================
=============
>>>
Stack currently contains:
1
2
3
Press any key when ready...
Stack is full!
Stack currently contains:
1
2
3
Press any key when ready...
Stack currently contains:
1
2
Press any key when ready...|
                                              Ln: 19 Col: 27
```

6. Press Enter.

The application tries to pop more values from the stack than it contains, resulting in an error, as shown in Figure 13-15. Any stack implementation that you create must be able to detect both overflows (too many entries) and underflows (too few entries).

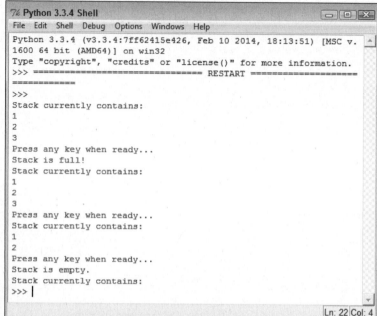

Figure 13-15:
Make sure
that your
stack imple-
mentation
detects
overflows
and
underflows.

Working with queues

A queue works differently from a stack. Think of any line you've ever stood in: You go to the back of the line, and when you reach the front of the line you get to do whatever you stood in the line to do. A queue is often used for task scheduling and to maintain program flow — just as it is in the real world. The following steps help you create a queue-based application. This example also appears with the downloadable source code as QueueData.py.

1. **Open a Python File window.**

   You see an editor in which you can type the example code.

2. **Type the following code into the window — pressing Enter after each line:**

   ```
   import queue

   MyQueue = queue.Queue(3)

   print(MyQueue.empty())
   input("Press any key when ready...")
   ```

```
MyQueue.put(1)
MyQueue.put(2)
print(MyQueue.full())
input("Press any key when ready...")

MyQueue.put(3)
print(MyQueue.full())
input("Press any key when ready...")

print(MyQueue.get())
print(MyQueue.empty())
print(MyQueue.full())
input("Press any key when ready...")

print(MyQueue.get())
print(MyQueue.get())
```

To create a queue, you must import the queue module. This module actually contains a number of queue types, but this example uses only the standard FIFO queue.

When a queue is empty, the empty() function returns True. Likewise, when a queue is full, the full() function returns True. By testing the state of empty() and full(), you can determine whether you need to perform additional work with the queue or whether you can add other information to it. These two functions help you manage a queue. It's not possible to iterate through a queue using a for loop as you have done with other collection types, so you must monitor empty() and full() instead.

The two functions used to work with data in a queue are put(), which adds new data, and get(), which removes data. A problem with queues is that if you try to put more items into the queue than it can hold, it simply waits until space is available to hold it. Unless you're using a *multithreaded application* (one that uses individual threads of execution to perform more than one task at one time), this state could end up freezing your application.

3. **Choose Run⇨Run Module.**

   You see a Python Shell window open. The application tests the state of the queue. In this case, you see an output of True, which means that the queue is empty.

4. **Press Enter.**

   The application adds two new values to the queue. In doing so, the queue is no longer empty, as shown in Figure 13-16.

Figure 13-16:
When the
application
puts new
entries in
the queue,
the queue
no longer
reports that
it's empty.

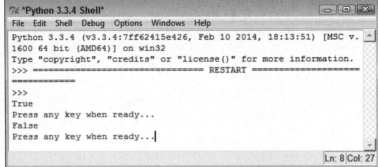

5. Press Enter.

The application adds another entry to the queue, which means that the queue is now full because it was set to a size of 3. This means that full() will return True because the queue is now full.

6. Press Enter.

To free space in the queue, the application gets one of the entries. Whenever an application gets an entry, the get() function returns that entry. Given that 1 was the first value added to the queue, the print() function should return a value of 1, as shown in Figure 13-17. In addition, both empty() and full() should now return False.

Figure 13-17:
Monitoring
is a key part
of work-
ing with
queues.

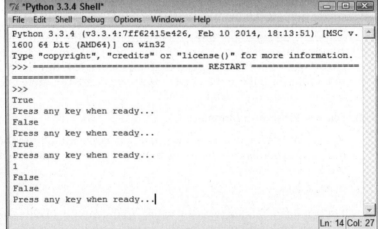

7. Press Enter.

The application gets the remaining two entries. You see 2 and 3 (in turn) as output.

Working with deques

A deque is simply a queue where you can remove and add items from either end. In many languages, a queue or stack starts out as a deque. Specialized code serves to limit deque functionality to what is needed to perform a particular task.

When working with a deque, you need to think of the deque as a sort of horizontal line. Certain individual functions work with the left and right ends of the deque so that you can add and remove items from either side. The following steps help you create an example that demonstrates deque usage. This example also appears with the downloadable source code as DequeData.py.

1. **Open a Python File window.**

   You see an editor in which you can type the example code.

2. **Type the following code into the window — pressing Enter after each line.**

```
import collections

MyDeque = collections.deque("abcdef", 10)

print("Starting state:")
for Item in MyDeque:
    print(Item, end=" ")

print("\r\n\r\nAppending and extending right")
MyDeque.append("h")
MyDeque.extend("ij")
for Item in MyDeque:
    print(Item, end=" ")
print("\r\nMyDeque contains {0} items."
    .format(len(MyDeque)))

print("\r\nPopping right")
print("Popping {0}".format(MyDeque.pop()))
for Item in MyDeque:
    print(Item, end=" ")

print("\r\n\r\nAppending and extending left")
MyDeque.appendleft("a")
MyDeque.extendleft("bc")
for Item in MyDeque:
    print(Item, end=" ")
print("\r\nMyDeque contains {0} items."
    .format(len(MyDeque)))
```

```
print("\r\nPopping left")
print("Popping {0}".format(MyDeque.popleft()))
for Item in MyDeque:
    print(Item, end=" ")

print("\r\n\r\nRemoving")
MyDeque.remove("a")
for Item in MyDeque:
    print(Item, end=" ")
```

The implementation of deque is found in the collections module, so you need to import it into your code. When you create a deque, you can optionally specify a starting list of *iterable items* (items that can be accessed and processed as part of a loop structure) and a maximum size, as shown.

A deque differentiates between adding one item and adding a group of items. You use append() or appendleft() when adding a single item. The extend() and extendleft() functions let you add multiple items. You use the pop() or popleft() functions to remove one item at a time. The act of popping values returns the value popped, so the example prints the value onscreen. The remove() function is unique in that it always works from the left side and always removes the first instance of the requested data.

Unlike some other collections, a deque is fully iterable. This means that you can obtain a list of items using a for loop whenever necessary.

3. Choose Run⇨Run Module.

You see a Python Shell window open. The example outputs the information shown in Figure 13-18.

It's important to follow the output listing closely. Notice how the size of the deque changes over time. After the application pops the j, the deque still contains eight items. When the application appends and extends from the left, it adds three more items. However, the resulting deque contains only ten items. When you exceed the maximum size of a deque, the extra data simply falls off the other end.

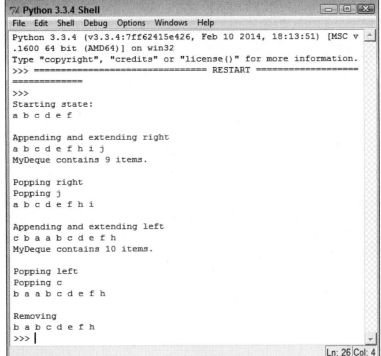

```
7% Python 3.3.4 Shell                                          [_][□][✖]
File  Edit  Shell  Debug  Options  Windows  Help
Python 3.3.4 (v3.3.4:7ff62415e426, Feb 10 2014, 18:13:51) [MSC v
.1600 64 bit (AMD64)] on win32
Type "copyright", "credits" or "license()" for more information.
>>> ================================ RESTART ====================
==============
>>>
Starting state:
a b c d e f

Appending and extending right
a b c d e f h i j
MyDeque contains 9 items.

Popping right
Popping j
a b c d e f h i

Appending and extending left
c b a a b c d e f h
MyDeque contains 10 items.

Popping left
Popping c
b a a b c d e f h

Removing
b a b c d e f h
>>> |
                                                          Ln: 26 Col: 4
```

Figure 13-18:
A deque provides the double-ended functionality and other features you'd expect.

Chapter 14

Creating and Using Classes

. . . .

In This Chapter

▶ Defining the characteristics of a class

▶ Specifying the class components

▶ Creating your own class

▶ Working with the class in an application

▶ Working with subclasses

. . . .

*Y*ou've already worked with a number of classes in previous chapters. Many of the examples are easy to construct and use because they depend on the Python classes. Even though classes are briefly mentioned in previous chapters, those chapters largely ignore them simply because discussing them wasn't immediately important.

Classes make working with Python code more convenient by helping to make your applications easy to read, understand, and use. You use classes to create containers for your code and data, so they stay together in one piece. Outsiders see your class as a black box — data goes in and results come out.

At some point, you need to start constructing classes of your own if you want to avoid the dangers of the spaghetti code that is found in older applications. *Spaghetti code* is much as the name implies — various lines of procedures are interwoven and spread out in such a way that it's hard to figure out where one piece of spaghetti begins and another ends. Trying to maintain spaghetti code is nearly impossible, and some organizations have thrown out applications because no one could figure them out.

Besides helping you understand classes as a packaging method that avoids spaghetti code, this chapter helps you create and use your own classes for the first time. You gain insights into how Python classes work toward making your applications convenient to work with. This is an introductory sort of chapter, though, and you won't become so involved in classes that your head begins to spin around on its own. This chapter is about making class development simple and manageable.

Understanding the Class as a Packaging Method

A class is essentially a method for packaging code. The idea is to simplify code reuse, make applications more reliable, and reduce the potential for security breaches. Well-designed classes are black boxes that accept certain inputs and provide specific outputs based on those inputs. In short, a class shouldn't create any surprises for anyone and should have known (quantifiable) behaviors. How the class accomplishes its work is unimportant, and hiding the details of its inner workings is essential to good coding practice.

Before you move onto actual class theory, you need to know a few terms that are specific to classes. The following list defines terms that you need to know in order to use the material that follows later in the chapter. These terms are specific to Python. (Other languages may use different terms for the same techniques or define terms that Python uses in different ways.)

- ✔ **Class:** Defines a blueprint for creating an object. Think of a builder who wants to create a building of some type. The builder uses a blueprint to ensure that the building will meet the required specifications. Likewise, Python uses classes as a blueprint for creating new objects.

- ✔ **Class variable:** Provides a storage location used by all methods in an instance of the class. A class variable is defined within the class proper but outside of any of the class methods. Class variables aren't used very often because they're a potential security risk — every method of the class has access to the same information. In addition to being a security risk, class variables are also visible as part of the class rather than a particular instance of a class, so they pose the potential problem of class contamination.

- ✔ **Data member:** Defines either a class variable or an instance variable used to hold data associated with a class and its objects.

- ✔ **Function overloading:** Creates more than one version of a function, which results in different behaviors. The essential task of the function may be the same, but the inputs are different and potentially the outputs as well. Function overloading is used to provide flexibility so that a function can work with applications in various ways.

- ✔ **Inheritance:** Uses a parent class to create child classes that have the same characteristics. The child classes usually have extended functionality or provide more specific behaviors than the parent class does.

- ✔ **Instance:** Defines an object created from the specification provided by a class. Python can create as many instances of a class to perform the work required by an application. Each instance is unique.

✔ **Instance variable:** Provides a storage location used by a single method of an instance of a class. The variable is defined within a method. Instance variables are considered safer than class variables because only one method of the class can access them. Data is passed between methods using arguments, which allows for controlled checks of incoming data and better control over data management.

✔ **Instantiation:** Performs the act of creating an instance of a class. The resulting object is a unique class instance.

✔ **Method:** Defines the term used for functions that are part of a class. Even though function and method essentially define the same element, method is considered more specific because only classes can have methods.

✔ **Object:** Defines a unique instance of a class. The object contains all the methods and properties of the original class. However, the data for each object differs. The storage locations are unique, even if the data is the same.

✔ **Operator overloading:** Creates more than one version of a function that is associated with an operator such as: +, -, /, or *, which results in different behaviors. The essential task of the operator may be the same, but the way in which the operator interacts with the data differs. Operator overloading is used to provide flexibility so that an operator can work with applications in various ways.

Considering the Parts of a Class

A class has a specific construction. Each part of a class performs a particular task that gives the class useful characteristics. Of course, the class begins with a container that is used to hold the entire class together, so that's the part that the first section that follows discusses. The remaining sections describe the other parts of a class and help you understand how they contribute to the class as a whole.

Creating the class definition

A class need not be particularly complex. In fact, you can create just the container and one class element and call it a class. Of course, the resulting class won't do much, but you can *instantiate it* (tell Python to build an object using your class as a blueprint) and work with it as you would any other class. The following steps help you understand the basics behind a class by creating the simplest class possible.

1. **Open a Python Shell window.**

   You see the familiar Python prompt.

2. **Type the following code (pressing Enter after each line and pressing Enter twice after the last line):**

   ```
   class MyClass:
       MyVar = 0
   ```

   The first line defines the class container, which consists of the keyword `class` and the class name, which is `MyClass`. Every class you create must begin precisely this way. You must always include `class` followed by the class name.

   The second line is the class suite. All the elements that comprise the class are called the *class suite*. In this case, you see a class variable named `MyVar`, which is set to a value of 0. Every instance of the class will have the same variable and start at the same value.

3. **Type** MyInstance = MyClass( ) **and press Enter.**

   You have just created an instance of `MyClass` named `MyInstance`. Of course, you'll want to verify that you really have created such an instance. Step 4 accomplishes that task.

4. **Type** MyInstance.MyVar **and press Enter.**

   The output of 0, as shown in Figure 14-1, demonstrates that `MyInstance` does indeed have a class variable named `MyVar`.

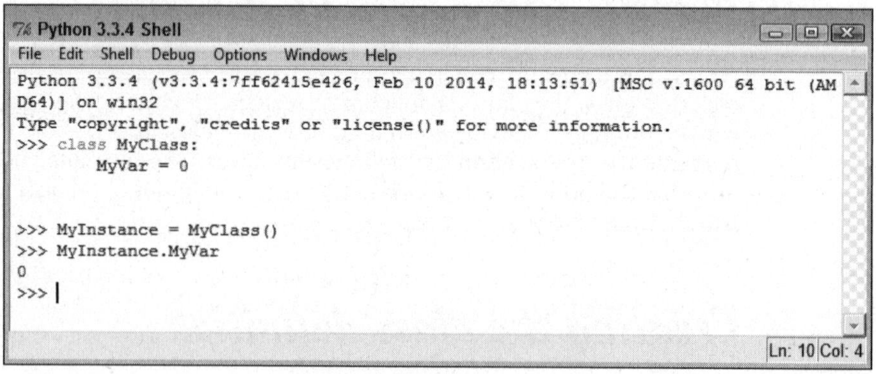

Figure 14-1: The instance contains the required variable.

5. **Type** MyInstance.__class__ **and press Enter.**

   Python displays the class used to create this instance, as shown in Figure 14-2. The output tells you that this class is part of the __main__ module, which means that you typed it directly into the shell.

6. **Retain this window and class for the next section.**

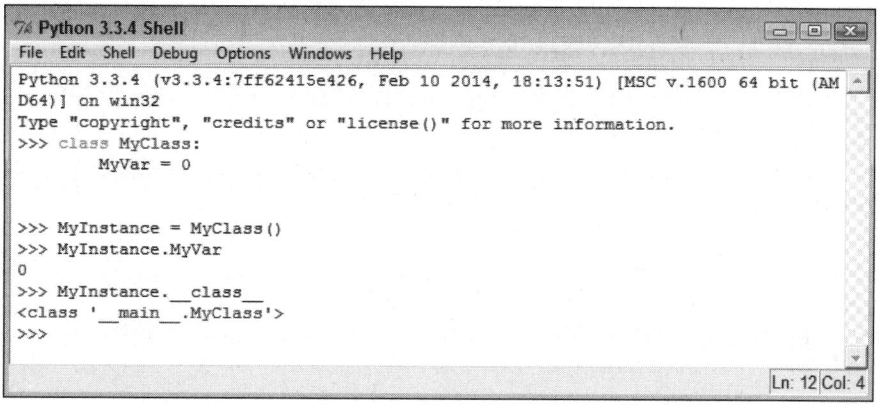

Figure 14-2:
The class
name is also
correct, so
you know
that this
instance
is cre-
ated using
MyClass.

```
Python 3.3.4 Shell
File  Edit  Shell  Debug  Options  Windows  Help
Python 3.3.4 (v3.3.4:7ff62415e426, Feb 10 2014, 18:13:51) [MSC v.1600 64 bit (AM
D64)] on win32
Type "copyright", "credits" or "license()" for more information.
>>> class MyClass:
        MyVar = 0

>>> MyInstance = MyClass()
>>> MyInstance.MyVar
0
>>> MyInstance.__class__
<class '__main__.MyClass'>
>>>
                                                                        Ln: 12 Col: 4
```

Considering the built-in class attributes

When you create a class, you can easily think that all you get is the class. However, Python adds built-in functionality to your class. For example, in the preceding section, you type __class__ and press Enter. The __class__ attribute is built in; you didn't create it. It helps to know that Python provides this functionality so that you don't have to add it. The functionality is needed often enough that every class should have it, so Python supplies it. The following steps help you work with the built-in class attributes.

1. **Use the Python Shell window that you open in the preceding section.**

   If you haven't followed the steps in the preceding section, "Creating the class definition," please do so now.

2. **Type dir(MyInstance) and press Enter.**

   A list of attributes appears, as shown in Figure 14-3. These attributes provide specific functionality for your class. They're also common to every other class you create, so you can count on always having this functionality in the classes you create.

3. **Type help('__class__') and press Enter.**

   Python displays information on the __class__ attribute, as shown in Figure 14-4. You can use the same technique for learning more about any attribute that Python adds to your class.

4. **Close the Python Shell window.**

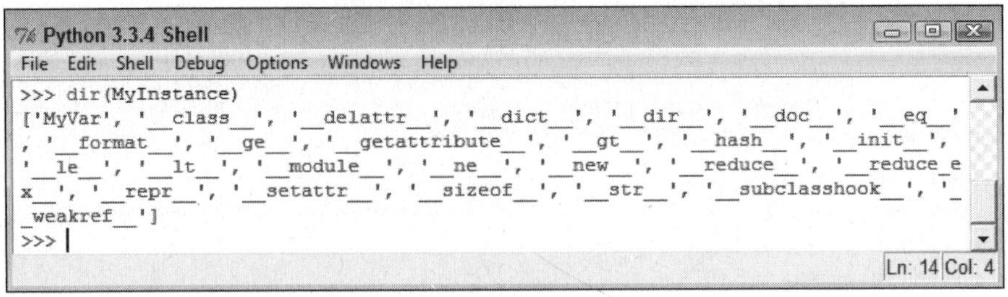

Figure 14-3:
Use the
dir()
function to
determine
which built-
in attributes
are present.

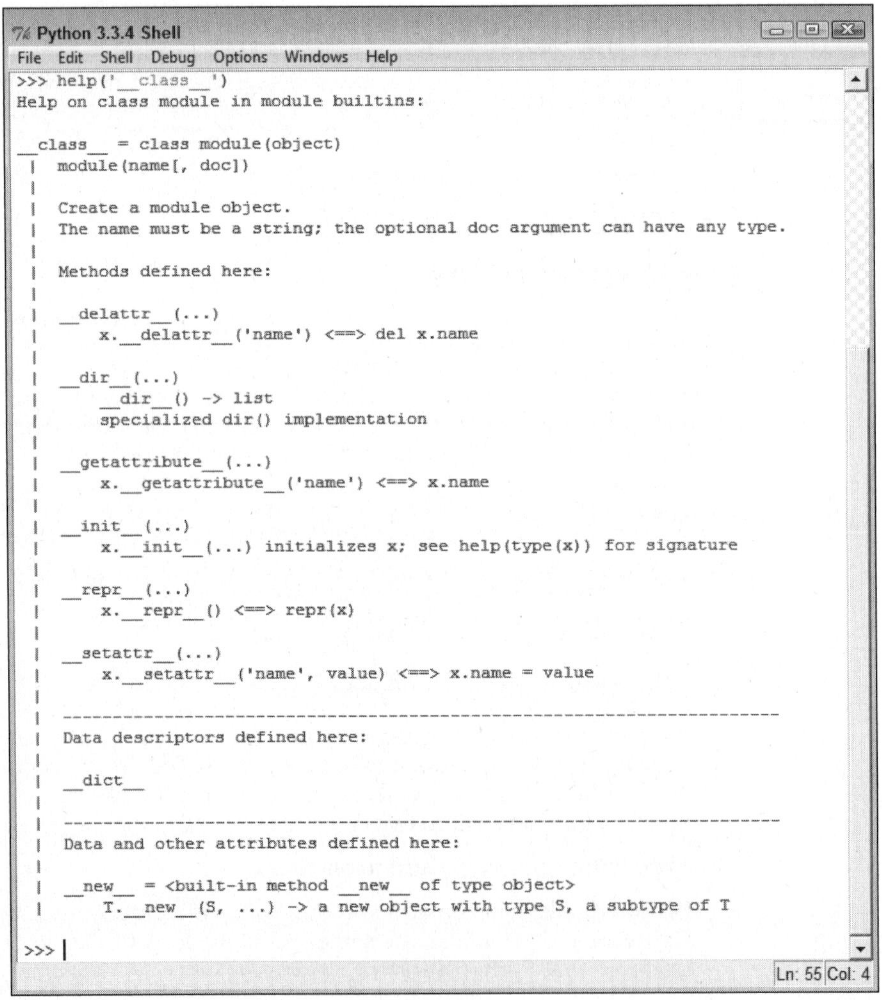

```
7 Python 3.3.4 Shell                                          [ - ] [ □ ] [ X ]
File  Edit  Shell  Debug  Options  Windows  Help
>>> dir(MyInstance)
['MyVar', '__class__', '__delattr__', '__dict__', '__dir__', '__doc__', '__eq__'
, '__format__', '__ge__', '__getattribute__', '__gt__', '__hash__', '__init__',
'__le__', '__lt__', '__module__', '__ne__', '__new__', '__reduce__', '__reduce_e
x__', '__repr__', '__setattr__', '__sizeof__', '__str__', '__subclasshook__', '__
_weakref__']
>>> |
                                                              Ln: 14 Col: 4
```

Figure 14-4:
Python
provides
help for
each of the
attributes it
adds to your
class.

```
7 Python 3.3.4 Shell                                          [ - ] [ □ ] [ X ]
File  Edit  Shell  Debug  Options  Windows  Help
>>> help('__class__')
Help on class module in module builtins:

__class__ = class module(object)
 |  module(name[, doc])
 |
 |  Create a module object.
 |  The name must be a string; the optional doc argument can have any type.
 |
 |  Methods defined here:
 |
 |  __delattr__(...)
 |      x.__delattr__('name') <==> del x.name
 |
 |  __dir__(...)
 |      __dir__() -> list
 |      specialized dir() implementation
 |
 |  __getattribute__(...)
 |      x.__getattribute__('name') <==> x.name
 |
 |  __init__(...)
 |      x.__init__(...) initializes x; see help(type(x)) for signature
 |
 |  __repr__(...)
 |      x.__repr__() <==> repr(x)
 |
 |  __setattr__(...)
 |      x.__setattr__('name', value) <==> x.name = value
 |
 |  ----------------------------------------------------------------------
 |  Data descriptors defined here:
 |
 |  __dict__
 |
 |  ----------------------------------------------------------------------
 |  Data and other attributes defined here:
 |
 |  __new__ = <built-in method __new__ of type object>
 |      T.__new__(S, ...) -> a new object with type S, a subtype of T
>>> |
                                                              Ln: 55 Col: 4
```

Working with methods

Methods are simply another kind of function that reside in classes. You create and work with methods in precisely the same way that you do functions, except that methods are always associated with a class (you don't see free-standing methods as you do functions). You can create two kinds of methods: those associated with the class itself and those associated with an instance of a class. It's important to differentiate between the two. The following sections provide the details needed to work with both.

Creating class methods

A *class method* is one that you execute directly from the class without creating an instance of the class. Sometimes you need to create methods that execute from the class, such as the functions you used with the str class in order to modify strings. As an example, the MultipleException4.py example in Chapter 9 uses the str.upper() function. The following steps demonstrate how to create and use a class method.

1. **Open a Python Shell window.**

   You see the familiar Python prompt.

2. **Type the following code (pressing Enter after each line and pressing Enter twice after the last line):**

   ```
   class MyClass:
       def SayHello():
           print("Hello there!")
   ```

   The example class contains a single defined attribute, SayHello(). This method doesn't accept any arguments and doesn't return any values. It simply prints a message as output. However, the method works just fine for demonstration purposes.

3. **Type MyClass.SayHello() and press Enter.**

   The example outputs the expected string, as shown in Figure 14-5. Notice that you didn't need to create an instance of the class — the method is available immediately for use.

4. **Close the Python Shell window.**

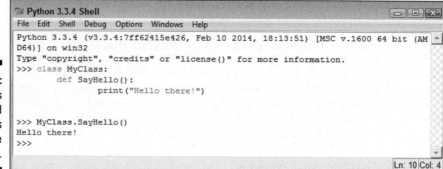

Figure 14-5:
The class
method
outputs
a simple
message.

A class method can work only with class data. It doesn't know about any data associated with an instance of the class. You can pass it data as an argument, and the method can return information as needed, but it can't access the instance data. As a consequence, you need to exercise care when creating class methods to ensure that they're essentially self-contained.

Creating instance methods

An *instance method* is one that is part of the individual instances. You use instance methods to manipulate the data that the class manages. As a consequence, you can't use instance methods until you instantiate an object from the class.

All instance methods accept a single argument as a minimum, `self`. The `self` argument points at the particular instance that the application is using to manipulate data. Without the `self` argument, the method wouldn't know which instance data to use. However, `self` isn't considered an accessible argument — the value for `self` is supplied by Python, and you can't change it as part of calling the method.

The following steps demonstrate how to create and use instance methods in Python.

1. **Open a Python Shell window.**

   You see the familiar Python prompt.

2. **Type the following code (pressing Enter after each line and pressing Enter twice after the last line):**

```
class MyClass:
    def SayHello(self):
        print("Hello there!")
```

The example class contains a single defined attribute, `SayHello()`. This method doesn't accept any special arguments and doesn't return any values. It simply prints a message as output. However, the method works just fine for demonstration purposes.

3. **Type** MyInstance = MyClass() **and press Enter.**

   Python creates an instance of `MyClass` named `MyInstance`.

4. **Type** MyInstance.SayHello() **and press Enter.**

   You see the message shown in Figure 14-6.

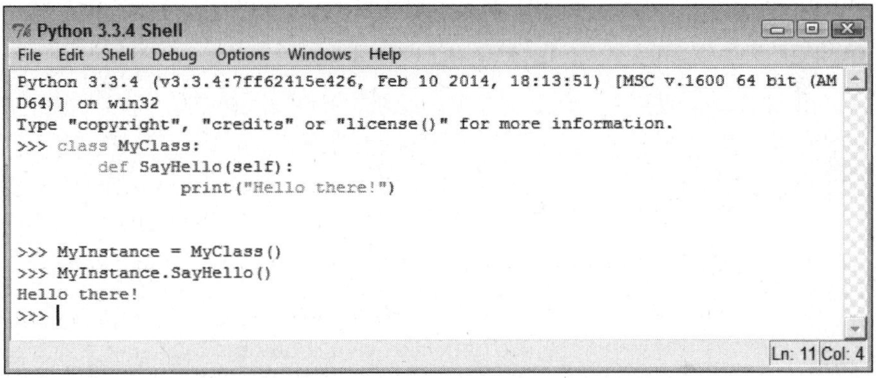

Figure 14-6: The instance message is called as part of an object and outputs this simple message.

```
7⅙ Python 3.3.4 Shell                                            □ □ ⊠
File   Edit   Shell   Debug   Options   Windows   Help
Python 3.3.4 (v3.3.4:7ff62415e426, Feb 10 2014, 18:13:51) [MSC v.1600 64 bit (AM
D64)] on win32
Type "copyright", "credits" or "license()" for more information.
>>> class MyClass:
        def SayHello(self):
                print("Hello there!")


>>> MyInstance = MyClass()
>>> MyInstance.SayHello()
Hello there!
>>> |
                                                               Ln: 11 Col: 4
```

5. **Close the Python Shell window.**

Working with constructors

A *constructor* is a special kind of method that Python calls when it instantiates an object using the definitions found in your class. Python relies on the constructor to perform tasks such as *initializing* (assigning values to) any instance variables that the object will need when it starts. Constructors can also verify that there are enough resources for the object and perform any other start-up task you can think of.

The name of a constructor is always the same, __init__(). The constructor can accept arguments when necessary to create the object. When you create a class without a constructor, Python automatically creates a default constructor for you that doesn't do anything. Every class must have a constructor, even if it simply relies on the default constructor. The following steps demonstrate how to create a constructor:

1. **Open a Python Shell window.**

   You see the familiar Python prompt.

2. **Type the following code (pressing Enter after each line and pressing Enter twice after the last line):**

```
class MyClass:
   Greeting = ""

   def __init__(self, Name="there"):
      self.Greeting = Name + "!"

   def SayHello(self):
      print("Hello {0}".format(self.Greeting))
```

   This example provides your first example of function overloading. In this case, there are two versions of __init__(). The first doesn't require any special input because it uses the default value for the Name of "there". The second requires a name as an input. It sets Greeting to the value of this name, plus an exclamation mark. The SayHello() method is essentially the same as previous examples in this chapter.

   Python doesn't support true function overloading. Many strict adherents to strict Object-Oriented Programming (OOP) principles consider default values to be something different from function overloading. However, the use of default values obtains the same result, and it's the only option that Python offers. In true function overloading, you see multiple copies of the same function, each of which could process the input differently.

3. **Type MyInstance = MyClass( ) and press Enter.**

   Python creates an instance of MyClass named MyInstance.

4. **Type MyInstance.SayHello( ) and press Enter.**

   You see the message shown in Figure 14-7. Notice that this message provides the default, generic greeting.

5. **Type MyInstance = MyClass("Amy") and press Enter.**

   Python creates an instance of MyClass named MyInstance.

6. **Type MyInstance.SayHello( ) and press Enter.**

   You see the message shown in Figure 14-8. Notice that this message provides a specific greeting.

7. **Close the Python Shell window.**

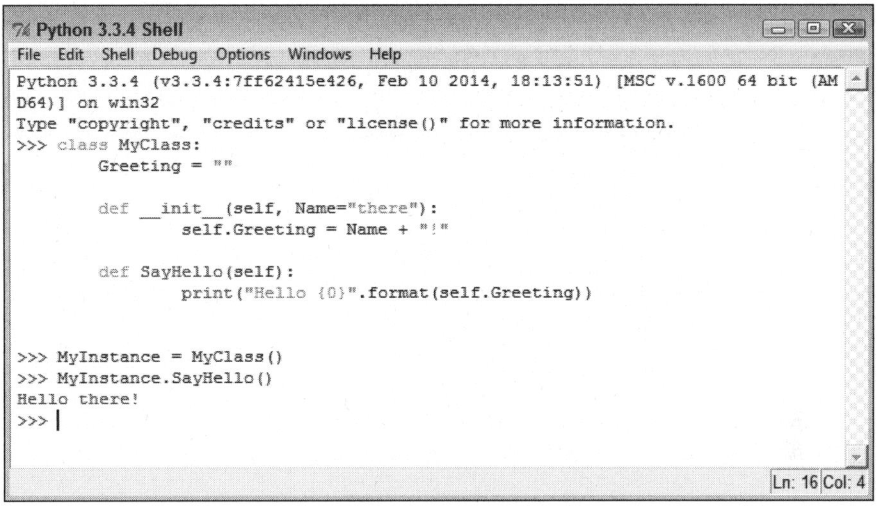

Figure 14-7:
The first version of the constructor provides a default value for the name.

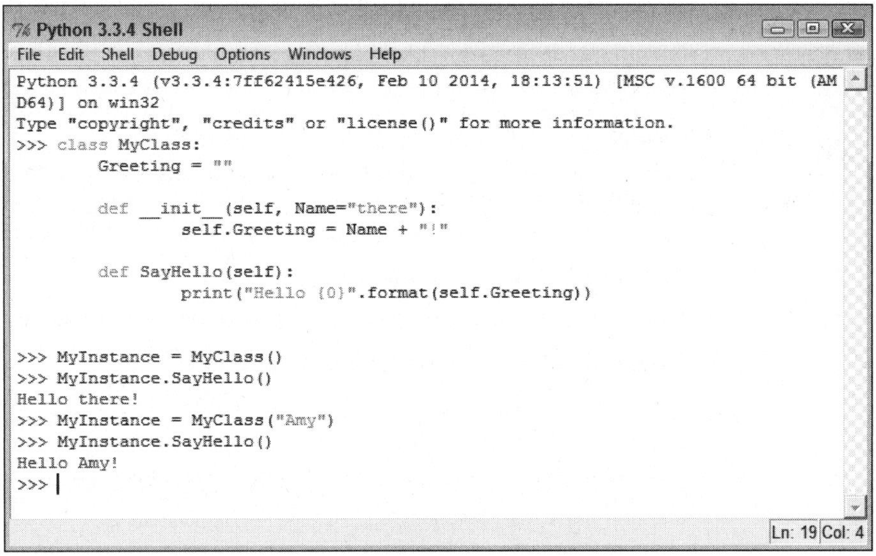

```
7% Python 3.3.4 Shell
File  Edit  Shell  Debug  Options  Windows  Help
Python 3.3.4 (v3.3.4:7ff62415e426, Feb 10 2014, 18:13:51) [MSC v.1600 64 bit (AM
D64)] on win32
Type "copyright", "credits" or "license()" for more information.
>>> class MyClass:
        Greeting = ""

        def __init__(self, Name="there"):
                self.Greeting = Name + "!"

        def SayHello(self):
                print("Hello {0}".format(self.Greeting))


>>> MyInstance = MyClass()
>>> MyInstance.SayHello()
Hello there!
>>> |
                                                              Ln: 16 Col: 4
```

Figure 14-8:
Supplying the constructor with a name provides a customized output.

```
7% Python 3.3.4 Shell
File  Edit  Shell  Debug  Options  Windows  Help
Python 3.3.4 (v3.3.4:7ff62415e426, Feb 10 2014, 18:13:51) [MSC v.1600 64 bit (AM
D64)] on win32
Type "copyright", "credits" or "license()" for more information.
>>> class MyClass:
        Greeting = ""

        def __init__(self, Name="there"):
                self.Greeting = Name + "!"

        def SayHello(self):
                print("Hello {0}".format(self.Greeting))


>>> MyInstance = MyClass()
>>> MyInstance.SayHello()
Hello there!
>>> MyInstance = MyClass("Amy")
>>> MyInstance.SayHello()
Hello Amy!
>>> |
                                                              Ln: 19 Col: 4
```

Working with variables

As mentioned earlier in the book, variables are storage containers that hold data. When working with classes, you need to consider how the data is stored and managed. A class can include both class variables and instance variables. The class variables are defined as part of the class itself, while instance variables are defined as part of methods. The following sections show how to use both variable types.

Creating class variables

Class variables provide global access to data that your class manipulates in some way. In most cases, you initialize global variables using the constructor to ensure that they contain a known good value. The following steps demonstrate how class variables work.

1. **Open a Python Shell window.**

   You see the familiar Python prompt.

2. **Type the following code (pressing Enter after each line and pressing Enter twice after the last line):**

   ```
   class MyClass:
       Greeting = ""

       def SayHello(self):
           print("Hello {0}".format(self.Greeting))
   ```

   This is a version of the code found in the "Working with constructors" section of the chapter, but this version doesn't include the constructor. Normally you do include a constructor to ensure that the class variable is initialized properly. However, this series of steps shows how class variables can go wrong.

3. **Type MyClass.Greeting = "Zelda" and press Enter.**

   This statement sets the value of Greeting to something other than the value that you used when you created the class. Of course, anyone could make this change. The big question is whether the change will take.

4. **Type MyClass.Greeting and press Enter.**

   You see that the value of Greeting has changed, as shown in Figure 14-9.

5. **Type MyInstance = MyClass() and press Enter.**

   Python creates an instance of MyClass named MyInstance.

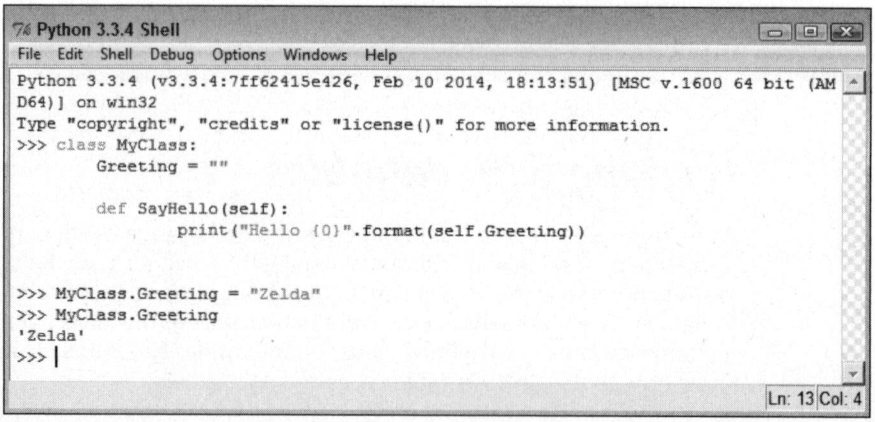

Figure 14-9:
You can change the value of Greeting.

```
Python 3.3.4 Shell
File  Edit  Shell  Debug  Options  Windows  Help
Python 3.3.4 (v3.3.4:7ff62415e426, Feb 10 2014, 18:13:51) [MSC v.1600 64 bit (AM
D64)] on win32
Type "copyright", "credits" or "license()" for more information.
>>> class MyClass:
        Greeting = ""

        def SayHello(self):
            print("Hello {0}".format(self.Greeting))

>>> MyClass.Greeting = "Zelda"
>>> MyClass.Greeting
'Zelda'
>>>
                                                              Ln: 13 Col: 4
```

6. **Type** MyInstance.SayHello() **and press Enter.**

    You see the message shown in Figure 14-10. The change that you made
    to `Greeting` has carried over to the instance of the class. It's true
    that the use of a class variable hasn't really caused a problem in this
    example, but you can imagine what would happen in a real application if
    someone wanted to cause problems.

    This is just a simple example of how class variables can go wrong. The
    two concepts you should take away from this example are as follows:

    - Avoid class variables when you can because they're inherently unsafe.

    - Always initialize class variables to a known good value in the con-
      structor code.

7. **Close the Python Shell window.**

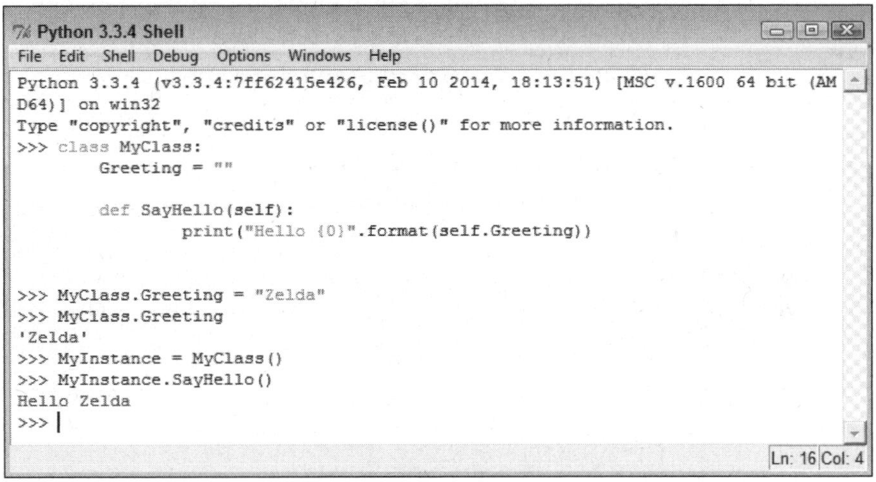

Figure 14-10:
The
change to
`Greeting`
carries
over to the
instance of
the class.

```
Python 3.3.4 Shell
File  Edit  Shell  Debug  Options  Windows  Help
Python 3.3.4 (v3.3.4:7ff62415e426, Feb 10 2014, 18:13:51) [MSC v.1600 64 bit (AM
D64)] on win32
Type "copyright", "credits" or "license()" for more information.
>>> class MyClass:
        Greeting = ""

        def SayHello(self):
                print("Hello {0}".format(self.Greeting))

>>> MyClass.Greeting = "Zelda"
>>> MyClass.Greeting
'Zelda'
>>> MyInstance = MyClass()
>>> MyInstance.SayHello()
Hello Zelda
>>>
```

Creating instance variables

Instance variables are always defined as part of a method. The input arguments to a method are considered instance variables because they exist
only when the method exists. Using instance variables is usually safer than
using class variables because it's easier to maintain control over them and
to ensure that the caller is providing the correct input. The following steps
show an example of using instance variables.

1. **Open a Python Shell window.**

   You see the familiar Python prompt.

2. **Type the following code (pressing Enter after each line and pressing Enter twice after the last line):**

   ```
   class MyClass:
       def DoAdd(self, Value1=0, Value2=0):
           Sum = Value1 + Value2
           print("The sum of {0} plus {1} is {2}."
                 .format(Value1, Value2, Sum))
   ```

   In this case, you have three instance variables. The input arguments, `Value1` and `Value2`, have default values of `0`, so `DoAdd()` can't fail simply because the user forgot to provide values. Of course, the user could always supply something other than numbers, so you should provide the appropriate checks as part of your code. The third instance variable is `Sum`, which is equal to `Value1 + Value2`. The code simply adds the two numbers together and displays the result.

3. **Type** MyInstance = MyClass() **and press Enter.**

   Python creates an instance of `MyClass` named `MyInstance`.

4. **Type** MyInstance.DoAdd(1, 4) **and press Enter.**

   You see the message shown in Figure 14-11. In this case, you see the sum of adding 1 and 4.

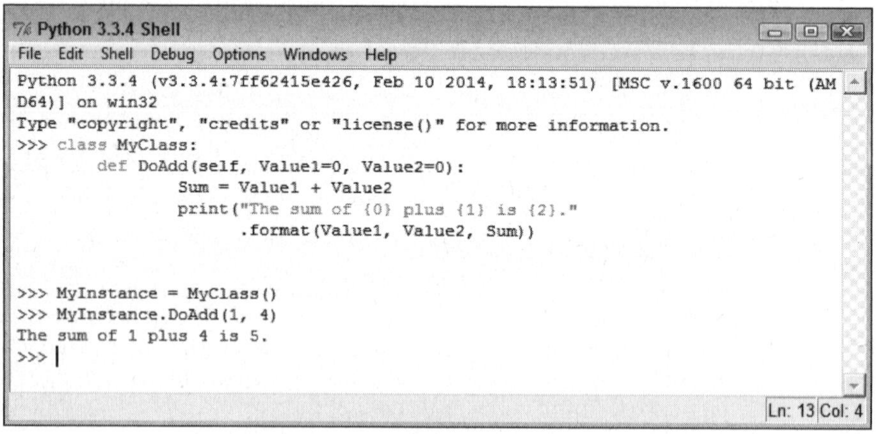

Figure 14-11:
The output is simply the sum of two numbers.

5. **Close the Python Shell window.**

Using methods with variable argument lists

Sometimes you create methods that can take a variable number of arguments. Handling this sort of situation is something Python does well. Here are the two kinds of variable arguments that you can create:

- ✔ `*args`: Provides a list of unnamed arguments.
- ✔ `**kwargs`: Provides a list of named arguments.

The actual names of the arguments don't matter, but Python developers use `*args` and `**kwargs` as a convention so that other Python developers know that they're a variable list of arguments. Notice that the first variable argument has just one asterisk (*) associated with it, which means the arguments are unnamed. The second variable has two asterisks, which means that the arguments are named. The following steps demonstrate how to use both approaches to writing an application. This example also appears with the downloadable source code as `VariableArgs.py`.

1. **Open a Python File window.**

   You see an editor in which you can type the example code.

2. **Type the following code into the window — pressing Enter after each line:**

```python
class MyClass:
    def PrintList1(*args):
        for Count, Item in enumerate(args):
            print("{0}. {1}".format(Count, Item))

    def PrintList2(**kwargs):
        for Name, Value in kwargs.items():
            print("{0} likes {1}".format(Name, Value))

MyClass.PrintList1("Red", "Blue", "Green")
MyClass.PrintList2(George="Red", Sue="Blue",
                   Zarah="Green")
```

For the purposes of this example, you're seeing the arguments implemented as part of a class method. However, you can use them just as easily with an instance method.

Look carefully at `PrintList1()` and you see a new method of using a `for` loop to iterate through a list. In this case, the `enumerate()` function outputs both a count (the loop count) and the string that was passed to the function.

The `PrintList2()` function accepts a dictionary input. Just as with `PrintList1()`, this list can be any length. However, you must process the `items()` found in the dictionary to obtain the individual values.

3. Choose Run➪Run Module.

You see the output shown in Figure 14-12. The individual lists can be of any length. In fact, in this situation, playing with the code to see what you can do with it is a good idea. For example, try mixing numbers and strings with the first list to see what happens. Try adding Boolean values as well. The point is that using this technique makes your methods incredibly flexible if all you want is a list of values as input.

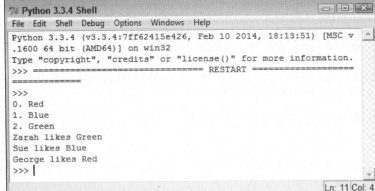

Figure 14-12: The code can process any number of entries in the list.

Overloading operators

In some situations, you want to be able to do something special as the result of using a standard operator such as add (+). In fact, sometimes Python doesn't provide a default behavior for operators because it has no default to implement. No matter what the reason might be, overloading operators makes it possible to assign new functionality to existing operators so that they do what you want, rather than what Python intended. The following steps demonstrate how to overload an operator and use it as part of an application. This example also appears with the downloadable source code as `OverloadOperator.py`.

1. Open a Python File window.

You see an editor in which you can type the example code.

2. **Type the following code into the window — pressing Enter after each line:**

```
class MyClass:
    def __init__(self, *args):
        self.Input = args

    def __add__(self, Other):
        Output = MyClass()
        Output.Input = self.Input + Other.Input
        return Output

    def __str__(self):
        Output = ""
        for Item in self.Input:
            Output += Item
            Output += " "
        return Output

Value1 = MyClass("Red", "Green", "Blue")
Value2 = MyClass("Yellow", "Purple", "Cyan")
Value3 = Value1 + Value2

print("{0} + {1} = {2}"
      .format(Value1, Value2, Value3))
```

The example demonstrates a few different techniques. The constructor, __init__(), demonstrates a method for creating an instance variable attached to the self object. You can use this approach to create as many variables as needed to support the instance.

When you create your own classes, no + operator is defined until you define one, in most cases. The only exception is when you inherit from an existing class that already has the + operator defined (see the "Extending Classes to Make New Classes" section, later in this chapter, for details). In order to add two MyClass entries together, you must define the __add__() method, which equates to the + operator.

The code used for the __add__() method may look a little odd, too, but you need to think about it one line at a time. The code begins by creating a new object, Output, from MyClass. Nothing is added to Output at this point — it's a blank object. The two objects that you want to add, self.Input and Other.Input, are actually tuples. (See "Working with Tuples," in Chapter 13, for more details about tuples.) The code places the sum of these two objects into Output.Input. The __add__() method then returns the new combined object to the caller.

Of course, you may want to know why you can't simply add the two inputs together as you would a number. The answer is that you'd end up with a tuple as an output, rather than a `MyClass` as an output. The type of the output would be changed, and that would also change any use of the resulting object.

To print `MyClass` properly, you also need to define a `__str__()` method. This method converts a `MyClass` object into a string. In this case, the output is a *space-delimited string* (in which each of the items in the string is separated from the other items by a space) containing each of the values found in `self.Input`. Of course, the class that you create can output any string that fully represents the object.

The main procedure creates two test objects, `Value1` and `Value2`. It adds them together and places the result in `Value3`. The result is printed onscreen.

3. Choose Run⇨Run Module.

Figure 14-13 shows the result of adding the two objects together, converting them to strings, and then printing the result. It's a lot of code for such a simple output statement, but the result definitely demonstrates that you can create classes that are self-contained and fully functional.

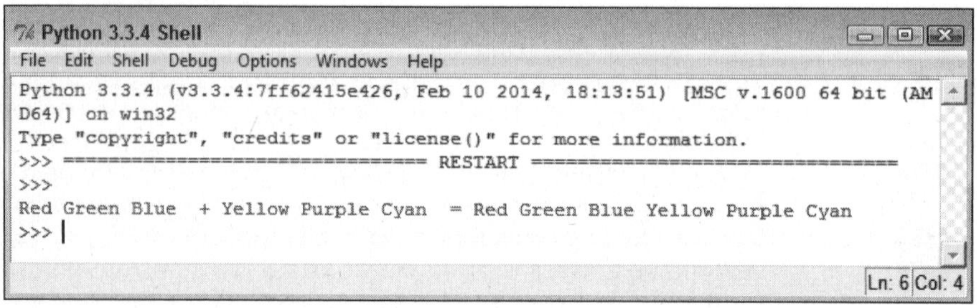

Figure 14-13: The result of adding two `MyClass` objects is a third object of the same type.

```
7k Python 3.3.4 Shell                                              [ _ ] [ □ ] [ x ]
File  Edit  Shell  Debug  Options  Windows  Help
Python 3.3.4 (v3.3.4:7ff62415e426, Feb 10 2014, 18:13:51) [MSC v.1600 64 bit (AM
D64)] on win32
Type "copyright", "credits" or "license()" for more information.
>>> ============================== RESTART ==============================
>>>
Red Green Blue  + Yellow Purple Cyan  = Red Green Blue Yellow Purple Cyan
>>> |
                                                                    Ln: 6 Col: 4
```

Creating a Class

All the previous material in this chapter has helped prepare you for creating an interesting class of your own. In this case, you create a class that you place into an external module and eventually access within an application. Listing 14-1 shows the code that you need to create the class. This example also appears with the downloadable source code as `MyClass.py`.

Listing 14-1: Creating an External Class

```
class MyClass:
    def __init__(self, Name="Sam", Age=32):
        self.Name = Name
        self.Age = Age

    def GetName(self):
        return self.Name

    def SetName(self, Name):
        self.Name = Name

    def GetAge(self):
        return self.Age

    def SetAge(self, Age):
        self.Age = Age

    def __str__(self):
        return "{0} is aged {1}.".format(self.Name,
                                        self.Age)
```

In this case, the class begins by creating an object with two instance variables: `Name` and `Age`. If the user fails to provide these values, they default to Sam and 32.

This example provides you with a new class feature. Most developers call this feature an *accessor*. Essentially, it provides access to an underlying value. There are two types of accessors: getters and setters. Both `GetName()` and `GetAge()` are *getters*. They provide read-only access to the underlying value. The `SetName()` and `SetAge()` methods are *setters*, which provide write-only access to the underlying value. Using a combination of methods like this allows you to check inputs for correct type and range, as well as verify that the caller has permission to view the information.

As with just about every other class you create, you need to define the `__str__()` method if you want the user to be able to print the object. In this case, the class provides formatted output that lists both of the instance variables.

Using the Class in an Application

Most of the time, you use external classes when working with Python. It isn't very often that a class exists within the confines of the application file because the application would become large and unmanageable. In addition, reusing the class code in another application would be difficult. The following steps help you use the `MyClass` class that you created in the previous section. This example also appears with the downloadable source code as `MyClassTest.py`.

1. **Open a Python File window.**

   You see an editor in which you can type the example code.

2. **Type the following code into the window — pressing Enter after each line:**

```
import MyClass

SamsRecord = MyClass.MyClass()
AmysRecord = MyClass.MyClass("Amy", 44)

print(SamsRecord.GetAge())
SamsRecord.SetAge(33)

print(AmysRecord.GetName())
AmysRecord.SetName("Aimee")

print(SamsRecord)
print(AmysRecord)
```

The example code begins by importing the `MyClass` module. The module name is the name of the file used to store the external code, not the name of the class. A single module can contain multiple classes, so always think of the module as being the actual file that is used to hold one or more classes that you need to use with your application.

After the module is imported, the application creates two `MyClass` objects. Notice that you use the module name first, followed by the class name. The first object, `SamsRecord`, uses the default settings. The second object, `AmysRecord`, relies on custom settings.

Sam has become a year old. After the application verifies that the age does need to be updated, it updates Sam's age.

Somehow, HR spelled Aimee's name wrong. It turns out that *Amy* is an incorrect spelling. Again, after the application verifies that the name is wrong, it makes a correction to `AmysRecord`. The final step is to print both records in their entirety.

3. **Choose Run➪Run Module.**

   The application displays a series of messages as it puts `MyClass` through its paces, as shown in Figure 14-14. At this point, you know all the essentials of creating great classes.

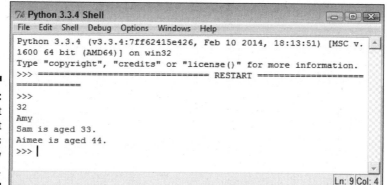

Figure 14-14:
The output
shows that
the class
is fully
functional.

Extending Classes to Make New Classes

As you might imagine, creating a fully functional, *production-grade class* (one that is used in a real-world application actually running on a system that is accessed by users) is time consuming because real classes perform a lot of tasks. Fortunately, Python supports a feature called *inheritance.* By using inheritance, you can obtain the features you want from a parent class when creating a child class. Overriding the features that you don't need and adding new features lets you create new classes relatively fast and with a lot less effort on your part. In addition, because the parent code is already tested, you don't have to put quite as much effort into ensuring that your new class works as expected. The following sections show how to build and use classes that inherit from each other.

Building the child class

Parent classes are normally supersets of something. For example, you might create a parent class named `Car` and then create child classes of various car types around it. In this case, you build a parent class named `Animal` and use it to define a child class named `Chicken`. Of course, you can easily add other child classes after you have `Animal` in place, such as a `Gorilla` class. However, for this example, you build just the one parent and one child class, as shown in Listing 14-2. This example also appears with the downloadable source code as `Animals.py`.

Listing 14-2:   Building a Parent and Child Class

```
class Animal:
    def __init__(self, Name="", Age=0, Type=""):
        self.Name = Name
        self.Age = Age
        self.Type = Type

    def GetName(self):
        return self.Name

    def SetName(self, Name):
        self.Name = Name

    def GetAge(self):
        return self.Age

    def SetAge(self, Age):
        self.Age = Age

    def GetType(self):
        return self.Type

    def SetType(self, Type):
        self.Type = Type

    def __str__(self):
        return "{0} is a {1} aged {2}".format(self.Name,
                                              self.Type,
                                              self.Age)

class Chicken(Animal):
    def __init__(self, Name="", Age=0):
        self.Name = Name
        self.Age = Age
        self.Type = "Chicken"

    def SetType(self, Type):
        print("Sorry, {0} will always be a {1}"
            .format(self.Name, self.Type))

    def MakeSound(self):
        print("{0} says Cluck, Cluck,
            Cluck!".format(self.Name))
```

The `Animal` class tracks three characteristics: `Name`, `Age`, and `Type`. A production application would probably track more characteristics, but these characteristics do everything needed for this example. The code also includes the required accessors for each of the characteristics. The `__str__()` method completes the picture by printing a simple message stating the animal characteristics.

The `Chicken` class inherits from the `Animal` class. Notice the use of `Animal` in parentheses after the `Chicken` class name. This addition tells Python that `Chicken` is a kind of `Animal`, something that will inherit the characteristics of `Animal`.

Notice that the `Chicken` constructor accepts only `Name` and `Age`. The user doesn't have to supply a `Type` value because you already know that it's a chicken. This new constructor overrides the `Animal` constructor. The three attributes are still in place, but `Type` is supplied directly in the `Chicken` constructor.

Someone might try something funny, such as setting her chicken up as a gorilla. With this in mind, the `Chicken` class also overrides the `SetType()` setter. If someone tries to change the `Chicken` type, that user gets a message rather than the attempted change. Normally, you handle this sort of problem by using an exception, but the message works better for this example by making the coding technique clearer.

Finally, the `Chicken` class adds a new feature, `MakeSound()`. Whenever someone wants to hear the sound a chicken makes, he can call `MakeSound()` to at least see it printed on the screen.

Testing the class in an application

Testing the `Chicken` class also tests the `Animal` class to some extent. Some functionality is different, but some classes aren't really meant to be used. The `Animal` class is simply a parent for specific kinds of animals, such as `Chicken`. The following steps demonstrate the `Chicken` class so that you can see how inheritance works. This example also appears with the downloadable source code as `ListStack.py`.

1. **Open a Python File window.**

   You see an editor in which you can type the example code.

2. Type the following code into the window — pressing Enter after each line:

```
import Animals

MyChicken = Animals.Chicken("Sally", 2)
print(MyChicken)
MyChicken.SetAge(MyChicken.GetAge() + 1)
print(MyChicken)
MyChicken.SetType("Gorilla")
print(MyChicken)
MyChicken.MakeSound()
```

The first step is to import the `Animals` module. Remember that you always import the filename, not the class. The `Animals.py` file actually contains two classes in this case: `Animal` and `Chicken`.

The example creates a chicken, `MyChicken`, named Sally, who is age 2. It then starts to work with `MyChicken` in various ways. For example, Sally has a birthday, so the code updates Sally's age by 1. Notice how the code combines the use of a setter, `SetAge()`, with a getter, `GetAge()`, to perform the task. After each change, the code displays the resulting object values for you. The final step is to let Sally say a few words.

3. Choose Run⇨Run Module.

You see each of the steps used to work with `MyChicken`, as shown in Figure 14-15. As you can see, using inheritance can greatly simplify the task of creating new classes when enough of the classes have commonality so that you can create a parent class that contains some amount of the code.

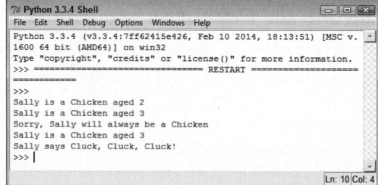

Figure 14-15:
Sally has a birthday and then says a few words.

Part IV

Performing Advanced Tasks

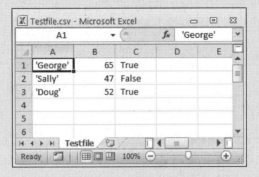

See an example of how you can interact with the directory structure of your platform at www.dummies.com/extras/beginningprogrammingwith python.

In this part . . .

- ✔ Create a file.
- ✔ Read a file.
- ✔ Update a file.
- ✔ Delete a file.
- ✔ Send an email.

Chapter 15

Storing Data in Files

● ●

In This Chapter

▶ Considering how permanent storage works with applications

▶ Deciding how to work with permanently stored content

▶ Writing to a file for the first time

▶ Obtaining content from the disk

▶ Changing file content as needed

▶ Removing a file from disk

● ●

*U*ntil now, application development might seem to be all about present-ing information onscreen. Actually, applications center around a need to work with data in some way. Data is the focus of all applications because it's the data that users are interested in. Be prepared for a huge disappoint-ment the first time you present a treasured application to a user base and find that the only thing users worry about is whether the application will help them leave work on time after creating a presentation. The fact is, the best applications are invisible, but they present data in the most appropriate manner possible for a user's needs.

If data is the focus of applications, then storing the data in a permanent manner is equally important. For most developers, data storage revolves around a permanent media such as a hard drive, Solid State Drive (SSD), Universal Serial Bus (USB) flash drive, or some other methodology. (Even cloud-based solutions work fine, but you won't see them used in this book because they require dif-ferent programming techniques that are beyond the book's scope.) The data in memory is temporary because it lasts only as long as the machine is running. A permanent storage device holds onto the data long after the machine is turned off so that it can be retrieved during the next session.

In addition to permanent storage, this chapter also helps you understand the four basic operations that you can perform on files: Create, Read, Update, and Delete (CRUD). You see the CRUD acronym used quite often in database circles, but it applies equally well to any application. No matter how your application stores the data in a permanent location, it must be able to perform these four tasks in order to provide a complete solution to the user. Of course,

CRUD operations must be performed in a secure, reliable, and controlled manner. This chapter also helps you set a few guidelines for how access must occur to ensure *data integrity* (a measure of how often data errors occur when performing CRUD operations).

Understanding How Permanent Storage Works

You don't need to understand absolutely every detail about how permanent storage works in order to use it. For example, just how the drive spins (assuming that it spins at all) is unimportant. However, most platforms adhere to a basic set of principles when it comes to permanent storage. These principles have developed over a period of time, starting with mainframe systems in the earliest days of computing.

Data is stored in *files*. You probably know about files already because every useful application out there relies on them. For example, when you open a document in your word processor, you're actually opening a data file containing the words that you or someone else has typed.

Files typically have an *extension* associated with them that defines the file type. The extension is generally standardized for any given application and is separated from the filename by a period, such as `MyData.txt`. In this case, `.txt` is the file extension, and you probably have an application on your machine for opening such files. In fact, you can likely choose from a number of applications to perform the task because the `.txt` file extension is relatively common.

Internally, files structure the data in some specific manner to make it easy to write and read data to and from the file. Any application you write must know about the file structure in order to interact with the data the file contains. The examples in this chapter use a simple file structure to make it easy to write the code required to access them, but file structures can become quite complex.

Files would be nearly impossible to find if you placed them all in the same location on the hard drive. Consequently, files are organized into *directories*. Many newer computer systems also use the term *folder* for this organizational feature of permanent storage. No matter what you call it, permanent storage relies on directories to help organize the data and make individual files significantly easier to find. To find a particular file so that you can open it and interact with the data it contains, you must know which directory holds the file.

Directories are arranged in hierarchies that begin at the uppermost level of the hard drive. For example, when working with the downloadable source code for this book, you find the code for the entire book in the BP4D directory. However, this directory doesn't actually contain any source code files. To locate the source code files, you must open one of the chapter directories contained in the BP4D directory first. To locate the source code files for this chapter, you look in the BP4D\Chapter 15 directory.

Notice that I've used a backslash (\) to separate the directory levels. Some platforms use the forward slash (/), while others use the backslash. You can read about this issue on my blog at http://blog.johnmuellerbooks. com/2014/03/10/backslash-versus-forward-slash/. The book uses backslashes when appropriate and assumes that you'll make any required changes for your platform.

A final consideration for Python developers (at least for this book) is that the hierarchy of directories is called a *path*. You see the term *path* in a few places in this book because Python must be able to find any resources you want to use based on the path you provide. For example, C:\ BP4D\Chapter 15 is the complete path to the source code for this chapter on a Windows system. A path that traces the entire route that Python must search is called an *absolute path*. An incomplete path that traces the route to a resource using the current directory as a starting point is called a *relative path*.

Creating Content for Permanent Storage

A file can contain structured or unstructured data. An example of *structured data* is a database in which each record has specific information in it. An employee database would include columns for name, address, employee ID, and so on. Each record would be an individual employee and each employee record would contain the name, address, and employee ID fields. An example of *unstructured data* is a word processing file whose text can contain any content in any order. There is no required order for the content of a paragraph, and sentences can contain any number of words. However, in both cases, the application must know how to perform CRUD operations with the file. This means that the content must be prepared in such a manner that the application can both write to and read from the file.

Even with word processing files, the text must follow a certain series of rules. Assume for a moment that the files are simple text. Even so, every paragraph must have some sort of delimiter telling the application to begin a new paragraph. The application reads the paragraph until it sees this delimiter, and then it begins a new paragraph. The more that the word processor offers in the way of features, the more structured the output becomes. For example, when the word processor offers a method of formatting the text, the formatting must appear as part of the output file.

The cues that make content usable for permanent storage are often hidden from sight. All you see when you work with the file is the data itself. The formatting remains invisible for a number of reasons, such as these:

✔ The cue is a control character, such as a carriage return or linefeed, that is normally invisible by default at the platform level.

✔ The application relies on special character combinations, such as commas and double quotes, to delimit the data entries. These special character combinations are consumed by the application during reading.

✔ Part of the reading process converts the character to another form, such as when a word processing file reads in content that is formatted. The formatting appears onscreen, but in the background the file contains special characters to denote the formatting.

✔ The file is actually in an alternative format, such as eXtensible Markup Language (XML) (see http://www.w3schools.com/xml/default. ASP for information about XML). The alternative format is interpreted and presented onscreen in a manner the user can understand.

Other rules likely exist for formatting data. For example, Microsoft actually uses a .zip file to hold its latest word processing files (the .docx) file. The use of a compressed file catalog, such as .zip, makes storing a great deal of information in a small space possible. It's interesting to see how others store data because you can often find more efficient and secure means of data storage for your own applications.

Now that you have a better idea of what could happen as part of preparing content for disk storage, it's time to look at an example. In this case, the formatting strategy is quite simple. All this example does is accept input, format it for storage, and present the formatted version onscreen (rather than save it to disk just yet). This example also appears with the downloadable source code as FormattedData.py (which contains the class used to format the information) and FormattedDataTest.py (which outputs the data onscreen).

1. **Open a Python File window.**

   You see an editor in which you can type the example code.

2. **Type the following code into the window — pressing Enter after each line:**

```
class FormatData:
    def __init__(self, Name="", Age=0, Married=False):
        self.Name = Name
        self.Age = Age
        self.Married = Married
```

```
def __str__(self):
    OutString = "'{0}', {1}, {2}".format(
        self.Name,
        self.Age,
        self.Married)
    return OutString
```

This is a shortened class. Normally, you'd add accessors (getter and setter methods) and error-trapping code. (Remember that *getter methods* provide read-only access to class data and *setter methods* provide write-only access to class data.) However, the class works fine for the demonstration.

The main feature to look at is the __str__() function. Notice that it formats the output data in a specific way. The string value, self. Name, is enclosed in single quotes. Each of the values is also separated by a comma. This is actually a form of a standard output format, comma-separated value (CSV), that is used on a wide range of platforms because it's easy to translate and is in plain text, so nothing special is needed to work with it.

3. Save the code as FormattedData.py.

4. Open another Python File window.

5. Type the following code into the window — pressing Enter after each line:

```
from FormattedData import FormatData

NewData = [FormatData("George", 65, True),
           FormatData("Sally", 47, False),
           FormatData("Doug", 52, True)]

for Entry in NewData:
    print(Entry)
```

The code begins by importing just the FormatData class from FormattedData. In this case, it doesn't matter because the FormattedData module contains only a single class. However, you need to keep this technique in mind when you need only one class from a module.

Most of the time, you work with multiple records when you save data to disk. You might have multiple paragraphs in a word processed document or multiple records, as in this case. The example creates a list of records and places them in NewData. In this case, NewData represents the entire document. The representation will likely take other forms in a production application, but the idea is the same.

Any application that saves data goes through some sort of output loop. In this case, the loop simply prints the data onscreen. However, in the upcoming sections, you actually output the data to a file.

6. **Choose Run⇨Run Module.**

You see the output shown in Figure 15-1. This is a representation of how the data would appear in the file. In this case, each record is separated by a carriage return and linefeed control character combination. That is, George, Sally, and Doug are all separate records in the file. Each *field* (data element) is separated by a comma. Text fields appear in quotes so that they aren't confused with other data types.

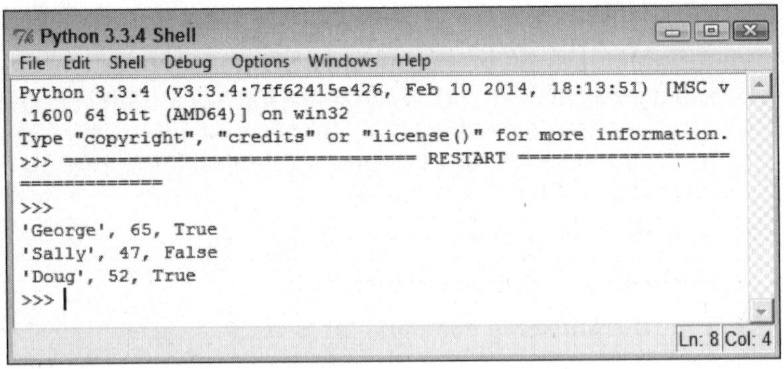

Figure 15-1:
The example presents how the data might look in CSV format.

```
7⁄6 Python 3.3.4 Shell                                    ▢ ▢ ▢ ✕
File  Edit  Shell  Debug  Options  Windows  Help
Python 3.3.4 (v3.3.4:7ff62415e426, Feb 10 2014, 18:13:51) [MSC v
.1600 64 bit (AMD64)] on win32
Type "copyright", "credits" or "license()" for more information.
>>> ============================== RESTART ==================
==============
>>>
'George', 65, True
'Sally', 47, False
'Doug', 52, True
>>> |
                                                   Ln: 8  Col: 4
```

Creating a File

Any data that the user creates and wants to work with for more than one session must be put on some sort of permanent media. Creating a file and then placing the data into it is an essential part of working with Python. You can use the following steps to create code that will write data to the hard drive. This example also appears with the downloadable source code as `FormattedData.py` and `CreateCSV.py`.

1. **Open the previously saved `FormattedData.py` file.**

You see the code originally created in the "Creating Content for Permanent Storage" section, earlier in this chapter, appear onscreen. This example makes modifications to the original code so that the class can now save a file to disk.

2. **Add the following `import` statement to the top of the file:**

```
import csv
```

The `csv` module contains everything needed to work with CSV files.

Python actually supports a huge number of file types natively, and libraries that provide additional support are available. If you have a file type that you need to support using Python, you can usually find a third-party library to support it when Python doesn't support it natively. Unfortunately, no comprehensive list of supported files exists, so you need to search online to find how Python supports the file you need. The documentation divides the supported files by types and doesn't provide a comprehensive list. For example, you can find all the archive formats at `https://docs.python.org/3/library/archiving.html` and the miscellaneous file formats at `https://docs.python.org/3/library/fileformats.html`.

3. **Type the following code into the window at the end of the existing code — pressing Enter after each line:**

```
def SaveData(Filename = "", DataList = []):
    with open(Filename,
              "w", newline='\n') as csvfile:
        DataWriter = csv.writer(
            csvfile,
            delimiter='\n',
            quotechar=" ",
            quoting=csv.QUOTE_NONNUMERIC)
        DataWriter.writerow(DataList)
        csvfile.close()
        print("Data saved!")
```

Make absolutely certain that `SaveData()` is properly indented. If you add `SaveData()` to the file but don't indent it under the `FormatData` class, Python will treat the function as a separate function and not as part of `FormatData`. The easiest way to properly indent the `SaveData()` function is to follow the same indentation used for the `__init__()` and `__str__()` functions.

Notice that the method accepts two arguments as input: a filename used to store the data and a list of items to store. This is a class method rather than an instance method. Later in this procedure, you see how using a class method is an advantage. The `DataList` argument defaults to an empty list so that if the caller doesn't pass anything at all, the method won't throw an exception. Instead, it produces an empty output file. Of course, you can also add code to detect an empty list as an error, if desired.

The `with` statement tells Python to perform a series of tasks with a specific resource — an open `csvfile` named `Testfile.csv`. The `open()` function accepts a number of inputs depending in how you use it. For this example, you open it in write mode (signified by the `w`). The `newline` attribute tells Python to treat the `\n` control character (linefeed) as a newline character.

In order to write output, you need a writer object. The DataWriter object is configured to use `csvfile` as the output file, to use `/n` as the record character, to quote records using a space, and to provide quoting only on nonnumeric values. This setup will produce some interesting results later, but for now, just assume that this is what you need to make the output usable.

Actually writing the data takes less effort than you might think. A single call to `DataWriter.writerow()` with the `DataList` as input is all you need. Always close the file when you get done using it. This action *flushes the data* (makes sure that it gets written) to the hard drive. The code ends by telling you that the data has been saved.

4. Save the code as `FormattedData.py`.

5. Open a new Python File window.

You see an editor in which you can type the example code.

6. Type the following code into the window — pressing Enter after each line:

```
from FormattedData import FormatData

NewData = [FormatData("George", 65, True),
           FormatData("Sally", 47, False),
           FormatData("Doug", 52, True)]

FormatData.SaveData("TestFile.csv", NewData)
```

This example should look similar to the one you created in the "Creating Content for Permanent Storage" section, earlier in the chapter. You still create `NewData` as a list. However, instead of displaying the information onscreen, you send it to a file instead by calling `FormatData.SaveData()`. This is one of those situations in which using an instance method would actually get in the way. To use an instance method, you would first need to create an instance of `FormatData` that wouldn't actually do anything for you.

7. Choose Run⇨Run Module.

The application runs, and you see a data saved message as output. Of course, that doesn't tell you anything about the data. In the source code file, you see a new file named `Testfile.csv`. Most platforms have a default application that opens such a file. With Windows, you can open it using Excel and WordPad (among other applications). Figure 15-2 shows the output in Excel, while Figure 15-3 shows it in WordPad. In both cases, the output looks surprisingly similar to the output shown in Figure 15-1.

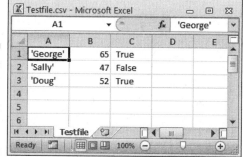

Figure 15-2:
The application output as it appears in Excel.

Figure 15-3:
The application output as it appears in WordPad.

Reading File Content

At this point, the data is on the hard drive. Of course, it's nice and safe there, but it really isn't useful because you can't see it. To see the data, you must read it into memory and then do something with it. The following steps show how to read data from the hard drive and into memory so that you can display it onscreen. This example also appears with the downloadable source code as `FormattedData.py` and `ReadCSV.py`.

1. **Open the previously saved `FormattedData.py` file.**

   You see the code originally created in the "Creating a File" section, earlier in this chapter, appear onscreen. This example makes modifications to the original code so that the class can now save a file to disk.

2. **Type the following code into the window at the end of the existing code — pressing Enter after each line:**

```python
def ReadData(Filename = ""):
    with open(Filename,
            "r", newline='\n') as csvfile:
        DataReader = csv.reader(
            csvfile,
            delimiter="\n",
            quotechar=" ",
            quoting=csv.QUOTE_NONNUMERIC)

        Output = []
        for Item in DataReader:
            Output.append(Item[0])

        csvfile.close()
        print("Data read!")
        return Output
```

As previously mentioned, make absolutely certain that `ReadData()` is properly indented. If you add `ReadData()` to the file but don't indent it under the `FormatData` class, Python will treat the function as a separate function and not as part of `FormatData`. The easiest way to properly indent `ReadData()` is to follow the same indentation used for the `__init__()` and `__str__()` functions.

Opening a file for reading is much like opening it for writing. The big difference is that you need to specify `r` (for read) instead of `w` (for write) as part of the `csv.reader()` constructor. Otherwise, the arguments are precisely the same and work the same.

It's important to remember that you're starting with a text file when working with a `.csv` file. Yes, it has delimiters, but it's still text. When reading the text into memory, you must rebuild the Python structure. In this case, `Output` is an empty list when it starts.

The file currently contains three records that are separated by the `/n` control character. Python reads each record in using a `for` loop. Notice the odd use of `Item[0]`. When Python reads the record, it sees the nonterminating entries (those that aren't last in the file) as actually being two list entries. The first entry contains data; the second is blank. You want only the first entry. These entries are appended to `Output` so that you end up with a complete list of the records that appear in the file.

As before, make sure that you close the file when you get done with it. The method prints a data read message when it finishes. It then returns `Output` (a list of records) to the caller.

3. **Save the code as** `FormattedData.py`.

4. **Open a Python File window.**

You see an editor in which you can type the example code.

5. **Type the following code into the window — pressing Enter after each line:**

```
from FormattedData import FormatData

NewData = FormatData.ReadData("TestFile.csv")

for Entry in NewData:
    print(Entry)
```

The `ReadCSV.py` code begins by importing the `FormatData` class. It then creates a `NewData` object, a list, by calling `FormatData.ReadData()`. Notice that the use of a class method is the right choice in this case as well because it makes the code shorter and simpler. The application then uses a `for` loop to display the `NewData` content.

6. **Choose Run➪Run Module.**

You see the output shown in Figure 15-4. Notice that this output looks similar to the output in Figure 15-1, even though the data was written to disk and read back in. This is how applications that read and write data are supposed to work. The data should appear the same after you read it in as it did when you wrote it out to disk. Otherwise, the application is a failure because it has modified the data.

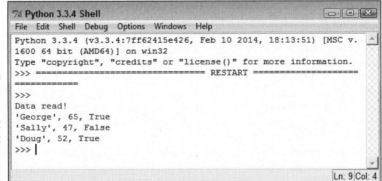

Figure 15-4:
The application input after it has been processed.

Updating File Content

Some developers treat updating a file as something complex. It can be complex if you view it as a single task. However, updates actually consist of three activities:

1. Read the file content into memory.

2. Modify the in-memory presentation of the data.

3. Write the resulting content to permanent storage.

In most applications, you can further break down the second step of modifying the in-memory presentation of the data. An application can provide some or all of these features as part of the modification process:

✔ Provide an onscreen presentation of the data.

✔ Allow additions to the data list.

✔ Allow deletions from the data list.

✔ Make changes to existing data, which can actually be implemented by adding a new record with the changed data and deleting the old record.

So far in this chapter, you have performed all but one of the activities in these two lists. You've already read file content and written file content. In the modification list, you've added data to a list and presented the data onscreen. The only interesting activity that you haven't performed is deleting data from a list. The modification of data is often performed as a two-part process of creating a new record that starts with the data from the old record and then deleting the old record after the new record is in place in the list.

Don't get into a rut by thinking that you must perform every activity mentioned in this section for every application. A monitoring program wouldn't need to display the data onscreen. In fact, doing so might be harmful (or at least inconvenient). A data logger only creates new entries — it never deletes or modifies them. An e-mail application usually allows the addition of new records and deletion of old records, but not modification of existing records. On the other hand, a word processor implements all the features mentioned. What you implement and how you implement it depends solely on the kind of application you create.

Separating the user interface from the activities that go on behind the user interface is important. To keep things simple, this example focuses on what needs to go on behind the user interface to make updates to the file you created in the "Creating a File" section, earlier in this chapter. The following steps demonstrate how to read, modify, and write a file in order to update it. The updates consist of an addition, a deletion, and a change. To allow you to run the application more than once, the updates are actually sent to another file. This example also appears with the downloadable source code as `FormattedData.py` and `UpdateCSV.py`.

1. **Open a Python File window.**

   You see an editor in which you can type the example code.

2. **Type the following code into the window — pressing Enter after each line:**

```
from FormattedData import FormatData
import os.path
```

```
if not os.path.isfile("Testfile.csv"):
    print("Please run the CreateFile.py example!")
    quit()

NewData = FormatData.ReadData("TestFile.csv")
for Entry in NewData:
    print(Entry)

print("\r\nAdding a record for Harry.")
NewRecord = "'Harry', 23, False"
NewData.append(NewRecord)
for Entry in NewData:
    print(Entry)

print("\r\nRemoving Doug's record.")
Location = NewData.index("'Doug', 52, True")
Record = NewData[Location]

NewData.remove(Record)
for Entry in NewData:
    print(Entry)

print("\r\nModifying Sally's record.")
Location = NewData.index("'Sally', 47, False")
Record = NewData[Location]
Split = Record.split(",")
NewRecord = FormatData(Split[0].replace("'", ""),
                       int(Split[1]),
                       bool(Split[2]))
NewRecord.Married = True
NewRecord.Age = 48
NewData.append(NewRecord.__str__())
NewData.remove(Record)
for Entry in NewData:
    print(Entry)

FormatData.SaveData("ChangedFile.csv", NewData)
```

This example has quite a bit going on. First, it checks to ensure that the
Testfile.csv file is actually present for processing. This is a check that
you should always perform when you expect a file to be present. In this
case, you aren't creating a new file, you're updating an existing file, so
the file must be present. If the file isn't present, the application ends.

The next step is to read the data into NewData. This part of the process
looks much like the data reading example earlier in the chapter.

You have already seen code for using list functions in Chapter 12. This
example uses those functions to perform practical work. The append()
function adds a new record to NewData. However, notice that the data
is added as a string, not as a FormatData object. The data is stored as

strings on disk, so that's what you get when the data is read back in. You can either add the new data as a string or create a FormatData object and then use the __str__() method to output the data as a string.

The next step is to remove a record from NewData. To perform this task, you must first find the record. Of course, that's easy when working with just four records (remember that NewData now has a record for Harry in it). When working with a large number of records, you must first search for the record using the index() function. This act provides you with a number containing the location of the record, which you can then use to retrieve the actual record. After you have the actual record, you can remove it using the remove() function.

Modifying Sally's record looks daunting at first, but again, most of this code is part of dealing with the string storage on disk. When you obtain the record from NewData, what you receive is a single string with all three values in it. The split() function produces a list containing the three entries as strings, which still won't work for the application. In addition, Sally's name is enclosed in both double and single quotes.

The simplest way to manage the record is to create a FormatData object and to convert each of the strings into the proper form. This means removing the extra quotes from the name, converting the second value to an int, and converting the third value to a bool. The FormatData class doesn't provide accessors, so the application modifies both the Married and Age fields directly. Using accessors (getter methods that provide read-only access and setter methods that provide write-only access) is a better policy.

The application then appends the new record to and removes the existing record from NewData. Notice how the code uses NewRecord.__str__() to convert the new record from a FormatData object to the required string.

The final act is to save the changed record. Normally, you'd use the same file to save the data. However, the example saves the data to a different file in order to allow examination of both the old and new data.

3. **Choose Run⇨Run Module.**

You see the output shown in Figure 15-5. Notice that the application lists the records after each change so that you can see the status of NewData. This is actually a useful troubleshooting technique for your own applications. Of course, you want to remove the display code before you release the application to production.

4. **Open the ChangedFile.csv file using an appropriate application.**

You see output similar to that shown in Figure 15-6. This output is shown using WordPad, but the data won't change when you use other applications. So, even if your screen doesn't quite match Figure 15-6, you should still see the same data.

Figure 15-5:
The application shows each of the modifications in turn.

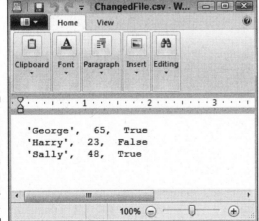

Figure 15-6:
The updated information appears as expected in `Changed File.csv`.

Deleting a File

The previous section of this chapter, "Updating File Content," explains how to add, delete, and update records in a file. However, at some point you may need to delete the file. The following steps describe how to delete files that you no longer need. This example also appears with the downloadable source code as DeleteCSV.py.

1. **Open a Python File window.**

   You see an editor in which you can type the example code.

2. **Type the following code into the window — pressing Enter after each line:**

   ```
   import os

   os.remove("ChangedFile.csv")
   print("File Removed!")
   ```

The task looks simple in this case, and it is. All you need to do to remove a file is call os.remove() with the appropriate filename and path (as needed, Python defaults to the current directory, so you don't need to specify a path if the file you want to remove is in the default directory). The ease with which you can perform this task is almost scary because it's too easy. Putting safeguards in place is always a good idea. You may want to remove other items, so here are other functions you should know about:

- **os.rmdir()**: Removes the specified directory. The directory must be empty or Python will display an exception message.

- **shutil.rmtree()**: Removes the specified directory, all subdirectories, and all files. This function is especially dangerous because it removes everything without checking (Python assumes that you know what you're doing). As a result, you can easily lose data using this function.

3. **Choose Run⇨Run Module.**

   The application displays the File Removed! message. When you look in the directory that originally contained the ChangedFile.csv file, you see that the file is gone.

Chapter 16

Sending an E-Mail

In This Chapter

▶ Defining the series of events for sending an e-mail

▶ Developing an e-mail application

▶ Testing the e-mail application

*T*his chapter helps you understand the process of sending an e-mail using Python. More important, this chapter is generally about helping you understand what happens when you communicate outside the local PC. Even though this chapter is specifically about e-mail, it also contains principles you can use when performing other tasks. For example, when working with an external service, you often need to create the same sort of packaging as you do for an e-mail. So, the information you see in this chapter can help you understand all sorts of communication needs.

To make working with e-mail as easy as possible, this chapter uses standard mail as a real-world equivalent of e-mail. The comparison is apt. E-mail was actually modeled on real-world mail. Originally, the term e-mail was used for any sort of electronic document transmission, and some forms of it required the sender and recipient to be online at the same time. As a result, you may find some confusing references online about the origins and development of e-mail. This chapter views e-mail as it exists today — as a storing and forwarding mechanism for exchanging documents of various types.

The examples in this chapter rely on the availability of a Simple Mail Transfer Protocol (SMTP) server. If that sounds like Greek to you, read the sidebar entitled "Considering the SMTP server" that appears later in the chapter.

Considering the simple mail transfer protocol

When you work with e-mail, you see a lot of references to Simple Mail Transfer Protocol (SMTP). Of course, the term looks really technical, and what happens under the covers truly *is* technical, but all you really need to know is that it works. On the other hand, understanding SMTP a little more than as a "black box" that takes an e-mail from the sender and spits it out at the other end to the recipient can be useful. Taking the term apart (in reverse order), you see these elements:

✔ **Protocol:** A standard set of rules. E-mail work by requiring rules that everyone agrees upon. Otherwise, e-mail would become unreliable.

✔ **Mail transfer:** Documents are sent from one place to another, much the same as what the post office does with real mail. In e-mail's case, the transfer process relies on short commands that your e-mail application issues to the SMTP server. For example, the MAIL FROM command tells the SMTP server who is sending the e-mail, while the RCPT TO command states where to send it.

✔ **Simple:** States that this activity goes on with the least amount of effort possible. The fewer parts to anything, the more reliable it becomes.

If you were to look at the rules for transferring the information, you would find they're anything but simple. For example, RFC1123 is a standard that specifies how Internet hosts are supposed to work (see http://www.faqs.org/rfcs/rfc1123.html for details). These rules are used by more than one Internet technology, which explains why most of them appear to work about the same (even though their resources and goals may be different).

Another, entirely different standard, RFC2821, describes how SMTP specifically implements the rules found in RFC1123 (see http://www.faqs.org/rfcs/rfc2821.html for details). The point is, a whole lot of rules are written in jargon that only a true geek could love (and even the geeks aren't sure). If you want a plain-English explanation of how e-mail works, check out the article at http://computer.howstuffworks.com/e-mail-messaging/email.htm. Page 4 of this article (http://computer.howstuffworks.com/e-mail-messaging/email3.htm) describes the commands that SMTP uses to send information hither and thither across the Internet. In fact, if you want the shortest possible description of SMTP, page 4 is probably the right place to look.

Understanding What Happens When You Send E-mail

E-mail has become so reliable and so mundane that most people don't understand what a miracle it is that it works at all. Actually, the same can be said of the real mail service. When you think about it, the likelihood of one particular letter leaving one location and ending up precisely where it should at the other end seems impossible — mind-boggling, even. However, both e-mail and its real-world equivalent have several aspects in common that improve the likelihood that they'll actually work as intended. The following sections examine what happens when you write an e-mail, click Send, and the recipient receives it on the other end. You might be surprised at what you discover.

Viewing e-mail as you do a letter

The best way to view e-mail is the same as how you view a letter. When you write a letter, you provide two pieces of paper as a minimum. The first contains the content of the letter, the second is an envelope. Assuming that the postal service is honest, the content is never examined by anyone other than the recipient. The same can be said of e-mail. An e-mail actually consists of these components:

- ✔ **Message:** The content of the e-mail, which is actually composed of two subparts:

  - *Header:* The part of the e-mail content that includes the subject, the list of recipients, and other features, such as the urgency of the e-mail.

  - *Body:* The part of the e-mail content that contains the actual message. The message can be in plain text, formatted as HTML, and consisting of one or more documents, or it can be a combination of all these elements.

- ✔ **Envelope:** A container for the message. The envelope provides sender and recipient information, just as the envelope for a physical piece of mail provides. However, an e-mail doesn't include a stamp.

When working with e-mail, you create a message using an e-mail application. As part of the e-mail application setup, you also define account information. When you click send:

1. The e-mail application wraps up your message, with the header first, in an envelope that includes both your sender and the recipient's information.

2. The e-mail application uses the account information to contact the SMTP server and send the message for you.

3. The SMTP server reads only the information found in the message envelope and redirects your e-mail to the recipient.

4. The recipient e-mail application logs on to the local server, picks up the e-mail, and then displays only the message part for the user.

The process is a little more complex than this explanation, but this is essentially what happens. In fact, it's much the same as the process used when working with physical letters in that the essential steps are the same. With physical mail, the e-mail application is replaced by you on one end and the recipient at the other. The SMTP server is replaced by the post office and the employees who work there (including the postal carriers). However, someone generates a message, the message is transferred to a recipient, and the recipient receives the message in both cases.

Defining the parts of the envelope

There is a difference in how the envelope for an e-mail is configured and how it's actually handled. When you view the envelope for an e-mail, it looks just like a letter in that it contains the address of the sender and the address of the recipient. It may not look physically like an envelope, but the same components are there. When you visualize a physical envelope, you see certain specifics, such as the sender's name, street address, city, state, and zip code. The same is true for the recipient. These elements define, in physical terms, where the postal carrier should deliver the letter or return the letter when it can't be delivered.

However, when the SMTP server processes the envelope for an e-mail, it must look at the specifics of the address, which is where the analogy of a physical envelope used for mail starts to break down a little. An e-mail address contains different information from a physical address. In summary, here is what the e-mail address contains:

- ✔ **Host:** The host is akin to the city and state used by a physical mail envelope. A host address is the address used by the card that is physically connected to the Internet, and it handles all the traffic that the Internet consumes or provides for this particular machine. A PC can use Internet resources in a lot of ways, but the host address for all these uses is the same.

- ✔ **Port:** The port is akin to the street address used by a physical mail envelope. It specifies which specific part of the system should receive the message. For example, an SMTP server used for outgoing messages normally relies on port 25. However, the Point-of-Presence (POP3) server used for incoming e-mail messages usually relies on port 110. Your browser typically uses port 80 to communicate with websites. However, secure websites (those that use https as a protocol, rather than http) rely on port 443 instead. You can see a list of typical ports at `http://en.wikipedia.org/wiki/List_of_TCP_and_UDP_port_numbers`.

✔ **Local hostname:** The local hostname is the human-readable form of the combination of the host and port. For example, the website www. myplace.com might resolve to an address of 55.225.163.40:80 (where the first four numbers are the host address and the number after the colon is the port). Python takes care of these details behind the scenes for you, so normally you don't need to worry about them. However, it's nice to know that this information is available.

Now that you have a better idea of how the address is put together, it's time to look at it more carefully. The following sections describe the envelope of an e-mail in more precise terms.

Host

A *host address* is the identifier for a connection to a server. Just as an address on an envelope isn't the actual location, neither is the host address the actual server. It merely specifies the location of the server.

The connection used to access a combination of a host address and a port is called a *socket*. Just who came up with this odd name and why isn't important. What is important is that you can use the socket to find out all kinds of information that's useful in understanding how e-mail works. The following steps help you see hostnames and host addresses at work. More important, you begin to understand the whole idea of an e-mail envelope and the addresses it contains.

1. **Open a Python Shell window.**

   You see the familiar Python prompt.

2. **Type** import socket **and press Enter.**

   Before you can work with sockets, you must import the socket library. This library contains all sorts of confusing attributes, so use it with caution. However, this library also contains some interesting functions that help you see how the Internet addresses work.

3. **Type** socket.gethostbyname("localhost") **and press Enter.**

   You see a host address as output. In this case, you should see 127.0.0.1 as output because localhost is a standard hostname. The address, 127.0.0.1, is associated with the host name, localhost.

4. **Type** socket.gethostbyaddr("127.0.0.1") **and press Enter.**

   Be prepared for a surprise. You get a tuple as output, as shown in Figure 16-1. However, instead of getting localhost as the name of the host, you get the name of your machine. You use localhost as a common name for the local machine, but when you specify the address, you get the machine name instead. In this case, Main is the name of my personal machine. The name you see on your screen will correspond to your machine.

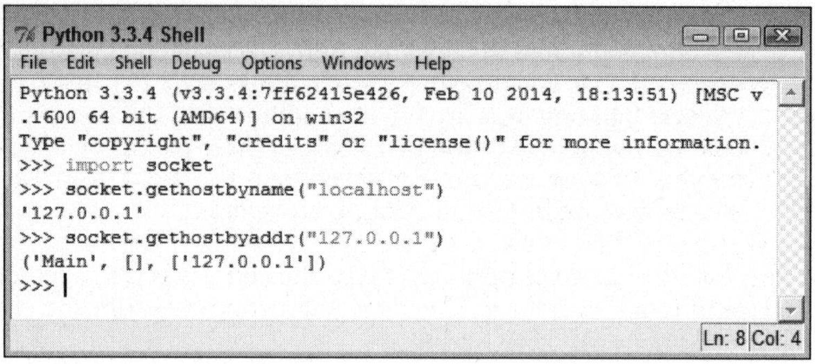

Figure 16-1:
The local-
host
address
actually cor-
responds
to your
machine.

5. **Type** socket.gethostbyname("www.johnmuellerbooks.com") **and press Enter.**

You see the output shown in Figure 16-2. This is the address for my web-site. The point is that these addresses work wherever you are and what-ever you're doing — just like those you place on a physical envelope. The physical mail uses addresses that are unique across the world, just as the Internet does.

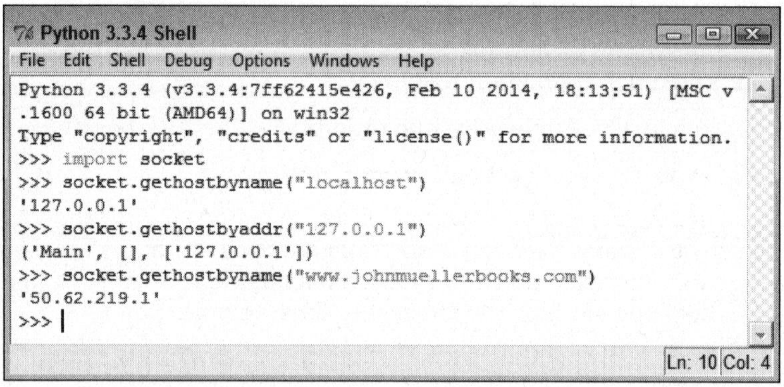

Figure 16-2:
The
addresses
that you
use to send
e-mail are
unique
across the
Internet.

6. **Close the Python shell.**

Port

A *port* is a specific entryway for a server location. The host address specifies the location, but the port defines where to get in. Even if you don't specify a port every time you use a host address, the port is implied. Access is always granted using a combination of the host address and the port. The following steps help illustrate how ports work with the host address to provide server access:

1. **Open a Python Shell window.**

   You see the familiar Python prompt.

2. **Type** import socket **and press Enter.**

   Remember that a socket provides both host address and port information. You use the socket to create a connection that includes both items.

3. **Type** socket.getaddrinfo("localhost", 110) **and press Enter.**

   The first value is the name of a host you want to obtain information about. The second value is the port on that host. In this case, you obtain the information about localhost port 110.

   You see the output shown in Figure 16-3. The output consists of two tuples: one for the Internet Protocol version 6 (IPv6) output and one for the Internet Protocol version 4 (IPv4) address. Each of these tuples contains five entries, four of which you really don't need to worry about because you'll likely never need them. However, the last entry, ('127.0.0.1', 110), shows the address and port for localhost port 110.

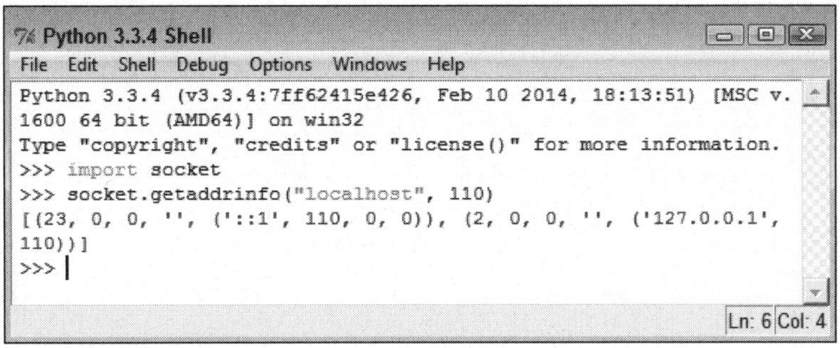

Figure 16-3:
The local-
host host
provides
both an IPv6
and an IPv4
address.

```
7% Python 3.3.4 Shell                                    □ □ ⊠
File  Edit  Shell  Debug  Options  Windows  Help
Python 3.3.4 (v3.3.4:7ff62415e426, Feb 10 2014, 18:13:51) [MSC v.
1600 64 bit (AMD64)] on win32
Type "copyright", "credits" or "license()" for more information.
>>> import socket
>>> socket.getaddrinfo("localhost", 110)
[(23, 0, 0, '', ('::1', 110, 0, 0)), (2, 0, 0, '', ('127.0.0.1',
110))]
>>> |
                                               Ln: 6 Col: 4
```

4. **Type** socket.getaddrinfo("johnmuellerbooks.com", 80) **and press Enter.**

   Figure 16-4 shows the output from this command. Notice that this Internet location provides only an IPv4 address, not an IPv6, address, for port 80. The socket.getaddrinfo() method provides a useful method for determining how you can access a particular location. Using IPv6 provides significant benefits over IPv4 (see http://www.networkcomputing.com/networking/six-benefits-of-ipv6/d/d-id/1232791 for details), but most Internet locations provide only IPv4 support now.

```
76 Python 3.3.4 Shell                                    [ _ ][ ▭ ][ ✕ ]
File  Edit  Shell  Debug  Options  Windows  Help
Python 3.3.4 (v3.3.4:7ff62415e426, Feb 10 2014, 18:13:51) [MSC v.  ▲
1600 64 bit (AMD64)] on win32
Type "copyright", "credits" or "license()" for more information.
>>> import socket
>>> socket.getaddrinfo("localhost", 110)
[(23, 0, 0, '', ('::1', 110, 0, 0)), (2, 0, 0, '', ('127.0.0.1',
110))]
>>> socket.getaddrinfo("johnmuellerbooks.com", 80)
[(2, 0, 0, '', ('50.62.219.1', 80))]
>>> |
                                                                   ▼
                                                         Ln: 8 Col: 4
```

Figure 16-4:
Most
Internet
locations
provide
only an IPv4
address.

5. **Type** socket.getservbyport(25) **and press Enter.**

You see the output shown in Figure 16-5. The `socket.getservbyport()` method provides the means to determine how a particular port is used. Port 25 is always dedicated to SMTP support on any server. So, when you access 127.0.0.1:25, you're asking for the SMTP server on localhost. In short, a port provides a specific kind of access in many situations.

```
76 Python 3.3.4 Shell                                    [ _ ][ ▭ ][ ✕ ]
File  Edit  Shell  Debug  Options  Windows  Help
Python 3.3.4 (v3.3.4:7ff62415e426, Feb 10 2014, 18:13:51) [MSC v.  ▲
1600 64 bit (AMD64)] on win32
Type "copyright", "credits" or "license()" for more information.
>>> import socket
>>> socket.getaddrinfo("localhost", 110)
[(23, 0, 0, '', ('::1', 110, 0, 0)), (2, 0, 0, '', ('127.0.0.1',
110))]
>>> socket.getaddrinfo("johnmuellerbooks.com", 80)
[(2, 0, 0, '', ('50.62.219.1', 80))]
>>> socket.getservbyport(25)
'smtp'
>>> |
                                                                   ▼
                                                         Ln: 10 Col: 4
```

Figure 16-5:
Standard-
ized ports
provide
specific
services
on every
server.

6. **Close the Python shell.**

Some people assume that the port information is always provided. However, this isn't always the case. Python will provide a default port when you don't supply one, but relying on the default port is a bad idea because you can't be certain which service will be accessed. In addition, some systems use nonstandard port assignments as a security feature. Always get into the habit of using the port number and ensuring that you have the right one for the task at hand.

Local hostname

A *hostname* is simply the human-readable form of the host address. Humans don't really understand 127.0.0.1 very well (and the IPv6 addresses make even less sense). However, humans do understand localhost just fine. There is a special server and setup to translate human-readable hostnames to host addresses, but you really don't need to worry about it for this book (or programming in general). When your application suddenly breaks for no apparent reason, it helps to know that one does exist, though.

The "Host" section, earlier in this chapter, introduces you to the hostname to a certain extent through the use of the `socket.gethostbyaddr()` method, whereby an address is translated into a hostname. You saw the process in reverse using the `socket.gethostbyname()` method. The following steps help you understand some nuances about working with the hostname:

1. **Open a Python Shell window.**

   You see the familiar Python prompt.

2. **Type** import socket **and press Enter.**

3. **Type** socket.gethostname() **and press Enter.**

   You see the name of the local system, as shown in Figure 16-6. The name of your system will likely vary from mine, so your output will be different than that shown in Figure 16-6, but the idea is the same no matter which system you use.

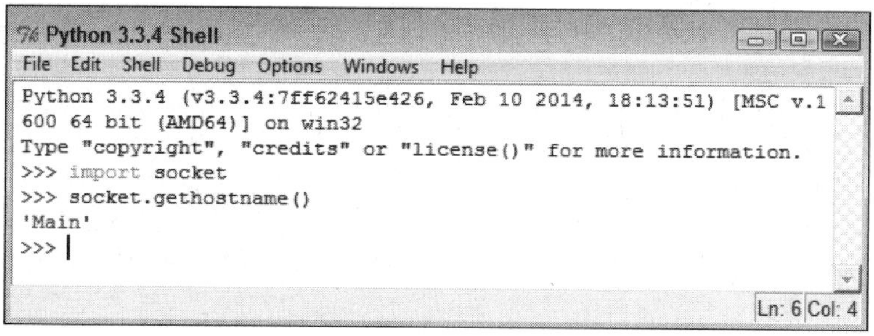
Python 3.3.4 Shell
File Edit Shell Debug Options Windows Help
Python 3.3.4 (v3.3.4:7ff62415e426, Feb 10 2014, 18:13:51) [MSC v.1
600 64 bit (AMD64)] on win32
Type "copyright", "credits" or "license()" for more information.
>>> import socket
>>> socket.gethostname()
'Main'
>>>
Ln: 6 Col: 4

Figure 16-6: Sometimes you need to know the name of the local system.

4. **Type** socket.gethostbyname(socket.gethostname()) **and press Enter.**

   You see the IP address of the local system, as shown in Figure 16-7. Again, your setup is likely different from mine, so the output you see will differ. This is a method you can use in your applications to determine the address of the sender when needed. Because it doesn't rely on any hard-coded value, the method works on any system.

5. **Close the Python shell.**

Figure 16-7:
Avoid using
hard-coded
values for
the local
system
whenever
possible.

```
7₄ Python 3.3.4 Shell                                    ▭ ▢ ✕
File  Edit  Shell  Debug  Options  Windows  Help
Python 3.3.4 (v3.3.4:7ff62415e426, Feb 10 2014, 18:13:51) [MSC v.1 ▲
600 64 bit (AMD64)] on win32
Type "copyright", "credits" or "license()" for more information.
>>> import socket
>>> socket.gethostname()
'Main'
>>> socket.gethostbyname(socket.gethostname())
'192.168.137.210'
>>> |
                                                          ▼
                                             Ln: 8 Col: 4
```

Defining the parts of the letter

The "envelope" for an e-mail address is what the SMTP server uses to route the e-mail. However, the envelope doesn't include any content — that's the purpose of the letter. A lot of developers get the two elements confused because the letter contains sender and receiver information as well. This information appears in the letter just like the address information that appears in a business letter — it's for the benefit of the viewer. When you send a business letter, the postal delivery person doesn't open the envelope to see the address information inside. Only the information on the envelope matters.

It's because the information in the e-mail letter is separate from its information in the envelope that nefarious individuals can spoof e-mail addresses. The envelope potentially contains legitimate sender information, but the letter may not. (When you see the e-mail in your e-mail application, all that is present is the letter, not the envelope — the envelope has been stripped away by the e-mail application.) For that matter, neither the sender nor the recipient information may be correct in the letter that you see onscreen in your e-mail reader.

The letter part of an e-mail is actually made of separate components, just as the envelope is. Here is a summary of the three components:

✔ **Sender:** The sender information tells you who sent the message. It contains just the e-mail address of the sender.

✔ **Receiver:** The receiver information tells you who will receive the message. This is actually a list of recipient e-mail addresses. Even if you want to send the message to only one person, you must supply the single e-mail address in a list.

✔ **Message:** Contains the information that you want the recipient to see. This information can include the following:

- **From:** The human-readable form of the sender.

- **To:** The human-readable form of the recipients.

- **CC:** Visible recipients who also received the message, even though they aren't the primary targets of the message.

- **Subject:** The purpose of the message.

- **Documents:** One or more documents, including the text message that appears with the e-mail.

E-mails can actually become quite complex and lengthy. Depending on the kind of e-mail that is sent, a message could include all sorts of additional information. However, most e-mails contain these simple components, and this is all the information you need to send an e-mail from your application. The following sections describe the process used to generate a letter and its components in more detail.

Defining the message

Sending an empty envelope to someone will work, but it isn't very exciting. In order to make your e-mail message worthwhile, you need to define a message. Python supports a number of methods of creating messages. However, the easiest and most reliable way to create a message is to use the Multipurpose Internet Mail Extensions (MIME) functionality that Python provides (and no, a MIME is not a silent person with white gloves who acts out in public).

As with many e-mail features, MIME is standardized, so it works the same no matter which platform you use. There are also numerous forms of MIME that are all part of the `email.mime` module described at `https://docs.python.org/3/library/email.mime.html`. Here are the forms that you need to consider most often when working with e-mail:

✔ **MIMEApplication:** Provides a method for sending and receiving application input and output

✔ **MIMEAudio:** Contains an audio file

✔ **MIMEImage:** Contains an image file

✔ **MIMEMultipart:** Allows a single message to contain multiple subparts, such as including both text and graphics in a single message

✔ **MIMEText:** Contains text data that can be in ASCII, HTML, or another standardized format

Although you can create any sort of an e-mail message with Python, the easiest type to create is one that contains plain text. The lack of formatting in the content lets you focus on the technique used to create the message, rather than on the message content. The following steps help you understand how the message-creating process works, but you won't actually send the message anywhere.

1. **Open a Python Shell window.**

   You see the familiar Python prompt.

2. **Type the following code (pressing Enter after each line):**

   ```
   from email.mime.text import MIMEText
   msg = MIMEText("Hello There")
   msg['Subject'] = "A Test Message"
   msg['From']='John Mueller <John@JohnMuellerBooks.com>'
   msg['To'] = 'John Mueller <John@JohnMuellerBooks.com>'
   ```

   This is a basic plain-text message. Before you can do anything, you must import the required class, which is `MIMEText`. If you were creating some other sort of message, you'd need to import other classes or import the `email.mime` module as a whole.

   The `MIMEText()` constructor requires message text as input. This is the body of your message, so it might be quite long. In this case, the message is relatively short — just a greeting.

   At this point, you assign values to standard attributes. The example shows the three common attributes that you always define: `Subject`, `From`, and `To`. The two address fields, `From` and `To`, contain both a human-readable name and the e-mail address. All you have to include is the e-mail address.

3. **Type** msg.as_string() **and press Enter.**

   You see the output shown in Figure 16-8. This is how the message actually looks. If you have ever looked under the covers at the messages produced by your e-mail application, the text probably looks familiar.

   The `Content-Type` reflects the kind of message you created, which is a plain-text message. The `charset` tells what kind of characters are used in the message so that the recipient knows how to handle them. The `MIME-Version` specifies the version of MIME used to create the message so that the recipient knows whether it can handle the content. Finally, the `Context-Transfer-Encoding` determines how the message is converted into a bit stream before it is sent to the recipient.

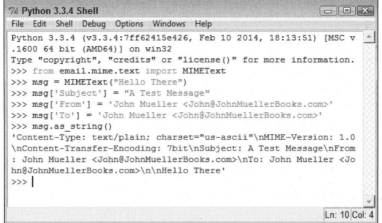

Figure 16-8:
Python
adds some
additional
information
required to
make your
message
work.

Specifying the transmission

An earlier section ("Defining the parts of the envelope") describes how the envelope is used to transfer the message from one location to another. The process of sending the message entails defining a transmission method. Python actually creates the envelope for you and performs the transmission, but you must still define the particulars of the transmission. The following steps help you understand the simplest approach to transmitting a message using Python. These steps won't result in a successful transmission unless you modify them to match your setup. Read the "Considering the SMTP server" sidebar for additional information.

1. **Use the Python Shell window that you opened if you followed the steps in the "Defining the message" section.**

   You should see the message that you created earlier.

2. **Type the following code (pressing Enter after each line and pressing Enter twice after the last line):**

   ```
   import smtplib
   s = smtplib.SMTP('localhost')
   ```

   The `smtplib` module contains everything needed to create the message envelope and send it. The first step in this process is to create a connection to the SMTP server, which you name as a string in the constructor. If the SMTP server that you provide doesn't exist, the application will fail at this point, saying that the host actively refused the connection.

3. **Type** s.sendmail('*SenderAddress*', ['*RecipientAddress*'], msg.as_string( )) **and press Enter.**

In order for this step to work, you must replace `SenderAddress` and `RecipientAddress` with real addresses. Don't include the human-readable form this time — the server requires only an address.

This is the step that actually creates the envelope, packages the e-mail message, and sends it off to the recipient. Notice that you specify the sender and recipient information separately from the message, which the SMTP server doesn't read.

4. **Close the Python shell.**

Considering the message subtypes

The "Defining the message" section, earlier in this chapter, describes the major e-mail message types, such as application and text. However, if e-mail had to rely on just those types, transmitting coherent messages to anyone would be difficult. The problem is that the type of information isn't explicit enough. If you send someone a text message, you need to know what sort of text it is before you can process it, and guessing just isn't a good idea. A text message could be formatted as plain text, or it might actually be an HTML page. You wouldn't know from just seeing the type, so messages require a subtype. The type is text and the subtype is html when you send an HTML page to someone. The type and subtype are separated by a forward slash, so you'd see text/html if you looked at the message.

Theoretically, the number of subtypes is unlimited as long as the platform has a handler defined for that subtype. However, the reality is that everyone needs to agree on the subtypes or there won't be a handler (unless you're talking about a custom application for which the two parties have agreed to a custom subtype in advance). With this in mind, you can find a listing of standard types and subtypes at `http://www.freeformatter.com/mime-types-list.html`. The nice thing about the table on this site is that it provides you with a common file extension associated with the subtype and a reference to obtain additional information about it.

Creating the E-mail Message

So far, you've seen how both the envelope and the message work. Now it's time to put them together and see how they actually work. The following sections show how to create two messages. The first message is a plain-text message and the second message uses HTML formatting. Both messages should work fine with most e-mail readers — nothing fancy is involved.

Working with a text message

Text messages represent the most efficient and least resource-intensive method of sending communication. However, text messages also convey the least amount of information. Yes, you can use emoticons to help get the point across, but the lack of formatting can become a problem in some situations. The following steps describe how to create a simple text message using Python. This example also appears with the downloadable source code as TextMessage.py.

1. **Open a Python File window.**

   You see an editor in which you can type the example code.

2. **Type the following code into the window — pressing Enter after each line:**

   ```
   from email.mime.text import MIMEText
   import smtplib

   msg = MIMEText("Hello There!")

   msg['Subject'] = 'A Test Message'
   msg['From']='SenderAddress'
   msg['To'] = 'RecipientAddress'

   s = smtplib.SMTP('localhost')
   s.sendmail('SenderAddress',
           ['RecipientAddress'],
           msg.as_string())

   print("Message Sent!")
   ```

   This example is a combination of everything you've seen so far in the chapter. However, this is the first time you've seen everything put together. Notice that you create the message first, and then the envelope (just as you would in real life).

3. **Choose Run⇨Run Module.**

   The application tells you that it has sent the message to the recipient.

Considering the SMTP server

If you tried the example in this chapter without modifying it, you're probably scratching your head right now trying to figure out what went wrong. It's unlikely that your system has an SMTP server connected to localhost. The reason for the examples to use localhost is to provide a placeholder that you replace later with the information for your particular setup.

In order to see the example actually work, you need an SMTP server as well as a real-world e-mail account. Of course, you could install all the software required to create such an environment on your own system, and some developers who work extensively with e-mail applications do just that. Most platforms come with an e-mail package that you can install, or you can use a freely available substitute such as Sendmail, an open source product available for download at `https://www.sendmail.com/sm/open_source/`

`download/`. The easiest way to see the example work is to use the same SMTP server that your e-mail application uses. When you set up your e-mail application, you either asked the e-mail application to detect the SMTP server or you supplied the SMTP server on your own. The configuration settings for your e-mail application should contain the required information. The exact location of this information varies widely by e-mail application, so you need to look at the documentation for your particular product.

No matter what sort of SMTP server you eventually find, you need to have an account on that server in most cases to use the functionality it provides. Replace the information in the examples with the information for your SMTP server, such as smtp.myisp.com, along with your e-mail address for both sender and receiver. Otherwise, the example won't work.

Working with an HTML message

An HTML message is basically a text message with special formatting. The following steps help you create an HTML e-mail to send off. This example also appears with the downloadable source code as `HTMLMessage.py`.

1. **Open a Python File window.**

    You see an editor in which you can type the example code.

2. **Type the following code into the window — pressing Enter after each line:**

```
from email.mime.text import MIMEText
import smtplib

msg = MIMEText(
    "<h1>A Heading</h1><p>Hello There!</p>","html")
```

```
msg['Subject'] = 'A Test HTML Message'
msg['From']='SenderAddress'
msg['To'] = 'RecipientAddress'

s = smtplib.SMTP('localhost')
s.sendmail('SenderAddress',
           ['RecipientAddress'],
           msg.as_string())

print("Message Sent!")
```

The example follows the same flow as the text message example in the previous section. However, notice that the message now contains HTML tags. You create an HTML body, not an entire page. This message will have an H1 header and a paragraph.

The most important part of this example is the text that comes after the message. The "html" argument changes the subtype from text/plain to text/html, so the recipient knows to treat the message as HTML content. If you don't make this change, the recipient won't see the HTML output.

3. **Choose Run⇨Run Module.**

   The application tells you that it has sent the message to the recipient.

Seeing the E-mail Output

At this point, you have between one and three application-generated messages (depending on how you've gone through the chapter) waiting in your Inbox. To see the messages you created in earlier sections, your e-mail application must receive the messages from the server — just as it would with any e-mail. Figure 16-9 shows an example of the HTML version of the message when viewed in Output. (Your message will likely look different depending on your platform and e-mail application.)

If your e-mail application offers the capability to look at the message source, you find that the message actually does contain the information you saw earlier in the chapter. Nothing is changed or different about it because after it leaves the application, the message isn't changed in any way during its trip.

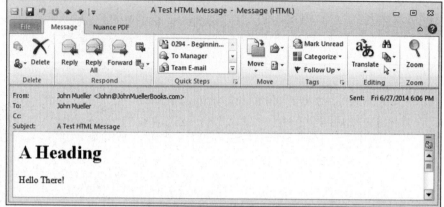

Figure 16-9:
The HTML
output
contains a
header and
a paragraph
as expected.

The point of creating your own application to send and receive e-mail isn't convenience — using an off-the-shelf application serves that purpose much better. The point is flexibility. As you can see from this short chapter on the subject, you control every aspect of the message when you create your own application. Python hides much of the detail from view, so what you really need to worry about are the essentials of creating and transmitting the message using the correct arguments.

Part V
The Part of Tens

 web extras Enjoy an additional Part of Tens article about ten sites with unique designs at www.dummies.com/extras/beginningprogrammingwithpython.

In this part

- ✔ Discover really cool resources that you can use to make your Python programming experience better.

- ✔ Earn a living with the Python knowledge you gain.

- ✔ Get the tools you need to work more efficiently with Python.

- ✔ Make Python do even more by adding libraries.

Chapter 17

Ten Amazing Programming Resources

In This Chapter

▶ Using the Python documentation

▶ Accessing an interactive Python tutorial

▶ Creating online applications using Python

▶ Extending Python using third-party libraries

▶ Obtaining a better editor than Python's for Python application development

▶ Getting the syntax for your Python application correct

▶ Working with XML

▶ Becoming a professional coder with less effort than usual

▶ Overcoming the Unicode obstacle

▶ Creating applications that run fast

*T*his book is a great start to your Python programming experience, but you'll want additional resources at some point. This chapter provides you with ten amazing programming resources that you can use to make your development experience better. By using these resources, you save both time and energy in creating your next dazzling Python application.

Of course, this chapter is only the beginning of your Python resource experience. Literally reams of Python documentation are out there, along with mountains of Python code. It might be possible to write an entire book (or two) on just the Python libraries. This chapter is designed to provide you with ideas of where to look for additional information that's targeted toward meeting your specific needs. Don't let this be the end of your search — consider this chapter the start of your search instead.

Working with the Python Documentation Online

An essential part of working with Python is knowing what is available in the base language and how to extend it to perform other tasks. The Python documentation at `https://docs.python.org/3/` (created for the 3.4.1 version of the product at the time of this writing; it may be updated by the time you read this chapter) contains a lot more than just the reference to the language that you receive as part of a download. In fact, you see these topics discussed as part of the documentation:

- New features in the current version of the language
- Access to a full-fledged tutorial
- Complete library reference
- Complete language reference
- How to install and configure Python
- How to perform specific tasks in Python
- Help with installing Python modules from other sources (as a means of extending Python)
- Help with distributing Python modules you create so that others can use them
- How to extend Python using C/C++ and then embed the new features you create
- Complete reference for C/C++ developers who want to extend their applications using Python
- Frequently Asked Questions (FAQ) pages

All this information is provided in a form that is easy to access and use. In addition to the usual table-of-contents approach to finding information, you have access to a number of indexes. For example, if you aren't interested in anything but locating a particular module, class, or method, you can use the Global Module Index.

The `https://docs.python.org/3/` web page is also the place where you report problems with Python. It's important to work through problems you're having with the product, but as with any other language, Python does have bugs in it. Locating and destroying the bugs will only make Python a better language.

Using the LearnPython.org Tutorial

Many tutorials are available for Python and many of them do a great job, but they're all lacking a special feature that you find when using the LearnPython. org tutorial at `http://www.learnpython.org/` — interactivity. Instead of just reading about a Python feature, you read it and then try it yourself using the interactive feature of the site.

You have already worked through all the material in the simple tutorials in this book. However, you haven't worked through the advanced tutorials yet. These tutorials present the following topics:

- ✔ **Generators:** Specialized functions that return iterators.

- ✔ **List comprehensions:** A method to generate new lists based on existing lists.

- ✔ **Multiple function arguments:** An extension of the methods described in the "Using methods with variable argument lists" in Chapter 14.

- ✔ **Regular expressions:** Wildcard setups used to match patterns of characters, such as telephone numbers.

- ✔ **Exception handling:** An extension of the methods described in Chapter 9.

- ✔ **Sets:** Demonstrates a special kind of list that never contains duplicate entries.

- ✔ **Serialization:** Shows how to use a data storage methodology called JavaScript Object Notation (JSON).

- ✔ **Partial functions:** A technique for creating specialized versions of simple functions that derive from more complex functions. For example, if you have a `multiply()` function that requires two arguments, a partial function named `double()` might require only one argument that it always multiplies by 2.

- ✔ **Code introspection:** Provides the ability to examine classes, functions, and keywords to determine their purpose and capabilities.

- ✔ **Decorator:** A method for making simple modifications to callable objects.

Performing Web Programming Using Python

This book discusses the ins and outs of basic programming, so it relies on desktop applications because of their simplicity. However, many developers specialize in creating online applications of various sorts using Python. The Web Programming in Python site at `https://wiki.python.org/moin/WebProgramming` helps you make the move from the desktop to online application development. It doesn't just cover one sort of online application — it covers almost all of them (an entire book free for the asking). The tutorials are divided into these three major (and many minor) areas:

- ✔ Server

  - Developing server-side frameworks for applications

  - Creating a Common Gateway Interface (CGI) script

  - Providing server applications

  - Developing Content Management Systems (CMS)

  - Designing data access methods through web services solutions

- ✔ Client

  - Interacting with browsers and browser-based technologies

  - Creating browser-based clients

  - Accessing data through various methodologies, including web services

- ✔ Related

  - Creating common solutions for Python-based online computing

  - Interacting with DataBase Management Systems (DBMSs)

  - Designing application templates

  - Building Intranet solutions

Getting Additional Libraries

The Pythonware site (`http://www.pythonware.com/`) doesn't look all that interesting until you start clicking the links. It provides you with access to a number of third-party libraries that help you perform additional tasks using Python. Although all the links provide you with useful resources, the "Downloads (`downloads.effbot.org`)" link is the one you should look at first. This download site provides you with access to

- ✔ **aggdraw:** A library that helps you create anti-aliased drawings.

- ✔ **celementtree:** An add-on to the elementtree library that makes working with XML data more efficient and faster.

- ✔ **console:** An interface for Windows that makes it possible to create better console applications.

- ✔ **effbot:** A collection of useful add-ons and utilities, including the EffNews RSS news reader.

- ✔ **elementsoap:** A library that helps you create Simple Object Access Protocol (SOAP) connections to Web services providers.

- ✔ **elementtidy:** An add-on to the elementtree library that helps you create nicer-looking and more functional XML tree displays than the standard ones in Python.

- ✔ **elementtree:** A library that helps you interact with XML data more efficiently than standard Python allows.

- ✔ **exemaker:** A utility that creates an executable program from your Python script so that you can execute the script just as you would any other application on your machine.

- ✔ **ftpparse:** A library for working with FTP sites.

- ✔ **grabscreen:** A library for performing screen captures.

- ✔ **imaging:** Provides the source distribution to the Python Imaging Library (PIL) that lets you add image-processing capabilities to the Python interpreter. Having the source lets you customize PIL to meet specific needs.

- ✔ **pil:** Binary installers for PIL, which make obtaining a good installation for your system easier. (There are other PIL-based libraries as well, such as pilfont — a library for adding enhanced font functionality to a PIL-based application.)

- ✔ **pythondoc:** A utility for creating documentation from the comments in your Python code that works much like JavaDoc.

- ✔ **squeeze:** A utility for converting your Python application contained in multiple files into a one- or two-file distribution that will execute as normal with the Python interpreter.

- ✔ **tkinter3000:** A widget-building library for Python that includes a number of subproducts. *Widgets* are essentially bits of code that create controls, such as buttons, to use in GUI applications. There are a number of add-ons for the tkinter3000 library, such as wckgraph, which helps you add graphing support to an application.

Creating Applications Faster Using an IDE

An Interactive Development Environment (IDE) helps you create applications in a specific language. The Integrated DeveLopment Environment (IDLE) editor that comes with Python worked well for the needs of the book, but you may find it limited after a while. For example, IDLE doesn't provide the advanced debugging functionality that many developers favor. In addition, you may find that you want to create graphical applications, which is difficult using IDLE.

You can talk to 50 developers and get little consensus as to the best tool for any job, especially when discussing IDEs. Every developer has a favorite product and isn't easily swayed to try another. Developers invest many hours learning a particular IDE and extending it to meet specific requirements (when the IDE allows such tampering).

An inability (at times) to change IDEs later is why it's important to try a number of different IDEs before you settle on one. (The most common reason for not wanting to change an IDE after you select one is that the project types are incompatible, which would mean having to re-create your projects every time you change editors, but there are many other reasons that you can find listed online.) The PythonEditors wiki at `https://wiki.python.org/moin/PythonEditors` provides an extensive list of IDEs that you can try. The table provides you with particulars about each editor so that you can eliminate some of the choices immediately.

Checking Your Syntax with Greater Ease

The IDLE editor provides some level of syntax highlighting, which is helpful in finding errors. For example, if you mistype a keyword, it doesn't change color to the color used for keywords on your system. Seeing that it hasn't changed makes it possible for you to know to correct the error immediately, instead of having to run the application and find out later that something has gone wrong (sometimes after hours of debugging).

The python.vim utility (`http://www.vim.org/scripts/script.php?script_id=790`) provides enhanced syntax highlighting that makes finding errors in your Python script even easier. This utility runs as a script, which makes it fast and efficient to use on any platform. In addition, you can tweak the source code as needed to meet particular needs.

Using XML to Your Advantage

The eXtensible Markup Language (XML) is used for data storage of all types in most applications of any substance today. You probably have a number of XML files on your system and don't even know it because XML data appears under a number of file extensions. For example, many `.config` files, used to hold application settings, rely on XML. In short, it's not a matter of if you'll encounter XML when writing Python applications, but when.

XML has a number of advantages over other means of storing data. For example, it's platform independent. You can use XML on any system, and the same file is readable on any other system as long as that system knows the file format. The platform independence of XML is why it appears with so many other technologies, such as web services. In addition, XML is relatively easy to learn and because it's text, you can usually fix problems with it without too many problems.

It's important to learn about XML itself, and you can do so using an easy tutorial such as the one found on the W3Schools site at `http://www.w3schools.com/xml/default.ASP`. Some developers rush ahead and later find that they can't understand the Python-specific materials that assume they already know how to write basic XML files. The W3Schools site is nice because it breaks up the learning process into chapters so that you can work with XML a little at a time, as follows:

- ✔ Taking a basic XML tutorial
- ✔ Validating your XML files
- ✔ Using XML with JavaScript (which may not seem important, but JavaScript is prominent in many online application scenarios)
- ✔ Gaining an overview of XML-related technologies
- ✔ Using advanced XML techniques
- ✔ Working with XML examples that make seeing XML in action easier

Using W3Schools to your advantage

One of the most used online resources for learning online computing technologies is W3Schools. You can find the main page at http://www.w3schools.com/. This single resource can help you discover every web technology needed to build any sort of modern application you can imagine. The topics include:

✔ HTML

✔ CSS

✔ JavaScript

✔ SQL

✔ JQuery

✔ PHP

✔ XML

✔ ASP.NET

However, you should realize that this is just a starting point for Python developers. Use the W3Schools material to get a good handle on the underlying technology, and then rely on Python-specific resources to build your skills. Most Python developers need a combination of learning materials to build the skills required to make a real difference in application coding.

After you get the fundamentals down, you need a resource that shows how to use XML with Python. One of the better places to find this information is the Python and XML Processing site at http://pyxml.sourceforge.net/topics/. Between these two resources, you can quickly build a knowledge of XML that will have you building Python applications that use XML in no time.

Getting Past the Common Python Newbie Errors

Absolutely everyone makes coding mistakes — even that snobby fellow down the hall who has been programming for the last 30 years (he started in kindergarten). No one likes to make mistakes and some people don't like to own up to them, but everyone does make them. So you shouldn't feel too bad when you make a mistake. Simply fix it up and get on with your life.

Of course, there is a difference between making a mistake and making an avoidable, common mistake. Yes, even the professionals sometimes make the common mistakes, but it's far less likely because they have seen the mistake in the past and have trained themselves to avoid it. You can gain an advantage over your competition by avoiding the newbie mistakes that everyone has to learn about sometime. To avoid these mistakes, check out this two-part series:

✔ Python: Common Newbie Mistakes, Part 1 (`http://blog.amir.rachum.com/blog/2013/07/06/python-common-newbie-mistakes-part-1/`)

✔ Python: Common Newbie Mistakes, Part 2 (`http://blog.amir.rachum.com/blog/2013/07/09/python-common-newbie-mistakes-part-2/`)

Many other resources are available for people who are just starting with Python, but these particular resources are succinct and easy to understand. You can read them in a relatively short time, make some notes about them for later use, and avoid those embarrassing errors that everyone tends to remember.

Understanding Unicode

Although this book tries to sidestep the thorny topic of Unicode, you'll eventually encounter it when you start writing serious applications. Unfortunately, Unicode is one of those topics that had a committee deciding what Unicode would look like, so we ended up with more than one poorly explained definition of Unicode and a multitude of standards to define it. In short, there is no one definition for Unicode.

You'll encounter a wealth of Unicode standards when you start working with more advanced Python applications, especially when you start working with multiple human languages (each of which seems to favor its own flavor of Unicode). Keeping in mind the need to discover just what Unicode is, here are some resources you should check out:

✔ The Absolute Minimum Every Software Developer Absolutely, Positively Must Know About Unicode and Character Sets (No Excuses!) (`http://www.joelonsoftware.com/articles/Unicode.html`)

✔ The Updated Guide to Unicode on Python (`http://lucumr.pocoo.org/2013/7/2/the-updated-guide-to-unicode/`)

✔ Python Encodings and Unicode (`http://eric.themoritzfamily.com/python-encodings-and-unicode.html`)

✔ Unicode Tutorials and Overviews (`http://www.unicode.org/standard/tutorial-info.html`)

✔ Explain it like I'm five: Python and Unicode? (`http://www.reddit.com/r/Python/comments/1g62eh/explain_it_like_im_five_python_and_unicode/`)

✔ Unicode Pain (`http://nedbatchelder.com/text/unipain.html`)

Making Your Python Application Fast

Nothing turns off a user faster than an application that performs poorly. When an application performs poorly, you can count on users not using it at all. In fact, poor performance is a significant source of application failure in enterprise environments. An organization can spend a ton of money to build an impressive application that does everything, but no one uses it because it runs too slowly or has other serious performance problems.

Performance is actually a mix of reliability, security, and speed. In fact, you can read about the performance triangle on my blog at `http://blog.johnmuellerbooks.com/2012/04/16/considering-the-performance-triangle/`. Many developers focus on just the speed part of performance but end up not achieving their goal. It's important to look at every aspect of your application's use of resources and to ensure that you use the best coding techniques.

Numerous resources are available to help you understand performance as it applies to Python applications. However, one of the best resources out there is "A guide to analyzing Python performance," at `http://www.huyng.com/posts/python-performance-analysis/`. The author takes the time to explain why something is a performance bottleneck, rather than simply tell you that it is. After you read this article, make sure to check out the PythonSpeed Performance Tips at `https://wiki.python.org/moin/PythonSpeed/PerformanceTips` as well.

Chapter 18

Ten Ways to Make a Living with Python

In This Chapter

▶ Using Python for QA

▶ Creating your own way in a smaller organization

▶ Employing Python for special product-scripting needs

▶ Working as an administrator

▶ Demonstrating programming techniques

▶ Delving into location data

▶ Mining data of various sorts

▶ Working with embedded systems

▶ Processing scientific data

▶ Analyzing data in real time

*Y*ou can literally write any application you want using any language you desire given enough time, patience, and effort. However, some undertakings would be so convoluted and time consuming as to make the effort a study in frustration. In short, most (possibly all) things are possible, but not everything is worth the effort. Using the right tool for the job is always a plus in a world that views time as something in short supply and not to be squandered.

Python excels at certain kinds of tasks, which means that it also lends itself to certain types of programming. The kind of programming you can perform determines the job you get and the way in which you make your living. For example, Python probably isn't a very good choice for writing device drivers, as C/C++ are, so you probably won't find yourself working for a hardware company. Likewise, Python can work with databases, but not at the same depth that comes natively to other languages such as Structured Query Language (SQL), so you won't find yourself working on a huge corporate database project. However, you may find yourself using Python in academic settings because Python does make a great learning language. (See my blog post on the topic at `http://blog.johnmuellerbooks.com/2014/07/14/python-as-a-learning-tool/`.)

The following sections describe some of the occupations that do use Python regularly so that you know what sorts of things you might do with your new-found knowledge. Of course, a single source can't list every kind of job. Consider this an overview of some of the more common uses for Python.

Working in QA

A lot of organizations have separate Quality Assurance (QA) departments that check applications to ensure that they work as advertised. Many different test script languages are on the market, but Python makes an excellent language in this regard because it's so incredibly flexible. In addition, you can use this single language in multiple environments — both on the client and on the server. The broad reach of Python means that you can learn a single language and use it for testing anywhere you need to test something, and in any environment.

In this scenario, the developer usually knows another language, such as C++, and uses Python to test the applications written in C++. However, the QA person doesn't need to know another language in all cases. In some situations, blind testing may be used to confirm that an application behaves in a practical manner or as a means for checking the functionality of an external service provider. You need to check with the organization you want to work with as to the qualifications required for a job from a language perspective.

Why you need to know multiple programming languages

Most organizations see knowledge of multiple programming languages as a big plus (some see it as a requirement). Of course, when you're an employer, it's nice to get the best deal you can when hiring a new employee. Knowing a broader range of languages means that you can work in more positions and offer greater value to an organization. Rewriting applications in another language is time consuming, error prone, and expensive, so most companies look for people who can support an application in the existing language, rather than rebuild it from scratch.

From your perspective, knowing more languages means that you'll get more interesting jobs and will be less likely to get bored doing the same old thing every day. In addition, knowing

multiple languages tends to reduce frustration. Most large applications today rely on components written in a number of computer languages. In order to understand the application and how it functions better, you need to know every language used to construct it.

Knowing multiple languages also makes it possible to learn new languages faster. After a while, you start to see patterns in how computer languages are put together, so you spend less time with the basics and can move right on to advanced topics. The faster you can learn new technologies, the greater your opportunities to work in exciting areas of computer science. In short, knowing more languages opens a lot of doors.

Becoming the IT Staff for a Smaller Organization

A smaller organization may have only one or two IT staff, which means that you have to perform a broad range of tasks quickly and efficiently. With Python, you can write utilities and in-house applications quite swiftly. Even though Python might not answer the needs of a large organization because it's interpreted (and potentially open to theft or fiddling by unskilled employees), using it in a smaller organization makes sense because you have greater access control and need to make changes fast. In addition, the ability to use Python in a significant number of environments reduces the need to use anything but Python to meet your needs.

Some developers are unaware that Python is available in some non-obvious products. For example, even though you can't use Python scripting with Internet Information Server (IIS) right out of the box, you can add Python scripting support to this product using the steps found in the Microsoft Knowledge Base article at `http://support.microsoft.com/kb/276494`. If you aren't sure whether a particular application can use Python for scripting, make sure that you check it out online.

Performing Specialty Scripting for Applications

A number of products can use Python for scripting purposes. For example, Maya (`http://www.autodesk.com/products/autodesk-maya/overview`) relies on Python for scripting purposes. By knowing which high-end products support Python, you can find a job working with that application in any business that uses it. Here are some examples of products that rely on Python for scripting needs:

- 3ds Max
- Abaqus
- Blender
- Cinema 4D
- GIMP
- Google App Engine
- Houdini
- Inkscape
- Lightwave
- Modo
- MotionBuilder
- Nuke
- Paint Shop Pro
- Scribus
- Softimage

This is just the tip of the iceberg. You can also use Python with the GNU debugger to create more understandable output of complex structures, such as those found in C++ containers. Some video games also rely on Python as a scripting language. In short, you could build a career around creating application scripts using Python as the programming language.

Administering a Network

More than a few administrators use Python to perform tasks such as monitoring network health or creating utilities that automate tasks. Administrators are often short of time, so anything they can do to automate tasks is a plus. In fact, some network management software, such as Trigger (`http://trigger.readthedocs.org/en/latest/`), is actually written in Python. A lot of these tools are open source and free to download, so you can try them on your network. Also, some interesting articles discuss using Python for network administration, such as "Intro to Python & Automation for Network Engineers" at `http://packetpushers.net/show-176-intro-to-python-automation-for-network-engineers/`. The point is that knowing how to use Python on your network can ultimately decrease your workload and help you perform your tasks more easily. If you want to see some scripts that are written with network management in mind, check out 25 projects tagged "Network Management" at `http://freecode.com/tags/network-management`.

Teaching Programming Skills

Many teachers are looking for a faster, more consistent method of teaching computer technology. Raspberry Pi (`http://www.raspberrypi.org/`) is a single-board computer that makes obtaining the required equipment a lot less expensive for schools. The smallish device plugs into a television or computer monitor to provide full computing capabilities with an incredibly simple setup. Interestingly enough, Python plays a big role into making the Raspberry Pi into a teaching platform for programming skills (`http://www.piprogramming.org/main/?page_id=372`).

In reality, teachers often use Python to extend native Raspberry Pi capabilities so that it can perform all sorts of interesting tasks (`http://www.raspberrypi.org/tag/python/`). The project entitled, Boris, the Twitter Dino-Bot (`http://www.raspberrypi.org/boris-the-twitter-dino-bot/`), is especially interesting. The point is that if you have a teaching goal in mind, combining Raspberry Pi with Python is a fantastic idea.

Helping People Decide on Location

A Geographic Information System (GIS) provides a means of viewing geographic information with business needs in mind. For example, you could use GIS to determine the best place to put a new business or to determine the optimum routes for shipping goods. However, GIS is used for more than simply deciding on locations — it also provides a means for communicating location information better than maps, reports, and other graphics, and a method of presenting physical locations to others. Also interesting is the fact that many GIS products use Python as their language of choice. In fact, a wealth of Python-specific information related to GIS is currently available, such as

- ✔ The GIS and Python Software Laboratory (`http://gispython.org/`)
- ✔ Python and GIS Resources (`http://www.gislounge.com/python-and-gis-resources/`)
- ✔ GIS Programming and Automation (`https://www.e-education.psu.edu/geog485/node/17`)

Many GIS-specific products, such as ArcGIS (`http://www.esri.com/software/arcgis`), rely on Python to automate tasks. Entire communities develop around these software offerings, such as Python for ArcGIS (`http://resources.arcgis.com/en/communities/python/`). The point is that you can use your new programming skills in areas other than computing to earn an income.

Performing Data Mining

Everyone is collecting data about everyone and everything else. Trying to sift through the mountains of data collected is an impossible task without a lot of fine-tuned automation. The flexible nature of Python, combined with its terse language that makes changes extremely fast, makes it a favorite with people who perform data mining on a daily basis. In fact, you can find an online book on the topic, *A Programmer's Guide to Data Mining,* at `http://guidetodatamining.com/`. Python makes data mining tasks a lot easier. The purpose of data mining is to recognize trends, which means looking for patterns of various sorts. The use of artificial intelligence with Python makes such pattern recognition possible. A paper on the topic, "Data Mining: Discovering and Visualizing Patterns with Python" (`http://refcardz.dzone.com/refcardz/data-mining-discovering-and`), helps you understand how such analysis is possible. You can use Python to create just the right tool to locate a pattern that could net sales missed by your competitor.

Of course, data mining is used for more than generating sales. For example, people use data mining to perform tasks such as locating new planets around stars or other types of analysis that increase our knowledge of the universe. Python figures into this sort of data mining as well. You can likely find books and other resources dedicated to any kind of data mining that you want to perform, with many of them mentioning Python as the language of choice.

Interacting with Embedded Systems

An embedded system exists for nearly every purpose on the planet. For example, if you own a programmable thermostat for your house, you're interacting with an embedded system. Raspberry Pi (mentioned earlier in the chapter) is an example of a more complex embedded system. Many embedded systems rely on Python as their programming language. In fact, a special form of Python, Embedded Python (`https://wiki.python.org/moin/EmbeddedPython`), is sometimes used for these devices. You can even find a YouTube presentation on using Python to build an embedded system at `http://www.youtube.com/watch?v=WZoeqnsY9AY`.

Interestingly enough, you might already be interacting with a Python-driven embedded system. For example, Python is the language of choice for many car security systems (`http://www.pythoncarsecurity.com/`). The remote start feature that you might have relies on Python to get the job done. Your home automation and security system (`http://www.linuxjournal.com/article/8513`) might also rely on Python.

Python is so popular for embedded systems because it doesn't require compilation. An embedded-system vendor can create an update for any embedded system and simply upload the Python file. The interpreter automatically uses this file without having to upload any new executables or jump through any of the types of hoops that other languages can require.

Carrying Out Scientific Tasks

Python seems to devote more time to scientific and numerical processing tasks than many of the computer languages out there. The number of Python's scientific and numeric processing modules is staggering (`https://wiki.python.org/moin/NumericAndScientific`). Scientists love Python because it's small, easy to learn, and yet quite precise in its treatment of data. It's possible to produce results using just a few lines code. Yes, you could produce the same result using another language, but the other language might not include the prebuilt modules to perform the task, and it would most definitely require more lines of code even if it did.

The two sciences that have dedicated Python modules are space sciences and life sciences. For example, there is actually a module for performing tasks related to solar physics. You can also find a module for working in genomic biology. If you're in a scientific field, the chances are good that your Python knowledge will significantly impact your ability to produce results quickly while your colleagues are still trying to figure out how to analyze the data.

Performing Real-Time Analysis of Data

Making decisions requires timely, reliable, and accurate data. Often, this data must come from a wide variety of sources, which then require a certain amount of analysis before becoming useful. A number of the people who report using Python do so in a management capacity. They use Python to probe those disparate sources of information, perform the required analysis, and then present the big picture to the manager who has asked for the information. Given that this task occurs regularly, trying to do it manually every time would be time consuming. In fact, it would simply be a waste of time. By the time the manager performed the required work, the need to make a decision might already have passed. Python makes it possible to perform tasks quickly enough for a decision to have maximum impact.

Previous sections have pointed out Python's data-mining, number-crunching, and graphics capabilities. A manager can combine all these qualities while using a language that isn't nearly as complex to learn as C++. In addition, any changes are easy to make, and the manager doesn't need to worry about learning programming skills such as compiling the application. A few changes to a line of code in an interpreted module usually serve to complete the task.

As with other sorts of occupational leads in this chapter, thinking outside the box is important when getting a job. A lot of people need real-time analysis. Launching a rocket into space, controlling product flow, ensuring that packages get delivered on time, and all sorts of other occupations rely on timely, reliable, and accurate data. You might be able to create your own new job simply by employing Python to perform real-time data analysis.

Chapter 19

Ten Interesting Tools

In This Chapter

▶ Keeping track of application bugs

▶ Creating a safe place to test applications

▶ Getting your application placed on a user system

▶ Documenting your application

▶ Writing your application code

▶ Looking for application errors

▶ Working within an interactive environment

▶ Performing application testing

▶ Sorting the `import` statements in your application

▶ Keeping track of application versions

*P*ython, like most other programming languages, has strong third-party support in the form of various tools. A *tool* is any utility that enhances the natural capabilities of Python when building an application. So, a debugger is considered a tool because it's a utility, but a library isn't. Libraries are instead used to create better applications. (You can see some of them listed in Chapter 20.)

Even making the distinction between a tool and something that isn't a tool, such as a library, doesn't reduce the list by much. Python enjoys access to a wealth of general-purpose and special tools of all sorts. In fact, the site at https://wiki.python.org/moin/DevelopmentTools breaks these tools down into the following 13 categories:

✔ AutomatedRefactoringTools

✔ BugTracking

✔ ConfigurationAndBuildTools

✔ DistributionUtilities

✔ DocumentationTools

- IntegratedDevelopmentEnvironments
- PythonDebuggers
- PythonEditors
- PythonShells
- SkeletonBuilderTools
- TestSoftware
- UsefulModules
- VersionControl

Interestingly enough, it's quite possible that the lists on the Python DevelopmentTools site aren't even complete. You can find Python tools listed in quite a few places online.

Given that a single chapter can't possibly cover all the tools out there, this chapter discusses a few of the more interesting tools — those that merit a little extra attention on your part. After you whet your appetite with this chapter, seeing what other sorts of tools you can find online is a good idea. You may find that the tool you thought you might have to create is already available, and in several different forms.

Tracking Bugs with Roundup Issue Tracker

You can use a number of bug-tracking sites with Python, such as the following: Github (https://github.com/); Google Code (https://code.google.com/); BitBucket (https://bitbucket.org/); and Launchpad (https://launchpad.net/). However, these public sites are generally not as convenient to use as your own specific, localized bug-tracking software. You can use a number of tracking systems on your local drive, but Roundup Issue Tracker (http://roundup.sourceforge.net/) is one of the better offerings. Roundup should work on any platform that supports Python, and it offers these basic features without any extra work:

- Bug tracking
- TODO list management

If you're willing to put a little more work into the installation, you can get additional features, and these additional features are what make the product special. However, to get them, you may need to install other products, such as a DataBase Management System (DBMS). The product instructions tell you what to install and which third-party products are compatible. After you make the additional installations, you get these upgraded features:

- Customer help-desk support with the following features:
  - Wizard for the phone answerers
  - Network links
  - System and development issue trackers
- Issue management for Internet Engineering Task Force (IETF) working groups
- Sales lead tracking
- Conference paper submission
- Double-blind referee management
- Blogging (extremely basic right now, but will become a stronger offering later)

Creating a Virtual Environment Using VirtualEnv

Reasons abound to create virtual environments, but the main reason for to do so with Python is to provide a safe and known testing environment. By using the same testing environment each time, you help ensure that the application has a stable environment until you have completed enough of it to test in a production-like environment. VirtualEnv (`https://pypi.python.org/pypi/virtualenv`) provides the means to create a virtual Python environment that you can use for the early testing process or to diagnose issues that could occur because of the environment. It's important to remember that there are at least three standard levels of testing that you need to perform:

- **Bug:** Checking for errors in your application
- **Performance:** Validating that your application meets speed, reliability, and security requirements
- **Usability:** Verifying that your application meets user needs and will react to user input in the way the user expects

Never test on a production server

A mistake that some developers make is to test their unreleased application on the production server where the user can easily get to it. Of the many reasons not to test your application on a production server, data loss has to be the most important. If you allow users to gain access to an unreleased version of your application that contains bugs that might corrupt the database or other data sources, the data could be lost or damaged permanently.

You also need to realize that you get only one chance to make a first impression. Many software projects fail because users don't use the end result. The application is complete, but no one uses it because of the perception that the application is flawed in some way. Users have

only one goal in mind: to complete their tasks and then go home. When users see that an application is costing them time, they tend not to use it.

Unreleased applications can also have security holes that nefarious individuals will use to gain access to your network. It doesn't matter how well your security software works if you leave the door open for anyone to come in. After they have come in, getting rid of them is nearly impossible, and even if you do get rid of them, the damage to your data is already done. Recovery from security breaches is notoriously difficult — and sometimes impossible. In short, never test on your production server because the costs of doing so are simply too high.

 Because of the manner in which most Python applications are used (see Chapter 18 for some ideas), you generally don't need to run them in a virtual environment after the application has gone to a production site. Most Python applications require access to the outside world, and the isolation of a virtual environment would prevent that access.

Installing Your Application Using PyInstaller

Users don't want to spend a lot of time installing your application, no matter how much it might help them in the end. Even if you can get the user to attempt an installation, less skilled users are likely to fail. In short, you need a surefire method of getting an application from your system to the user's system. Installers, such as PyInstaller (http://www.pyinstaller.org/), do just that. They make a nice package out of your application that the user can easily install.

Avoid the orphaned product

Some Python tools floating around the Internet are *orphaned*, which means that the developer is no longer actively supporting them. Developers still use the tool because they like the features it supports or how it works. However, doing so is always risky because you can't be sure that the tool will work with the latest version of Python. The best way to approach tools is to get tools that are fully supported by the vendor who created them.

If you absolutely must use an orphaned tool (such as when an orphaned tool is the only one available to perform the task), make sure that the tool still has good community support. The vendor may not be around any longer, but at least the community will provide a source of information when you need product support. Otherwise, you'll waste a lot of time trying to use an unsupported product that you might never get to work properly.

Fortunately, PyInstaller works on all the platforms that Python supports, so you need just the one tool to meet every installation need you have. In addition, you can get platform-specific support when needed. For example, when working on a Windows platform, you can create code-signed executables. Mac developers will appreciate that PyInstaller provides support for bundles. In many cases, avoiding the platform-specific features is best unless you really do need them. When you use a platform-specific feature, the installation will succeed only on the target platform.

A number of the installer tools that you find online are platform specific. For example, when you look at an installer that reportedly creates executables, you need to be careful that the executables aren't platform specific (or at least match the platform you want to use). It's important to get a product that will work everywhere it's needed so that you don't create an installation package that the user can't use. Having a language that works everywhere doesn't help when the installation package actually hinders installation.

Building Developer Documentation Using pdoc

Two kinds of documentation are associated with applications: user and developer. User documentation shows how to use the application, while developer documentation shows how the application works. A library requires only one sort of documentation, developer, while a desktop application may require only user documentation. A service might actually require both kinds of documentation depending on who uses it and how the service is put together. The majority of your documentation is likely to affect developers, and pdoc (`https://github.com/BurntSushi/pdoc`) is a simple solution for creating it.

The pdoc utility relies on the documentation that you place in your code in the form of docstrings and comments. The output is in the form of a text file or an HTML document. You can also have pdoc run in a way that provides output through a web server so that people can see the documentation directly in a browser. This is actually a replacement for epydoc, which is no longer supported by its originator.

Developing Application Code Using Komodo Edit

Several chapters have discussed the issue of Interactive Development Environments (IDEs), but none have made a specific recommendation. The IDE you choose depends partly on your needs as a developer, your skill level, and the kinds of applications you want to create. Some IDEs are better than others when it comes to certain kinds of application development. One of the better general-purpose IDEs for novice developers is Komodo Edit (`http://komodoide.com/komodo-edit/`). You can obtain this IDE free, and it includes a wealth of features that will make your coding experience much better than what you'll get from IDLE. Here are some of those features:

✔ Support for multiple programming languages

✔ Automatic completion of keywords

✔ Indentation checking

✔ Project support so that applications are partially coded before you even begin

✔ Superior support

However, the thing that sets Komodo Edit apart from other IDEs is that it has an upgrade path. When you start to find that your needs are no longer met by Komodo Edit, you can upgrade to Komodo IDE (`http://komodoide.com/`), which includes a lot of professional level support features, such as code profiling (a feature that checks application speed) and a database explorer (to make working with databases easier).

Debugging Your Application Using pydbgr

A high-end IDE, such as Komodo IDE, comes with a complete debugger. Even Komodo Edit comes with a simple debugger. However, if you're using something smaller, less expensive, and less capable than a high-end IDE, you might not have a debugger at all. A *debugger* helps you locate errors in your application and fix them. The better your debugger, the less effort required to locate and fix the error. When your editor doesn't include a debugger, you need an external debugger such as pydbgr (`https://code.google.com/p/pydbgr/`).

A reasonably good debugger includes a number of standard features, such as code colorization (the use of color to indicate things like keywords). However, it also includes a number of nonstandard features that set it apart. Here are some of the standard and nonstandard features that make pydbgr a good choice when your editor doesn't come with a debugger:

- ✔ **Smart eval:** The `eval` command helps you see what will happen when you execute a line of code, before you actually execute it in the application. It helps you perform "what if" analysis to see what is going wrong with the application.

- ✔ **Out-of-process debugging:** Normally you have to debug applications that reside on the same machine. In fact, the debugger is part of the application's process, which means that the debugger can actually interfere with the debugging process. Using out-of-process debugging means that the debugger doesn't affect the application and you don't even have to run the application on the same machine as the debugger.

- ✔ **Thorough byte-code inspection:** Viewing how the code you write is turned into *byte code* (the code that the Python interpreter actually understands) can sometimes help you solve tough problems.

- ✔ **Event filtering and tracing:** As your application runs in the debugger, it generates events that help the debugger understand what is going on. For example, moving to the next line of code generates an event, returning from a function call generates another event, and so on. This feature makes it possible to control just how the debugger traces through an application and which events it reacts to.

Entering an Interactive Environment Using IPython

The Python shell works fine for many interactive tasks. You've used it extensively in this book. However, you may have already noted that the default shell has certain deficiencies (and if you haven't, you'll notice them as you work through more advanced examples). Of course, the biggest deficiency is that the Python shell is a pure text environment in which you must type commands to perform any given task. A more advanced shell, such as IPython (http://ipython.org/), can make the interactive environment friendlier by providing GUI features so that you don't have to remember the syntax for odd commands.

IPython is actually more than just a simple shell. It provides an environment in which you can interact with Python in new ways, such as by displaying graphics that show the result of formulas you create using Python. In addition, IPython is designed as a kind of front end that can accommodate other languages. The IPython application actually sends commands to the real shell in the background, so you can use shells from other languages such as Julia and Haskell. (Don't worry if you've never heard of these languages.)

One of the more exciting features of IPython is the ability to work in parallel computing environments. Normally a shell is single threaded, which means that you can't perform any sort of parallel computing. In fact, you can't even create a multithreaded environment. This feature alone makes IPython worthy of a trial.

Testing Python Applications Using PyUnit

At some point, you need to test your applications to ensure that they work as instructed. You can test them by entering in one command at a time and verifying the result, or you can automate the process. Obviously, the automated approach is better because you really do want to get home for dinner someday and manual testing is really, really slow (especially when you make mistakes, which are guaranteed to happen). Products such as PyUnit (https://wiki.python.org/moin/PyUnit) make unit testing (the testing of individual features) significantly easier.

The nice part of this product is that you actually create Python code to perform the testing. Your script is simply another, specialized, application that tests the main application for problems.

You may be thinking that the scripts, rather than your professionally written application, could be bug ridden. The testing script is designed to be extremely simple, which will keep scripting errors small and quite noticeable. Of course, errors can (and sometimes do) happen, so yes, when you can't find a problem with your application, you do need to check the script.

Tidying Your Code Using Isort

It may seem like an incredibly small thing, but code can get messy, especially if you don't place all your `import` statements at the top of the file in alphabetical order. In some situations, it becomes difficult, if not impossible, to figure out what's going on with your code when it isn't kept neat. The Isort utility (`http://timothycrosley.github.io/isort/`) performs the seemingly small task of sorting your `import` statements and ensuring that they all appear at the top of the source code file. This small step can have a significant effect on your ability to understand and modify the source code.

Just knowing which modules a particular module needs can be a help in locating potential problems. For example, if you somehow get an older version of a needed module on your system, knowing which modules the application needs can make the process of finding that module easier.

In addition, knowing which modules an application needs is important when it comes time to distribute your application to users. Knowing that the user has the correct modules available helps ensure that the application will run as anticipated.

Providing Version Control Using Mercurial

The applications you created while working through this book aren't very complex. In fact, after you finish this book and move on to more advanced training applications, you're unlikely to need version control. However, after you start working in an organizational development environment in which you create real applications that users need to have available at all times, version control becomes essential. *Version control* is simply the act of keeping track of the changes that occur in an application between application releases to the production environment. When you say you're using MyApp 1.2, you're referring to version 1.2 of the MyApp application. Versioning lets everyone know which application release is being used when bug fixes and other kinds of support take place.

Numerous version control products are available for Python. One of the more interesting offerings is Mercurial (`http://mercurial.selenic.com/`). You can get a version of Mercurial for almost any platform that Python will run on, so you don't have to worry about changing products when you change platforms. (If your platform doesn't offer a binary, executable, release, you can always build one from the source code provided on the download site.)

Unlike a lot of the other offerings out there, Mercurial is free. Even if you find that you need a more advanced product later, you can gain useful experience by working with Mercurial on a project or two.

The act of storing each version of an application in a separate place so that changes can be undone or redone as needed is called *source code management.* For many people, source code management seems like a hard task. Because the Mercurial environment is quite forgiving, you can learn about source control management in a friendly environment. Being able to interact with any version of the source code for a particular application is essential when you need to go back and fix problems created by a new release.

The best part about Mercurial is that it provides a great online tutorial at `http://mercurial.selenic.com/wiki/Tutorial`. Following along on your own machine is the best way to learn about source control management, but even just reading the material is helpful. Of course, the first tutorial is all about getting a good installation of Mercurial. The tutorials then lead you through the process of creating a repository (a place where application versions are stored) and using the repository as you create your application code. By the time you finish the tutorials, you should have a great idea of how source control should work and why versioning is an important part of application development.

Chapter 20

Ten Libraries You Need to Know About

In This Chapter

▶ Securing your data using cryptology

▶ Working with databases

▶ Getting to where you're going and finding new locations

▶ Presenting the user with a GUI

▶ Creating tables that users will enjoy viewing

▶ Working with graphics

▶ Finding the information you need

▶ Allowing access to Java code from your Python application

▶ Obtaining access to local network resources

▶ Using resources found online

*P*ython provides you with considerable power when it comes to creating average applications. However, most applications aren't average and require some sort of special processing to make them work. That's where libraries come into play. A good library will extend Python functionality so that it supports the special programming needs that you have. For example, you might need to plot statistics or interact with a scientific device. These sorts of tasks require the use of a library.

One of the best places to find a library listing online is the UsefulModules site at `https://wiki.python.org/moin/UsefulModules`. Of course, there are many other places to look for libraries as well. For example, the article entitled "7 Python Libraries you should know about" (`http://doda.co/7-python-libraries-you-should-know-about`) provides you with a relatively complete description of the seven libraries its title refers to. If you're working on a specific platform, such as Windows, you can find platform-specific sites, such as Unofficial Windows Binaries for Python Extension Packages (`http://www.lfd.uci.edu/~gohlke/pythonlibs/`). The point is that you can find lists of libraries everywhere.

The purpose of this chapter isn't to add to your already overflowing list of potential library candidates. Instead, it provides you with a list of ten libraries that work on every platform and provide basic services that just about everyone will need. Think of this chapter as a source for a core group of libraries to use for your next coding adventure.

Developing a Secure Environment Using PyCrypto

Data security is an essential part of any programming effort. The reason that applications are so valued is that they make it easy to manipulate and use data of all sorts. However, the application must protect the data or the efforts to work with it are lost. It's the data that is ultimately the valuable part of a business — the application is simply a tool. Part of protecting the data is to ensure that no one can steal it or use it in a manner that the originator didn't intend, which is where cryptographic libraries such as PyCrypto (`https://www.dlitz.net/software/pycrypto/`) come into play.

The main purpose of this library is to turn your data into something that others can't read while it sits in permanent storage. The purposeful modification of data in this manner is called *encryption*. However, when you read the data into memory, a *decryption* routine takes the mangled data and turns it back into its original form so that the application can manage it. At the center of all this is the *key*, which is used to encrypt and decrypt the data. Ensuring that the key remains safe is part of your application coding as well. You can read the data because you have the key; no others can because they lack the key.

Interacting with Databases Using SQLAlchemy

A *database* is essentially an organized manner of storing repetitive or structured data on disk. For example, customer *records* (individual entries in the database) are repetitive because each customer has the same sort of information requirements, such as name, address, and telephone number. The precise organization of the data determines the sort of database you're using. Some database products specialize in text organization, others in tabular information, and still others in random bits of data (such as readings taken from a scientific instrument). Databases can use a tree-like structure or a flat-file configuration to store data. You'll hear all sorts of odd terms when you start looking into DataBase Management System (DBMS) technology — most of which mean something only to a DataBase Administrator (DBA) and won't matter to you.

The most common type of database is called a Relational DataBase Management System (RDBMS), which uses tables that are organized into records and fields (just like a table you might draw on a sheet of paper). Each *field* is part of a column of the same kind of information, such as the customer's name. Tables are related to each other in various ways, so creating complex relationships is possible. For example, each customer may have one or more entries in a purchase order table, and the customer table and the purchase order table are therefore related to each other.

An RDBMS relies on a special language called the Structured Query Language (SQL) to access the individual records inside. Of course, you need some means of interacting with both the RDBMS and SQL, which is where SQLAlchemy (http://www.sqlalchemy.org/) comes into play. This product reduces the amount of work needed to ask the database to perform tasks such as returning a specific customer record, creating a new customer record, updating an existing customer record, and deleting an old customer record.

Seeing the World Using Google Maps

Geocoding (the finding of geographic coordinates, such as longitude and latitude from geographic data, such as address) has lots of uses in the world today. People use the information to do everything from finding a good restaurant to locating a lost hiker in the mountains. Getting from one place to another often revolves around geocoding today as well. Google Maps (https://pypi.python.org/pypi/googlemaps/) lets you add directional data to your applications.

In addition to getting from one point to another or finding a lost soul in the desert, Google Maps can also help in Geographic Information System (GIS) applications. The "Helping People Decide on Location" section of Chapter 18 describes this particular technology in more detail, but essentially, GIS is all about deciding on a location for something or determining why one location works better than another location for a particular task. In short, Google Maps presents your application with a look at the outside world that it can use to help your user make decisions.

Adding a Graphical User Interface Using TkInter

Users respond to the Graphical User Interface (GUI) because it's friendlier and requires less thought than using a command-line interface. Many products out there can give your Python application a GUI. However, the most commonly used product is TkInter (https://wiki.python.org/moin/TkInter). Developers like it so much because TkInter keeps things simple. It's actually an interface for the Tool Command Language (Tcl)/Toolkit (Tk) found at http://www.tcl.tk/. A number of languages use Tcl/Tk as the basis for creating a GUI.

You might not relish the idea of adding a GUI to your application. Doing so tends to be time consuming and doesn't make the application any more functional (it also slows the application down in many cases). The point is that users like GUIs, and if you want your application to see strong use, you need to meet user requirements.

Providing a Nice Tabular Data Presentation Using PrettyTable

Displaying tabular data in a manner the user can understand is important. From the examples you've seen throughout the book, you know that Python stores this type of data in a form that works best for programming needs. However, users need something that is organized in a manner that humans understand and that is visually appealing. The PrettyTable library (https://pypi.python.org/pypi/PrettyTable) makes it easy to add an appealing tabular presentation to your command-line application.

Enhancing Your Application with Sound Using PyAudio

Sound is a useful way to convey certain types of information to the user. Of course, you have to be careful in using sound because special-needs users might not be able to hear it, and for those who can, using too much sound can interfere with normal business operations. However, sometimes audio is an important means of communicating supplementary information to users who can interact with it (or of simply adding a bit of pizzazz to make your application more interesting).

One of the better platform-independent libraries to make sound work with your Python application is PyAudio (http://people.csail.mit.edu/hubert/pyaudio/). This library makes it possible to record and play back sounds as needed (such as a user recording an audio note of tasks to perform later and then playing back the list of items as needed).

Classifying Python sound technologies

It's important to realize that sound comes in many forms in computers. The basic multimedia services provided by Python (see the documentation at `https://docs.python.org/3/library/mm.html`) provide essential playback functionality. You can also write certain types of audio files, but the selection of file formats is limited. In addition, some modules, such as winsound (`https://docs.python.org/3/library/winsound.html`), are platform dependent, so you can't use them in an application designed to work everywhere. The standard Python offerings are designed to provide basic multimedia support for playing back system sounds.

The middle ground, augmented audio functionality designed to improve application usability, is covered by libraries such as PyAudio. You can see a list of these libraries at `https://wiki.python.org/moin/Audio`. However, these libraries usually focus on business needs, such as recording notes and playing them back later. Hi-fidelity output isn't part of the plan for these libraries.

Gamers need special audio support to ensure that they can hear special effects, such as a monster walking behind them. These needs are addressed by libraries such as PyGame (`http://www.pygame.org/news.html`). When using these libraries, you need higher-end equipment and have to plan to spend considerable time working on just the audio features of your application. You can see a list of these libraries at `https://wiki.python.org/moin/PythonGameLibraries`.

Working with sound on a computer always involves trade-offs. For example, a platform-independent library can't take advantage of special features that a particular platform might possess. In addition, it might not support all the file formats that a particular platform uses. The reason to use a platform-independent library is to ensure that your application provides basic sound support on all systems that it might interact with.

Manipulating Images Using PyQtGraph

Humans are visually oriented. If you show someone a table of information and then show the same information as a graph, the graph is always the winner when it comes to conveying information. Graphs help people see trends and understand why the data has taken the course that it has. However, getting those pixels that represent the tabular information onscreen is difficult, which is why you need a library such as PyQtGraph (`http://www.pyqtgraph.org/`) to make things simpler.

Even though the library is designed around engineering, mathematical, and scientific requirements, you have no reason to avoid using it for other purposes. PyQtGraph supports both 2D and 3D displays, and you can use it to generate new graphics based on numeric input. The output is completely interactive, so a user can select image areas for enhancement or other sorts of manipulation. In addition, the library comes with a wealth of useful widgets (controls, such as buttons, that you can display onscreen) to make the coding process even easier.

Unlike many of the offerings in this chapter, PyQtGraph isn't a free-standing library, which means that you must have other products installed to use it. This isn't unexpected because PyQtGraph is doing quite a lot of work. You need these items installed on your system to use it:

- Python version 2.7 or above
- PyQt version 4.8 or above (`https://wiki.python.org/moin/PyQt`) or PySide (`https://wiki.python.org/moin/PySide`)
- numpy (`http://www.numpy.org/`)
- scipy (`http://www.scipy.org/`)
- PyOpenGL (`http://pyopengl.sourceforge.net/`)

Locating Your Information Using IRLib

Finding your information can be difficult when the information grows to a certain size. Consider your hard drive as a large, free-form, tree-based database that lacks a useful index. Any time such a structure becomes large enough, data simply gets lost. (Just try to find those pictures you took last summer and you'll get the idea.) As a result, having some type of search capability built into your application is important so that users can find that lost file or other information.

A number of search libraries are available for Python. The problem with most of them is that they are hard to install or don't provide consistent platform support. In fact, some of them work on only one or two platforms. However, IRLib (`https://github.com/gr33ndata/irlib`) is written in pure Python, which ensures that it works on every platform. If you find that IRLib doesn't meet your needs, make sure the product you do get will provide the required search functionality on all the platforms you select and that the installation requirements are within reason.

IRLab works by creating a search index of whatever information you want to work with. You can then save this index to disk for later use. The search mechanism works through the use of metrics — you locate one or more entries that provide a best fit for the search criteria.

Creating an Interoperable Java Environment Using JPype

Python does provide access to a huge array of libraries, and you're really unlikely to use them all. However, you might be in a situation in which you find a Java library that is a perfect fit but can't use it from your Python application unless you're willing to jump through a whole bunch of hoops. The JPype library (http://jpype.sourceforge.net/) makes it possible to access most (but not all) of the Java libraries out there directly from Python. The library works by creating a bridge between the two languages at the byte-code level. Consequently, you don't have to do anything weird to get your Python application to work with Java.

Converting your Python application to Java

There are many different ways to achieve interoperability between two languages. Creating a bridge between them, as JPype does, is one way. Another alternative is to convert the code created for one language into code for the other language. This is the approach used by Jython (https://wiki.python.org/jython/). This utility converts your Python code into Java code so that you can make full use of Java functionality in your application while maintaining the features that you like about Python.

 You'll encounter trade-offs in language interoperability no matter which solution you use. In the case of JPype, you won't have access to some Java libraries. In addition, there is a speed penalty in using this approach because the JPype bridge is constantly converting calls and data. The problem with Jython is that you lose the ability to modify your code after conversion. Any changes that you make will create an incompatibility between the original Python code and its Java counterpart. In short, no perfect solutions exist for the problem of getting the best features of two languages into one application.

Accessing Local Network Resources Using Twisted Matrix

Depending on your network setup, you may need access to files and other resources that you can't reach using the platform's native capabilities. In this case, you need a library that makes such access possible, such as Twisted Matrix (https://twistedmatrix.com/trac/). The basic idea behind this library is to provide you with the calls needed to establish a connection, no matter what sort of protocol is in use.

The feature that makes this library so useful is its event-driven nature. This means that your application need not get hung up while waiting for the network to respond. In addition, the use of an event-driven setup makes asynchronous communication (in which a request is sent by one routine and then handled by a completely separate routine) easy to implement.

Accessing Internet Resources Using Libraries

Although products such as Twisted Matrix can handle online communication, getting a dedicated HTTP protocol library is often a better option when working with the Internet because a dedicated library is both faster and more feature complete. When you specifically need HTTP or HTTPS support, using a library such as httplib2 (https://github.com/jcgregorio/httplib2) is a good idea. This library is written in pure Python and makes handling HTTP-specific needs, such as setting a Keep-Alive value, relatively easy. (A Keep-Alive is a value that determines how long a port stays open waiting for a response so that the application doesn't have to continuously re-create the connection, wasting resources and time as a result.)

You can use httplib2 for any Internet-specific methodology — it provides full support for both the GET and POST request methods. This library also includes routines for standard Internet compression methods, such as deflate and gzip. It also supports a level of automation. For example, httplib2 adds ETags back into PUT requests when resources are already cached.

Index

• Symbols and Numerics •

– (minus sign), 97, 98, 103
!= (not equal) operator, 98, 103
(number sign), 74, 76
% operator, 98, 103
%= operator, 101, 103
& operator, 100, 103
( ) parentheses, 103, 106, 246
* (asterisk)
  multiplication operator, 98, 103, 236
  variable argument lists, 111, 281
** operator, 98, 103
**= operator, 101, 103
*= operator, 101, 103
/ (forward slash), 98, 103, 295
// operator, 98
/= operator, 101, 103
//= operator, 101, 103
: (colon), 106, 118, 125, 219
[ ] square brackets, 211, 226, 229
\ (backslash), 209–210, 295
^ operator, 100, 103
{ } curly brackets, 219
| operator, 100
~ operator, 97, 100, 103
+ (plus sign)
  addition operator, 98
  concatenation using, 212, 236
  operator precedence, 103
  overloading, 283–284
  as unary operator, 97
  using indentation with, 72
  using with tuples, 247
+= operator, 101, 103
< (less-than) operator, 99, 103
<< operator, 100, 103
<= (less-than or equal) operator, 99, 103
= (assignment) operator, 85, 101, 103
-= operator, 101, 103
== (equality) operator, 98, 103, 118
> (greater-than) operator, 98, 103
>= (greater-than or equal) operator,
  99, 103
>> operator, 100, 103
" (double quotes), 74, 207, 209
' (single quote), 207, 209
3ds Max, 342

• A •

\a escape sequence, 210
Abaqus, 342
absolute paths, 295
accented characters, 209
accessors, 285
action warning level, 43
Add to Path option, 26
__add__() function, 246, 247, 283
Additional Help Sources feature, IDLE, 66
aggdraw library, 333
AIX (Advanced IBM Unix), 21
Alice Educational Software, 17
alignment, string, 220
American Standard Code for Information
  Interchange (ASCII), 206, 210
Amiga Research OS (AROS), 21
and operator, 99, 103
append() function, 193, 232, 257,
  264, 305
appendleft() function, 264
Apple Siri, 7

Application System 400 (AS/400), 22
applications
  commands in, 68–69
  commercial, written in Python, 18
  compile time errors, 152
  creating in Edit window, 67–68
  CRUD and, 39
  debugging, 353
  decision-making and, 117
  defined, 9
  designing, 13–14
  installing using PyInstaller, 350–351
  loading in Edit window, 79
  multithreaded, 261
  overview, 12
  procedures and, 10
  purpose of, 13
  quitting, 237
  README files, 40
  running from command line, 78
  running from IDLE, 71–72, 79–80
  runtime errors, 152
  saving files for, 69–70
  usage types, 16–17
`apt-get` command, 30–31
ArcGIS, 344
`*args` argument list, 281
arguments, command-line, 42
arguments, exception
  listing, 163–164
  overview, 161–163
arguments, function
  accessing using keywords, 110
  default values for, 110–111
  overview, 108
  positional, 110
  required, 108–110
  variable number of, 111–112
arguments, method, 281–282
arithmetic operators
  listing of, 97–98
  precedence, 103

`ArithmeticError` exception, 167, 169
AROS (Amiga Research OS), 21
as clause, 162
`as_string()` function, 320
AS/400 (Application System 400), 22
ASCII (American Standard Code for
  Information Interchange), 206, 210
ASP.NET, 336
assignment operators
  assigning value to variable, 85
  listing of, 101
  precedence, 103
asterisk (*)
  multiplication operator, 98, 103, 236
  variable argument lists, 111, 281
attributes, module, 184, 193–197
audio, 360–361

• B •

backslash (\ ), 209–210, 295
backspace character, 210
Base 2, 86
Base 8, 86
Base 10, 86
Base 16, 86
b command, 199
\b escape sequence, 210
-b option, 42
-bb option, 42
-B option, 42, 44
BeOS, 22
`bin()` function, 86
binary codes, 12
binary operators, 96, 103
Binary to Decimal to Hexadecimal
  Converter, 100
BitBucket, 348
bitwise operators, 99–100, 103
Blender, 342
blue text in IDLE, 61
`bool()` function, 306

Boolean type, 89–90
break statements
  overview, 136–138
  for while statements, 144
bugs
  defined, 150
  tracking sites for, 348
  using virtual environments, 349
  __builtins__ attribute, 194
byte code, 353
byte type, 42, 45
bytearray type, 42
-c option, 43

● **C** ●

C#
  job opportunities and, 15
  Python versus, 19
  user interfaces, 17
  __cached__ attribute, 194
caller, 105, 175–176
capitalization, 154, 171
capitalize() function, 213
car security systems, 345
Carnegie Mellon University, 17
carriage return character, 210
Cascading Style Sheets (CSS), 336
CASE (Computer Aided Software
    Engineering), 17
case sensitivity, 154
catching exceptions. *See* exceptions,
    handling
category warning level, 43
C/C++, 15, 340
celementtree library, 333
center() function, 213, 216
CentOS, 29
CGI (Common Gateway Interface), 332
characters
  ASCII, 206–207
  creating strings from, 207–208

escape sequences, 209–210
selecting individual in string, 211–213
sets of, 207
special, 208–211
child classes, 287
Cinema 4D, 342
__class__ attribute, 271
classes
  built-in attributes, 271–272
  class suite, 270
  constructors, 275–277
  creating, 269–271
  creating external, 284–285
  explained, 268–269
  extending, 287–290
  importance of application organization,
      267
  importing module for, 286
  inheritance, 287
  method arguments, 281–282
  methods, 273–275
  overloading operators, 282–284
  using external, 285–287
  variables, 277–280
clear() function, 232, 234, 241, 253
client (web) applications, 332
CMS (Content Management System), 332
code
  blocks of, 120–121
  cleaning using Isort, 355
  color coding, 61, 63–64
  commenting out, 75–77
  comments in, 74–75
  common mistakes, 336–337
  grouping into collections, 184–185
  highlighting, 63–64
  indentation, 72–73
  inspecting, 43
  introspection, 331
  optimizing, 43
  readability, 1, 15
  reusability, 104–105

code *(continued)*
runnable, 184
spaghetti code, 267
understandable, 93
using Edit window, 67–68
version control, 355–356
collections, 241, 243–244
colon (:), 106, 118, 125, 219
color coding, 61, 63–64
Comma Separated Values (CSV), 297
command-line Python. *See also* IDLE
accessing from command prompt, 34–35
advantages of, 40
arguments, 42
close button of terminal, 55
commands in, 46
Enter key in, 46
environment variables and, 44–45
exiting, 54–56
help mode, 48–49
IDLE versus, 58
options for, 42–44
running applications, 78
starting, 41
viewing result in, 46–47
comments
commenting out code, 75–77
multiline, 74–75
single-line, 74
uses for, 75
Common Gateway Interface (CGI), 332
communication
applications and, 9, 13
computers and, 7–8
exceptions and, 150–151
comparisons
function output, 114
if statements, 121–123
overview, 94–95
precedence, 103
compile time errors, 152, 154
complex numbers, 88

Computer Aided Software Engineering
(CASE), 17
computers
characters and, 206–207
communication with, 7–8
comparisons and, 95
CRUD, 39
data storage, 84
exceptions, 150–151
lists and, 225–226
preciseness of, 11
procedures, 10–11
programming languages, 12
purpose of applications, 9
strings and, 205
concatenation
creating lists using, 236
defined, 72
using + operator, 212
using with tuples, 247
conditions for if statements, 118
configuration
environment variables, 44–45
IDLE, 63–66
console library, 333
constants, 193
constructors, 275–277
Content Management System (CMS), 332
Content-Type header, 320
Context-Transfer-Encoding
header, 320
continue statements
overview, 138–139
pass clause versus, 140
for while statements, 144
control characters, 208–209, 296
control statements
if statements, 118–123
if...elif statements, 125–128
if...else statements, 124–125
nesting, 129–132
switch statement and, 128

`copy()` function, 232, 234
`copyright()` function, 48
copyright messages, 43
`count()` function, 217, 218, 244
`Counter` object, 240–242
Create, Read, Update, Delete.
    See CRUD
`credits()` command, 48–49
cross-platform support, 19, 21–22
CRUD (Create, Read, Update, Delete)
  applications and, 83
  defined, 39
  file storage, 293–294
  for lists, 232
CSS (Cascading Style Sheets), 336
CSV (Comma Separated Values), 297
curly brackets { }, 219
current directory, 191
`-d` option, 43, 44

• D •

data analysis, real-time, 346
data integrity, 294
data mining, 344–345
data storage
  assigning values, 85
  creating files, 298–301
  deleting files, 308
  file storage, 294–295
  purpose of, 83
  reading files, 301–303
  structure of content, 295–298
  variables, 84
  writing data to files, 303–307
data types
  Boolean, 89–90
  complex numbers, 88
  dates and times, 91–92
  defined, 85
  determining for variable, 90
  floating-point values, 87–88

integers, 86–87
numeric types, 89
strings, 90–91
Database Administrator (DBA), 358
Database Management Systems
  (DBMSs), 332, 349, 358
databases, 16, 358–359
`Datalist` argument, 299
`DataReader` class, 302
`DataWriter` class, 299–300
dates and times, 45, 91–92
`day` value, 92
DBA (Database Administrator), 358
DBMSs (Database Management
  Systems), 332, 349, 358
debugging
  defined, 150
  starting debugger, 43
  using pydbgr, 353
decryption, 358
default values for arguments, 110–111
`del` command, 253
deleting files, 308
delimiters, 214, 296
`deque` type
  defined, 244
  sequence types, 224
  using, 263–265
development tools, 18
dictionaries
  creating, 249
  defined, 244
  overview, 248–249
  sequence types, 224
  as switch statement, 253–256
  using, 250–253
`dir()` function, 164, 193, 228, 271
directories, 294
division operator (/), 98, 103
`doc()` function, 198
`__doc__` attribute, 194

documentation
  accessing from IDLE, 62–63
  in comments, 75
  creating using pdoc, 351–352
  online, 330
  opening pydoc application, 198–200
  quick-access links, 200–201
  searching, 202–204
  .docx files, 296
double quotes ("), 74, 207, 209
downloading Python, 22–23
drawing characters, 209
dynamic systems, 88
-E option, 43

• E •

Edit window, IDLE, 67–68, 79
effbot library, 333
elementsoap library, 333
elementtidy library, 333
elementtree library, 333
elif clause, 125–126, 237
else clause
  for if statements, 124–125
  for loops, 141–142
  try block and, 157
  for while statements, 144
email
  creating HTML message, 324–325
  creating text message, 323–324
  envelope analogy, 312–313
  host address, 313–314
  hostname, 317–318
  HowStuffWorks article, 310
  letter analogy, 311–312, 318–319
  MIME types, 319–321
  ports, 312, 314–316
  sending transmission, 321–322
  SMTP, 309–310
  subtypes, 322
  viewing output, 325–326

email.mime module, 319
Embedded Python, 345
empty() function, 261
encryption, 358
endless loops, 143
endswith() function, 217
engineering applications, 16, 88
Enter key, 46
enumerate() function, 281
envelope analogy, 311, 312–313
environment variables
  ERRORLEVEL environment variable, 54
  ignoring, 43
  PATH environment variable, 26, 34–35
  Python configuration, 35, 44–45, 191
equality (==) operator, 98, 103, 118
errno argument, 162
ERRORLEVEL environment variable, 54
errors. See also exceptions; exceptions,
      handling
  compile time, 152
  handling, 149
  logical, 154–155
  runtime, 152–153
  semantic, 154
  syntactical, 154
  types of, 153
escape sequences, 209–210
ETags, 364
eval command, 353
except clause
  combining specific clauses with
      generic, 167–170
  defined, 157
  listing exception arguments, 164
  multiple clauses, 165–167
  single clause, 164–165
  using, 158–161
Exception exception, 155
exceptions. See also errors
  arguments for, 161–163
  built-in, 155

custom, 176–178
defined, 122, 149
listing arguments, 163–164
online resources, 331
raising, 174–175
exceptions, handling
except clause, 158–161
finally clause, 178–180
length checking, 137
multiple exceptions, 164–167
nesting, 170–173
passing error information to caller,
175–176
raising exceptions, 174–175
range checking, 123
single exception, 156–158
specific and unknown exceptions,
167–170
exec() command, 79
exemaker library, 333
exit() command, 54–56
expandtabs() function, 213
exponents, 87, 89
expressions, 95, 113
extend() function, 232, 264
extending classes, 287–290
extendleft() function, 264
Extensible Markup Language (XML), 16,
296, 335–336
extensions, file, 294

● **F** ●

\f escape sequence, 210
features, 13, 58
Fedora Core, 29
Fermilab, 17
fields, database, 359
FIFO (first in/first out), 244
file storage
creating files, 298–301
deleting files, 308

overview, 294–295
reading files, 301–303
structure of content, 295–298
supported file types, 299
writing data to files, 303–307
__file__ attribute, 194
FileNotFoundError exception, 155
fill character, 220
finally clause
exceptions and, 150
overview, 178–180
find() function, 217, 218
first in/first out (FIFO), 244
float() function, 90
float type, 87
floating-point values
formatting strings, 221
overview, 87–88
reasons for multiple numeric types, 89
flow control. *See* control statements
fluid dynamics, 88
flushing data, 300
folders, 294
Fonts/Tabs tab, IDLE, 63–64
for loops
break statements, 136–138
continue statements, 138–139
creating, 135
deque type and, 264
else clause, 141–142
nesting, 145–147
pass clause, 140–141
for statement, 134
using with lists, 231
while statement versus, 144
format() function, 219–221
formfeed character, 210
forward slash (/), 98, 103, 295
freezing applications, 152, 261
from...import statements, 188–191
ftpparse library, 333
full() function, 261

function arguments
  default values, 110–111
  overview, 108
  required, 108–110
  using keywords, 110
  variable number of, 111–112
functions
  calling, 107–108
  code reusability and, 104–105
  comparing output from, 114
  defined, 104
  defining, 105–107
  overloading, 268
  partial, 331
  purpose of, 104
  returning data from, 112–113
  user input, 114–116
FUNCTIONS topic, 50

● *G* ●

GCC (GNU Compiler Collection), 28
General tab, IDLE, 65–66
generators, 331
geocoding, 359
Geographic Information System (GIS),
  344, 359
get() function, 241, 261
getaddrinfo() function, 315
__getattribute__() function, 164
gethostbyaddr() function, 313, 317
gethostbyname() function, 313, 317
gethostname() function, 317
getserverbyport() function, 316
getters/setters, 285, 297
GIMP, 342
GIS (Geographic Information System),
  344, 359
Github, 348
GNU Compiler Collection (GCC), 28
Go.com, 17
Google, 17

Google App Engine, 342
Google Code, 348
Google Maps, 359
grabscreen library, 333
Graphic User Interface (GUI), 17,
  359–360
graphs, 361–362
greater-than (>) operator, 98, 103
greater-than or equal (>=) operator,
  99, 103
green text in IDLE, 61
GUI (Graphic User Interface), 17, 359–360
-h option, 43

● *H* ●

handling exceptions. *See* exceptions,
  handling
headers, email, 311
help
  Additional Help Sources feature, 66
  command for, 48–49, 53–54
  displaying, 43
  help mode, 48–49, 50–52
  in IDLE, 62–63
  for specific commands or topics,
    52–54
Hewlett-Packard Unix (HP-UX), 22
hex() function, 86
hexadecimal values, 86, 210
hierarchy of tuples, 247–248
highlighting code, 63–64, 334–335
horizontal tab character, 210
host address, 313–314
hostname, 317–318
Houdini, 342
hour value, 92
HP-UX (Hewlett-Packard Unix), 22
HTML (Hypertext Markup Language),
  324–325, 336
-i option, 43, 45

• I •

IDE (Integrated Development Environment), 45, 334, 352
identity operators, 102, 103
IDLE (Interactive Development Environment). *See also* command-line Python
  accessing on Mac, 36
  accessing on Windows, 32–33
  color coding in, 37, 61, 63–64
  command-line Python versus, 58
  commands in, 60
  comments in, 74–77
  configuration, 63–66
  Edit window, 67–68
  exiting, 80
  feature overview, 58
  help in, 62–63
  indentation in, 72–73
  overview, 58
  Python versions and, 29
  running applications from, 71–72, 79–80
  saving files, 69–70
  shortcut keys, 65
  starting, 59
  testing installation, 36–37
IETF (Internet Engineering Task Force), 349
if statements
  code blocks for, 120–121
  if...elif statements, 125–128
  if...else statements, 124–125
  multiple comparisons for, 121–123
  nesting, 129–132
  overview, 118
  using relational operators, 119–120
IIS (Internet Information Server), 342
imaging library, 333
immutable types, 245
import statements
  ignoring case in, 44

importing entire module, 187–188
importing only needed attributes, 188–191
overview, 183, 185–186
using, 162
in operator, 102, 103, 236
indentation, 63, 72–73
index
  for dictionaries, 250
  for lists, 229
  for lists, negative, 230
  for tuples, 247
index() function, 217, 244, 306
Industrial Light & Magic, 17
inheritance, 268, 287
__init__() constructor function, 275–276
initializing values, 275
__initializing__ attribute, 194
Inkscape, 342
input() function, 114–115
insert() function, 232, 233
insertion pointer, 208–209
inspecting code, 43
installing applications, 350–351
installing Python
  on Linux, 30–32
  on Mac, 27–29
  testing installation, 36–38
  on Windows, 25–27
instances
  creating, 270
  defined, 268
  methods, 274–275
  variables, 279–280
instantiation, 269
int() function, 90, 306
integers, 86–87, 220
Integrated Development Environment (IDE), 45, 334, 352
Interactive Development Environment. *See* IDLE

interactive environment, 354
Internet Engineering Task Force (IETF), 349
Internet Information Server (IIS), 342
IOError exception, 162
IPv4 (Internet Protocol version 4), 315
IPv6 (Internet Protocol version 6), 315
IPython, 354
IRLib library, 362–363
is not operator, 102, 103
is operator, 102, 103
isalnum() function, 213
isalpha() function, 213
isdecimal() function, 213
isdigit() function, 214
islower() function, 214
isnumeric() function, 214
Isort, 355
isspace() function, 214
istitle() function, 214
isupper() function, 214
items() function, 282
iterable items, 264

• J •

j identifier, 88
Java
  development time, 15
  Python versus, 19
  using libraries in Python, 363
JavaScript, 16, 336
job opportunities
  data mining, 344–345
  embedded systems interaction, 345
  GIS, 344
  IT departments, 341–342
  network administration, 343
  programming languages and, 15
  QA, 340
  real-time data analysis, 346
  scientific tasks, 345–346

  specialty scripting, 342–343
  teaching, 343
join() function, 214
JPype library, 363
jQuery, 336
Jython, 363

• K •

KeyboardInterrupt exception, 155, 172
keys() function, 250–251
key/value pairs. *See* dictionaries
keywords topic, 50
Komodo Edit, 58, 352
**kwargs argument list, 281

• L •

Language Integrated Query (LINQ), 16
last in/first out (LIFO), 244
Launchpad, 348
Lawrence Livermore National Library, 17
learning curve, 15
LearnPython.org tutorial, 331
len() function, 214, 232, 253
length checking, 137
less-than (<) operator, 99, 103
less-than or equal (<=) operator, 99, 103
letter analogy, 311–312, 318–319
libraries
  defined, 183
  finding online, 357
  Google Maps, 359
  httplib2, 364
  IRLib, 362–363
  JPype, 363
  NumPy, 16
  PrettyTable, 360
  PyAudio, 360–361
  PyCrypto, 358
  PyQtGraph, 361–362

SciPy, 16
socket, 313, 315, 316, 317
SQLAlchemy, 358–359
third-party libraries, 332–333
TkInter, 359–360
Twisted Matrix, 364
license() command, 49
LIFO (last in/first out), 244
Lightwave, 342
linefeed character, 210
lineno warning level, 43
LINQ (Language Integrated Query), 16
Linux
    accessing Python on, 36
    installing Python, 30–32
    Python support, 22
lists
    accessing items in, 228–230
    computer view of, 225–226
    Counter object for, 240–242
    creating, 226–227
    creating stacks using, 256–260
    functions for, 228
    looping through, 231
    modifying items in, 232–235
    mutable types, 245
    negative indexes, 230
    overview, 223–225
    range of values in, 229
    searching in, 236–238
    sorting, 238–240
    using operators with, 236
    zero-based indexes, 229
ljust() function, 214
__loader__ attribute, 194
local hostname, 317–318
logical errors, 154–155
logical operators
    listing of, 99
    multiple comparisons for if
        statements, 121–123
    precedence, 103

loops
    break statements, 136–138
    continue statements, 138–139
    deque type and, 264
    else clause, 141–142
    endless, 143
    for loops, 134–135
    nesting, 145–147
    overview, 133–134
    pass clause, 140–141
    using with lists, 231
    while statements, 143–145
lower() function, 214
lstrip() function, 214
-m option, 43

• M •

Mac OS X
    accessing Python, 35–36
    installing Python, 27–29
    Python support, 22
mantissa, 89
mathematic applications, 16
max() function, 214, 216
Maya, 342
members, class, 268
membership operators, 102, 103
memory, and floating-point values, 89
MemoryError exception, 155
Mercurial version control, 355–356
message warning level, 43
methods
    class, 273–274
    defined, 269
    instance, 274–275
    instance variables and, 279
    variable argument lists for,
        281–282
microsecond value, 92
Microsoft Disk Operating System
    (MS-DOS), 22

Microsoft Windows
  accessing IDLE, 32–33
  accessing Python from command
    prompt, 34–35
  ignoring case in import statements, 44
  installing Python, 25–27
  opening pydoc application, 198
  platform support, 22
MIME (Multipurpose Internet Mail
    Extensions), 319–321
min() function, 214
minus sign (-), 97, 98, 103
minute value, 92
Modo, 342
module warning level, 43
modules
  defined, 183
  finding on disk, 191–193
  finding online, 357
  from...import statements, 188–191
  grouping code and, 184–185
  ignoring paths for, 43
  importing, 92, 185–188
  numeric processing, 345
  opening pydoc application, 198–200
  quick-access documentation links,
    200–201
  running, 43
  scientific, 345
  searching documentation, 202–204
  viewing attributes in, 193–197
modules topic, 50
month value, 92
MorphOS, 22
MotionBuilder, 342
MS-DOS (Microsoft Disk Operating
    System), 22
multiline comments, 74–75
multiplatform support, 19, 21–22
multiple processors, 245
multiplication operator (*), 98,
    103, 236

Multipurpose Internet Mail Extensions
    (MIME), 319–321
multithreaded applications, 261
mutable types, 245, 248

• N •

\n escape sequence, 210, 215, 299
__name__ attribute, 194
NASA (National Space and Aeronautics
    Administration), 17
negation operator (-), 97
nesting
  defined, 129
  exception handling, 170–173
  if statements, 129–132
  loops, 145–147
network administration, 343
New York Stock Exchange, 17
newline attribute, 299
not equal (!=) operator, 98, 103
not in operator, 102, 103
not operator, 99, 103
now() function, 92
Nuke, 342
number sign (#), 74, 76
numeric types
  complex numbers, 88
  floating-point values, 87–88
  integers, 86–87
  reasons for multiple, 89
NumPy library, 16, 362
-O option, 43

• O •

ObjectDomain, 17
objects, 269
oct() function, 86
octal numeric values, 210
-OO option, 43, 45
open() function, 79, 162, 299

open source, 19
operands, 96
Operating System 2 (OS/2), 22
Operating System 390 (OS/390), 22
operators
  arithmetic, 97–98
  assignment, 101
  binary, 96
  bitwise, 99–100
  comparisons and, 95
  identity, 102
  logical, 99
  membership, 102
  overloading, 269, 282–284
  overview, 95–97
  precedence, 103
  relational, 98–99
  ternary, 96
  unary, 96, 97
  using with lists, 236
optimizing code, 43
or operator, 99
ord() function, 90
orphaned projects, 351
os._exit() command, 56
OS/2 (Operating System 2), 22
OS/390 (Operating System 390), 22
os.environ[ ] attributes, 192–193
os.pathsep constant, 193
os.remove() function, 308
os.rmdir() function, 308
overloading
  functions, 268
  operators, 269, 282–284

● *P* ●

__package__ attribute, 194
padding strings with zeroes, 215
Paint Shop Pro, 342
PalmOS, 22
parent classes, 287

parentheses ( ), 103, 106, 246
partial functions, 331
pass clause
  overview, 140–141
  for while statements, 144
PATH environment variable, 26, 34–35
paths, directory, 295
pdoc, 351–352
performance
  resources for, 338
  using virtual environments, 349
Perl, 20
PHP, 336
PIL (Python Imaging Library), 333
platform support, 21–22
Playstation, 22
plus sign (+)
  addition operator, 98
  concatenation using, 212, 236
  operator precedence, 103
  overloading, 283–284
  as unary operator, 97
  using indentation with, 72
  using with tuples, 247
Pocket PC, 22
pop() function, 232, 234, 257, 264
POP3 (Post Office Protocol 3), 312
popleft() function, 264
ports, 314–316
positional arguments, 110
Post Office Protocol 3 (POP3), 312
precedence, operator, 103
precision of decimal number, 220
PrettyTable library, 360
print() function
  testing installation, 36–37
  typing commands, 46
  using in application, 68–69
  viewing command result, 46–47
procedures
  commands and, 46
  computers and, 10–11

procedures *(continued)*
  defined, 9
  separating from user interface, 304
  tasks as, 9–10
processors, multiple, 245
production servers, 350
production-grade classes, 287
Program Files directory, 26
programming
  application usage types, 16–17
  code reusability, 104–105
  common mistakes, 336–337
  communication with computer, 94
  exceptions and, 150–151
  knowing multiple languages, 341
  languages, 12, 14, 19–20
  Python advantages, 15
protocol, defined, 310
prototypes, 16
Psion, 22
purple text in IDLE, 61
put() function, 261
.py files, 42
PyAudio library, 360–361
.pyco files, 42
PyCrypto library, 358
pydbgr, 353
pydoc application
  opening, 198–200
  quick-access links, 200–201
  searching, 202–204
PyGame library, 361
PyInstaller, 350–351
PyOpenGL, 362
PyQtGraph library, 361–362
Python
  advantages of, 15
  applications written in, 18
  C# versus, 19
  documentation, 62–63
  downloading, 22–23
  Embedded Python, 345

  environment variables for, 35
  installing on Linux, 30–32
  installing on Mac, 27–29
  installing on Windows, 25–27
  Java versus, 19
  language comparisons online, 19
  online documentation, 330
  online tutorial, 331
  organizations using, 17–18
  Perl versus, 20
  platform support, 21–22
  popularity of, 15
  reporting problems, 330
  uses for, 16–17
  using Java libraries in, 363
  web programming using, 332
Python and XML Processing site, 336
python command, 78
Python GUI. *See* IDLE
Python Imaging Library (PIL), 333
PYTHONCASEOK environment variable,
    35, 44
PYTHONDEBUG environment
    variable, 44
PYTHONDEFAULTHANDLER environment
    variable, 45
pythondoc library, 333
PythonEditors wiki, 334
PYTHONFAULTHANDLER environment
    variable, 35
PYTHONHASHSEED environment variable,
    35, 45
PYTHONHOME environment variable,
    35, 45
PYTHONINSPECT environment
    variable, 45
PYTHONIOENCODING environment
    variable, 35, 45
PYTHONNOUSERSITE environment
    variable, 45
PYTHONOPTIMIZE environment
    variable, 45

PYTHONPATH environment variable, 35, 45, 191
PYTHONSTARTUP environment variable, 35, 45
PYTHONUNBUFFERED environment variable, 45
PYTHONVERBOSE environment variable, 45
python.vim utility, 335
Pythonware site, 332–333
PYTHONWARNINGS environment variable, 45
PYTHONWRITEBYTECODE environment variable, 44
PyUnit, 354–355

• *Q* •

q command, 199
-q option, 43
QA (Quality Assurance), 340
QNX, 22
quantum mechanics, 88
queue type
  defined, 244
  sequence types, 224
  using, 260–262
quit() command, 38, 54–55

• *R* •

\r escape sequence, 210
raising exceptions. *See also* exceptions, handling
  defined, 150
  overview, 174–175
  passing error information to caller, 175–176
range checking, 121, 123
range of values in list, 229
Raspberry Pi, 343, 345
RDBMS (Relational Database Management System), 359

read() function, 79
readability of code, 1, 15
reading files, 301–303
README files, 40
real-time data analysis, 346
records, database, 358
Red Hat, 17, 29
Red Hat Package Manager (RPM), 29
regular expressions, 331
Relational Database Management System (RDBMS), 359
relational operators
  listing of, 98–99
  precedence, 103
  using with if statements, 119–120
relative paths, 295
remove() function, 193, 232, 234, 264, 306
repetition, 212
repetitive tasks. *See* loops
replace() function, 217
reporting problems, 330
required arguments, 108–110
resources
  common mistakes, 336–337
  IDEs, 334
  LearnPython.org tutorial, 331
  online documentation, 330
  performance, 338
  third-party libraries, 332–333
  Unicode characters, 337
  web programming, 332
  XML, 335–336
ResourceWarning exception, 155
returning data from functions, 112–113
reusable code, 104–105
reverse() function, 240
rfind() function, 217, 218
rindex() function, 217
RISC OS, 22
rjust() function, 214
rmtree() function, 308

Roundup Issue Tracker, 348
RPM (Red Hat Package Manager), 29
`rstrip()` function, 214
runnable code, 184
running applications
  from command line, 78
  defined, 68
  from Edit window, 79
  in IDLE, 71–72, 79–80
runtime errors, 152–153

• S •

-s option, 43, 45
-S option, 43
scientific applications, 16, 345–346
scientific notation, 87
SciPy library, 16, 362
screenshots in book, 32
Scribus, 342
SD (Secure Digital), 83
searching
  IRLib library, 362–363
  in lists, 236–238
  module documentation, 202–204
  in strings, 217–219
`second` value, 92
Secure Digital (SD), 83
seeding with random values, 45
selection tree, 129
`self` object, 274, 283
semantic errors, 154
sequences, 224–225, 243–244. *See also*
  lists
serialization, 331
Series 60, 22
server applications, 332
sets, 331
setters, 285, 297
shell, 54
shortcut keys for IDLE, 65
`shutil.rmtree()` function, 308

Simple Mail Transfer Protocol (SMTP),
  309–310, 321–322, 324
Simple Object Access Protocol
  (SOAP), 333
single quote ('), 207, 209
single-line comments, 74–75
`__sizeof__` attribute, 194, 196
SMTP (Simple Mail Transfer Protocol),
  309–310, 321–322, 324
`smtplib` module, 321
SOAP (Simple Object Access
  Protocol), 333
socket library, 313, 315, 316, 317
Softimage, 342
Solaris, 22
Solid State Drive (SSD), 293
`sort()` function, 239
sorting lists, 238–240
sound technologies, 361
spaghetti code, 267
special characters, 208–211
`split()` function, 193, 214, 216, 306
`splitlines()` function, 215
SQL (Structured Query Language), 16,
  336, 359
SQLAlchemy library, 358–359
square brackets [ ], 211, 226, 229
squeeze library, 333
SSD (Solid State Drive), 293
stacks
  defined, 244
  sequence types, 224
  using, 256–260
`startswith()` function, 217
`str()` function, 42, 91
`str` type, 45
`__str__()` function, 284, 285, 297
`strerror` attribute, 162, 175–176, 177
strings
  creating from characters, 207–208
  as dictionary keys, 250
  formatting, 219–222

functions for, 213–216, 217
overview, 90–91
searching in, 217–219
selecting individual characters in, 211–213
upper() function, 171
using special characters, 208–211
as viewed by computers, 206
strip() function, 215, 216
structured data, 295
Structured Query Language (SQL), 16, 336, 359
subtraction operator (-), 98, 103
sudo command, 31
SUSE Linux, 29
swapcase() function, 215
switch statements, 128, 253–256
switches, command-line, 42–44
syntax
  concise, 1
  errors in, 154
  highlighting, 334–335
sys.exit() command, 56
sys.path variable, 43, 45, 192

● *T* ●

\t (tab character), 210
Tcl (Tool Command Language), 360
ternary operator, 96
testing
  C++ applications, 340
  installation, 36–38
  production servers and, 350
  using PyUnit, 354–355
third-party libraries, 332–333
throwing exceptions, 150, 174–175. *See also* exceptions, handling
time() function, 92
TIOBE web site, 15
title() function, 215
TkInter library, 333, 359–360

TODO list management, 348
Tool Command Language (Tcl), 360
tools
  bug-tracking sites, 348
  IPython, 354
  Isort, 355
  Komodo Edit, 352
  Mercurial version control, 355–356
  pdoc, 351–352
  pydbgr, 353
  PyInstaller, 350–351
  PyUnit, 354–355
  Roundup Issue Tracker, 348–349
  VirtualEnv, 349–350
topics keyword, 50
traceback, 45
Trigger, 343
try block, 156, 164
tuples
  defined, 244
  hierarchy of, 247–248
  sequence types, 224
  using, 245–248
Twisted Matrix, 364
type() method, 90
typographical characters, 209

● *U* ●

\u escape sequence, 210
-u option, 43, 45
UAC (User Access Control), 26
Ubuntu, 31
unary operators
  defined, 96
  listing of, 97
  precedence, 103
uncommenting lines, 77
Unicode characters, 210, 337
unit testing, 354–355
Universal Serial Bus (USB), 83, 293
unstructured data, 295

update() function, 241, 252
upper() function, 171, 215
USB (Universal Serial Bus), 83, 293
UsefulModules site, 357
User Access Control (UAC), 26
user input, 114–116
user interfaces, 17, 304

\v escape sequence, 210
-V option, 43
-v option, 43, 45
ValueError exception, 168, 177
variables
  assigning values, 85
  class, 268, 278–279
  defined, 84
  determining type of, 90
  instance, 269, 279–280
  returning data from functions, 113
    verbose mode, 43
version control, 355–356
--version option, 43
vertical tab character, 210
VirtualEnv, 349–350
Visual Basic, 15
VMS (Virtual Memory System), 22
-W option, 43, 45

W3Schools site, 335–336
warning level, 43
web programming, 16, 332

while statements
  nesting, 145–147
  overview, 143–144
  using, 144–145
whitespace, removing, 215
widgets library, 333
winsound module, 361
with statement, 299•
writerow() function, 300
writing data to files, 303–307

\x escape sequence, 210
-x option, 44
-X option, 44
XML (Extensible Markup Language), 16,
    296, 335–336

Yahoo!, 18
year value, 92
Yellow Dog Linux, 29
YouTube, 18

• **Z** •

zero-based indexes, 229
ZeroDivisionError exception, 167, 169
zeroes, padding with, 215
zfill() function, 215
.zip files, 296
Zope, 18
z/OS, 22

About the Author

John Mueller is a freelance author and technical editor. He has writing in his blood, having produced 95 books and more than 300 articles to date. The topics range from networking to artificial intelligence and from database management to heads-down programming. Some of his current books include a Windows command-line reference, books on VBA and Visio 2007, a C# design and development manual, and an IronPython programmer's guide. His technical editing skills have helped more than 63 authors refine the content of their manuscripts. John has provided technical editing services to both *Data Based Advisor* and *Coast Compute* magazines. He has also contributed articles to magazines such as *Software Quality Connection, DevSource, InformIT, SQL Server Professional, Visual C++ Developer, Hard Core Visual Basic, asp.netPRO, Software Test and Performance,* and *Visual Basic Developer.* Be sure to read John's blog at http://blog.johnmuellerbooks.com/.

When John isn't working at the computer, you can find him outside in the garden, cutting wood, or generally enjoying nature. John also likes making wine, baking cookies, and knitting. When not occupied with anything else, he makes glycerin soap and candles, which come in handy for gift baskets. You can reach John on the Internet at John@JohnMuellerBooks.com. John is also setting up a website at http://www.johnmuellerbooks.com/. Feel free to take a look and make suggestions on how he can improve it.

Dedication

Some people are simply there in your life — as reliable as the day is long. Scott and Pegg Conderman are two such people — they have helped me through an extremely hard time simply by being themselves and knowing just what to do to make the day a little better.

Author's Acknowledgments

Thanks to my wife, Rebecca. Even though she is gone now, her spirit is in every book I write, in every word that appears on the page. She believed in me when no one else would.

Russ Mullen deserves thanks for his technical edit of this book. He greatly added to the accuracy and depth of the material you see here. Russ is always providing me with great URLs for new products and ideas. However, it's the testing that Russ does that helps most. He's the sanity check for my work. Russ also has different computer equipment from mine, so he's able to point out flaws that I might not otherwise notice.

Matt Wagner, my agent, deserves credit for helping me get the contract in the first place and taking care of all the details that most authors don't really consider. I always appreciate his assistance. It's good to know that someone wants to help.

A number of people read all or part of this book to help me refine the approach, test the coding examples, and generally provide input that all readers wish they could have. These unpaid volunteers helped in ways too numerous to mention here. I especially appreciate the efforts of Eva Beattie, Glenn A. Russell, Emanuel Jonas, and Michael Sasseen, who provided general input, read the entire book, and selflessly devoted themselves to this project.

Finally, I would like to thank Kyle Looper, Susan Christophersen, and the rest of the editorial and production staff.

Publisher's Acknowledgments

Senior Acquisitions Editor: Kyle Looper

Project and Copy Editor: Susan Christophersen

Technical Editor: Russ Mullen

Editorial Assistant: Claire Johnson

Sr. Editorial Assistant: Cherie Case

Project Coordinator: Patrick Redmond

Cover Image: © iStock.com / Glam-Y

...ple & Mac

...d For Dummies,
... Edition
...-1-118-72306-7

...one For Dummies,
... Edition
...-1-118-69083-3

...cs All-in-One
... Dummies, 4th Edition
...-1-118-82210-4

... X Mavericks
... Dummies
...-1-118-69188-5

...ogging & Social Media

...cebook For Dummies,
... Edition
...-1-118-63312-0

...cial Media Engagement
... Dummies
...-1-118-53019-1

...ordPress For Dummies,
... Edition
...-1-118-79161-5

...usiness

...ock Investing
... Dummies, 4th Edition
...-1-118-37678-2

...vesting For Dummies,
... Edition
...-0-470-90545-6

Personal Finance
For Dummies, 7th Edition
978-1-118-11785-9

QuickBooks 2014
For Dummies
978-1-118-72005-9

Small Business Marketing
Kit For Dummies,
3rd Edition
978-1-118-31183-7

Careers

Job Interviews
For Dummies, 4th Edition
978-1-118-11290-8

Job Searching with Social
Media For Dummies,
2nd Edition
978-1-118-67856-5

Personal Branding
For Dummies
978-1-118-11792-7

Resumes For Dummies,
6th Edition
978-0-470-87361-8

Starting an Etsy Business
For Dummies, 2nd Edition
978-1-118-59024-9

Diet & Nutrition

Belly Fat Diet For Dummies
978-1-118-34585-6

Mediterranean Diet
For Dummies
978-1-118-71525-3

Nutrition For Dummies,
5th Edition
978-0-470-93231-5

Digital Photography

Digital SLR Photography
All-in-One For Dummies,
2nd Edition
978-1-118-59082-9

Digital SLR Video &
Filmmaking For Dummies
978-1-118-36598-4

Photoshop Elements 12
For Dummies
978-1-118-72714-0

Gardening

Herb Gardening
For Dummies, 2nd Edition
978-0-470-61778-6

Gardening with Free-Range
Chickens For Dummies
978-1-118-54754-0

Health

Boosting Your Immunity
For Dummies
978-1-118-40200-9

Diabetes For Dummies,
4th Edition
978-1-118-29447-5

Living Paleo For Dummies
978-1-118-29405-5

Big Data

Big Data For Dummies
978-1-118-50422-2

Data Visualization
For Dummies
978-1-118-50289-1

Hadoop For Dummies
978-1-118-60755-8

Language &
Foreign Language

500 Spanish Verbs
For Dummies
978-1-118-02382-2

English Grammar
For Dummies, 2nd Edition
978-0-470-54664-2

French All-in-One
For Dummies
978-1-118-22815-9

German Essentials
For Dummies
978-1-118-18422-6

Italian For Dummies,
2nd Edition
978-1-118-00465-4

---

e Available in print and e-book formats.

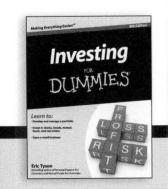
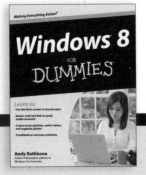

Available wherever books are sold. **For more information or to order direct visit www.dummies.com**

Math & Science

Algebra I For Dummies,
2nd Edition
978-0-470-55964-2

Anatomy and Physiology
For Dummies, 2nd Edition
978-0-470-92326-9

Astronomy For Dummies,
3rd Edition
978-1-118-37697-3

Biology For Dummies,
2nd Edition
978-0-470-59875-7

Chemistry For Dummies,
2nd Edition
978-1-118-00730-3

1001 Algebra II Practice
Problems For Dummies
978-1-118-44662-1

Microsoft Office

Excel 2013 For Dummies
978-1-118-51012-4

Office 2013 All-in-One
For Dummies
978-1-118-51636-2

PowerPoint 2013
For Dummies
978-1-118-50253-2

Word 2013 For Dummies
978-1-118-49123-2

Music

Blues Harmonica
For Dummies
978-1-118-25269-7

Guitar For Dummies,
3rd Edition
978-1-118-11554-1

iPod & iTunes
For Dummies, 10th Edition
978-1-118-50864-0

Programming

Beginning Programming
with C For Dummies
978-1-118-73763-7

Excel VBA Programming
For Dummies, 3rd Edition
978-1-118-49037-2

Java For Dummies,
6th Edition
978-1-118-40780-6

Religion & Inspiration

The Bible For Dummies
978-0-7645-5296-0

Buddhism For Dummies,
2nd Edition
978-1-118-02379-2

Catholicism For Dummies,
2nd Edition
978-1-118-07778-8

Self-Help & Relationships

Beating Sugar Addiction
For Dummies
978-1-118-54645-1

Meditation For Dummies,
3rd Edition
978-1-118-29144-3

Seniors

Laptops For Seniors
For Dummies, 3rd Edition
978-1-118-71105-7

Computers For Seniors
For Dummies, 3rd Edition
978-1-118-11553-4

iPad For Seniors
For Dummies, 6th Edition
978-1-118-72826-0

Social Security
For Dummies
978-1-118-20573-0

Smartphones & Tablets

Android Phones
For Dummies, 2nd Edition
978-1-118-72030-1

Nexus Tablets
For Dummies
978-1-118-77243-0

Samsung Galaxy S 4
For Dummies
978-1-118-64222-1

Samsung Galaxy Tabs
For Dummies
978-1-118-77294-2

Test Prep

ACT For Dummies,
5th Edition
978-1-118-01259-8

ASVAB For Dummies,
3rd Edition
978-0-470-63760-9

GRE For Dummies,
7th Edition
978-0-470-88921-3

Officer Candidate Tests
For Dummies
978-0-470-59876-4

Physician's Assistant Exam
For Dummies
978-1-118-11556-5

Series 7 Exam For Dummie
978-0-470-09932-2

Windows 8

Windows 8.1 All-in-One
For Dummies
978-1-118-82087-2

Windows 8.1 For Dummie:
978-1-118-82121-3

Windows 8.1 For Dummie:
Book + DVD Bundle
978-1-118-82107-7

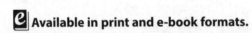 **Available in print and e-book formats.**

   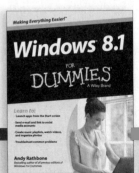

Available wherever books are sold. **For more information or to order direct visit www.dummies.com**

Take Dummies with you everywhere you go!

Whether you are excited about e-books, want more from the web, must have your mobile apps, or are swept up in social media, Dummies makes everything easier.

Visit Us

bit.ly/JE0O

Like Us

on.fb.me/1f1ThNu

Follow Us

bit.ly/ZDytkR

Watch Us

bit.ly/gbOQHn

Join Us

linkd.in/1gurkMm

Pin Us

bit.ly/16caOLd

Circle Us

bit.ly/1aQTuDQ

Shop Us

bit.ly/4dEp9

Leverage the Power

For Dummies is the global leader in the reference category and one of the most trusted and highly regarded brands in the world. No longer just focused on books, customers now have access to the For Dummies content they need in the format they want. Let us help you develop a solution that will fit your brand and help you connect with your customers.

Advertising & Sponsorships

Connect with an engaged audience on a powerful multimedia site, and position your message alongside expert how-to content.

Targeted ads • Video • Email marketing • Microsites • Sweepstakes sponsorship

21 Million Monthly Page Views & 13 Million Unique Visitors

For Dummies is a registered trademark of John Wiley & Sons, Inc.

Custom Publishing

Reach a global audience in any language by creating a solution that will differentiate you from competitors, amplify your message, and encourage customers to make a buying decision.

Apps • Books • eBooks • Video • Audio • Webinars

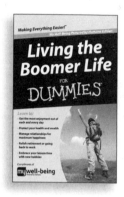   

Brand Licensing & Content

Leverage the strength of the world's most popular reference brand to reach new audiences and channels of distribution.

For more information, visit www.Dummies.com/biz

A Wiley Brand

Dummies products make life easier!

- DIY
- Consumer Electronics
- Crafts

- Software
- Cookware
- Hobbies

- Videos
- Music
- Games
- and More!

For more information, go to **Dummies.com** and search the store by category.

For Dummies is a registered trademark of John Wiley & Sons, Inc.

A Wiley Brand